Donut Forget™
Bible Story Lessons

Teacher's Guide

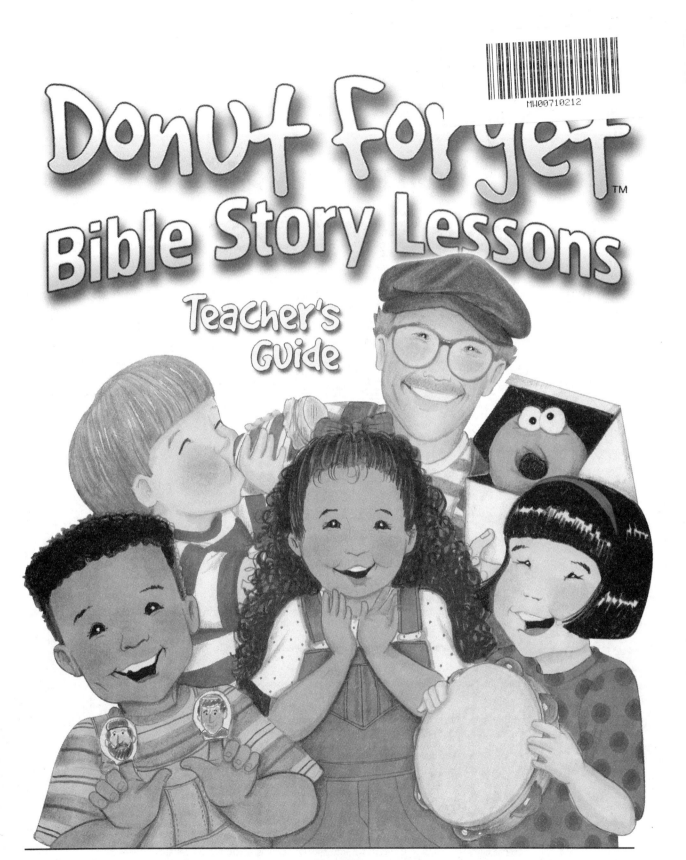

STANDARD PUBLISHING™

Cincinnati, Ohio

Donut Forget™
Bible Story Lessons

Standard Publishing, Cincinnati, Ohio
A division of Standex International Corporation
© 1999 Standard Publishing
All rights reserved
Printed in the United States of America

Donut Man® is used under license. ©1999 by Rob Evans.
All recordings used courtesy of Integrity Incorporated.
For more information please call 1-800-239-7000 or visit www.integritymusic.com.
Duncan created by Steve Axtell and © 1999 Rob Evans. Used under license.

Donut Forget™ is a trademark of Rob Evans. Used under license.

Credits
Cover design and inside illustrations: Liz Howe, Jan Knudson, Sam Thiewes, Glenna Buck
Cover illustration: Priscilla Burris
Creative consultant: Rob Evans
Writing team: Diana Crawford, Sarah Lyons, Nancy I. Sanders, Patricia Senseman,
Angela Smith, Bonnie Temple, Kristi Walter, Jennifer Root Wilger
Editors: Jennifer Root Wilger, Bonnie Temple
Syllabus development: Carol A. Jackson, Jennifer Root Wilger
Acquisitions editor: Ruth Frederick

Scriptures quoted from the *International Children's Bible, New Century Version,* ©1986,
1988 by word Publishing, Dallas, Texas 75039. Used by permission.

06 05 04 03 02 01 00 99   5 4 3 2 1

ISBN 0-7847-0999-8

CONTENTS

Donut
forget™
Bible Story
Lessons

Donut Forget™ Bible Story Lessons

Welcome . . . to a brand-new Bible learning adventure! *Donut Forget Bible Story Lessons* will provide the four- to eight-year-olds in your church with a year's worth of unforgettable learning experiences based on engaging Bible stories and the fun, Bible-based music of Rob Evans, The Donut Man®. Since 1982, The Donut Man has captivated audiences with his kid-friendly, singable songs. *Donut Forget Bible Story Lessons* features your favorite Donut Man songs—plus 22 brand new ones—all wrapped up in an easy-to-teach lesson format your kids will love.

Your complete curriculum package includes

- *Donut Forget Bible Story Lessons* teacher's guide (52 lessons)
- *Donut Forget Bible Story Lessons Songbook* (words and music with accompaniment for 52 songs, plus an index to help you use the songs anytime)
- *Donut Forget CDs* (52 songs)
- *Duncan* puppet (13 scripts included in the songbook)

Donut Forget Distinctives

BUILDS BIBLE KNOWLEDGE. As a teacher, you want to make sure the kids in your class are really learning the Bible. *Donut Forget Bible Story Lessons* will help you reach that goal. Research shows that repetition is an important part of young children's learning. So instead of rushing through a new Bible lesson each week, you'll spend an entire unit on one or two important Bible stories. Each lesson offers a wide variety of active, hands-on, easy-to-do activities, so the children won't get bored—and neither will you!

"The Lord listens when I pray to him." "Christ died for our sins, as the Scriptures say." "If we love each other, God lives in us." These are just a sampling of the Bible truths the children will learn. And since the best Bible knowledge comes straight from the Bible, each unit includes a Bible memory verse. All memory verses in *Donut Forget Bible Story Lessons* are taken from the *International Children's Bible*, so the children's learning won't be hindered by difficult or unfamiliar words.

It's every teacher's heartfelt prayer that students would hide God's Word in their hearts. Bible memorization comes easy to children—especially when Bible verses are paired with fun, memorable music. Think about the Bible verses you've committed to memory. How many of them were learned from praise songs or worship choruses? At the end of a year, your students will be able to sing thirteen Bible verses that will stay in their minds—and hearts—for years to come.

BUILDS CHRISTIAN RELATIONSHIPS. *Donut Forget Bible Story Lessons* helps you focus on what's most important—your students. Each lesson is packed with active, fun, age-appropriate activities that kids can do themselves. Once you've completed the minimal advance preparation, you're free to participate alongside the children. Instead of struggling to hold kids' attention as they wiggle and squirm, you'll join them in singing, shouting, marching, jumping, and praising their way through each lesson time. The Christian walk is often better "caught" than "taught." Your participation in the lesson activities will let your love for the Lord shine through.

The children will also build relationships with each other. From the Bible lessons, they'll learn that helping others is something that Jesus wants us to do. They'll discover from Jesus' example how to be true friends to each other. Through the course of the curriculum, the children will get to know each other by working in pairs or small groups. As the children choose the activities they want to work on, they'll work alongside different classmates each week. In addition, completion of a unit-long project will help build class unity. With the encouragement of their friends from your class, life application will come naturally. "Peer pressure" can be turned into a positive phenomenon!

Sound exciting? Well, it doesn't stop there. *Donut Forget Bible Story Lessons* will challenge the children—and their teachers—to build relationships beyond your classroom walls. Unit projects and activities provide opportunities for the children to build relationships with godly men and women in your church, and to share their developing faith with nonbelievers in your community. Babies, peers in other classes, teenagers, parents, senior adults, and church staff will all be invited to share in your children's learning as they experience the dynamic life and mission of your church community.

How to Use the Lessons

Donut Forget Bible Story Lessons are easy to use. From opening Learning Centers to closing Donut Forget Time activities, you'll find a variety of Bible-based activities your four- to eight-year-olds will love. Here's why:

LEARNING CENTERS offer children choices about their learning. In *Your Child's Growing Mind*, author and education specialist Jane Healy points out that children are more motivated to learn when they're offered choices. Each *Donut Forget Bible Story Lesson* includes three learning centers. Because each learning center activity is integrally connected to the Bible story or memory verse, you'll know the children are learning, regardless of which center they choose.

CENTERS 1 AND 2 are generally projects the children complete from start to finish, then use later in the lesson. Many of these centers help the children produce musical instruments, motions, or other projects to reinforce the Bible-based Donut Man songs. Through the course of the year, the children will make tambourines, chimes, kazoos, and more kinds of shakers than you can shake a stick at! And they'll love playing the instruments they've made themselves as they sing and celebrate God's love each week.

CENTER 3 is a unit-long project that the children add to each week. Here are just a few of the faith-stretching projects children will participate in:

- *The Marvelous Miracle Variety Show* (a puppet and musical extravaganza put on for parents)
- *Barnabas Project* (encouragement projects delivered to various members of your church)
- *Go Everywhere Quilt* (a wall hanging that demonstrates their commitment to tell others about Jesus)
- *The Do-Good Wagon Train* (a fun-filled ride around the room to celebrate their do-good words and actions)

GATHERING TIME gives the children an opportunity to share what they've learned. Four- to eight-year-olds are proud of their accomplishments, and they'll accomplish a lot in these lessons! Each week during Gathering Time, you'll recognize the work the children have done in their Learning Centers, then help them cement the connection between their Learning Center projects and the lessons' Bible truth.

BIBLE STORY TIME teaches children key Bible stories in fun, memorable ways. Four- to eight-year-olds love stories! *Donut Forget Bible Story Lessons* is chock full of songs, puppets, finger plays, and other creative Bible story-telling activities. Each unit focuses on one or two important Bible stories, told in multiple ways to reach children of all learning styles. Each unit also features one or more Bible story songs that will keep Bible lessons alive in kids' minds long after they've left your classroom.

SING-ALONG FUN TIME lets kids keep learning while they wear out their wiggles. Kids will be kids, and four- to eight-year-olds are full of energy that is just bursting to get out. During this time, children will sing their favorite Donut Man songs as they move around the room, use rhythm instruments, or play listening games. The Donut Man song "Sing and Skip and Dance" sums up this lesson component best: *Kids love to sing and skip and dance and shout hallelujah!*

DONUT FORGET TIME challenges the children to reflect on and apply the Bible truths they've learned. They'll learn about encouragement and tell an encouraging Bible story to a group of senior adults. They'll learn about sharing the good news and pray for the people they'll talk to about Jesus. They'll learn that God forgives us and quietly ask forgiveness for the wrong things they've done. Donut Forget Time ties the lesson together and equips kids to practice what they've learned.

Just for you . . . we've added **Bite Idea** tips. Sprinkled throughout the lessons, Bite Ideas suggest ways to adapt activities for younger or older children, modifications for large or small class sizes, and extra impact ideas that require a little more preparation but really bring home the lesson's point. In addition to the Bite Idea tips, you can find extra ideas for each unit at **www.donutforget.com**.

Let the Holy Spirit guide you as you adapt these lessons for the students in your class. And "Donut Forget" to have fun as you teach. May God bless you as you use *Donut Forget Bible Story Lessons* to share the joy of the Lord with the children in your church and community.

Use the Donut Man's object lesson of repairing a donut when it will help you reinforce the application of the unit. The following paragraph is the basic lesson; adapt it for different units in the curriculum.

Something is missing without Jesus in your heart! Hold up a donut and point to the hole. **This donut reminds us that we are empty without Jesus. The sad news is that Jesus had to die to take away our emptiness, our sin. The good news is that Jesus didn't leave us empty.** Get the "Donut Repair Kit" (a pastry donut hole) and repair the hole in the donut. As you do, talk about how Jesus has filled us up with his love, his forgiveness, his Holy Spirit (who helps us do good), his joy (or the specific application for the unit you are studying).

Look for additional Donut Man® resources from Standard Publishing and Integrity Music's JUST-FOR-KIDS on pages 42, 204, 222, and 240 in this book!

Also, for more information about Standard Publishing, Integrity Music, and The Donut Man, visit these web sites:
www.standardpub.com
www.integritymusic.com   www.donutman.net

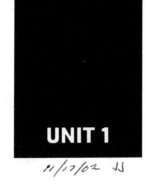

11/17/02 JJ

Donut Forget to Worship God

BY THE END OF THIS UNIT, LEARNERS WILL

Know   Name some wonderful things God made.

Feel   Feel amazed at the variety and greatness of God's creation.

Do   Worship God for making everything.

MEMORY VERSE

"I praise you because you made me in an amazing and wonderful way" (Psalm 139:14).

When we think about creation, we think of how awesome the Creator is. God created everything from nothing, and his creation is more varied than any human can grasp. We praise God for his amazing handiwork. Together with the stars, the trees, and all God's creatures, we offer our humble praise to the one who made us in an amazing and wonderful way.

Four- to eight-year-olds can't fully fathom God's incredible work in creation. But they can appreciate the variety of plants, trees, and animals and the amazing ability of the human body. This unit will lead the children to praise God with their voices, their hands, and their bodies for creating the world and all that is in it.

	LESSON 1	LESSON 2	LESSON 3	LESSON 4
Center 1	finger paint bags	handprint tree	animal shadows	children chain
Center 2	paper sculptures	star shakers	animal hands & feet	babies
Center 3	mini-world, days 1 & 2	mini-world, days 3 & 4	mini-world, animals	mini-world, people
Gathering Time	rain sounds	human tree	animal shadows	amazing prints
Bible Story Time	Genesis 1, days 1 & 2	Genesis 1, days 3 & 4	Genesis 1, animals	Genesis 1, people
Sing-Along Fun Time	singing praise	memory verse game	sing & skip & dance	hallelujah bells
Donut Forget Time	praise pictures	popcorn praise	thanking prayers	lead worship

Donut Forget™ Bible Story Lessons

LEARNING CENTERS

Set up the following activities for the children to do as they arrive. Assign an equal number of children to each activity. Have a teacher or helper available to assist the children with each activity.

At each Learning Center, welcome the children to your class. Make sure you know each child's name. Explain that today you'll be talking about all the wonderful things God has created and learning that we worship God for creating us in an amazing and wonderful way.

Center 1: Finger Paint Bags

Classroom supplies: one 2-gallon plastic resealable bag for each child, packaging tape, liquid poster paint, CD player

Curriculum supplies: Donut Forget CD ("In the Beginning")

BITE IDEA
You may choose to prepare single-color or multi-color paint bags. Bags with more than one paint color will allow children to swirl and mix colors as they draw. Eventually the colors will completely blend together, so you may want to limit your "blends" to primary colors such as red and yellow, blue and yellow, or red and blue.

Before the children arrive, place about 1/2 cup of poster paint in each resealable bag. Close the bags, then tape the tops with packaging tape.

Lay a paint bag flat on a table or the floor. With your finger, draw a simple outline of an animal, tree, flower, landscape, or person. Let the children guess what you've drawn, then smooth the paint to "erase" the drawing. Draw another creation and let the children guess again.

Give each child a finger paint bag. Play "In the Beginning" from the Donut Forget CD and let the children draw the items as they're mentioned in the song. After the song, if time allows, form pairs and let the children take turns painting and guessing each other's favorite creations.

Center 2: Paper Sculptures

Classroom supplies: newsprint, newspaper, scissors, stapler, markers or crayons, other art supplies (optional), CD player

Curriculum supplies: Donut Forget CD ("In the Beginning")

BITE IDEA
If you have mostly younger children in your class, you may want to draw and cut out some simple paper shapes before class. Children can decorate and stuff the shapes.

Before class, prepare a sample paper sculpture as described below.

Play "In the Beginning" from the Donut Forget CD. As you listen, help children pick out the things God made on each day. Show the sample you made, then let each child choose one item mentioned in the song for his own paper sculpture.

Set out a double layer of newsprint. Have the children draw large, simple outlines on the top layer, then cut out the drawings through both layers. This will create a top and bottom.

Let the children decorate their shapes with markers, crayons, or other art supplies. Have older children who can work more quickly make extras to share with the rest of the class. As the children work, talk about the unique features of their projects. Point out that God made each creation in a special way.

When the children finish decorating their paper pieces, staple the edges together, leaving an opening large enough for children to stuff the sculptures with newspaper. After the shapes are stuffed, staple the openings shut.

Set the sculptures aside to use during Sing-Along Fun Time.

Center 3: Mini-World Project

Classroom supplies: large cardboard box, black spray paint, blue construction paper, cotton balls or fiberfill stuffing, silver tinsel or glitter glue, blue or clear cellophane, glue, scissors, CD player
Curriculum supplies: Donut Forget CD ("In the Beginning")

Before the children arrive, trim a cardboard box to approximately 12 inches deep. Spray the inside and outside of the box with black spray paint. Allow the box to dry completely.

Invite the children to name some of the things God created. Hold up the painted box, then explain that they'll use it to make a mini-world to represent God's creations. Point out that just as it took God more than one day to create the earth, it will take several class times to finish the mini-world.

Play "In the Beginning" from the Donut Forget CD. Help the children understand that darkness and light, sky, and water were created on the first two days.

Point out that the mini-world is black and dark, just as everything was black and dark before

BITE IDEA
If the children have extra time each week, have them decorate the outside of their mini-world to look like a globe. They can add blue water, green and brown land shapes, a red ribbon equator, and white North and South Poles.

God created the world. Help the children work together to add sky and water to their mini-world. Encourage the children to come up with their own decorating ideas, or offer the following suggestions to get them started:

- Create a sky by covering the top half of the box with blue paper, inside and out.
- Attach cotton or fiberfill clouds to the sky.
- Use silver tinsel or glitter glue to create rain.
- Cover the bottom half of the box with blue or clear cellophane "water."

Help the children move the mini-world to the Gathering Time area.

GATHERING TIME

Classroom supplies: mini-world from Center 3, squirt bottle filled with water
Curriculum supplies: none

Have the children sit down in the Gathering Time area. Invite them to tell you about the things they did at their Learning Centers. Then say: **You all did different things, but you were all learning about God's creations. If you finger-painted God's creations, wiggle your fingers in the air. If you made paper sculptures of God's creations, wave your hand. If you worked on a mini-world to represent God's creations, come up and stand by me.**

Have children describe the mini-world and point out each creation they've added. Say: **Great job! Now we can imagine what the world would be like without any plants, animals, or people. Today our mini-world has only sky and water, but we'll be adding other creations in the next few weeks.**

Have the children who worked on the mini-world join the rest of the class. Say: **Before God created our world, water was everywhere. By the time God finished, the world had sky and land, too. Right now, let's think about all the places we find water on earth. When you hear me name a type of water, make a sound or do an action that matches the kind of water I name. For example, if I said "raindrops," you might pat your hands on your legs. If I said "ocean," you might move your hands up and down like waves.**

Donut Forget™ Bible Story Lessons

9

Read the following list of water types and let the children come up with sounds or actions for each one. When you say "squirt bottle," lightly spray children with water. Water types: raindrops, ocean waves, drinking water, swimming pool, river, lake, hail, snow, fountain, squirt bottle.

Say: **Wow! Isn't God amazing? He made so many different kinds of water for us to enjoy. I hope you enjoyed your little squirt. Let's listen to our Bible story now and hear about all the other amazing things God created.**

BIBLE STORY TIME

Classroom supplies: Bible, CD player
Curriculum supplies: Donut Forget CD ("In the Beginning")

Open your Bible to Genesis 1 and show the passage to the children. Say: **Our Bible story today comes from the very first page of the book of Genesis. We're going to go on a pretend journey as we learn about the days of creation. Listen carefully, and do what I do.**

As you tell the story, use an exaggerated tone and motions to get the children to follow you. Say: **In the beginning, there was nothing: no light, no people, no animals—only God. Cover your eyes and imagine what the world was like without any light.**

On the first day, God said, "Let there be light." Open your eyes and see the light God created. It was light for awhile, and then it was dark, just like our days and nights. What do you do when it's nighttime? What do you do when it's daytime?

Let children respond, then continue: **When I wake up I like to stand up and stretch. Let's all do that now. Stretch as high as you can. Reach for the sky—remember God made sky and water on the second day. On the third day, God made the land and plants. Let's climb the mountains God made. Up, up, up, then run down into the valley. Stop to pick a flower. Climb up a tree and pick a piece of fruit. What kind of fruit did you pick? How did it taste? Jump down from the tree and wade across the river.**

On the fourth day, God made the sun, the moon, and lots and lots of stars. Use your fingers to make twinkling stars.

On the fifth day God made thousands of different kinds of fish and birds for his sky and seas. Flop around like a fish. Touch a friend with an octopus arm. Flutter like a hummingbird. Soar like an eagle. Dive down into the water like a pelican catching a fish. Gulp!

On the sixth day God created animals and his greatest creation—people. Let's have an animal parade as we listen to "In the Beginning" and review the days of creation. I'll call out an animal, and we'll all walk like that animal. Listen carefully, because God made a lot of different animals.

Play "In the Beginning" from the Donut Forget CD as you lead the children around the room. Encourage them to sing along. Use the following animals: crab, duck, snail, bird, fish, alligator, horse, elephant.

After the song, lead the children back to the story area. Say: **Whew! Now we know why God rested on the seventh day. Let's rest here for a minute before our next activity.**

Pause for a few moments, then say: **God was very pleased with his world. We worship God for making everything. Let's sing some worship songs together now.**

SING-ALONG FUN TIME

Classroom supplies: paper sculptures from Center 2, scissors, CD player
Curriculum supplies: Donut Forget CD ("I Praise You, Lord, With the Hands You Made," "In the Beginning")

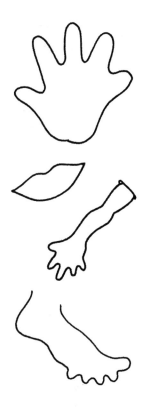

Before class, draw simple illustrations of hands, mouth, arms, and feet on sheets of newsprint. Post the illustrations in easy-to-see locations around your room.

Open your Bible to Psalm 139:14 and show it to the children. Say: **Psalm 139:14 says, "I praise you because you made me in an amazing and wonderful way." Let's learn a song about the amazing way God made us.**

Have the children gather near the hands illustration. As you sing "I Praise You, Lord, With the Hands You Made" with the Donut Forget CD, lead the children to the appropriate illustration (hands, mouth, arms, feet). Encourage them to march, skip, or jump as they move between the illustrations. As you sing the words "I praise you because you made me . . . ," join hands and walk in a circle.

Then say: **Now let's sing our story song "In the Beginning." If you made a paper sculpture at your Learning Center, hold it up when we sing about that day's creation.**

Distribute the paper sculptures and lead the children in singing "In the Beginning" with the Donut Forget CD. Encourage them to hold up their sculptures as they sing. After you're through, set the sculptures aside for use in Lesson 2.

DONUT FORGET TIME

Classroom supplies: papers, scissors, markers or crayons, CD player
Curriculum supplies: Donut Forget CD ("I Praise You, Lord, With the Hands You Made")

Set paper, scissors, and markers or crayons near each illustration you've posted in the room.

Say: **We worship God for making everything on earth. We've just been singing a song about all the ways we can praise God with the amazing bodies he's given us. Now we're going to think of some examples of how we can praise God with our hands, mouth, arms, and feet. Choose which body part you'd like to use to praise God and go sit by that picture.**

After the children are all seated, help them form pairs. Have partners draw and cut out the body part they've chosen. Then have them think of ways they could praise God with that body part. Inside the cutout, have them draw a picture or write a sentence describing what they'll do. Remind them that we can praise and honor God in many different ways, such as obeying parents, showing kindness to others, and doing what the Bible tells us to do. If some children need help, offer the following ideas:

Hands—fold in prayer, help set the table, make cookies for a sick friend
Mouth—read the Bible, say a prayer, tell someone about God
Arms—hug a friend or family member, help carry groceries, wave a friendly "hello" to
    someone
Feet—take a walk and enjoy God's creation, walk someone's dog, jump for joy

After the children finish, sing "I Praise You, Lord, With the Hands You Made" once more. As you make reference to each body part, have the corresponding group of children toss their papers up in the air and catch them. When you sing "I praise you because you made me . . . ," have all the children toss and catch their papers.

After the song, say a brief prayer thanking God for making each child in an amazing and wonderful way. Have the children take their papers home with them as a reminder to praise God this week.

Donut Forget™ Bible Story Lessons

LESSON TWO

H/24/02 JJ

LEARNING CENTERS

Set up the following activities for the children to do as they arrive. Assign an equal number of children to each activity. Have a teacher or helper available to assist the children with each activity.

At each Learning Center, welcome children to your class. Make sure you know each child's name. Explain that today you'll be talking about all the wonderful things God has created and learning that we worship God for creating us in an amazing and wonderful way.

Center 1: Handprint Tree

Classroom supplies: newspapers, newsprint, pie pans, tempera paint, paint shirts, pre-moistened wipes, CD player
Curriculum supplies: Donut Forget CD ("In the Beginning")

Before children arrive, cover a work area with newspapers. If you'll be working on a table, you may want to put a plastic tablecloth under the table. Decide what color handprint "leaves" children will make and prepare tempera paint in those colors. Add a drop of dish soap to each pan of paint for easier cleanup.

Set out a large sheet of newsprint and pans of tempera paint. Review with the children what God made on Days 1 and 2. Then explain that on Day 3, God made land and plants and trees. Tell children that they'll be making handprint leaves for a tree you'll use during Gathering Time.

Help the children draw a tree outline on the newsprint, then cover it with "leaf" handprints. Explain that you'll add the tree trunk during Gathering Time. As children work, play "In the Beginning" from the Donut Forget CD.

Hang the finished print on the wall in the Gathering Time Area.

Center 2: Star Shakers

Classroom supplies: scissors, marker, felt, several staplers, staples, large dried beans (such as pinto or lima beans), CD player
Curriculum supplies: copy of star pattern (page 23), Donut Forget CD ("In the Beginning")

Before class, enlarge and photocopy the star pattern and cut out the star shape. Trace the pattern onto felt. You'll need two felt stars for each child. If you have mostly younger children, you may want to cut out the felt stars ahead of time.

BITE IDEA
Older children would also enjoy sewing the star shakers with blunt needles and colored yarn.

Review with the children what God created on Days 1 and 2 of creation. Tell the children that on the third day, God made the land and plants, and that on the fourth day, God made the sun and moon and stars. Explain that they'll be making star shakers to praise God for these amazing creations.

Give each child two felt stars. Help younger children with cutting as necessary. Show the children how to stack their star shapes, then staple around the edges, leaving one point open. Encourage the children to place their staples close together to keep the beans inside once the stars are filled.

Set out a bowl of dried beans, and let the children fill their stars. To prevent the staples from tearing out, remind children not to fill the stars too full. (About 1/2 cup of beans is plenty.) After children have added the beans, help them staple around the open point. If time allows, have some children make additional stars for other children in the class.

Play "In the Beginning" from the Donut Forget CD as children work. Set the finished star shakers aside for use during Sing-Along Fun Time.

Center 3: Mini-World Project

Classroom supplies: decorated mini-world from Lesson 1, colored construction paper or felt, glue, scissors, very small plant branches, brown felt or sand paper, Mylar, silver glitter or glitter glue, glow-in-the-dark adhesive stars, CD player

Curriculum supplies: Donut Forget CD ("In the Beginning")

Review with the children what God created on Days 1 and 2 of creation. Then help children identify what was created on Days 3 and 4 as you read Genesis 1:9-19. Let the children use the craft supplies you've provided to add land, plants, trees, and a sun, moon, and stars to their mini-world. As the children work, play "In the Beginning" from the Donut Forget CD.

Invite the children to show and explain what they've added to the mini-world during Gathering Time.

GATHERING TIME

Classroom supplies: Bible, handprint tree leaves from Center 1, green crepe paper, brown crepe paper, CD player

Curriculum supplies: Donut Forget CD ("I Praise You, Lord, With the Hands You Made")

Before class, cut green crepe paper into 12-inch strips. You'll need one crepe-paper strip for each child. Set the crepe-paper strips near the Gathering Time area.

Have the children sit down in the Gathering Time area. Invite them to tell you about the things they did at their Learning Centers. Then say: **Today we are talking some more about all the wonderful things God created for the earth. Some of you worked on our mini-world. Can you show us what you've added?**

Let the Center 3 children point out new additions to the mini-world. Say: **Some of you made star shakers that we'll use during Sing-Along Fun Time. If you made a star shaker, raise your hands and say, "I'm a star!" Some of you made a handprint tree to remind us of all the plants and trees God created. If you put your handprints on the tree, wave your arms in the air like tree branches.**

There's a Bible verse that talks about the trees praising God. Listen to what it says. Read Psalm 96:12 from an easy-to-understand translation. Say: **Just like the trees, we can sing for joy when we see all the amazing things that God has made. In just a minute we're going to sing a praise song together, but first we need a tree trunk for our handprint tree. Do you think you can help turn me into a tree trunk?**

Give the children the brown crepe paper and help them wrap it around you. Stand near the hand print tree poster. Point out the pile of green crepe-paper strips. Either find a volunteer or say: **I'll be the tree trunk, and you can be the leafy green branches. Wave your green crepe paper in the air as we sing "I Praise You, Lord, With the Hands You Made."**

Lead children in singing "I Praise You, Lord, With the Hands You Made" with the Donut Forget CD. Then collect all the crepe paper and place it out of sight. Say: **That was fun! Now let's have some more fun praising God and learning more about the days of creation.**

BIBLE STORY TIME

Classroom supplies: paper plates, marker, paper sculptures from Lesson 1, CD player
Curriculum supplies: Donut Forget CD ("In the Beginning")

Before class, write the numbers 1-7 on paper plates. Make the numbers large enough for children to see them from several feet away.

Donut Forget™ Bible Story Lessons

13

Open your Bible to Genesis 1 and show it to the children. Read Genesis 1:1. Say: **This verse sounds just like our song "In the Beginning." Today we're going to do some fun things with that song to help us remember the days of creation. Do you think you can remember what was created on each day? Let's see how many days we can guess, then we'll listen to the song and see if we're right.**

One at a time, hold up the paper sculptures from Lesson 1. Have the children name the day each item was created. Then listen to "In the Beginning" from the Donut Forget CD. Praise the children for the items they placed on the correct days.

Give each child a paper sculpture. Then say: **This time, I'll hold up a number for each day of creation. When you see the number that matches your paper sculpture, stand up and hold it over your head.**

Play the song again and let children hold up their sculptures. Then say: **Are you ready for even more fun? This time we're going to sing the song without the CD. I'm going to choose seven volunteers to hold the paper plate numbers. The rest of you will hold up your paper sculptures again. But here's the catch—the paper plate number may not be in order. So you'll need to watch and listen carefully to hold up your sculpture on the right day.**

Choose seven children to hold the paper plates. (If you have fewer than ten children in your class, you may want to hold two plates yourself and choose three older children to hold one or two plates each.) Have the plate holders stand with their backs to the rest of the class. When you tap a plate holder's head, have her turn around and face the rest of the class as you lead them in singing the words for that day. Don't forget to sing the chorus "In the beginning God made the heavens and the earth . . ." after every few numbers. Repeat until all the children have had a chance to be plate holders, or as time allows.

SING-ALONG FUN TIME

Classroom supplies: Bible, star shakers from Center 2, CD player
Curriculum supplies: Donut Forget CD ("I Praise You, Lord, With the Hands You Made," "In the Beginning," "I'm So Wonderfully Made")

Open your Bible to Psalm 139:14 and show it to the children. Say: **We worship God for making everything on the earth. Psalm 139:14 says, "I praise you because you made me in an amazing and wonderful way." Let's play a game to help us learn this verse.**

Have children sit in a circle. As you sing along with "I Praise You, Lord, With the Hands You Made," have the children pass two or three star shakers around the circle. Stop the music periodically. Each time you stop the music, have the children who are holding the star shakers stand. Encourage other children to name amazing "star qualities" they see in those children. Repeat the game until each child has been affirmed.

Then form pairs and let the children toss and catch the star shakers in time to the music as you sing along with "In the Beginning." You may need to coach them at first to throw and catch with the beat of the song. If time allows, continue tossing and catching as you listen to "I'm So Wonderfully Made." (You'll spend more time on this song in Lessons 3 and 4).

Use the **Duncan** puppet and the script from the Donut Forget Songbook to talk about the memory verse, Psalm 139:14.

DONUT FORGET TIME

Classroom supplies: air-pop popcorn popper, popcorn, sheet
Curriculum supplies: none

Lay a sheet on the floor and place the air-pop popcorn popper in the center. Have the children sit around the edge of the sheet far enough from the popper to avoid being burned by hot popcorn. Hold up a handful of unpopped popcorn. Say: **Today we learned that God made the land, plants, and trees. This popcorn came from one of the plants that God made. We're going to use the popcorn to help us pray a prayer of thanks for all the wonderful things God has created.**

In just a minute, I'm going to turn on the popcorn popper. When the popcorn starts flying out of the popper, we'll take turns naming things God created. For example, someone might say, "God made trees." Then we'll all say, "Thank you God, for making trees." When you name something God made, then you may eat a piece of popcorn.

Fill the popper with popcorn kernels and plug it in. But leave the top off so that when a kernel pops, it flies out of the popper and lands on the sheet. As the corn begins to pop, lead children in thanking God for the amazing things he created for our world.

Let children "graze" on the popped popcorn, then have them help you clean up any leftovers.

LEARNING CENTERS

Set up the following activities for the children to do as they arrive. Assign an equal number of children to each activity. Have a teacher or helper available to assist the children with each activity.

At each Learning Center, welcome the children to your class. Make sure you know each child's name. Explain that today you'll be talking about all the wonderful things God has created and learning that we worship God for creating us in an amazing and wonderful way.

Center 1: Animal Shadows

Classroom supplies: strong light source (such as a large flashlight, a slide or overhead projector, or a lamp with lampshade removed), white sheet or projection screen, CD player
Curriculum supplies: copies of "Animal Shadows" handout (page 22), Donut Forget CD

Before the children arrive, set up a projection screen or hang a white sheet on the wall in the Gathering Time area. Set up a light source that will shine onto the screen or sheet. Photocopy the "Animal Shadows" handout. You'll need a copy for each child. Practice making the animal shadow figures so you'll be able to demonstrate them for the children.

Give each child a copy of the "Animal Shadows" handout. Demonstrate how to make each animal pictured. Play the unit songs from the Donut Forget CD as the children practice making the animal figures. Then turn on the light source and let the children make the animal shadows on the screen. Encourage them to create additional animal shadows of their own. Point out that God made all the different kinds of animals. Remind the children that we worship God for making everything.

BITE IDEA
IMPORTANT! Use a single-use camera to take pictures of children as they arrive today. You'll need the developed pictures for next week's Center 3. If some regular attenders are absent, call their parents and ask them to bring a non-Polaroid photo of their child to class next week.

Center 2: Animal Hands & Feet

Classroom supplies: construction paper, markers, scissors, glue, yarn, chenille wire, fabric scraps, sequins, cotton balls or fiberfill stuffing, CD player
Curriculum supplies: Donut Forget CD ("I Praise You, Lord, With the Hands You Made")

Set out construction paper, markers, scissors, and the other craft supplies you've brought. Help the children trace and cut out their hands or feet, then decorate the cutouts to look like animal hands or feet. For example, they could add sequins to create turtle or lizard feet, fiberfill stuffing for sheep feet, or pieces of yarn for lion paws. Have some children create extra hands and feet for the rest of the class.

As the children work, play "I Praise You, Lord, With the Hands You Made" from the Donut Forget CD. Remind the children that we worship God for making us in an amazing way. Point out that God made some pretty amazing animals, too.

Set the animal hands and feet aside for use later in the lesson.

Center 3: Mini-World Project

Classroom supplies: decorated mini-world from Lessons 1 and 2, construction paper, glue, scissors, chenille wire, aluminum foil, sequins or glitter, yarn, modeling clay, CD player
Curriculum supplies: Donut Forget CD

Review with the children what God created on Days 1–4. Then help the children identify what was created on Days 5 and 6 as you read Genesis 1:20-27.

Form three groups: the Fish Formers, the Bird Builders, and the Animal Architects. Have the Fish Formers glue fish-shaped yarn loops to the mini-world, then fill the loops with sequin or glitter "scales." Have the Bird Builders shape birds from aluminum foil or chenille wire, then suspend them from the top of the mini-world box. Have the Animal Architects sculpt animals out of modeling clay and place them inside the mini-world.

As the children work, play the unit songs from the Donut Forget CD. Invite the children to show and explain what they've added to the mini-world during Gathering Time.

GATHERING TIME

Classroom supplies: Bible, light source and projection screen from Center 1, CD player
Curriculum supplies: Donut Forget CD ("Sing and Skip and Dance")

Have the children sit down in the Gathering Time area. Invite them to tell you about the things they did at their Learning Centers. Then hold up the mini-world and say: **We've all been learning about the amazing animals God created. Look at the amazing animals in our mini-world. Let's give a big clap for the Fish Formers, the Bird Builders, and the Animal Architects who made all these amazing animals for our mini-world. Now let's give a big clap for Paws and Pads—the group that worked at Center 2. You made animal hands and feet that we'll get to use later. And last, but not least, Center 1. Please come up and show us all how to make animal shadows.**

Turn on the light source, and have the children from Center 1 demonstrate the animal shadows they practiced. Announce each shadow form with an introduction such as, "Introducing God's amazing crab!" As children practice each animal shadow, help them point out unique features of that animal.

After you've practiced all four shadows, say: **Amazing! God sure made a lot of wonderful animals. We worship God for making all of his wonderful creation. But did you know that animals can praise God, too? They don't praise God the way we do, but in their own special way, they praise God, too.**

16

Read Psalm 148:7-13. Say: **Animals, people, and all of creation can praise the God who created us. That makes me want to sing a praise song right now. Let's make our animal shadows skip and dance on the screen as we sing "Sing and Skip and Dance."**

Lead the children in singing "Sing and Skip and Dance" with the Donut Forget CD. As they sing, have them move their animal shadows up and down on the screen.

BIBLE STORY TIME

Classroom supplies: Bible
Curriculum supplies: none

Open your Bible to Genesis 1 and show it to the children. Say: **Our Bible story comes from the first book in the Bible, the book of Genesis. We've been learning about all the amazing creations God made for our world.**

Help the children review the things God created on Days 1-4. Then say: **God made the sky, water, land, plants, sun, moon, and stars in just four days. That's pretty amazing! On Days 5 and 6, God added a lot more living things to his world—animals and people. Let's have some more fun learning about God's amazing animals now.**

Form pairs and assign an animal to each pair. Say: **Work with your partner to act out a way your animal might praise God. For example, a bird might praise God by flapping its wings. A crocodile might praise God by opening and shutting its strong jaws.**

Help partners come up with ideas and actions to show how their animal might praise God. Then gather the children back together. Say: **Now let's see some animal praise. I'll ask each set of partners to tell the name of their animal. For example, suppose your animal is a crocodile. We'll all say, "Amazing crocodile, how do you praise?" Let me hear you say that all together.**

Then the partners can tell us and show us their crocodile praise. After they've shown us, we'll all do the actions with them as we say, "Crocodile praise! Crocodile praise! Yeah God! Hooray!" Let's practice that once.

Let partners take turns demonstrating their actions. For each animal, lead the children in asking, **Amazing (name of animal), how do you praise?** Then lead them in the chant, **(Animal) praise! (Animal) praise! Yeah God! Hooray!** as you do the actions together.

After all the pairs have demonstrated their animals, say: **That was fun. Now let's have some people praise during Sing-Along Fun Time.**

SING-ALONG FUN TIME

Classroom supplies: CD player
Curriculum supplies: Donut Forget CD ("Sing and Skip and Dance," "I'm So Wonderfully Made")

Have the children stand in a circle as you sing the chorus of "Sing and Skip and Dance." Have them turn and skip to the right the first time you sing "I love to sing and skip and dance." The first time you sing "shout hallelujah," have them stop and wave their hands in the air. The second time you sing "shout hallelujah," have them jump into the circle and wave their hands again. The third time, have them jump back to their original positions and wave their hands. Repeat the motions the second time through, only this time skip to the left. Encourage the children to make up their own motions to the verses.

Donut
Forget™
Bible Story
Lessons

After you sing "Sing and Skip and Dance" a few times, have the children sit in their circle and catch their breath as you listen to "I'm So Wonderfully Made." Then have the children sing the song with the CD.

DONUT FORGET TIME

Classroom supplies: animal hands and feet from Center 2
Curriculum supplies: none

BITE IDEA
Before children leave, check to make sure you've photographed each child. Plan to develop the pictures this week.

Have the children help you lay the animal hands and feet in a path on the floor. Lead children in this traveling prayer of thanks for the animals God made. As you come to each set of animal hands or feet, have the child who made them say: **We praise you, God, for the (name of animal).** Then have all the children say together: **Your amazing and wonderful creation.** Let children who didn't make their own animal hands or feet lead in thanking God for the animal of their choice.

Say: **God sure made some amazing animals. Animals, people, and all God's creations were made in a wonderful way.**

Close by singing "I'm So Wonderfully Made."

LEARNING CENTERS

Set up the following activities for the children to do as they arrive. Assign an equal number of children to each activity. Have a teacher or helper available to assist the children with each activity.

At each Learning Center, welcome the children to your class. Make sure you know each child's name. Explain that today you'll be talking about God creating people in an amazing and wonderful way.

Center 1: Children Chain

Classroom supplies: newsprint, scissors, markers, yarn, fabric scraps, glue, CD player
Curriculum supplies: copies of children chain pattern (page 23), Donut Forget CD ("I'm So Wonderfully Made")

Before the children arrive, photocopy the child pattern. Practice cutting the children chain.

Show the sample children chain you've prepared. Help the children fold and cut the children chain. Have the children use the markers and other craft supplies you've provided to decorate a child on the chain to represent each child in your class. Encourage them to use the yarn and fabric scraps to add hair and clothing to each child on the chain.

As the children work, play "I'm So Wonderfully Made" from the Donut Forget CD. Point out how each child on the chain is different, just as each child in your class is different. Remind the children that God made each of us in an amazing and wonderful way. Hang the chain near the Gathering Time area.

Center 2: Babies

Classroom supplies: baby clothes, baby bottles, pacifiers, baby toys, CD player
Curriculum supplies: Donut Forget CD ("I'm So Wonderfully Made")

Set out the baby clothes and supplies you've brought. Have children pretend they're babies again. Help them discuss and act out the things babies do during the first year of their lives. Encourage the children to compare the things they can do now with the things babies can do. Point out God's wonderful plan for them to grow.

Sing "I'm So Wonderfully Made" from the Donut Forget CD.

Center 3: Mini-World Project

Classroom supplies: decorated mini-world from Lessons 1–3, construction paper, glue, scissors, children's pictures taken last week, CD player
Curriculum supplies: Donut Forget CD ("I'm So Wonderfully Made")

Review with the children what God created on Days 1–6. Point out that people are God's greatest creation, then explain that the children will add themselves to the mini-world.

Give each child his photo. Help the children cut out the heads from the pictures, then glue the trimmed photos onto construction paper. Let the children draw bodies to go with their photo heads, then decorate the photo people as they wish. When the children finish their photo people, have them create photo people for the rest of the class.

As children work, play "I'm So Wonderfully Made" from the Donut Forget CD. When all the people are finished, set them aside. (You'll attach them to the mini-world during Gathering Time.)

GATHERING TIME

Classroom supplies: photo people from Center 3, mini-world box, washable ink pad, CD player, tape
Curriculum supplies: copy of "Amazing Prints" (page 24), Donut Forget CD ("I Praise You, Lord, With the Hands You Made")

Before class, fill in the children's names on the "Amazing Prints" page. Bring the completed page with you to Gathering Time.

Have the children sit down in the Gathering Time area. Invite them to tell you about the things they did at their Learning Centers. Then say: **Today we're talking about people, God's greatest creation. If you made a chain of all the amazing and wonderful people in our class, say, "Chugga-chugga, chain, chain!"** Point to the chain and say: **Look at all the wonderful people on our children chain. God made each of us special! Be sure to find yourself on the chain after class.**

If you discovered the amazing ways you've grown since you were babies, put your thumb in your mouth and say, "Goo-goo." If you made amazing people to add to our mini-world, please join me at the front.

Have the Center 3 children show the photo people. Let each child tape her own photo person to the outside of the mini-world box.

Point to the inside of the mini-world box. Say: **Look at all the beautiful things God created for the earth.** Then turn the box around so the outside is facing the children. Say: **And look at all the beautiful people God put on our world. I'm so glad each one of you is a part of our class. You know why? Because there is no one else like you. You are one of a kind. Even your fingerprints are different from everyone else's. No one in the world has fingerprints like yours.**

19

One at a time, invite the children to come up and print their thumbprint on the handout. When all the children have added their prints, pass the handout around and let the children observe the unique prints. Hold up the handout and say: **Let's post this handout on our classroom door so anyone who walks by will know that we have some amazing and wonderful people in this class!**

Post the handout on the door, then lead the children in celebrating their uniqueness by singing "I Praise You, Lord, With the Hands You Made" with the Donut Forget CD.

BIBLE STORY TIME

Classroom supplies: Bible, paper or plastic cups, pitcher of water, CD player
Curriculum supplies: Donut Forget CD ("I'm So Wonderfully Made")

Open your Bible to Genesis 1 and show it to the children. Say: **We've learned about all that God created. How many days did God take to create the world?** Let the children respond.

Say: **We've learned about all the wonderful plants and animals God put in our world. Today we're talking about people, God's most amazing creation. After God made all the other creations in the world, God made people to take care of the world and enjoy all the beautiful things he'd put in it. First God made a man, Adam. Then he made a woman, Eve, so that Adam wouldn't be lonely. God told Adam and Eve to take care of the world and everything in it.**

Beginning with the very first people, Adam and Eve, God made people's bodies in a very special way. He thought of everything. Just think about our thumbs. What would it be like if we didn't have thumbs?

Demonstrate trying to pick up a cup without using your thumb. Give the children cups and let them try. Then ask: **What would it be like if we didn't have elbows?**

Demonstrate trying to drink from the glass without bending your elbow. Have the children try this, too.

Continue the demonstration, letting the children suggest body parts that we rely on for drinking from a cup. For example, ask what would happen if we had no arms, if our mouths didn't open and close, or if we couldn't swallow.

Say: **We praise God for making us in an amazing way. He thought of everything. Let's use our amazing thumbs, fingers, hands, mouths, and throats to enjoy some cool water now.**

Fill the children's cups half-full with water. Play "I'm So Wonderfully Made" from the Donut Forget CD as they enjoy their drinks.

BITE IDEA
If you have fewer than six children in your class, you may want to make only one set of "hallelujah bells." Instead of echoing the verses, have children all sing together. If you have outgoing or musical students in any size class, invite them to sing "solos" on one or two phrases from the verses. The rest of the class can echo.

SING-ALONG FUN TIME

Classroom supplies: colored yarn, one jingle bell for each child, CD player
Curriculum supplies: Donut Forget CD

Before class, arrange for the children to lead worship in an adult class or church service using the Donut Man songs they've learned.

Let the children "warm up" with their favorite unit songs. Then say: **We worship God because he made us. We've been having a great time singing and skipping and dancing and praising God together with our unit songs. Today we're going to share our worship by singing "Sing and Skip and Dance" for another group. Let's make "hallelujah bells" to go along with our singing.**

Form two groups. As you practice singing "Sing and Skip and Dance" with the CD, have the children in each group thread the jingle bells onto a long strand of yarn. Knot the yarn around the end bells on each strand.

Have children form two single-file lines by holding onto the string between the bells. Let them practice skipping and dancing with the hallelujah bells as you listen to "Sing and Skip and Dance." Encourage them to shake the bells each time they sing, "hallelujah." On the verses, have the groups take turns echoing the words to each other.

Ten to fifteen minutes before the end of your class time, have the children line up at the door. Have them hold the bells in their hands as they walk to the class where you'll lead in worship. When you arrive, pray with the children outside the door before you go in. Pray: **Lord, we worship you because you made us. Be with us as we lead others to worship you, too. In Jesus' name, amen.**

DONUT FORGET TIME

Classroom supplies: Bible, hallelujah bells from Sing-Along Fun Time, CD player
Curriculum supplies: Donut Forget CD ("Sing and Skip and Dance")

Have the children wait outside the door with their hallelujah bells. Enter the class and thank the leader for having you. Read Psalm 139:14. Say: **Our class has been learning that we worship God for making people and all the other amazing things in our world. We want to share our worship with you as we sing and skip and dance to praise God for making people in such an amazing and wonderful way.**

Start the CD, then cue the children to skip into the room with their bell strings and sing the song. Repeat the song if time allows, and invite adults to sing along on the chorus.

Close in prayer, thanking God for each unique child and adult in your gathering.

21

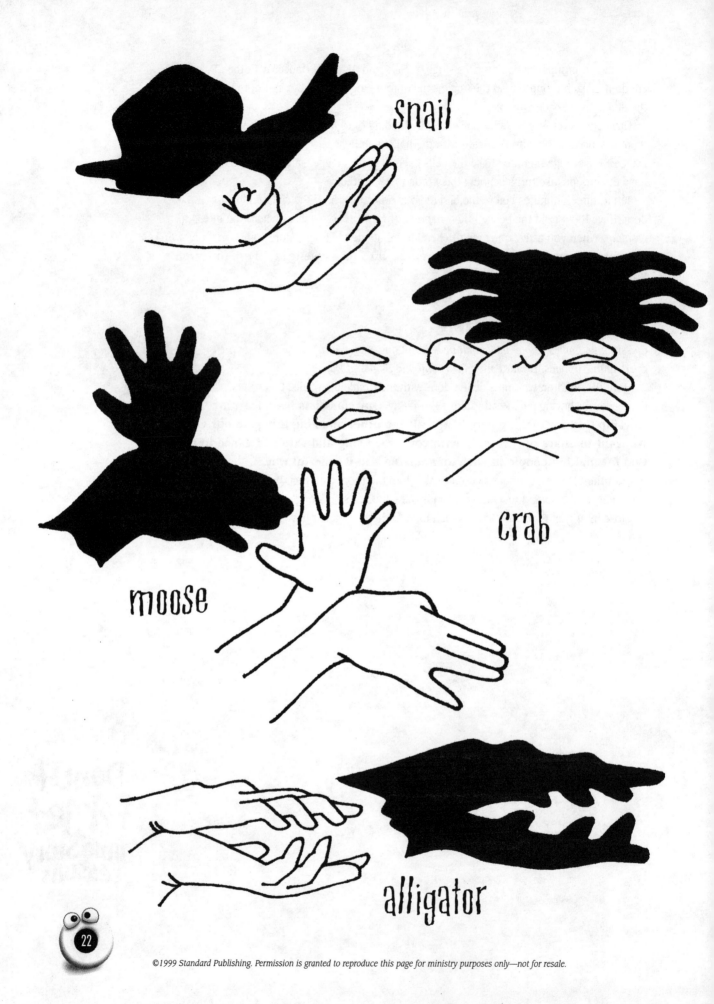

snail

crab

moose

alligator

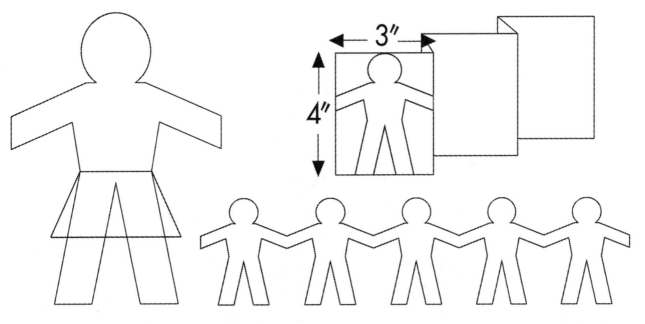

3"

4"

Child chain

Star Shaker

Donut forget™
Bible Story Lessons

23

AMaZiNG PRINTS

"I praise you because you made me in an amazing and wonderful way."

(Psalm 139:14)

24

Donut Forget to Obey the Bible

BY THE END OF THIS UNIT, LEARNERS WILL

Know Tell how two Bible people obeyed God's Word.
Feel Feel thankful for the Bible.
Do Obey the Bible, God's Word.

MEMORY VERSE

"How can a young person live a pure life? He can do it by obeying your word" (Psalm 119:9).

Josiah became a king at the tender age of eight. His evil father, Amon, had worshiped idols and disobeyed God. Instead of following in his father's footsteps, Josiah chose to seek God. He obeyed the Lord, and when he was a young adult he tore down altars to other gods his people had set up. Later he sought diligently to repair the temple.

Like Josiah, Samuel too was called by the Lord as a young child. He listened to and obeyed God from the first time he heard the Lord until he died an old man.

Josiah and Samuel loved God so much that they determined to keep God's commandments with all their hearts and to live out the word of God. Their deeds and example caused people to follow the Lord throughout their lifetimes and beyond.

Josiah and Samuel provide exciting examples of children who were devoted to hearing God's Word and then doing it. The children in your class can have this same devotion to God's Word. Use these lessons to help children see the importance of obeying God by listening to his Word and then doing it.

	LESSON 1	LESSON 2	LESSON 3	LESSON 4
Center 1	dough cross	Bible memory book	puzzle pictures	hands & heart banner
Center 2	edible Josiahs	guiros	soda can shakers	bleached hearts
Center 3	Josiah poster	crowns	Samuel poster	paper sack robes
Gathering Time	find the treat	guiro partners	no arguing	holding the banner
Bible Story Time	2 Chronicles 34, poster	2 Chronicles 34, actions	1 Samuel 3, poster	1 Samuel 3, actions
Sing-Along Fun Time	Josiah game	Josiah songleaders	song motions	practice for parade
Donut Forget Time	obey flags	getting rid of idols	picture puzzles	Bible parade

LEARNING CENTERS

Set up the following activities for the children to do as they arrive. Assign an equal number of children and a teacher or helper to each activity.

At each Learning Center, welcome the children to your class. Make sure you know each child's name. Explain that today you'll be talking about ways we can obey God's Word, the Bible.

Center 1: Dough Cross

Classroom supplies: modeling dough, CD player
Curriculum supplies: Donut Forget CD ("Josiah")

Explain that today you'll be learning about a boy named Josiah who became a king when he was eight years old. Briefly summarize Josiah's story. Point out that Josiah tore down the idols the people had created.

Give each child a lump of modeling dough. Have the children work by themselves or with partners to create model "idols." Encourage them to make their idols as elaborate as they want. As the children work, play "Josiah" from the Donut Forget CD.

After the children have finished their idols, talk about how silly it would be to worship what they made out of dough. Then have the children punch down and flatten their idols.

Repeat the building and smashing if time allows. After all the idols have been smashed, have the children put their dough in the center of the table. Invite them to help you form the dough into a cross shape. Point out that instead of following idols, we obey and follow Jesus.

Leave the cross shape in the center of the table. You'll refer to it during Donut Forget Time.

Center 2: Edible Josiahs

Classroom supplies: bananas, plastic knives, paper plates, peanut butter, chocolate chips or raisins, pretzel sticks, fruit leather, CD player
Curriculum supplies: Donut Forget CD ("Josiah")

Before class, cut the fruit leather into 2-by-3-inch rectangular pieces. You'll need one fruit leather piece for each child in your class. (The children will make enough figures to share the snack during Gathering Time.)

BITE IDEA
If the children have trouble with the bananas tipping over, have them assemble the figures with the bananas lying down on the plate.

Set out the bananas, plastic knives, small paper plates, and bowls of peanut butter, chocolate chips or raisins, and pretzel sticks. Explain to the children that if they follow instructions carefully they will make special edible Bible action figures!

Form four groups: the Body Builders, the Eye Poppers, the Strong Arms, and the Crazy Capers. Have the Body Builders peel and halve bananas, then set them on paper plates. Have the Eye Poppers dip chocolate chips or raisins in peanut butter "glue" and stick them on the banana halves to create facial features for the figures. Have the Strong Arms add two pretzel arms to each figure. The Crazy Capers will "glue" the fruit leather capes to the backs of the figures.

As the children work, play "Josiah" from the Donut Forget CD. Tell the children that the figures they're making are Josiah figures, and that Josiah was a boy who became a great king who loved God. Explain that they'll add edible crowns and eat the figures during Gathering Time.

Center 3: Josiah Poster

Classroom supplies: large sheet of poster board, markers, glue, glitter glue, aluminum foil or gold foil gift wrap, fabric scraps or purple or red tissue paper, CD player.
Curriculum supplies: Donut Forget CD ("Josiah")

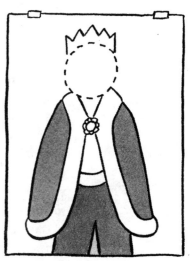

Before class, cut a hole about 6 inches from the top of a large sheet of poster board. Make the hole large enough for a child's face to show through. The poster needs to be large enough so that when a child stands behind it with his face peeking out, his legs show only from the knees down.

Read James 1:22 from an easy-to-understand translation. Point out that today they'll be learning about a boy who was a doer of God's Word, not just a listener. Have the children repeat the verse with you, then invite them to help you prepare a Josiah figure for use later in the lesson.

Place the poster board on the floor and have a child lie on top of it face up. Make sure the child's head is in the face cutout. Trace the child's body lightly with a pencil. Leave the legs open at the bottom. Show the children how to put their faces in the figure's cutout.

Place the poster on the table. Draw a crown above the cutout and a cape around the arms, as shown in the illustration. Have the children decorate Josiah's clothes using markers. Encourage them to add "kingly" features such as an aluminum or gold foil belt and glitter glue buttons or patterns on his crown, shirt, and pants. Help them glue pieces of fabric or purple or red tissue paper to the cape.

As the children work, play "Josiah" from the Donut Forget CD. When you finish the poster, let the children take turns standing behind it.

Set the poster aside to use later during Bible Story Time.

GATHERING TIME

Classroom supplies: bag of Hershey's chocolate kisses
Curriculum supplies: none

Before class, hide the chocolate kisses where the children won't be able to find them, such as in a purse, backpack, or coat pocket.

Have the children sit down in the Gathering Time area. Invite them to tell you about the things they made at their Learning Centers. Then say: **That's great! You all made a lot of things today. If you helped build a modeling dough cross, stand up and take a bow, then sit down.**

Wait for the children to respond, then hold up the Josiah poster and peek through it. Say: **Oh my. Who is this royal-looking fellow? Can someone from Center 3 tell me about him?**

Invite the Center 3 children to tell you about the Josiah figure. Then say: **And I believe some of you made us a yummy snack. Center 2 group, what have you made for us to eat?**

Invite the Center 2 children to show and describe an edible Josiah figure, but don't distribute them yet. Look at the Josiah figure, then scratch your head. Say: **Hmm. These Josiahs look yummy, but they don't look very kingly. I think something's missing. Can anyone figure out what it is?**

Let the children respond, then say: **I've hidden some chocolate kiss crowns for our Josiahs somewhere in the classroom! I need a few volunteers to find them.**

Donut Forget™ Bible Story Lessons

Choose two or three children to look for the kisses without any instructions. After a few minutes have them sit down and let others try. Then say: **No one was able to find the crowns. What should we do?**

Let the children respond, then say: **I think I need to give you more instructions. Listen carefully to my words. If you follow my directions, you'll be able to find the treat.**

Choose a child who hasn't had a chance to look for the kisses. Tell the child where to look, then have the child bring you the kisses.

Ask: **Why was (name of child) able to find the candy when the others couldn't? Yes, I told (name) what to do. (Name) listened to my words and obeyed them. God's Word, the Bible, is like that. If we obey God's words to us, we'll receive good things. Who wants to obey God's Word? That's great that all of you want to obey God's Word. Josiah wanted to obey God's Word, too. That's why he was a great king. I think these Josiah figures look pretty great, too. Let's give them some chocolate kiss crowns and gobble them up. Then we'll hear more about Josiah.**

Give each child a Josiah figure and a chocolate kiss crown. Let the children enjoy the snack, then have them throw their plates away and join you in the story area.

BIBLE STORY TIME

Classroom supplies: Bible, Josiah poster from Center 2, CD player
Curriculum supplies: Donut Forget CD ("Josiah")

Open your Bible to 2 Chronicles 34 and show the passage to the children. Say: **Our Bible story today comes from the second book of Chronicles. It's about Josiah. Josiah became a king when he was only eight years old. That's not much older than you! Can you imagine being a king? We're going to find out how Josiah became king in just a moment, but first I need some helpers.**

Hold up the Josiah poster and choose two children to stand near you and hold it up. Say: **I'm looking for the quietest, most kingly looking person in this room. (Name of child), you are being so quiet and respectful, you'd make an excellent king, just like Josiah.**

Have the child stand behind the poster with her face showing. Say: **Josiah's father before him had been a bad, bad king. Show me a bad face. Oh, you look so mean! Josiah's father disobeyed God and let people build altars and statues to other gods. They worshiped them instead of worshiping God.**

When Josiah became king, he did not act like his father—he loved God! Show me a happy face. Yes, I'm sure that's just how Josiah looked! After Josiah was king for a little while, he did a brave thing. He went through the town and tore down all the idols and statues people had made to other gods. Show me some muscle with your arms! Yes, you look strong, just like Josiah! Let's pretend to tear down the idols.

Make pounding actions in the air, then say: **Parts of God's temple where the people were supposed to worship God were broken and old. Josiah told workers to build it back up. One day, the priest in the temple found something important. It was the book of the laws of God. It had been forgotten for many years. Josiah read the book. He studied it. Then he said, "We must obey these laws. We must do what God says." And they did. God was happy with Josiah and he blessed him with a good life. As long as he lived, the people did not turn from following God.**

Take the poster and ask the children to sit down. Say: **Thank you, (name of children), for helping us with our story. Now I need two other poster holders and a new Josiah. I also have an important job for everyone else.**

Choose three new children, get them in position, and say: **The rest of you can help, too. I need you to tell me the story this time.**

Have the remaining children tell you the story of Josiah. Then set the poster aside. Say: **Let's learn a song now about Josiah and how he was strong and tore the idols down.**

Play "Josiah" from the Donut Forget CD. Let the children listen to the song once, then play it again and invite them to sing along.

Ask:

- **How do you think Josiah felt being a king?**
- **How can you be like Josiah?**

Say: **We act like Josiah when we obey God's Word, our parents, and our teachers. You make lots of people happy when you obey! Let's sing our memory verse song now to remind us to obey God with all our hearts.**

SING-ALONG FUN TIME

Classroom supplies: CD player
Curriculum supplies: Donut Forget CD ("Live a Pure Life," "Josiah")

Lead the children in repeating the memory verse, then play "Live a Pure Life" from the Donut Forget CD. Play the song a second time and have the children sing along. Then say: **Obeying God is so fun and exciting, it's hard to sit still. Let's get up and play a game as we sing "Josiah."**

As we sing I'm going to tag some of you when we get to the part about the idols being knocked down. If you get tagged, fall down like one of the idols. Please walk, don't run, as we sing and play. And be sure to watch out for fallen "idols!"

Play the song "Josiah" and walk around the room singing. Tag some children at the appropriate parts of the song. Repeat the song and tag other children. At the end of the song, tag everyone so that all the children are lying down. Let the children rest for a few moments, then continue with the lesson.

DONUT FORGET TIME

Classroom supplies: plastic drinking straw for each child, scissors, index cards, marker, CD player
Curriculum supplies: Donut Forget CD ("Live a Pure Life")

Before class, cut a 3-inch slit at the end of each drinking straw.

Say: **One way we worship God is by doing the things he tells us. We want to be "doers of the word." James 1:22 says, "Do what God's teaching says; do not just listen and do nothing." I'm going to read some other verses. Think about them like Josiah did. Then tell me what you think God is telling you to do.**

Read the following verses (or ask older children to read them) and ask the children to give examples of how they can obey each one. As they respond, write one or two words on each index card to represent what they'll do. Suggestions are given after the verses.

- "Love each other deeply with all your heart," 1 Peter 1:22. (Be kind, love.)
- "Do everything without complaining or arguing," Philippians 2:14. (No arguing.)

29

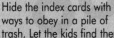

- "Be sure that no one pays back wrong for wrong. But always try to do what is good for each other," 1 Thessalonians 5:15. (No paybacks.)
- "Children, obey your parents the way the Lord wants. This is the right thing to do," Ephesians 6:1. (Obey your parents.)
- "Loving God means obeying his commands," 1 John 5:3 (Obey God.)

Give each child one of the index cards and a drinking straw. Show the children how to make flag by slipping the index card into the slit. If time allows, let the children decorate their flags with crayons or markers.

BITE IDEA
Hide the index cards with ways to obey in a pile of trash. Let the kids find them just like the priest found God's Word in the temple rubble.

When everyone has a flag, sing "Live a Pure Life." As the children sing the words "obeying your Word," have them wave their flags in the air.

After the song, gather around the modeling dough cross. Say: **Let's take turns putting our flags into the modeling dough cross. When it's your turn to put your flag in the cross, ask God to help you obey his Word by saying, "God, help me to . . ."** (repeat the verse on each card). Give each child a chance to put his flag in the dough, and help him to repeat the verse written on it.

Then pray: **Jesus, we love you. We want to show you that we love you by obeying your Word. Help us listen to your Word and obey it. Amen.**

LEARNING CENTERS

Set up the following activities for the children to do as they arrive. Assign an equal number of children and a teacher or helper to each activity.

At each Learning Center, welcome the children to your class. Make sure you know each child's name. Explain that today you'll be talking about ways we can obey God's Word, the Bible.

Center 1: Bible Memory Book

Classroom supplies: one colored or manila file folder for each child, scissors, glue, markers, glitter glue
Curriculum supplies: photocopies of "Bible Memory Book" handout (page 41)

Before class, cut the tabs off the file folders. Photocopy and cut apart the "Bible Memory Book" handout. You'll need a copy for each child.

Remind the children that knowing about God's Word, the Bible, can help us obey God as Josiah did. Tell the children they'll be making a Bible Memory Book to help them remember and obey God's Word.

Give each child a file folder and a copy of the "My Bible Memory Book" section of the handout. Have the children glue the sections to the front of the folders. Next have them glue the bottom half of the handout inside the folder. Explain that they'll use the Bible Memory Books to help them learn their memory verse, Psalm 119:9. Read the verse and have the children repeat it with you.

Let the children decorate their Bible Memory Books with markers. Show them how to "emboss" their names on the front cover with glitter glue. As the children finish their books, let them help you prepare extra books for the other children in the class. Set the finished books aside to dry.

30

Center 2: Guiro

Classroom supplies: two wooden skewers for each child; small wood or plastic beads with holes large enough to fit on the skewers, about 22-24 per child; slightly larger wood or plastic beads, one per child; different colors of electrical tape; glue; CD player
Curriculum supplies: Donut Forget CD ("Live a Pure Life")

Before class, make a sample guiro (pronounced GWEER-oh) as described below. Show the children how to play the guiro by scraping the beads backward and forward with the bead scraper. Explain that it's a South American rhythm instrument.

Give each child a wooden skewer. Have the children wrap electrical tape around one end of their skewers until they've created a raised edge large enough to keep the beads from sliding off. (The raised edge will be the handle of the guiro.)

Next, have the children thread the beads onto the skewer, saving room at the top for one large bead. Glue the large bead in place. (If large beads aren't available, wind several layers of electrical tape around the skewer tip until it's thick enough to keep the beads in place.)

Give each child a second skewer. Have the children make bead scrapers by covering both tips of their skewers with electrical tape. Help them cover the handle end of the skewer with a wider band of tape.

Play "Live a Pure Heart" from the Donut Forget CD and encourage the children to play their guiros as they listen. Have them experiment with different rhythms and tempos as they rub the beads with the scraper.

Set the guiros aside to use during Donut Forget Time. Caution the children to handle the guiros carefully so no one gets poked.

Center 3: Crowns

Classroom supplies: poster board, scissors, aluminum foil (optional), glitter glue, markers, foil star stickers, stapler, CD player
Curriculum supplies: Donut Forget CD ("Josiah")

Before class, cut out a large, pointy poster board crown for each child. If you have mostly older children, trace the crowns for the children to cut out during class.

Give each child a poster board crown. Have the children write their names on the crowns, then decorate them using glitter glue, markers, and foil star stickers.

As the children work, invite them to review what they learned about Josiah last week.

As the children finish decorating their crowns, measure each child's crown to her head. Cut off any excess and staple the crown's ends together. Have the children wear the crowns as you sing along with the Donut Man song "Josiah."

BITE IDEA
For a special touch, cover the crowns with foil before decorating.

Have the children wear their crowns to Gathering Time. Explain that they'll use the crowns later today and during the next few lessons, then they may take them home.

GATHERING TIME

Classroom supplies: guiros from Center 2, additional rhythm instruments if needed, CD player
Curriculum supplies: Donut Forget CD ("Live a Pure Life")

Have the children sit down in the Gathering Time area. Invite them to tell you about the things they made at their Learning Centers. Then say: **What great things you made to help us learn more about Josiah! He's a great Bible friend. When I say Josiah's**

Donut Forget™ Bible Story Lessons

name again, if you made a Josiah crown, stand up and say, **"God has given you a crown."** Pause, then repeat: **Josiah.**

Wait for the children to respond, then continue: **Some of you made Bible Memory Books to help us learn our memory verse. If you made a Bible Memory Book, turn and tell someone sitting near you where our Bible verse is found.** (If necessary, remind the children that the Bible verse comes from Psalm 119:9.)

Let the children share the verse reference, then say: **Great! Later we'll all get to have a Bible Memory Book to take home to help us with the memory verse. Right now let's have some fun learning what our memory verse says.**

Have the children who made guiros stand up. Say: **Some of you made some special rhythm instruments called guiros. If you made a guiro, play it as we sing our memory verse song.**

Let the children play their guiros as you sing "Live a Pure Life" with the Donut Forget CD. Then say: **Everyone with a guiro, find a partner. If you don't have a partner, come stand by me.**

Help the children form pairs. If some pairs don't have a guiro partner, give one child another rhythm instrument. Help the children designate who will be the player and who will be the singer. (Or have one child hold the guiro while the other child plays. Both can sing.)

Say: **We're going to sing our memory verse song again. This time each pair will sing and play on one word of the song's chorus. When I point to you, stand up. Have the singer sing the next word of the song while the player plays the guiro. We'll start out slowly, then see how fast we can go.**

Lead the children in singing the song. Have pairs take turns singing the words of the chorus as they play their guiros. Have everyone sing the verses together. Pick up the tempo each time you repeat the song.

Then say: **How can a young person live a pure life?** Let the children respond, then continue: **By obeying God's Word. Now let's review how Josiah obeyed God's Word.**

BIBLE STORY TIME

Classroom supplies: Bible, CD player
Curriculum supplies: Donut Forget CD ("Josiah")

Open your Bible to 2 Chronicles 34 and show it to the children. Then say: **I'm going to tell Josiah's story, and you can help me. First listen, then say what I say and do what I do.**

As you tell the following story, do the actions in parentheses. Pause after you say each line to allow the children to repeat the words and actions.

I'm Josiah. I'm the king. (Make a crown on head with hands.)
I'm only eight years old. (Hold up eight fingers.)
My father, Amon, was a bad king. (Wag finger as if scolding.)
But I don't want to follow in his footsteps. (Shake head no.)
Nope. I want to walk in God's ways. (Walk in place.)
It won't be easy. (Shake head no.)
My people might not listen to me. (Cover ears.)
But I'm going to follow God. (Use thumbs to point to self.)
Listen. What's that sound? (Cup hand to ear.)
It sounds like hammering. (Pretend to hammer.)
I wonder what it is? (Hold up hands, look perplexed.)

32

Oh no! Oh no! (Place hands on cheeks, drop mouth open.)

People are building statues and altars to other gods. And they're bowing down to them. (Pretend to bow down.)

That's not right. (Fold arms to chest.)

I must tear those idols down. (Nod head.)

Smash! Crash! Don't worship idols! (Pound fist in hand.)

Worship the true God instead! (Point up to heaven.)

Hey, what's this? (Bend down as if picking up something from the ground.)

It looks like a piece of God's temple. (Pretend to examine the object you've picked up.)

I'll have my workers repair the temple right away. (Touch finger to temple as if you've come up with a brilliant idea.)

My workers cleaned up the temple. (Pretend to sweep.)

And guess what they found? (Hold out hands, palms up.)

The book of the laws of God! (Hold hands together, palms up, as if reading a book.)

I read it to my people, and they agreed to obey God. Hurray! (Jump up and down as if cheering.)

I hope you'll obey God's Word, too. (Point to the children.)

Good-bye! (Wave good-bye.)

SING-ALONG FUN TIME

Classroom supplies: Josiah poster from Lesson 1, CD player
Curriculum supplies: Donut Forget CD ("Josiah," "I Like the Bible," "I'm So Wonderfully Made")

Bring out the Josiah poster from Lesson 1. Choose three children to be poster holders and Josiah. Say: **Josiah will be our song leader. Josiah, remember to sing nice and loud while we sing with you. After a few minutes, I'll choose another Josiah to be our leader.**

Use the **Duncan** puppet and the script from the Donut Forget Songbook to talk about the memory verse, Psalm 119:9.

Sing "Josiah" and "I Like the Bible." Change Josiahs several times during each song. Make sure each child gets a chance to be Josiah and lead the singing. If you need to sing another song to allow time for all the children to be Josiahs, sing "I'm So Wonderfully Made" from Unit 1.

Point out that just as everyone got to be Josiah, we can all obey God as Josiah did. Put the Josiah poster away for use in future lessons.

DONUT FORGET TIME

Classroom supplies: magazines, scissors, stickers, CD player
Curriculum supplies: Donut Forget CD ("Josiah")

Before class, cut out pictures that represent things that might be idols for the children, such as toys, candy, houses, cars, pets, clothes, money, and friends. Set a waste basket or empty box near you in the Bible story area.

Ask: **What did Josiah do that made God happy? What can you do to make God happy?**

Let the children respond, then say: **Josiah told people to stop worshiping idols and to worship God. Today we don't worship statues, but whenever something is more important to us than obeying God, that thing could be an idol. Name one of your favorite things.** Let children respond. **Do you love God more than that thing? If you do, then you are making that thing an idol.**

Hold up the magazine pictures. Say: **Here are some pictures of some of the idols we've mentioned. Choose one that might be an idol for you.**

Let the children choose their idols. Then say: **Let's listen to our Josiah song once more. When we get to the part about Josiah tearing down the idols, I'm going to stop the tape. Then we'll crumple our paper idols and throw them in this waste basket.**

Play "Josiah." After the words, "So he tore their idols down, drove the evil out of town and led the nation of Judah back to God again," have the children crumple their pictures and throw them into the basket.

Play the rest of the song. Say: **You did a good job of getting rid of those idols! Let's pray together. Dear God, please help us to see whenever there is something in our life that is more important to us than you. We love you, God. Amen.**

Before the children leave, give them their Bible Memory Books. Encourage the children who think they know the memory verse to say it to you. Place stickers in children's books if they're able to say the verse. Let the children take their books with them so they can work on learning the verse at home. Remind them to bring the books back next week.

LEARNING CENTERS

Set up the following activities for the children to do as they arrive. Assign an equal number of children and a teacher or helper to each activity.

At each Learning Center, welcome the children to your class. Make sure you know each child's name. Explain that today you'll be talking about ways we can obey God's Word, the Bible.

Center 1: Puzzle Pictures

Classroom supplies: poster board, markers or crayons, scissors, CD player
Curriculum supplies: Donut Forget CD ("I Like the Bible")

Before class, cut large sheets of poster board in half. You'll need one half-sheet of poster board for every two children.

Explain to the children that today you'll learn about another young person who obeyed God. Invite the children to share ways they've obeyed God this week. Help them brainstorm other ways they can obey God.

Form pairs. Give each pair a half-sheet of poster board. Set out markers and have pairs draw a large picture of a way they can obey God. As the children work, play "I Like the Bible" from the Donut Forget CD.

When the children finish their pictures, invite them to describe what they've drawn. Then distribute scissors and have pairs cut their pictures into puzzles. Explain that you'll use the puzzles later in the lesson.

BITE IDEA
Invite children who have brought their Bible Memory Books to say the memory verse (Psalm 119:9). Place stickers in the children's books after they've said the verse. Encourage them to bring their books and say the verse again next week.

Center 2: Soda Can Shaker

Classroom supplies: one clean, empty soda can for each child, transparent tape, different colors of electrical tape, construction paper, stickers, markers, a funnel, small dried beans, CD player
Curriculum supplies: Donut Forget CD ("I Like the Bible")

Before class, cut different colors of construction paper into 4-by-9-inch strips, long enough to fit around a soda can.

Remind the children that when we obey God's Word, good things happen. Explain that if they obey your instructions, they'll be able to create a fun rhythm instrument.

Give each child an empty soda can. Help the children use the funnel to pour about 2 tablespoons of dried beans into their cans. Cover the top of the can with pieces of electrical tape so that nothing will spill out. (It's okay if the tape ends hang over the edges of the can. They'll be covered up later.)

Help each child wrap a construction paper strip around the outside of her can, then secure it with transparent tape. Wrap a strip of colorful electrical tape along the top and bottom edges of the paper. Have the children decorate the cans with markers and stickers.

When the children finish their shakers, let them play along as you sing "I Like the Bible" with the Donut Forget CD. Have the children take their shakers with them to Gathering Time.

Center 3: Samuel Poster

Classroom supplies: large sheet of poster board, markers, construction paper, glue, fabric scraps or colored tissue paper, CD player
Curriculum supplies: Donut Forget CD ("Speak, Lord, I'm Listening")

Before class, prepare a sheet of poster board for a Samuel poster, similar to the Josiah poster from Lesson 1. (For detailed instructions, see page 27.)

Read Philippians 2:14 from an easy-to-understand translation. Point out that today you'll be learning about a boy who didn't argue or complain, but listened to God's instructions. Have the children repeat the verse with you, then invite them to help you prepare a Samuel figure for use later in the lesson.

Trace a child's body onto the poster as directed on page 27. Then place the poster on the table for the children to decorate. Explain that Samuel lived with the priest at the temple, so he didn't have kingly clothes like Josiah. Have the children decorate Samuel's clothes using markers or solid color fabric scraps. Encourage them to draw or attach a rolled construction paper scroll to represent God's Word. Have an older child write the memory verse on the scroll.

As the children work, play "Speak, Lord, I'm Listening" from the Donut Forget CD. When you finish the poster, let the children take turns standing behind it.

Set the poster aside to use later during Bible Story Time.

GATHERING TIME

Classroom supplies: Bible, shakers from Center 2, Samuel poster from Center 3
Curriculum supplies: none

Invite the children to tell you what they did at their learning centers. Say: **Some of you made puzzle pictures to show how you obey God. If you made a puzzle picture, clap your hands three times.**

Let the children respond, then say: **Some of you made shakers to accompany our music during Sing-Along Fun Time. If you made a shaker, shake it three times.**

Let the children respond, then hold up the Samuel poster. Say: **Some of you made a Samuel poster to help tell our Bible story. If you worked on the Samuel poster, stomp your feet three times.**

Let the children respond, then continue: **All three groups did great on their projects. And we sure don't want to argue about who did the best project! In Philippians 2:14 the Bible tells us not to argue or complain.**

Read Philippians 2:14. Say: **Tell me about a time you argued with someone. How did it make you feel?**

Say: **Arguing and complaining makes us feel bad inside. So to show we're in agreement that all the projects are great, we'll give each other high fives. Make sure you give a high five to at least one person from another group.**

Let the children give each other high fives, then continue: **Remember, we want to be doers of God's Word, and God's Word tells us not to argue or complain. Let's hear a story now about a boy who didn't argue or complain, but followed God's instructions right away.**

BIBLE STORY TIME

Classroom supplies: Bible, CD player
Curriculum supplies: Donut Forget CD ("Speak Lord, I'm Listening")

Open your Bible to 1 Samuel 3 and show it to the children. Say: **Our Bible story comes from the book of Samuel. Today we're going to learn a song that tells this story. It's about a boy named Samuel who heard God speak to him. Samuel obeyed God right away.**

Play "Speak, Lord, I'm Listening" from the Donut Forget CD. After the song, say: **Samuel obeyed God right away. God told Samuel to do something that was hard. But he did what God asked. Samuel was a doer of the Word.**

Ask:

■ **How can you be a doer of the Word like Samuel?**
■ **How can God talk to you?**

Say: **God speaks to us through his Word, the Bible. God can also speak to you through your parents. That's why it's important that we obey them.**

Let's review Samuel's story again. This time we'll do some actions along with the song.

Choose a child and two poster holders to play Samuel. Choose a child to be Eli. Have three children be Samuel's bed and three children be Eli's bed. Have Samuel and Eli lie down gently on the "beds." Play the song one more time and have the children sing along and act out their parts with the tape. If you have a large class, you may want to repeat the song until everyone has played a part.

SING-ALONG FUN TIME

Classroom supplies: CD player
Curriculum supplies: Donut Forget CD ("I Like the Bible," "Speak, Lord, I'm Listening")

Play the song "I Like the Bible." Help the children make up motions to the words. Accept and use their suggestions. If they have trouble coming up with ideas, suggest motions such as the following:

I like the Bible (Nodding head)
I read it (Open palms like a book)
I do it (Run in place)
When I'm reading through it (Hold one hand like a book, use other hand to page through it)
I'm a doer of the Word (March in place and nod head)

Suggest a big gesture on the last "I like the Bible," such as jumping up with legs spread and arms towards the sky. Practice the song several times until the children know the motions.

Say: **That was good work on those motions! Everyone stand up! Now let's make up motions for "Speak, Lord, I'm Listening."**

As you play the song, have the children suggest motions. Then play the song again and have everyone sing and do the motions together.

DONUT FORGET TIME

Classroom supplies: puzzles from Center 1, transparent tape, CD player
Curriculum supplies: Donut Forget CD ("I Like the Bible")

Form groups of two to four. Give each group one of the picture puzzles the children made at Center 1. (Make sure children don't get their own puzzles.) Have groups work with each other to put the puzzle together. Have the children tape their finished puzzles together and place them on a table.

Gather the children around the puzzles. Say: **Each puzzle shows a way we can obey God. Tell me what you see in these pictures.**

Let the children respond, then say: **Just as you worked together to figure out your puzzles, we learn God's Word together in class—so we can figure out what God wants us to do! Let's thank God for the Bible now. Dear God, we're glad you talk to us through your Word, the Bible. Help us remember to read the Bible and do what it says this week. Amen.**

Close by singing "I Like the Bible" with the Donut Forget CD. Display the finished puzzles on a classroom wall or bulletin board.

LEARNING CENTERS

Set up the following activities for the children to do as they arrive. Assign an equal number of children and a teacher or helper to each activity.

At each Learning Center, welcome the children to your class. Make sure you know each child's name. Explain that today you'll be learning more about how Samuel obeyed God.

BITE IDEA
Invite the children who have brought their Bible Memory Books to say the memory verse (Psalm 119:9). Place stickers in children's books after they've said the verse. Encourage them to take their books home to remind them to obey God's Word every day.

Center 1: Banner

Classroom supplies: butcher paper, markers, tempera paints, liquid soap, a sponge, scissors, towels, plastic tub, warm water, CD player
Curriculum supplies: Donut Forget CD ("Live a Pure Life")

Before class, cut a heart shape out of a large sponge. Write the words "Doers of the Word!" in large letters on a large sheet of butcher paper.

Read James 1:22. Show the children the sponge heart and invite them to tell you how our hearts can help us do God's Word. Let the children respond, then talk about ways they can use their hands to obey God's Word. Explain that they'll be making a "hearts and hands" banner to demonstrate their commitment to obey God.

Lay the butcher paper on a table or the floor. Add a few drops of liquid soap to pans of two or three colors of tempera paint and stir gently. Set the pans in the center of the work area.

Help the children each make one or two hand prints and several sponge heart prints. Set a tub of warm soapy water nearby for quick clean up. Have the children use a marker to write

37

their names near their handprints. Play "Live a Pure Life" from the Donut Forget CD as the children work.

Set the banner aside for use later in the lesson.

Center 2: Bleached Hearts

Classroom supplies: construction paper, scissors, liquid bleach, cotton swabs, small bowls, CD player

Curriculum supplies: Donut Forget CD ("Live a Pure Life")

Before class, cut out a large construction-paper heart for each child.

Set out cotton swabs, the hearts, and small bowls of bleach. Read Psalm 119:11. Talk with the children about what it means to hide God's Word in our hearts. Point out that hiding God's Word in our hearts helps us remember to do what the Bible says.

Using cotton swabs dipped in bleach, help the children draw or write something on their hearts to show they are doers of the Word. As the children work, tell them that when they memorize God's Word, it's like writing it on their hearts, like what they're doing with the bleach on the paper. Play "Live a Pure Life" from the Donut Forget CD as the children work.

Set the finished hearts aside for use during Donut Forget Time.

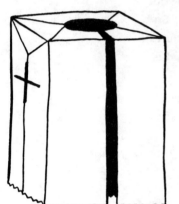

Center 3: Robes

Classroom supplies: paper grocery sack for each child; scissors; blue, purple, and red yarn; glue; CD player

Curriculum supplies: Donut Forget CD ("Speak, Lord, I'm Listening")

Before class, cut the grocery sacks as shown in the illustration.

If possible, have a child try on the grocery sack "robe" to make sure the armholes are right. Otherwise, fit and cut the armholes individually in class.

Set out the grocery sacks, glue, scissors, and yarn. Explain that while Samuel was living at the temple, his mother brought him a new robe each year. Since priests' clothing contained purple, blue, and red yarn, Samuel's robe may have been these colors, too.

Let the children decorate the grocery bag "robes" with the yarn. As they work, play "Speak, Lord, I'm Listening" from the Donut Forget CD.

Set the finished robes aside for use later in the lesson.

GATHERING TIME

Classroom supplies: Bible, banner from Center 1, markers

Curriculum supplies: none

Gather the children around you and invite them to tell you what they made at their Learning Centers. Begin with Center 3 and end with Center 1. Say: **This is a great banner you made. You put hearts on it to show you love God. You put hands on it to show that you'll use your hands to obey God's Word. But something is missing. Only the Center 1 group's names are on this banner. Does anyone from Center 2 or Center 3 want to be a doer of God's Word?**

Let the children respond, then invite them to come up and write their names on the banner. If time allows, they could even trace around their hands.

Have the children return to their seats, then hold up the banner in the center. It will droop on the ends. Say: **Hmm. I don't seem to be supporting this banner very well. I want to be a doer of God's Word, but sometimes it's hard to remember what the Bible says when we're on our own—just as it's hard for me to hold up this banner on my own. Will somebody come and help me?**

Choose a volunteer to help hold up the banner. Have the child stand as close to you as possible so the banner still droops. Say: **That's better, but I think we could use a little more support. Will another doer of God's Word join us behind the banner?**

Continue inviting the children to join you, one at a time, until everyone is behind the banner. Then say: **Wow! When we all stand together, there's no doubt our banner can be seen. Anyone who walked into this room right now would know for sure that we're all doers of God's Word. A little later we'll use our banner to tell others in our church how much we love God's Word. But right now, let's hear about our Bible friend Samuel—another doer of God's Word.**

BIBLE STORY TIME

Classroom supplies: Bible, CD player
Curriculum supplies: Donut Forget CD ("Josiah," "Speak Lord, I'm Listening")

Open the Bible to 1 Samuel 3. Say: **The book of 1 Samuel tells how God talked to Samuel when he was just a little boy. Stand with me and repeat what I say and do what I do.**

As you tell the following story, do the actions in parentheses. Pause after you say each line to allow the children to repeat the words and actions.

Hi, I'm Samuel. (Point to self with thumb.)
When I was little (Hold out index finger and thumb.)
I went to live in the temple. (Point over shoulder with thumb.)
Eli, an old priest, was my teacher. (Stroke chin like a beard.)
One night while I was asleep (Lay head on folded hands.)
I heard Eli call me. "Samuel!" (Cup hands around mouth.)
I ran to Eli. (Run in place.)
"Here I am, you called me." (Hold hands out, palms up.)
"But Eli said, "It wasn't me." (Shake head no.)
I went back to bed. (Lay head on folded hands.)
Then I heard it again. "Samuel!" (Cup hands around mouth.)
I jumped up! I ran to Eli! (Jump, then run in place.)
Eli said, "Samuel, God was calling you." (Shake index finger.)
I was surprised! (Look surprised, throw hands in air.)
I was happy! (Smile and put hand over heart.)
I went back and lay down. (Lay head on hands.)
Then I heard it again. "Samuel!" (Cup hands around mouth.)
I said, "Speak, Lord, your servant is listening." (Look toward heaven.)
Then God spoke to me. (Point to self.)
I did exactly what God told me. (Nod head.)
God used me to talk to his people. (Point to self with both hands.)
And now I'm talking to you. (Point to children.)
Please listen to God and obey (Point index finger up.)
Because he's calling YOU today! (Point to each child.)

Have the children sit down, then ask:

■ **How did Samuel obey the Lord?**
■ **How can you obey the Lord?**

Say: **When Samuel knew God was calling him, he responded right away. When you hear something in this class and go home and do it, you are being like Samuel. You are doers of the Word!**

Lead the children in singing "Speak, Lord, I'm Listening." Have them add the motions they made up last week.

SING-ALONG FUN TIME

Classroom supplies: props and instruments from Lessons 1-4 Learning Centers, CD player
Curriculum supplies: Donut Forget CD ("Josiah," "Speak, Lord, I'm Listening," "Live a Pure Life," "I Like the Bible")

Say: **We're doers of the Word! To celebrate that, we're going to have a Bible Celebration Parade. We'll march through the church as we sing our unit songs and let everyone know how much we love the Bible. Let's practice singing now.**

Give the children the props and instruments they made. Have the children who worked on the banner lead a march around the room as you practice singing the songs. Other children can wave their bleached hearts, shake their shakers, or wear their Samuel and Josiah attire.

When you're ready to take your parade out of the room, line the children up at the door and go over your planned route. Say: **We like the Bible! It's time to celebrate!**

DONUT FORGET TIME

Classroom and Curriculum supplies: parade supplies listed in Sing-Along Fun Time

Before class, plan a route for your Bible Celebration Parade. Let other classes know that you'll be passing by. Encourage other teachers to cheer the children on. Other classes may even want to join your parade!

Lead the Bible Celebration Parade along your planned route. After the parade, lead the children back to your room. Say: **I can tell you like the Bible! Let's have three cheers for all the doers of God's Word. Hip, hip, hooray! Hip, hip, hooray! Hip, hip, hooray!**

Hang the banner and posters in your classroom. Let the children take home their bleached hearts, shakers, crowns, and robes.

40

MY
BIBLE MEMORY
BOOK

"How can a young person live
a pure life? He can do it
by obeying your word."

Psalm 119:9

I know my Bible memory verse!

Date:

_____ _____ _____ _____ _____

Donut
forget™
Bible Story
Lessons

41

Teaching children Christian values just got a whole lot easier. ◆

ON TOUR
Kids will learn the value of knowing God as they sing and dance and learn of the David and Goliath story in this first video by Rob Evans. Code: IKV001

BARNYARD FUN
Kids will learn the value of God's creation when Uncle Jim hurts his leg and The Donut Repair Club helps take care of his farm. Code: IKV005

AT THE ZOO
Kids will learn the value of kindness in this episode of nonstop adventure. Code: IKV004

BIBLE SONGS VOLUME 1 & 2
Don't think learning Christian values can be fun? Think again and give a listen to The Donut Man's Bible Songs Volume 1 & 2. With real kids singing high-energy Scripture songs, you will find your kids singing right along with this incredible album. Features songs like:
* In the Beginning
* You Are My Friend
* I've Got No Doubt
* The Lord Listens When I Pray to Him
* The Golden Rule
Codes: Vol. 1 CD–16242   Vol. 2 CD–16252
CS–16244   CS–16254

CALEB'S RESCUE
In this Part 2 of the value of honesty, Caleb runs away from the Royal Academy and falls in with the wrong crowd. Will he learn from his mistakes? Kids can watch as Caleb learns the story of Ananais and Sapphira. Code: 09683

CALEB AND THE SILVER CUP
Caleb learns the value of honesty and courage after he meets an unknown traveler at the Royal Academy. Watch as he learns that honesty is the best policy from the story of Joshua, Achan, and the Battle of Jericho. Code: 09673

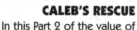

THE VALLEY OF MIRACLES
Teacher Windwright's tale from The Great Book about Noah's Ark teaches Caleb and his friends the value of patience and perseverance. Join Caleb and his friends as they have fun exploring the Valley of Miracles. Code: 09923

BEST PRESENT OF ALL
Join The Donut Repair Club as they learn the value of giving when they present a play about the very first Christmas. Old familiar carols and festive new songs provide a delightful way for kids to learn about God's greatest gift of all. Code: 09473

To locate the Christian bookstore nearest you, call 1-800-991-7747.
www.integritymusic.com   www.donutman.net

© 1999 Integrity Incorporated

Donut Forget to Pray to God

BY THE END OF THIS UNIT, LEARNERS WILL

Know   Describe two times when Bible people prayed to God.

Feel   Feel confident that God listens when we pray to him.

Do   Pray to God anytime.

MEMORY VERSE

"The Lord listens when I pray to him" (Psalm 4:3).

The Old Testament is full of stories of men and women who talked to God daily. They prayed in times of ease and times of trouble. They prayed prayers for help and prayers of thanksgiving. Daniel was thrown into a den of lions, because he would rather have died than to have missed his prayer time. In the lion's den, he called out to God for salvation. Moses and Miriam prayed for God's deliverance and then praised and thanked him for gloriously rescuing them by parting the Red Sea. God heard the prayers of these people, just as he hears the prayers of all his children who pray to him.

Four- to eight-year-olds are great imitators. They copy older brothers and sisters or mimic friends' behavior. Children learn by our example whether we realize it or not. Use these lessons to teach the children that we can talk to God anytime. Children will be eager to follow the biblical examples of Daniel, Moses, and Miriam. They will pray to God, too, expecting great answers.

	LESSON 1	LESSON 2	LESSON 3	LESSON 4
Center 1	cereal shakers	lion masks	tambourines	praise streamers
Center 2	paw print trail	rhythm bottles	pop-up puppets	praise poster
Center 3	prayer-time machine	timers for machine	clocks	song pictures
Gathering Time	prayer-time machine	prayer cards	times to pray	thankful prayers
Bible Story Time	Daniel 6, paw print trail	Daniel 6, story song	Exodus 15, pop-up puppets	Exodus 15, song actions
Sing-Along Fun Time	memory verse song	"anytime" song	circle song game	all unit songs
Donut Forget Time	thank-you song	clock pictures	prayer banner	ways to talk to God

LEARNING CENTERS

Set up the following activities for the children to do as they arrive. Assign an equal number of children and a teacher or helper to each activity.

At each Learning Center, welcome the children to your class. Make sure you know each child's name. Explain that today you'll be learning that we can talk to God anytime.

Center 1: Cereal Shakers

Classroom supplies: lunch-sized paper bags; markers; assortment of stickers; rubber bands; large mixing bowls; 1-cup measuring cups; large spoon; a variety of treats such as raisins, chocolate or butterscotch chips, mini-M&Ms; a variety of cereals (toasted oat rings or corn cereal); CD player
Curriculum supplies: Donut Forget CD ("With All My Heart")

BITE IDEA
If you have a large class, you'll save time if you make the extra shakers beforehand.

Explain to the children that we can talk to God anytime. Tell them that even though God sees us and knows everything about us, he wants us to talk to him and to tell him what we're thinking and feeling.

Give each child several bags to decorate with stickers and markers. Decorate enough bags for each child in the classroom to have one. Tell the children they're making Cereal Shakers to use during Sing-Along Fun Time.

Have everyone wash their hands. Ask for volunteers to choose one of three jobs: Dumper, Scooper, or Twister.

Dumpers should dump the ingredients for the snack mix into a large bowl and take turns stirring it with the spoon. Next, have the Scoopers scoop 1 cup of the cereal snack mix into each of the decorated bags. The Twisters can then make handles on the Cereal Shakers by twisting the top half of each bag tightly closed and wrapping a rubber band around it.

As the children work, listen to "With All My Heart." As they finish the Cereal Shakers, let them try shaking the shakers in rhythm to the song.

Set the finished shakers aside for use during Sing-Along Fun Time.

Center 2: Paw Print Trail

Classroom supplies: colored copier paper, masking tape, scissors, CD player
Curriculum supplies: lion paw print (page 59), Donut Forget CD ("With All My Heart")

Before class, photocopy the lion paw print onto colored copier paper. Photocopy enough paw prints to make a trail for the activity at Bible Story Time. Cut out several of the prints but leave some for the children to cut out.

BITE IDEA
If you have a large class, make two trails so there's enough room for everyone to be on a trail without crowding.

Have several children cut out paw prints while the others help you tape the prints to the floor around the room. Space the paw prints about 1 foot or more apart to form a continuous trail around the room. Be sure to make the trail long enough for every child to be on it during the story. Explain that you'll be using the trail during Bible Story Time. Tell the children that you'll be learning about Daniel and how he talked to God every day.

Play the song "With All My Heart" while the children work.

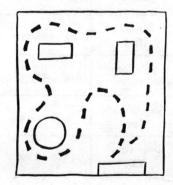

Center 3: Prayer-Time Machine

Classroom supplies: large appliance box; aluminum foil or brightly-colored gift wrap; recyclable items such as empty cereal or cracker boxes, yogurt or margarine containers, or soda bottles; scissors; tape; glue; CD player
Curriculum supplies: Donut Forget CD ("With All My Heart")

Before class, cut away the top half of the backside of the box so that a child can step into the box and stand or crawl inside it. Cut a slot along the bottom front of the box large enough for your hand to fit through to operate the CD player comfortably. (You'll put the CD player inside the box in Lesson 2.) Cut a 3-by-12-inch slot in the top front of the box. Write the words "Prayer-Time Machine" in large letters on a piece of poster board and cut out around the shape of the words (don't cut out individual letters). Use the illustration as a guide.

At the Center, ask the children to tell you about times when they pray. Then tell them that they'll be making a pretend Prayer-Time Machine to help us learn that we can talk to God anytime.

Help the children glue the poster board title "Prayer-Time Machine" to the front of the box. Have the children cover the recyclable items with aluminum foil or gift-wrap, then mount the items to the Prayer-Time Machine with tape. These items can be mounted to the top and any sides but the back. Have the children add any other decorations they want to the front of the box with markers. (Don't decorate the other sides—they'll be decorated in the upcoming weeks.)

As the children work, listen to the song "With All My Heart." Set the Prayer Time Machine in the Gathering Time area.

BITE IDEA
If tape isn't strong enough to hold some of the items to the box, have an adult helper poke holes in the box with a screwdriver and then thread chenille wire through the holes and around the item, twisting the ends of the wire together inside the box to hold it in place. For safety, have the children stand out of the way while the holes are being poked.

You may need an extension cord to reach the electrical outlet-in from inside the Prayer Time Machine.

GATHERING TIME

Classroom supplies: Prayer-Time Machine
Curriculum supplies: none

Invite the children to sit down in the Gathering Time area. Say: **Some of you made Cereal Shakers for Sing-Along Fun time. If you made Cereal Shakers, stand up and shake, shake, shake your body, then sit down. Good job! Some of you used lion paw prints to make a trail around the room for Bible Story Time. If you helped build the trail, give a great big roar!**

Point out the Prayer-Time Machine and say: **This is our Prayer-Time Machine that some of you helped make. Tick like a clock if you helped at this center.**

Say: **Our Prayer-Time Machine is going to help us learn that we can pray to God anytime. But first I need some volunteers to act out things that I whisper in your ear. Let's see if the rest of us can guess what the volunteers are doing.**

Choose a few children and whisper to them to act out eating a meal, then going to sleep and waking up. After the children guess the actions, say: **Before you eat is a great time to pray and thank God for your food!**

Ask: **What kinds of things can you talk to God about before you go to sleep? What can you pray about when you wake up?**

Say: **Think about some other times when you might want to talk to God. You can get inside the Prayer-Time Machine and tell us about it.**

Let several children get inside the machine and talk to the class about times they might want to pray.

After several children share, say: **Praying means talking to God. He wants us to talk to him anytime! He never goes to sleep. The Bible tells us about a man named Daniel who prayed to God many times every day, even when the king's evil men told him not to. Let's get ready to hear our Bible story now about Daniel and some hungry lions!**

BIBLE STORY TIME

Classroom supplies: Bible, CD player, paw print trail made during Center 2
Curriculum supplies: Donut Forget CD ("Daniel and the Lions")

Stand near the trail of paw prints and say: **Go find a lion's paw print and stand on it!**

When everyone is standing on a paw print, open your Bible to Daniel 6 and show it to the children. Say: **Our Bible story comes from the book of Daniel. Daniel was a wise and good man who loved God. Three times a day Daniel would stop what he was doing and kneel down to pray and thank God. Let's kneel down three times now. Kneel down, get up. Kneel down, get up. Kneel down, get up.**

Now there were some wicked men who were jealous of Daniel and wanted to get rid of him. So they tricked the king into making a law. The law said that no one could pray to any god except the king. If anyone disobeyed, they would be thrown into a den of lions! Let me hear some lions roaring. Roar! What do you think would happen to a person thrown into a deep hole with a bunch of hungry lions? Let kids respond.

But Daniel wasn't afraid. He loved God very much and prayed to God even though the law said he shouldn't. The wicked men saw Daniel praying, so they told the king. The king's men threw Daniel into the lions' den! What do you think Daniel did? Get on your knees again, because Daniel prayed to God and God helped him!

Let's listen to a new song about Daniel. When the song is over, tell me how God answered Daniel's prayers and saved him from the lions. When you hear the part about the lions, act like a lion and creep slowly along the trail of paw prints. When you hear the parts about the angel or the king, stop and stand quietly on a paw print and listen to the story. Are you ready? Let's listen!

Play the song "Daniel and the Lions." When the song ends, have everyone sit down on a paw print. Ask:

- **How did God save Daniel from the lions?**
- **Why did Daniel decide to pray and not obey the king's law?**

After the children respond, say: **Just like Daniel, we can pray to God anytime. We can pray when we wake up or before we eat and we can pray when we're in trouble or when we just want to thank God for something.**

SING-ALONG FUN TIME

Classroom supplies: Cereal Shakers from Center 1, CD player

Curriculum supplies: Donut Forget CD ("I Like the Bible," "The Lord Listens When I Pray," "Daniel and the Lions")

Pass out the Cereal Shakers and let children shake them to the rhythm of "I Like the Bible." Play the song once or twice, then collect the Cereal Shakers.

Open the Bible to Psalm 4:3 and show it to the children. Say: **Here's a Bible verse you'll really like! Psalm 4:3 says, "The Lord listens when I pray to him." Say that with me, then we'll learn a new song with these words.**

Repeat the verse and lead the children in singing the "The Lord Listens When I Pray." Ask: **Where is a quiet place where you can go to pray?**

Have the children choose partners. Play the song "Daniel and the Lions." Encourage the children to move around the room with their partners and to act out the story as they sing.

DONUT FORGET TIME

Classroom supplies: Cereal Shakers, CD player

Curriculum supplies: Donut Forget CD ("The Lord Listens When I Pray")

Gather the children around you and say: **One way we can talk to God is to tell him thank-you for the good things he does and praise him for being so good! Think of some things you are thankful for and in a minute you can tell me about them. I think Daniel was thankful that God saved him from the lions. I'm going to sing a thank-you prayer to God for helping Daniel.**

Sing to the tune of the first few lines of "Twinkle, Twinkle Little Star":

Thank you, God, for saving Daniel
From the den of hungry lions.

Ask the children to tell you things they want to thank God for. Then make up a verse about it and sing it together to God. For example, if a child says she's thankful for her dog, sing, "Thank you, God, for Awbrey's dog; Thank you, God, you're good to her." If a child says he's thankful for his fort, sing, "Thank you, God, for Johnny's fort; Thank you, God, you're good to him."

When you finish singing, say: **When you go home, remember that you can pray anytime. At our next class I'm going to ask you to tell me about the times you prayed at home. Remember, God always hears your prayers.**

Pray: **Jesus, please help us to be like Daniel and talk to you often. Thank you for hearing us and loving us. We love you, Jesus. Amen.**

Pass out the Cereal Shakers and let children open them and eat the treats while you listen to the "The Lord Listens When I Pray."

BITE IDEA
For Lesson 2 you'll need several kitchen or household timers or wind-up clocks with alarms. If you need help collecting these, ask parents today when they pick up their children if they have any you could borrow. Ask them to send the timers to class next week.

Donut Forget™ Bible Story Lessons

LEARNING CENTERS

Set up the following activities for the children to do as they arrive. Assign an equal number of children and a teacher or helper to each activity.

At each Learning Center, welcome the children to your class. Make sure you know each child's name. Explain that today you'll be learning that we can talk to God anytime.

Center 1: Lion Masks

Classroom supplies: poster board; brown construction paper; brown, orange, and gold crayons or markers; an eyeliner or eyebrow pencil; scissors; glue; CD player
Curriculum supplies: Donut Forget CD ("Daniel and the Lions")

Before class, cut poster board into 11-by-14-inch rectangles, one for each child. Cut a 5-inch circle in the center of each piece.

Give each child one of the pieces of poster board with a hole cut in it. Have the children make lion's masks by coloring a large, curly mane around the poster board cutouts. Show the children how to cut two triangles out of the brown construction paper and glue them onto their manes for ears. If they fold the triangles in half and glue the left and right corners down with the fold sticking up they'll get a 3D effect.

Have the children hold their masks up to their faces while you draw whiskers on their cheeks with the makeup pencil. As you work, remind the children that God answered Daniel's prayers when he was in the lions' den. Tell them that God listens to our prayers, too, and that we can talk to God anytime.

Play the song "Daniel and the Lions." Let the children wear the masks and roar along with the chorus of the song. Practice singing the chorus together without the music.

Set the masks aside to use during Bible Story Time.

Center 2: Roarin' Rhythm Bottles

Classroom supplies: 16-ounce plastic bottles with ridges on their sides (found in the grocery store with water inside), craft sticks, lion or other wild animal stickers, scissors, CD player
Curriculum supplies: Donut Forget CD ("Daniel and the Lions")

Have the children decorate the sides and bottoms of the plastic bottles with lion stickers. Don't put stickers over the ridges on the bottles. Demonstrate how to play the Roarin' Rhythm Bottles by rubbing a craft stick back and forth over the ridges. Play "Daniel and the Lions" from the Donut Forget CD and practice playing along with the beat.

After singing the song, ask the children how Daniel might have felt when he was in the lions' den. Have them tell about times they were scared.

Remind the children that Daniel prayed when he was scared. Tell them that they can be like Daniel and pray to God anytime.

Center 3: Prayer-Time Machine

Classroom supplies: an assortment of kitchen or household timers, wind-up alarm clocks, or watches with alarms; poster board; markers; 8-by-11-inch or larger box; old magazines; CD player
Curriculum supplies: Donut Forget CD ("The Lord Listens When I Pray")

48

Before class, cut out pictures from magazines that suggest situations when it would be good to pray (such as a picture of a sick child in bed, a family sitting at the dinner table, or a child with a pet). Cut poster board into 8-by-11-inch cards. Glue the pictures to the poster board cards and set them in the box. Set the Prayer-Time Machine next to the area where the children will be working. Put the CD player inside the box. (You may need an extension cord to make it reach the electrical outlet.)

Set out the timers and clocks and show the children how they work. Explain that the timers are going to help us learn that we can talk to God anytime, no matter what time it is. Help the children set the timers to go off at different intervals during class, such as 15 minutes, 30 minutes, 45 minutes. Make sure that one of the timers is set to go off during Gathering Time. Tell the children that when the timers go off, everyone will stop what they're doing and go to the Prayer-Time Machine to learn about praying to God.

If there's time, show the children one of the poster board prayer cards. Give them magazines and have them find more pictures that show times we should pray. Have them glue the pictures to poster board cards and add them to the box inside the Prayer-Time Machine.

While they work, play the song "The Lord Listens When I Pray" from inside the Prayer-Time Machine.

GATHERING TIME

Classroom supplies: Prayer-Time Machine, a timer set to go off during Gathering Time, prayer cards made in Center 3

Curriculum supplies: none

Have everyone sit down in front of the Prayer-Time Machine. Invite the children to tell you about the things they did at their Learning Centers. Then say: **Today we are learning that we can talk to God anytime. Some of you made lion masks to use during Bible Story Time. We see your whiskers! Give us a mighty roar! Some of you made special instruments for singing time and some of you made something special for the Prayer-Time Machine. If you did one of those things, stand up and take a bow, then sit down.**

Remind the children that at the last class you told them you would ask them to tell about times they prayed at home during the week. Ask for volunteers and have them stand inside the Prayer-Time Machine as they share.

When the timer rings sometime during this discussion, stop everything and say: **The timer is telling us it's time for the Prayer-Time Machine to teach us something about praying. Let's see what it is.**

Have one child stand outside the front of the Prayer-Time Machine. Have another child go inside the machine, choose one of the prayer cards from the box, and stick it through the top slot at the front of the Machine for the other child to take. That child should show the prayer card to the class.

Have the children describe the picture on the prayer card. Point out that it shows a time to pray. Discuss what you might pray about at such a time. Say things such as, "God is never too busy to help us when we're sick," or "God loves to hear you say thank-you when you're happy." Always end by telling the children that we can talk to God anytime.

During the rest of the class, whenever a timer goes off, have everyone stop what they're doing and gather around the Prayer-Time Machine and repeat this activity. (Plan on having the timers go off no more than five times during the class, or it will be too disruptive.)

49

BIBLE STORY TIME

Classroom supplies: Bible, lion masks from Center 1
Curriculum supplies: Donut Forget Songbook

BITE IDEA
Remember to stop and visit the Prayer-Time Machine each time a timer goes off!

Have the children who worked at Center 1 stand in front of the group. Give them their masks and have them be ready to hold them up to their faces.

Open your Bible to Daniel 6. Say: **Not only did Daniel pray to God three times a day, but he also talked to God other times throughout the day. He asked God to help him when he was in danger. I'm going to read the verses from our Daniel song to you like it's a story. The kids that made lion masks will help me tell the story when we get to the chorus. They'll hold up their masks and sing the lion part with me without the CD. Those of you without a mask can fold your hands together like you're praying whenever you hear Daniel's name mentioned. Let's try that. Good job!**

Read the first verse from the song aloud to the children. Encourage the children with no masks to fold their hands when they hear Daniel's name. At the chorus, lead the "lions" in singing the chorus together without the CD. Continue through the rest of the lyrics. Refer to the song in the Donut Forget Songbook.

When the story is finished, say:

- **Tell me some times when you think Daniel prayed to God.**
- **Tell me some times when you could pray to God.**

Say: **God wants us to be like Daniel. He wants us to talk to him anytime. That is good news! Let's get ready to sing some songs now. Our songs are like prayers to God.**

SING-ALONG FUN TIME

Classroom supplies: lion masks, rhythm bottles and sticks, several of the clocks whose alarms have already rung, CD player
Curriculum supplies: Donut Forget CD ("Daniel and the Lions," "I Like the Bible," "Sing and Skip and Dance," "With All My Heart")

Let the children who weren't in Center 1 take a turn wearing the lion masks while you sing "Daniel and the Lions."

Distribute the rhythm bottles and have the children play along as you sing "I Like the Bible" and "Sing and Skip and Dance."

Use the **Duncan** puppet and the script from the Donut Forget Songbook to talk about the memory verse, Psalm 4:3.

Say: **Last week we learned a memory verse song from Psalm 4:3. It says, "The Lord listens when I pray to him." Say that with me. That is awesome news! Let's sing "With All My Heart." It's a fun song of praise to God for always listening to us.**

Play the song "With All My Heart." Sing the song a second time and have the children stand up and then sit down whenever they hear the word "anytime." Pass out the timers or clocks. Have some of the children hold up their timers when they stand. When the children sing the word "anywhere," have them stand up and point in any direction and then sit down.

DONUT FORGET TIME

Classroom supplies: construction paper, crayons or markers, CD player

Curriculum supplies: Donut Forget CD ("The Lord Listens When I Pray")

Before class, cut 6-to-8-inch diameter circles out of construction paper. You'll need one circle for each child.

Say: **We can talk to God anytime. He hears us when we pray. One way we talk to God is when we ask him to help someone else. Let's make something that will help us pray for each other.**

Distribute the paper circles. Give the children crayons or markers and have them make clocks by drawing hands on their circles. Have them write their names on their clocks. The older children can help the younger ones if they need it. Then say: **Now we're going to draw a picture on our clocks of something you need God's help with.**

Have the children think of something they want to ask God to help them with and draw a picture of it. When they finish, invite volunteers to talk about what they drew.

Then help the children form pairs and say: **Show your clock to your partner and explain your picture. Then pray out loud for the thing your partner needs God's help with. You can pray something like, "Jesus, help Jason feel better," or "Jesus, please help Mary find her puppy."**

Circulate among the children and help the ones who may be unsure of what to do or how to pray. With extremely shy children, have them repeat a simple prayer after you.

Say: **Let's each hold our partner's clock now while we sing "The Lord Listens When I Pray" Remember that God always hears our prayers. He heard the prayers you just prayed for your friend.**

Lead the children in singing "The Lord Listens When I Pray." Then pray: **Thank you, God, that you listen to our prayers. Please help our friends with everything they need.**

Encourage the children to take their partner's clocks home and pray for them through the week.

BITE IDEA
Mail postcards to the children during the week, reminding them to pray for their partners. Remind them that they can pray to God anytime.

LEARNING CENTERS

Set up the following activities for the children to do as they arrive. Assign an equal number of children and a teacher or helper to each activity.

At each Learning Center, welcome the children to your class. Make sure you know each child's name. Explain that today you'll be learning that we can talk to God anytime.

Center 1: Tambourines

Classroom supplies: sturdy paper plates of various sizes, assorted sizes of jingle bells, chenille wire, hole punch, CD player

Curriculum supplies: Donut Forget CD ("With All My Heart")

Before class, cut the chenille wire into 4-inch lengths and punch four holes around the edge of each plate.

Let each child choose a paper plate. Show the children how to attach bells to the plates by threading pieces of chenille wire through the bells, then through the holes in the plates. Help

Donut Forget™ Bible Story Lessons

the children secure the bells by twisting the wire ends together. Have the children attach a bell to each hole on their plates.

Play the song "With All My Heart" as you work. Explain that in Bible days as well as today people use instruments to praise God for the good things he does. Encourage the children to try out their tambourines as they finish them.

Set the tambourines aside to use during Sing-Along Fun Time.

Center 2: Pop-Up Puppets

Classroom supplies: poster board or construction paper, markers, scissors, jumbo craft sticks, paper or Styrofoam cups that are shorter than the craft sticks, glue, fabric scraps, CD player
Curriculum supplies: Donut Forget CD ("The Lord Listens When I Pray")

Before class, cut the poster board or construction paper into 2½-inch circles and the fabric into 3-inch squares. Cut a 1-inch slit in the bottom of each cup.

Help the children make Miriam and Moses pop-up puppets by having them draw smiley faces on two poster board circles. Add curly hair for a Miriam circle and a beard for a Moses circle.

Help the children glue the smiley faces back-to-back with the tip of a craft stick in between them. Then have them wrap a fabric "robe" around the stick underneath the faces and glue it in place.

While the glue dries, play "The Lord Listens When I Pray." Ask the children to share about good things that happened to them this week that they're thankful for. Be sure to share something yourself. Explain to the children that it's good to thank God when good things happen.

When the glue is dry, carefully insert each puppet through the slit on the inside of a cup. (The figure should be hidden inside the cup with the craft stick sticking out the bottom.) Tell the children that one side of the puppet is Moses and the other Miriam and that they'll be hearing a Bible story about Moses and Miriam today.

Set the puppets aside for use during the Bible Story Time.

Center 3: Prayer-Time Machine

Classroom supplies: Prayer-Time Machine, old magazines or catalogs, markers, glue, scissors, CD player
Curriculum supplies: photocopies of clocks (page 60), Donut Forget CD ("The Lord Listens When I Pray")

Before class, make photocopies of the clocks from page 60. (You'll need two or three extra copies of the same handout for Sing-Along Fun Time.) Put the CD player in the Prayer-Time Machine and plug it in.

Have the children cut out the clock shapes from the photocopies. Help them find additional pictures of clocks and watches in magazines and cut them out. Have them glue the clock pictures at random on one side of the Prayer-Time Machine.

As you work, listen to "The Lord Listens When I Pray."

When the clock pictures are glued in place, give the children markers and have them draw pictures on the box of things that represent times they pray, such as a pillow for bedtime or a table for meal times.

Remind the children that we can talk to God anytime, all through the day.

GATHERING TIME

Classroom supplies: Prayer-Time Machine, markers
Curriculum supplies: none

BITE IDEA
If you didn't discuss all the prayer cards from last week's lesson, you may want to repeat the activity here. See Gathering Time, Lesson 2, page 49.

Gather the children around the Prayer-Time Machine. Invite the children to share what they did during the Learning Centers. Have everyone stand. Say: **If you made a Moses or Miriam pop-up puppet, pop up and then sit down. Good job, puppeteers! If you made a tambourine to use during Sing-Along Time say, "Jingle bells!" and sit down. You sound great! If you helped decorate the Prayer-Time Machine shout, "We can talk to God anytime!" Then sit down. I'm proud of you!**

Brainstorm with the children about times in the Bible story that Daniel prayed to God. Remind them that Daniel prayed to God every day, not just when he was in the lions' den.

Ask for volunteers from Center 3 to come up to the Prayer-Time Machine and point out the pictures they made. Have them explain what their picture tells us about praying. Add any other pictures to the box that represent things the children talk about.

Say: **Last week you each prayed for a friend and took a clock home to remind you to pray for her. Raise your hand if you remembered to pray for your partner this week. Tell us what you did.**

Give the children time to share about praying and praise any efforts that are reported. Encourage the children to pray to God anytime.

When finished, say: **Daniel was a man who loved to pray. Let's get ready to hear a story about Moses and his sister Miriam and how they prayed to God.**

BIBLE STORY TIME

Classroom supplies: Bible, pop-up puppets from Center 2, CD player
Curriculum supplies: Donut Forget CD ("The Horse and Its Rider")

Open your Bible to Exodus 15:1-21 and show the passage to the children. Say: **Our Bible story comes from the book of Exodus. Moses and God's people, the Israelites, were slaves to the wicked Pharaoh. God sent Moses to set the people free. They followed him until they reached the Red Sea. They were trapped! Pharaoh's army was chasing them from behind and the Red Sea was in front of them. How could they escape? Who knows what happened?**

Give the children time to tell what they know about the story of Moses and how God parted the sea for the people to walk across on dry land. Then say: **I'm going to tell you a story rhyme using one of our pop-up puppets. Each time I make the Miriam or Moses puppet pop up, you pop up and say, "Praise the Lord!" Then sit back down. Listen carefully to find out what Moses and his sister Miriam did after God saved them.**

Hold up a pop-up puppet and say:
The children of Israel were slaves.
They worked hard day after day.
But one day God sent Moses
To take them far away.
Here comes Moses! Pop up Moses, then put him back down inside the cup. Have the children pop up and say, "Praise the Lord!"
Moses led God's people straight to the sea.
But look—who followed their tracks?

**Mean old Pharaoh and his army
ready to take them all back.
Pray, Moses, pray!** (Pop up Moses. Children pop up.)

**God made the sea dry right up
so the Israelites crossed at last.
But when Pharaoh's army ran across, too,
the water came down with a crash!
Look, Miriam, look!** (Pop up Miriam. Children pop up.)

**Now Moses and Miriam praised the Lord
For rescuing all of them.
They sang a song to thank the Lord
And everyone joined right in.
Sing, everyone, sing!** (Pop up Moses or Miriam. Children pop up.)

Ask:

- **What happened to God's people? To Pharaoh's army?**
- **What did Moses and Miriam and the people do when they realized God saved them?**

Say: **Everyone was happy that God had saved them. They could hardly believe what happened! They broke into joyful singing and dancing, saying thank-you to God. We can thank God like Moses and Miriam did. Let's sing the song "The Horse and Its Rider."**

Pass out all the puppets made in Center 2. Play the song "The Horse and Its Rider." Encourage the children to pop up the puppets during the parts about Moses and Miriam. Play the song again so each child has a chance to use a puppet.

SING-ALONG FUN TIME

Classroom supplies: paper, masking tape, tambourines from Center 1, rhythm bottles from Lesson 2, CD player
Curriculum supplies: copies of the clocks (page 60), Donut Forget CD ("The Horse and Its Rider," "Sing and Skip and Dance")

BITE IDEA
If you have a large group, make more than one circle on the floor with the tape and clocks. If you're unsure of attendance, allow enough space between spots so that extras can be added if more children attend than planned.

Before class, copy and cut out several of the clocks from page 60. Make a large circle on the floor with pieces of masking tape and several of the clocks taped to the floor. Each tape piece and clock in the circle is a place marker. You will need one for each child in your class.

Have all the children stand on a tape spot or a clock until the circle is full. Give tambourines to the children standing on the clocks. Play the song "The Horse and Its Rider" and have the children move from spot to spot around the circle as the music plays. Stop the music at various intervals and give whoever is standing on a clock a tambourine to play for the next round. Start the music again and continue the song.

Repeat this activity several times. Then pass out the rhythm bottles and tambourines and sing "Sing and Skip and Dance." Take turns sharing the instruments so that everyone has a chance to use them.

DONUT FORGET TIME

Classroom supplies: Bible, butcher paper, markers, crepe paper, balloons, tape or stapler, CD player, tambourines from Center 1, rhythm bottles from Lesson 2

Curriculum supplies: Donut Forget CD ("With All My Heart," "The Horse and Its Rider," "Daniel and the Lions," "The Lord Listens When I Pray")

Show the children your Bible. Open it to Psalm 147 and say: **Psalm 147:1 says: "Praise the Lord! It is good to sing praises to our God. It is good and pleasant to praise him." Today is a good time to thank God for the things he does for us. Let's worship him like Moses and Miriam and the Israelites did by having a celebration parade!**

Set out a 3-foot sheet of butcher paper. Have older children write "Praise the Lord!" in large letters across the paper or write the words yourself lightly in pencil and have them trace the letters with marker. Have younger children draw smiley faces and colorful pictures of things to thank God for. If you have a large class, make more than one banner. Tape a few crepe paper streamers and balloons to the banner.

When the banners are finished, pass out the instruments and assign two children to carry the banner at the front of the parade. Play the song "With All My Heart" and march around the classroom. Repeat the song or play "The Horse and Its Rider" or "Daniel and the Lions."

When the songs are over, collect the instruments and hang the banners on the walls. Gather the children on the floor around you. Say: **That was a fun way to praise the Lord! Worshiping God makes us feel happy inside.**

Pray: **Thank you, God, that we can pray to you anytime. Thank you that you answer our prayers just like you answered Moses' and Miriam's prayers. We love you. Amen.**

Lead the children in singing "The Lord Listens When I Pray" before going home.

LEARNING CENTERS

Set up the following activities for the children to do as they arrive. Assign an equal number of children and a teacher or helper to each activity.

At each Learning Center, welcome the children to your class. Make sure you know each child's name. Explain that today you'll be learning that we can talk to God anytime.

Center 1: Praise Streamers

Classroom supplies: chenille wire, crepe paper, scissors, stapler, CD player

Curriculum supplies: Donut Forget CD ("The Horse and Its Rider")

Before class, cut different colors of crepe paper into 4-foot lengths. You'll need at least two for each child.

Help each child form a loop with a chenille wire and twist the ends together. Show them how to thread two pieces of the crepe paper through the loop and fold them in half over the chenille wire. The fold should cover the twisted ends of the chenille wire. Staple the crepe paper at the fold.

Have the children make extra praise streamers so that every child will have one. As the children work, play the song "The Horse and Its Rider." Tell them that they'll use the praise

55

streamers later in class to worship God. Explain that it makes God happy to hear words and see actions of praise.

When the streamers are finished, encourage the children to hold the chenille wire by the loop and wave them back and forth to the music.

Set the praise streamers aside for use during Sing-Along Fun Time.

Center 2: Praise Poster

Classroom supplies: butcher paper, markers or crayons, tape, CD player
Curriculum supplies: Donut Forget CD ("With All My Heart")

Before class, mount with tape a piece of butcher paper on the wall at the approximate height of the children. It needs to be long enough so that each child's body can be traced on it. If your class is large, the paper can be put up in several sections. Across the top of the paper, write the words in large letters, "We're Praising God!"

BITE IDEA
If you have a very large class, you may want to trace the outlines of the rest of the children now so that during Gathering Time the children need only to add faces and clothing.

Have the children stand with their backs against the butcher paper. Trace each child's outline on the paper from the waist up. Have them raise their hands as if they are pointing to God or praising him. If you use marker to trace their shapes, be careful not to get marker on their clothing. As you trace each child's outline, thank God for him. Remind the children that we can talk to God anytime.

Once their outlines are drawn, have the children use markers to draw in happy faces and clothing details. Have them write their names inside their pictures.

Sing "With All My Heart" as the children work.

During Gathering Time, the children who didn't work at this center will have their shapes traced, too. They will be added between the others from shoulder up to make it look like they're standing behind the other children in a crowd.

Center 3: Prayer-Time Machine

Classroom supplies: Prayer-Time Machine, markers, and CD player
Curriculum supplies: Donut Forget CD ("With All My Heart")

Before class, place the CD player inside the Prayer-Time Machine and move it close to the area where they'll be working. Play the song "With All My Heart." As the children listen to the song, have them list things we give to God, such as our heart, mind, soul, strength, muscles, and so on. Write the words as they mention them.

When the song is over, have the children draw pictures of the things from their list on the remaining undecorated side of the Prayer-Time Machine. Sing the song while they decorate the box.

Next have the children make up motions for the song. Tell them that they'll be sharing their drawings and motions with the rest of the class later.

GATHERING TIME

Classroom supplies: praise poster from Center 2, markers or crayons
Curriculum supplies: none

Gather the children around you and invite them to share what they did during the Learning Centers. Say: **If you helped make praise streamers, wave your hands in the air. If you helped decorate the Prayer-Time Machine, put both hands over your heart. Good job, all of you! If you helped make our praise poster, go stand next to your outline now. You look great. You can help me add the other kids to the poster by getting them in position, then I'll trace their shapes.**

56

Have the children who have not been traced stand between the figures of the others on the poster. Trace their bodies from the shoulder up, so it looks like they're standing behind the other children in a crowd. Pray out loud over each child as you trace the children's shapes. Give the children markers to write their names and draw faces on their outlines.

After everyone's picture is on the praise poster, have them stand back and admire their work. Say: **I prayed a thank-you prayer to God for each of you as I traced your shape. Think of something you want to thank God for. Then we'll each pray and then sit down. Stand in front of your outline. You can say things like, "Thank you, God, for my puppy," or whatever you're thankful for.**

Have each child thank God for something. If you have a shy or reluctant child, ask them to tell you what they're thankful for and have the whole class say the prayer together.

Say: **God loves to hear our prayers! Our poster can help us remember to praise God and thank him for the good things he does for us, just like Moses and Miriam did in our Bible story. Let's go over to the story area now and hear our Bible story.**

BIBLE STORY TIME

Classroom supplies: Bible, CD player
Curriculum supplies: Donut Forget CD ("The Horse and Its Rider")

Open your Bible to Exodus 15:1-21 and show it to the children. Say: **Our Bible story comes from the book of Exodus. Think about our story from last week about Miriam and Moses. Why did they sing a song of thanks to God?**

Give the children time to respond, then say: **Moses and Miriam gave thanks to God after he helped them escape from Pharaoh by parting the Red Sea. We're going to play our Bible story song now. As we listen to it, let's think of ways to act out the story. Then we'll perform it for each other.**

Play "The Horse and Its Rider" and help the children make up actions for the story. When they're finished, play and sing the song again. Have half the children act it out while the other half watches. Repeat the activity with the children reversing the roles.

SING-ALONG FUN TIME

Classroom supplies: praise streamers from Center 1, instruments made during this unit, CD player
Curriculum supplies: Donut Forget CD ("With All My Heart," "Daniel and the Lions," "The Horse and Its Rider," "The Lord Listens when I Pray")

Gather around the Prayer-Time Machine and say: **The words in the song "With All My Heart" say, "Anytime, anywhere, when I pray you are there." God always hears us when we talk to him. Our songs can be like prayers to God!**

Have one or two children who worked at Center 3 point out the pictures they drew on the side of the Prayer-Time Machine and explain how they represent the song. Play "With All My Heart" and have the Center 3 children show the others the motions they made up to go with the song.

Pass out the praise streamers and sing "Daniel and the Lions." Encourage the children to move around the room and praise God while they sing.

Lead the children in singing other songs from this unit, such as "The Horse and Its Rider" and "The Lord Listens When I Pray." Have the praise streamers and instruments made during this unit available. Encourage the children to move around the room, play instruments, or make up motions as they sing. Remind them that whatever they do they should praise the Lord with all their heart.

DONUT FORGET TIME

Classroom supplies: Bible; bookmarks or pieces of paper; piece of sheet music or photocopy of a song with music; book of poetry or photocopy of a poem; storybook; instruction manual from an appliance or a game; map; personal letter in its envelope; CD player
Curriculum supplies: Donut Forget CD ("I Like the Bible," "The Lord Listens When I Pray")

Before class, gather the items mentioned above. Place them in a stack in the order mentioned. Put bookmarks in your Bible at Exodus 15, Psalms, Matthew, Acts, Romans, and 1 Timothy.

Show your Bible to the children. Say: **The Bible is full of people who talked to God. It's also full of God talking to people! That's why we call the Bible God's Word. It's his words to us. When we talk to him, he talks back!**

Hold up the sheet music and ask the children to tell you what it is. Then open the Bible to Exodus 15. Say: **People write songs when they want to tell others how they feel. There are many songs written in the Bible. It's one way of talking to God and telling him how we feel. We learned that Miriam and Moses sang a thankful song to God in Exodus 15.**

BITE IDEA
Write a poem with the children. Here's an idea to get you started:
We love you, God.
You are great!
You hear each word
that we pray.

Hold up the poem and explain what it is. Say: **David wrote many songs and poems to tell God how much he loved him. We can write poems to God, too. It's another way we can talk to God.**

Continue with each of the items and explain that there are many ways to talk to God and for him to talk to us. For example, someone wrote the storybook to tell a story the way Matthew wrote his story about Jesus. The instruction manual goes with Acts because God shows us how to love one another. The map goes with Romans as an example of how God helps us with direction for our life. The letter goes with 1 Timothy because God used Paul's letters to teach the church about him.

When all items have been discussed say: **The Bible reminds us in many ways that we can talk to God anytime, anywhere. We can talk to him, sing to him, dance for him, even draw or write to him! He always listens to us.**

Lead the children in singing "I Like the Bible" together. Then say the memory verse and sing "The Lord Listens When I Pray."

When the song is over, pray: **Dear God, thank you that we can talk to you anytime, day or night. Thank you that you always hear us. Help us to remember that you love us and are never too busy to listen. Amen.**

Pass out the instruments and praise streamers for the children to take home. As they leave, remind them to talk to God anytime.

Lion Paw Print

59

clocks

Donut forget to celebrate Jesus' Birth

BY THE END OF THIS UNIT, LEARNERS WILL

Know   Describe special things that happened when Jesus was born.

Feel   Feel happy that Jesus was born.

Do   Celebrate Jesus' birth.

MEMORY VERSE

"Today your Savior was born in David's town. He is Christ, the Lord" (Luke 2:11).

When Jesus was born, the town of Bethlehem was crowded with people. But in this crowded city, the only ones who took notice of God's Son's humble entry into the world were his earthly parents and a few barnyard animals. Quiet cries soon gave way to joyful shouts as first angels, then shepherds spread the joyful news of Jesus' birth. The God of creation became a baby boy!

Children love the surprise and delight that accompany Christmas. They thrill to unwrap carefully packed ornaments, decorate the family tree, and, most of all, open Christmas gifts. Use the lessons in this unit to help the children celebrate the best present of all—God's Son, Jesus.

	LESSON 1	LESSON 2	LESSON 3	LESSON 4
Center 1	bulletin board	story picture board	angel choir	story transparencies
Center 2	tambourines	present shakers	staff rhythm sticks	birthday cake
Center 3	celebration gifts	celebration streamers	celebration invitations	celebration decorations
Gathering Time	birthdays	opening gifts	shining lights	party items
Bible Story Time	Luke 2, story actions	Luke 2, story scene	Luke 2, shepherds & angels	Luke 2, transparencies
Sing-Along Fun Time	dancing songs	rhythm orchestra	marching songs	caroling
Donut forget Time	birthday cards	people wrapping	giving invitations	birthday celebration

Donut forget™ Bible Story Lessons

61

LEARNING CENTERS

Set up the following activities for the children to do as they arrive. Assign an equal number of children and a teacher or helper to each activity.

At each Learning Center, welcome the children to your class. Make sure you know each child's name. Explain that today you'll be talking about Jesus, the greatest gift of all.

Center 1: Bulletin Board

Classroom supplies: construction paper, wrapping paper or wallpaper squares; ribbon and sticky-back gift bows; department store or mail order catalogs; scissors; glue; CD player
Curriculum supplies: baby Jesus picture (page 65); Donut Forget CD ("The Best Present of All")

Before class, prepare a bulletin board with red or green background paper and a contrasting border. Letter the words "The Best Present of All!" at the top. Enlarge and photocopy the illustration of baby Jesus (page 65) and glue it to construction paper. Lay a second sheet of construction paper on top of the picture, then staple the two sheets together only at the top. Attach a sticky-back gift bow to the top sheet.

As the children arrive, invite them to tell you about Christmas presents they've received in the past and presents they'd like to receive this Christmas. Point out that it's fun to give and receive toys and other presents. Remind the children that Jesus is the best present of all.

Show the children the bulletin board you've decorated and explain that they'll be adding to the bulletin board. Assign several children to find and cut out pictures of "gifts" in catalogs. Have other children create "presents" by decorating construction paper with ribbons and bows. As the children work, play "The Best Present of All" from the Donut Forget CD.

Have the children work together to glue the gift-pictures onto construction paper. Show them how to place the decorated presents on top of the gift pictures. Help the children staple the presents to the gift pictures only at the top. As the children finish, attach the presents to the board. In the center, place the present with the picture of baby Jesus in the manger.

After all the presents are attached, have the children lift the flaps and discuss each gift.

Center 2: Tambourines

Classroom supplies: small paper plates (not coated paper or plastic); watercolors and brushes; individual jingle bells; green or red chenille wire; glue; hole punch; CD player
Curriculum supplies: Donut Forget CD ("Happy Birthday, Jesus!")

Before the children arrive, make a sample tambourine. Decorate the bottoms of two paper plates with watercolors, then glue the plates together, decorated sides out. Punch holes around the edge of the plates, then use pieces of chenille wire to attach a jingle bell to each hole.

Explain that today you'll be learning new songs to celebrate Jesus' birthday. Show the children the sample tambourine and tell them that they'll be making tambourines to help the whole class celebrate Jesus' birth.

Set out the supplies and guide the children in making the tambourines according to the instructions. Younger children will probably need help attaching the bells to their tambourines. As the children work, play the unit songs from the Donut Forget CD.

Have each child make two or three tambourines, one to keep and one or two to share.

Have the children take the tambourines with them to Gathering Time.

Center 3: Celebration Gifts

Classroom supplies: cardboard tubes, wrapped Christmas candy, red and green tissue paper, tape, yarn or ribbon, foil star stickers (optional)
Curriculum supplies: none

BITE IDEA
You may want to consider inviting a younger class to join you for the celebration that will take place at the end of Lesson 4. If you decide to try this, be sure to check with the teacher(s) from the other class ahead of time.

Before class, cut the yarn or ribbon into 8-inch pieces. Set up an assembly line by setting out supplies in the order they'll be used.

As the children arrive, talk about the excitement of celebrating Christmas. Point out that giving gifts to others is one way we celebrate Jesus' birth. Explain that today they'll be making presents to give to each other at a Christmas party you'll have in a few weeks.

Form pairs, then show the children the supplies you've set out. Have the first pair roll a tube in tissue paper and tape it. Have the second pair tie the tissue paper at one end. Have the third pair fill the tube with candy, then have the fourth pair tie the other end closed. If desired, another pair of children can decorate the presents with foil stars. Try to assign each pair of children a job that is challenging, but not overwhelming.

As the children work, let them listen to the unit songs from the Donut Forget CD. After pairs have completed several gifts, they may want to switch jobs. Have the children prepare a gift for everyone who will attend your celebration.

Set the finished presents aside to be distributed during Lesson 4.

GATHERING TIME

Classroom supplies: tambourines made in Center 2
Curriculum supplies: none

Gather all of the children together. Hand out the tambourines. Make sure every child has one. Say: **Stand up and shake your tambourine when I name the Center you worked in. Who helped to decorate a bulletin board?** (Let the children respond.) **Stand up and shake your tambourine if you made special gifts for a birthday celebration we'll have soon.** (Let the children respond.) **Who helped to make these wonderful tambourines?** (Let the children respond.) **You all did a super job! Shake your tambourine if you had a fun time at your Center.**

Let the children shake their tambourines, then collect them. Gather the tambourines, then have the children stand in a circle. Say: **Today we're learning about the first Christmas, Jesus' birthday. But before we do that, let's have some fun celebrating *our* birthdays. How many people have a birthday in January?**

Continue naming months and asking about the children's birthdays. (Younger children may need help remembering their birthdays. Check with parents before class.) Then lead the children in playing this game. Have the children form a large circle. Call out a birthday month and have all the children with birthdays in that month stand inside the circle. Have the children in the circle walk around and sing to the tune of "Mary Had a Little Lamb":

The birthday month is January, January, January.
The birthday month is January.
Stand inside our circle.

Continue until each child has had a turn to be in the circle. When the game is finished, invite the children to tell you about special birthday parties they've attended. Conclude the discussion by saying: **Everyone has a birthday. Birthdays are a lot of fun to celebrate. We have Christmas just to celebrate a very special birthday. The birthday we celebrate at Christmas is Jesus' birthday. Let's hear a story about Jesus' birthday now.**

BIBLE STORY TIME

Classroom supplies: Bible; box "manger" filled with "straw" (real straw, shredded newspaper, or construction paper); doll wrapped up in cloths; CD player
Curriculum supplies: Donut Forget CD ("No Room in the Inn")

Open your Bible to Luke 2. Say: **Our Bible story comes from the book of Luke. It tells us about Jesus' birthday. Listen carefully as I tell the Bible story. When I say "Joseph," I want you to pretend you are a carpenter like Joseph was.** Show the children how to make "hammers" with their fists and pound on a nail, then continue: **When I say "Mary," pretend to hold a baby in your arms.** Show the children how to hold their arms together as if they are rocking a baby. Let the children practice the actions several times. Before you tell the story, choose two children to play Mary and Joseph. When you talk about the baby, place the wrapped doll in the box manger. Pause each time you say *Mary* or *Joseph* to allow the children to do their actions.

Say: **An angel had told *Mary* and *Joseph* that they were going to have a special baby. They would call this baby Jesus, and he would be the Son of God. The angel said that Jesus would save all people from their sins!**

When it was time for *Mary* to have her baby, she and *Joseph* had to take a long trip to the town of Bethlehem to register for taxes. *Mary* was tired and needed a place to rest, but Bethlehem was very busy. There were no hospitals to have the baby in. There weren't even any rooms left in an inn or hotel. *Mary* had to have the baby Jesus in a stable, a barn full of animals.

When the baby arrived, *Mary* wrapped him in cloths and laid him in a manger full of hay. This was a box for the animals to eat from. Even though they were in a barn, *Mary* and *Joseph* were happy to celebrate Jesus' birthday!

Say: **We're happy to celebrate Jesus' birthday, too. At Christmas, we decorate a special tree, eat special yummy Christmas treats, and sing special Christmas songs. Let's sing a song about Jesus' birth now. Listen carefully—you can do your *Mary* and *Joseph* motions as we sing.**

Lead the children in singing "No Room in the Inn" with the Donut Forget CD. Then say: **Christmas is a time for singing. Let's sing some more songs about Jesus' birth!**

SING-ALONG FUN TIME

Classroom supplies: bulletin board from Center 1, tambourines from Center 2, CD player
Curriculum supplies: Donut Forget CD ("The Best Present of All!" "Happy Birthday, Jesus")

Let the children who helped in Center 1 explain the board that they made. Say: **There are many nice things we could receive as presents for Christmas. But none of those presents are as special as the best present of all. God sent us baby Jesus on the very first Christmas. Let's listen to a song about that.**

Have the children listen to "The Best Present of All." Then say: **Now let's make up a dance to go with our song.**

Distribute the tambourines and encourage the children to incorporate them into the dance. Point out that the tambourines can be shaken, waved in the air, or tapped against their hands, heads, hips, knees, elbows, or feet.

When the children are ready, play the song several times and let them sing and dance along with it. Then have them sing and play with "Happy Birthday, Jesus" before putting their instruments away. Keep the instruments to use throughout the unit.

DONUT FORGET TIME

Classroom supplies: construction paper, Christmas cookie cutters or stencils, markers, paper bag, CD player

Curriculum supplies: photocopy of Celebrate Jesus cards (page 76), Donut Forget CD ("Happy Birthday, Jesus")

Before class, color the Celebrate Jesus cards (page 76) and cut them apart.

Say: **The Bible says in 1 Corinthians 10:31, "Do everything for the glory of God." When we celebrate Christmas, we remember that we are celebrating Jesus' birthday. We praise and worship and glorify him in all that we do.**

Hold up each card and have the children identify what the children are doing in each picture. Invite the children to tell you about times they've done those things. Then say: **There are many fun ways we can celebrate Jesus' birthday. Let's celebrate now by making Christmas cards to share Jesus' love with some older people.**

Help the children fold their papers in half, then decorate them by tracing around the cookie cutter shapes or stencils. Help them write messages on the insides of the cards and sign their names. As the children work, play "Happy Birthday, Jesus."

Have the children bring their finished cards and sit in a circle. Say: **We have learned today that we celebrate Jesus' birthday at Christmas. The cards you've made will remind others of Jesus' love. As I play "Happy Birthday, Jesus," I will pass around a paper bag. When the bag comes to you, drop your Christmas card in the bag and say, "Happy Birthday, Jesus."**

After you've collected all the cards, stop the CD. Lead the children in thanking God for sending his Son, Jesus, at Christmas.

After class, make arrangements to have the cards delivered. If possible, arrange for the children (with their families or as a class) to deliver the cards themselves.

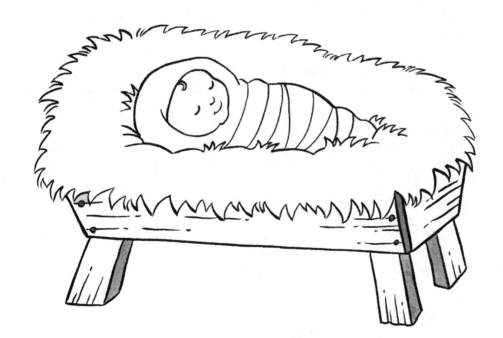

LEARNING CENTERS

Set up the following activities for the children to do as they arrive. Assign an equal number of children and a teacher or helper to each activity.

At each Learning Center, welcome the children to your class. Make sure you know each child's name. Explain that today you'll be talking about Jesus, the greatest gift of all.

Center 1: Story Picture Board

Classroom supplies: markers or crayons, scissors, Velcro tape, large piece of poster board, craft sticks, chenille wire, paper grocery bag, dried grass or straw, cotton, fabric scraps
Curriculum supplies: photocopies of nativity figures (page 77)

Before class, photocopy the nativity figures. If you want additional animals or shepherds for your scene, make more than one copy. Glue the copies to poster board or stiff paper, then cut apart the figures. Unless you have mostly younger children, don't cut closely around the figure outlines. The children will do this themselves in class.

Set out the nativity figures, markers, fabric scraps, and glue. Assign each child one or more figures to color and cut out. Talk about the story of Jesus' birth as they work.

After the children make the figures, set out additional supplies. Have the children use the supplies to design a background nativity scene on a sheet of poster board. For example, pieces of a paper sack and craft sticks could be glued on for the stable. Chenille wire could make a shepherd's staff. Dried grass or straw could be used in the manger.

When the background is completed, help the children put Velcro on the back of each figure. They can then place matching Velcro pieces where they'd like to place the figures on the scene.

Set the figures and poster board scene aside for use during Bible Story Time.

Center 2: Present Shakers

Classroom supplies: small box for each child (empty gelatin or pudding boxes work great), dried beans or rice, tape, tissue paper or Christmas gift wrap, scissors, ribbons and bows, CD player
Curriculum supplies: Donut Forget CD ("The Best Present of All")

Before class, set out the supplies on a large table. You may want to make a few shakers ahead of time, especially if your Center group is small.

Remind the children that Christmas is the time we celebrate Jesus' birthday. Point out that one way to celebrate Jesus' birth is by singing songs and making music. Explain that you'll be making present shakers to use while you sing.

Let the children put beans or rice in the boxes and tape them shut. Then show them how to wrap the gifts in paper and decorate them with ribbons and bows. Make sure there are enough present shakers for everyone in the class.

When the children are finished, let them try the shakers while singing "The Best Present of All" with the Donut Forget CD.

Set the shakers aside for use later in the lesson.

Center 3: Celebration Streamers

Classroom supplies: 1-by-12-inch strips of cardboard; red, green, and white crepe pape; scissors; tape or glue; CD player
Curriculum supplies: Donut Forget CD ("Happy Birthday, Jesus")

Remind the children that Christmas is the time we celebrate Jesus' birthday. Explain that today they'll make streamers for the Christmas celebration you'll have during Lesson 4.

Help the children cut strips of red, green, and white crepe paper into various lengths. Then give each child a strip of cardboard. Have the children glue or tape several crepe paper streamers to one end of their cardboard strips. Encourage the children to make extra streamers for class members working at other Learning Centers. If you'll be inviting another class to join you at the celebration, have the children make additional streamers to share.

When the children finish their streamers, play "Happy Birthday, Jesus" from the Donut Forget CD. Invite the children to practice waving the streamers and dancing with the music.

GATHERING TIME

Classroom supplies: large wrapped Christmas box with removable lid, wrapped sample Christmas gifts that the children might receive (toy cars, action figures, dolls, clothing, books, or art supplies), one construction-paper heart for each child in your class, manila envelope, CD player
Curriculum supplies: Donut Forget CD ("The Best Present of All")

Before class, place the construction-paper hearts in the manila envelope. Place the envelope in the bottom of the Christmas box. Put the sample gifts in the box on top of the envelope.

Gather the children in a circle around the Christmas box and invite them to tell you about their Learning Center activities. Say: **I see people at each Center who did something special. Wave your arms above your head if you helped make streamers. If you helped make our Bible story picture board, shake your finger at a neighbor and say, "No room!" If you made present shakers, shake your hands in front of you and say, "Merry Christmas!"**

Oh, that was so much fun. Let's all say it together. Merry Christmas! It looks like we'll all be having a merry Christmas with this giant present! What do you think is inside?

Let the children take a few guesses, then invite pairs of children to take turns opening the wrapped gifts. (Make sure the children know that these gifts are not for them to keep.) After the children have opened all the sample gifts, say: **What a lot of fun that was! It's great to unwrap presents and discover the neat gifts our friends and family have picked out for us. These are some great examples of the kinds of gifts you might receive. But we haven't even opened the very best gift yet.**

Invite a child to remove the envelope from the box. Hold it up and say: **This doesn't look like a very neat gift. It's just a plain old envelope. I wonder what's inside?**

Let the children take a few guesses, then let a child open and remove the hearts. Say: **Of course! God's love is the best gift anyone can ever receive. God loves us so much that he sent Jesus to be born on Christmas. And that's the best gift ever!**

Play "The Best Present of All" from the Donut Forget CD as you give each child a heart. As you hand the child the heart, say: **(Name of child), God loves you.** After the song, have all the children join you in saying, **And that's the greatest gift of all!**

BIBLE STORY TIME

Classroom supplies: Bible, Bible story board from Center 1, CD player
Curriculum supplies: Donut Forget CD ("No Room in the Inn")

Gather the children together around the Bible story board. Distribute the figures to the children who made them. Open your Bible to Luke 2. Say: **The Bible tells us in the book of Luke about Jesus' birth in Bethlehem. The children in one of our Learning Centers made figures to help us remember that story.**

Invite each child to tell about her figure, then place it on the scene. Say: **Now let's all act out the story using the song "No Room in the Inn."**

Choose two children to be Joseph and Mary and one child to be the innkeeper. Let the rest of the children decide which stable animal they would like to pretend to be. Help the children come up with animal actions for the first verse and people actions for the second verse and chorus. For example, the children might pretend to knock or open a door as they sing, "When will you open the door?" They could touch their hearts, then point to heaven as they sing, "You will find room in my heart, Lord Jesus."

Have Mary, Joseph, and the innkeeper act out the first verse as the animals do their animal motions. Then have everyone do the people motions on the second verse and chorus.

When you're ready to move on to Sing-Along Fun Time, say: **Even though there was no room in the inn, we can make room for Jesus in our hearts. Let's sing some more songs to help us praise and worship Jesus.**

SING-ALONG FUN TIME

Classroom supplies: present shakers from Center 2; bulletin board from Lesson 1; tambourines from Lesson 1 and rhythm instruments from previous units; CD player
Curriculum supplies: Donut Forget CD ("The Best Present of All")

Pass out present shakers to all of the children. Let them sing along and shake their shakers as you sing "The Best Present of All" with the Donut Forget CD. Then show them the bulletin board. Say: **Let's look at these presents. When you see the best present of all, shake your present shaker.** Open each gift, saving the one with baby Jesus for last.

Form two groups. Give one group the tambourines and the other the present shakers. Say: **We are going to be a rhythm orchestra. I am the conductor, so you'll have to watch me closely. When I point to your group and wave my arms, play your instruments. When I lower my arms, stop playing. Are you ready?**

Use the **Duncan** puppet and the script from the Donut Forget Songbook to talk about the memory verse, Luke 2:11.

Let the children practice following your arm movements, then play "The Best Present of All" and conduct as the children play their instruments. Let each group play alone, then let both groups play together. Test the children's attention by starting and stopping the groups unexpectedly. Then repeat the song and have the children switch instruments.

DONUT FORGET TIME

Classroom supplies: one sticky-back Christmas bow for each child; one roll of wrapping paper for every two children; tape; Bible; CD player
Curriculum supplies: Donut Forget CD ("No Room in the Inn," "The Best Present of All")

Form pairs. Give each pair a roll of wrapping paper. Set out rolls of tape in a central location. Say: **We've been talking today about the best gift God has given us. Who can tell me what that is?**

Let the children respond, then continue: **That's right. Jesus is God's best gift to us. Now what do you think is our best gift to God?**

Let the children respond, then say: **The best gift we can give God is ourselves. We please God by loving and following his Son, Jesus. To remind us that we're all gifts to God, you and your partner are going to make Christmas gifts out of each other. Use the wrapping paper and tape to wrap each other as a Christmas gift.**

68

Play "No Room in the Inn" and "The Best Present of All" as the children decorate one another. Circulate among the pairs and offer help as needed.

When everyone is wrapped, call the children back together. Say: **This is John 3:16: "For God loved the world so much that he gave his only Son. God gave his Son so that whoever believes in him may not be lost, but have eternal life." God sent Jesus as the best gift that was ever given. We can give ourselves as gifts, too. We can give our hearts to Jesus by loving him and living for him each day. As I play "No Room in the Inn," think about how you can love and live for Jesus this week.**

As you distribute bows for the children to stick on, play "No Room in the Inn." After the song, lead the children in praying: **Dear God, thank you for sending Jesus to be our Savior. Help us remember to make room in our hearts for him this week. In Jesus' name, amen.**

today

Savior

born

"B" for Bethlehem

Lord

Christ

he (God)

LEARNING CENTERS

Set up the following activities for the children to do as they arrive. Assign an equal number of children and a teacher or helper to each activity.

At each Learning Center, welcome the children to your class. Make sure you know each child's name. Explain that today you'll be talking about Jesus, the greatest gift of all.

Center 1: Angel Choir

Classroom supplies: gold or silver garland, tape, Bible, CD player
Curriculum supplies: Donut Forget CD ("Today a Savior Is Born")

Before class, cut garland into pieces long enough to circle the children's heads. Review the sign language motions for "Today a Savior Is Born."

Read Luke 2:8-14 aloud. Talk about how the shepherds may have felt when they first saw the angels, and how their emotions might have changed when they heard the angels' news.

Help each child make an angel halo using the garland and tape. Then have the children take turns repeating the angels' message: "Do not be afraid! Today your Savior was born in David's town." Then play "Today a Savior Is Born" from the Donut Forget CD and encourage your "angels" to sing along. Explain that they'll be your angel choir as you tell the Bible story.

If time allows, teach the children some or all of the sign language motions. Have the children practice doing the signs with the song several times, so they'll be prepared to do them for the class during Bible Story time.

Center 2: Shepherd Staff Rhythm Sticks

Classroom supplies: two wooden chopsticks for each child; red and green colored tape, Bible, CD player
Curriculum supplies: Donut Forget CD ("Happy Birthday, Jesus," "The Best Present of All")

Explain that you'll be making shepherd staff rhythm sticks to use as you sing the unit songs. Show the children how to decorate each rhythm stick by wrapping red and green tape around it. As the children wrap the tape, have them repeat the memory verse. Encourage them to say one word of the verse each time they wrap the tape around a stick. Have the children prepare two sticks for each child in your class.

When the children finish, encourage them to experiment with different ways of playing the rhythm sticks. For example, they might tap or rub the sticks together, tap them on the floor or wall, or roll them on the table. Help them tap out a rhythm as they repeat the Bible verse. If time allows, let the children play their sticks in time to "Happy Birthday, Jesus" or "The Best Present of All!"

Center 3: Celebration Invitations

Classroom supplies: black or dark blue construction paper, metallic markers or crayons, glitter glue, colored chalk, regular markers, foil star stickers, glue, CD player
Curriculum supplies: photocopies of Christmas party invitation (page 78), Donut Forget CD ("Today a Savior Is Born")

Before class, write the date, time, and place of your Christmas celebration on the reproducible invitation handout (page 78). Then copy the invitation. (If you have mostly seven- or eight-year-olds, they may be able to fill in this information themselves.)

Read Isaiah 9:2a. Explain that God's gift of his Son, Jesus, brought light to the world. Remind the children that they'll be celebrating Jesus' birthday at your class Christmas party next week.

Set out the photocopied invitations, black or dark blue construction paper, and the metallic markers or crayons, glitter glue, and colored chalk. Show the children how to fold a sheet of construction paper in half, then glue the invitation inside. If you have a class of older children, help them fill in the information on the invitation. Then have the children use the supplies you've provided to draw a star or candle on the front of their invitations. As they work, play "Today a Savior Is Born" from the Donut Forget CD.

Have the children make one invitation for themselves and two or three others to share with other class members. If time runs short, have the children simply decorate the extra invitations with foil star stickers.

GATHERING TIME

Classroom supplies: various lights (candle, match, flashlights, lamps), Bible, CD player
Curriculum supplies: Donut Forget CD ("Today a Savior Is Born")

Invite the children to tell you what they did during their Learning Centers. Say: **It sounds like you've all been very busy at your Learning Centers today. If you were part of an angel choir, hold your hands over your head like a halo. If you helped to make rhythm sticks to play with our music, nod your head and tap the floor with your toes. If you made celebration invitations, jump up and say, "Let's celebrate!"**

Let the children respond, then continue: **Everyone has been busy because we are celebrating a special holiday, Christmas. At Christmas we celebrate Jesus' birthday. In the book of Isaiah, it says that before Jesus came, people were living in darkness because of sin and death. But when Jesus was born, light came into the world (Isaiah 9:2). In John 8:12, Jesus says, "I am the light of the world."**

Ask: **How is Jesus like a light? Why are things dark without Jesus?**

Say: **Without Jesus, our lives would be full of sin and sadness. But when we know Jesus, his love fills our lives with joy and light. I've brought some different lights with me to class today to help us see how Jesus lights up our lives.**

Turn off the lights in the classroom and show the children the different lights that you brought. Have them rank the lights in order from dimmest to brightest.

70

Say: **When it's totally dark, even a little light makes a big difference! But Jesus is more than just a little light. He's the light that can light up the whole world. As we sing our memory verse song about Jesus' birth, we'll use these lights to light up our whole room. We'll start with the dimmest light first.**

Play "Today a Savior Is Born." Help the children turn on the lights, one at a time, as you sing the song with the CD.

BIBLE STORY TIME

Classroom supplies: Bible, halos from Center 1, bright light from Gathering Time, CD player
Curriculum supplies: Donut Forget CD ("Today a Savior Is Born")

Form three groups: the angels, the shepherds, and the sheep. Have the children who worked at Center 1 be the angels. Other children may choose to be shepherds or sheep. Talk with the children about how shepherds and sheep act. As you tell the following story, have the children act their parts.

Open the Bible to Luke 2. Say: **In the book of Luke, the Bible tells us that Jesus was born in a stable in Bethlehem. Do you think Jesus' birth was written about in the newspaper or put on TV? No, of course not! There weren't any newspapers or TVs, but God made sure some people heard about Jesus' birthday.**

The night Jesus was born, some shepherds in the fields were just watching over their sheep like they usually did. Here sheepy-sheepy. Want to eat some yummy grass? Oh, yes, that's a nice sheep. Baa, baa, baa.

Encourage the shepherds to pretend to feed and pet their sheep. Then continue in a hushed voice: **It was very dark and quiet that night. The shepherds were getting sleepy. Ahhh! they yawned as they stretched their arms above their heads. Maybe if we took turns watching the sheep we could each take a little nap. . . .**

Encourage the shepherds and sheep to lie or sit down. Then shine the brightest light you brought from Gathering Time on the children. Continue in a loud, surprised voice: **Suddenly a bright light shone from the sky all around the shepherds. The shepherds were scared! They fell to the ground and covered their faces. Then they heard a voice speaking to them. It was an angel! The angel spoke, then many others joined him and they all sang praises to God.**

Have the angel choir speak their lines, then sing the first verse of "Today a Savior Is Born" with the signs, while the shepherds and sheep listen.

After they finish, continue: **The angels told the shepherds to look for Jesus wrapped in cloths and lying in a manger. The shepherds wanted to see the new King, so they left their sheep and ran to Bethlehem to look for baby Jesus. They found him and worshiped him. The shepherds were so excited to see Jesus, they went out and told everyone they met about the baby King!**

The shepherds wanted to tell the good news of Jesus' birth to everyone. We can tell the good news just like they did. And we can sing the good news as the angels did. Let's sing about Jesus' birth now.

SING-ALONG FUN TIME

Classroom supplies: rhythm sticks from Center 2; tambourines and present shakers from previous lessons; CD player
Curriculum supplies: Donut Forget CD ("Today a Savior Is Born," "Happy Birthday, Jesus")

Have the angel choir lead the children in the signs they learned to go with "Today a Savior Is Born." Encourage the children to sing along as they do the signs.

Then pass out the rhythm sticks and other instruments. Say: **Jesus' birth is good news! Let's celebrate by singing and playing our instruments.**

Lead the children in playing the instruments and marching around the room as you sing "Happy Birthday, Jesus." Have the children take turns leading the line. Let the line leader also set a rhythm for the children to follow with their rhythm instruments. Encourage the children to shout out "Happy Birthday!" along with the CD.

When you're ready to move on to the next activity, lead the line back to your story area as you sing the song one last time.

BITE IDEA
If you've invited another class to your celebration, take the children to the other classroom at this time. Have each child hand someone an invitation. Then return to your room for the closing song and prayer time.

DONUT FORGET TIME

Classroom supplies: lights used in Gathering Time; invitations made in Center 3
Curriculum supplies: none

Have the children gather in a circle. Refer to the different kinds of lights you've brought. Say: **In Matthew 5:16, Jesus tells his followers that they should "be a light for other people." Not everyone knows about the good news of Jesus' birth. As followers of Jesus, it's our job to tell these people that Jesus is the light, and we celebrate Christmas because it's his birthday. Who can you tell about the light of Jesus?**

Allow a few moments for the children to think of a friend or family member they can tell about Jesus. Then have the children who participated in Center 3 pass out the celebration invitations. Say: **One way you can let your light shine is to invite your friends and family to come to church with you. We will be having a birthday celebration for Jesus next week. Think of someone you can invite.**

Let the children share the names of the people they'll invite. Then lead the children in singing "Today a Savior Is Born." After you sing the song, invite the children to pray for the people they want to tell about Jesus.

LEARNING CENTERS

Set up the following activities for the children to do as they arrive. Assign an equal number of the children and a teacher or helper to each activity.

At each Learning Center, welcome the children to your class. Make sure you know each child's name. Explain that today you'll be talking about Jesus, the greatest gift of all.

Center 1: Story Transparencies

Classroom supplies: blank transparencies; white paper; colored transparency markers; damp and dry cloths; overhead projector; blank wall, screen, or white board; CD player

Curriculum supplies: Donut Forget CD ("Today a Savior Is Born")

Before class, set out the blank transparencies, transparency markers, paper, and cloths on a table. Set up an overhead projector where you can display the children's transparency pictures.

Review the details of the Christmas story with the children. Then form pairs. Assign each pair one of the following scenes to illustrate with the transparencies.

- Mary, Joseph, and baby Jesus in the manger
- Angels talking to shepherds in a field
- Shepherds visiting baby Jesus
- Excited shepherds telling people about the baby Jesus

Show the children how to place a sheet of white paper underneath the transparencies to make drawing easier. Have cloths available so that they can erase or change portions of their drawings as needed. As the children work, play "Today a Savior Is Born."

When the children finish their pictures, let pairs take turns telling about their pictures as you display them on the overhead projector.

Center 2: Birthday Cake

Classroom supplies: frosted sheet cake; plastic knives; tubes or red, green, and white frosting; colored sprinkles; CD player

Curriculum supplies: Donut Forget CD ("Happy Birthday, Jesus")

Before class, prepare and frost a sheet cake. Set out the tubes of frosting, as well as various kinds of colorful sprinkles.

Remind the children that Christmas is the time we celebrate Jesus' birthday. Invite them to tell you what their families do to celebrate birthdays. Ask them how Jesus' birthday is different from our birthdays.

Let the children squeeze the tubes of frosting in various designs all over the cake, then decorate it with the sprinkles. As they work, play "Happy Birthday, Jesus" from the Donut Forget CD. Set the finished birthday cake aside until you're ready to eat it later.

Center 3: Celebration Decorations

Classroom supplies: red, green, and white balloons and crepe paper; scissors; construction paper; markers; Christmas stickers; tape; CD player

Curriculum supplies: Donut Forget CD ("Happy Birthday, Jesus")

Before class, blow up ten or twelve balloons. Write the words "Happy Birthday, Jesus!" on a chalkboard or sheet of newsprint. (If you use newsprint, hang it up where the children can easily see it.)

Have younger children decorate the room by taping up crepe paper and balloons. Let older children make construction paper birthday signs and banners to hang up. Show them where you've written the words "Happy Birthday, Jesus!" and help them copy the words if necessary. Set out Christmas stickers for the children to decorate the signs and banners as desired. As the children work, play "Happy Birthday, Jesus!" from the Donut Forget CD.

73

GATHERING TIME

Classroom supplies: blank transparency, transparency markers, overhead projector, party hats, small candy canes, tape, CD player
Curriculum supplies: Donut Forget CD ("Happy Birthday, Jesus")

Before class, write the words "Happy Birthday, Jesus!" on an overhead transparency. Leave space for small illustrations. Tape a small candy cane inside a party hat for each child.

Gather the children together. Say: **I see that some of you decorated our room for a birthday celebration for Jesus. And others made a yummy birthday treat we'll get to enjoy later. Everything looks great! Give yourselves a big hand.**

Let the children applaud each other, then set the "Happy Birthday, Jesus!" transparency on the overhead. Say: **Some of you made some special story transparencies that we'll get to use later. If you made a story transparency, please join me now.**

Wait for the children to join you, then turn on the overhead projector. Say: **We're having a birthday party for Jesus. I've written "Happy Birthday, Jesus!" on this transparency. This can represent a birthday card. Besides birthday cards, what other items would you expect to find at a birthday party?**

Let the children suggest items such as presents, cake, friends, games, noisemakers, and party hats. Have the children who worked on the overhead transparencies take turns drawing (or helping you draw) the items other children name. If the children don't mention hats, prompt them by saying, "What about party hats?" After you've added a party hat to the transparency, say: **Party hats! What a great idea! Let's all get our party hats on right now.**

Place a party hat on each child's head. Be careful not to let the children see the candy canes hidden inside the hats. Then say: **Now everyone looks ready for a party. Let's sing "Happy Birthday, Jesus."**

Lead the children in singing "Happy Birthday, Jesus" with the Donut Forget CD. Then say: **Our song talks about how the angels, wise men, and shepherds celebrated the birth of Jesus. The angels sang, the wise men brought gifts, and the shepherds ran to see Jesus. What a great surprise they had!**

And if you look inside your party hats, you'll find a surprise to remind you of the shepherds in our Bible story. You can take your candy canes home to remind you of the shepherds' Christmas surprise.

Set the candy canes and party hats aside for the children to have during your party.

BIBLE STORY TIME

Classroom supplies: Bible, transparencies from Center 1, overhead projector and screen, CD player
Curriculum supplies: Donut Forget CD ("Today a Savior Is Born")

Open your Bible to Luke 2 and show it to the children. Say: **The book of Luke in the Bible tells us about the shepherds' Christmas surprise. Some of our friends have drawn pictures that tell us the Christmas story.**

Invite the children who worked on the Christmas story transparencies to come up. Let pairs take turns placing their pictures on the screen and telling about what they drew. Encourage the children to ask respectful questions (no making fun of others' artwork!) and elaborate on details of the story that may be missing from the pictures.

Say: **We celebrate Christmas because Jesus was born. An angel told Mary that she was going to have a baby who would be the Son of God, Jesus. More angels told shepherds that they'd find the baby Jesus wrapped in cloths and lying in a**

manger. "Today your Savior was born in David's town," the angels sang. "He is Christ, the Lord." What wonderful news! Let's sing about that news.

Have the children stand and sing "Today a Savior Is Born" using the sign language motions they learned last week. Then lead the children in a prayer similar to this one: **Dear God, thank you for surprising the shepherds with the birth of your Son. Jesus is the best present anyone can ever receive. We're so glad he's part of our lives, and we thank you for the joy of celebrating his birthday at Christmas. Amen.**

SING-ALONG FUN TIME

Classroom supplies: streamers made in Lesson 3, rhythm instruments, CD player
Curriculum supplies: Donut Forget CD ("Happy Birthday, Jesus!" "Today a Savior Is Born," "The Best Present of All," "No Room in the Inn")

Before class, arrange to go caroling to another class. Make arrangements with the teacher, but ask the teacher not to tell his students that you'll be coming. Plan to sing some or all of the unit songs, as well as familiar carols the children might suggest. If you've invited others to join you for your Christmas celebration, have them come along for the caroling.

Say: **The shepherds were so excited to hear the surprising news about Jesus, they went and told everyone. We're going to share the news about Jesus by surprising another class with some of our Christmas music.**

Practice singing the unit songs and familiar carols, then lead the children to the other class to surprise them with the good news about Jesus. After you finish singing, lead the children back to your room for your Christmas celebration.

DONUT FORGET TIME

Classroom supplies: cake from Center 2; birthday candles and matches; paper plates, plastic forks, and napkins; presents made in Lesson 2; CD player
Curriculum supplies: Donut Forget CD ("Happy Birthday, Jesus")

Say: **We've already begun to celebrate Jesus' birthday by singing. Let's enjoy our birthday cake for Jesus now.**

Place several candles on the birthday cake, then light them. Lead the children in singing the traditional "Happy Birthday" to Jesus, then let them all help blow out the candles. Cut and serve the cake. As the children enjoy it, play "Happy Birthday, Jesus" from the Donut Forget CD.

When the children finish their cake, have them dispose of their plates, forks, and napkins. Then gather in a circle. Say: **Another way we celebrate Jesus' birthday is by giving and receiving gifts. Let's pass gifts out to our friends.**

Give a gift to a child and say: **Merry Christmas, (name of child.)** Then have that child give a gift to another child. Continue until each child has received a gift.

Say: **If you're visiting our class today, you may have been surprised that we had a gift for you. The surprise gift you received is just a little reminder of God's greatest Christmas surprise—his Son, Jesus. Jesus is the best present of all, and God sent him to earth to save each person here. Let's thank God for that gift before we go home today.**

Invite the children to pray if they want to. Then pray: **Dear God, thank you for sending baby Jesus to us. Thank you for Christmas. Help us to remember to celebrate Jesus' birthday every Christmas. Amen.**

Nativity figures

Jesus is Our Light!

Please join our
Christmas celebration:

Date _____

Time _____

Place _____

Donut Forget to Help Others

BY THE END OF THIS UNIT, LEARNERS WILL

Know   Tell what Jesus said about being great (be a servant).
Feel   Feel willing and happy to be a servant/helper.
Do   Help other people to show love for Jesus.

MEMORY VERSE

"No one should try to do what will help only himself. He should try to do what is good for others"
(1 Corinthians 10:24).

When James and John asked Jesus to give them places of greatness in his kingdom, they were surprised by his response. They'd been hoping he'd say yes; wondering whether he'd say no. But they certainly didn't expect him to issue a call to servanthood. James and John didn't understand that serving others is an important part of loving and serving God. The priest and the Levite in Jesus' story of the Good Samaritan may have understood what it means to be a servant, but refused to help a man who was hurt.

Many four- to eight-year-olds will help when asked. They often enjoy helping at home with household tasks and are eager to volunteer to be "teacher's helper." This unit will teach the children that helping others is a way to show Jesus' love.

	LESSON 1	LESSON 2	LESSON 3	LESSON 4
Center 1	water chimes	sand blocks	twangers	coin instruments
Center 2	lookout glasses	building contest	finger puppets	good Samaritans
Center 3	Lookout Luke	Luke, dressed up	Luke, the nerd	Luke, helping
Gathering Time	lookout walk	block creation	helping situations	servant seat game
Bible Story Time	Mark 10, story song	Mark 10, rap story	Luke 10, finger play	Luke 10, on the road
Sing-Along Fun Time	memory verse rhythm	instruments	helping motions	unit songs
Donut Forget Time	service project	heart toss	serving pictures	helping drawings

Donut forget™
Bible Story Lessons

LEARNING CENTERS

Set up the following activities for the children to do as they arrive. Assign an equal number of children and a teacher or helper to each activity.

At each Learning Center, welcome the children to your class. Make sure you know each child's name. Explain that today you'll be talking about different ways of helping others and learning that we help others because we love Jesus.

Center 1: Water Chimes

Classroom supplies: empty glass jars and bottles, water, plastic dishpan or bucket, wooden or metal spoons, paper towels, CD player
Curriculum supplies: Donut Forget CD ("Be a Helper")

Before the children arrive, fill a dishpan or bucket with water. If you'll have more than six children doing this activity, you may want to provide a second dishpan to reduce crowding (and spills). Set out the jars, bottles, and spoons. Plug in the CD player in a location away from the water.

Help the children form pairs. Hold up a partially filled jar and tap it with a spoon. Explain that partners will practice helping others by helping each create musical instruments like the one you've demonstrated. Have pairs choose one partner to be the chimer and one partner to be the filler. Explain that the filler will fill a container with water, and the chimer will tap the filled container to see what kind of sound it makes.

BITE IDEA
You may want to cover your work area with towels. They'll soak up most of the spilled water, and will also cushion any wet jars that slip out of little hands.

Help the children choose roles, then fill and test their water chimes. Encourage the children to experiment with different water levels to hear the different sounds they make. Children using bottles may even want to try blowing on the tops for a different kind of sound. After several tests, invite the children to switch roles if they want. As the children work, play "Be a Helper" from the Donut Forget CD.

About 5 minutes before you're ready to move on to Gathering Time, have the children practice playing their chimes with the music. Remind them that they'll get to use their chimes again during Sing-Along Fun Time.

Center 2: Lookout Glasses

Classroom supplies: chenille wires (several different colors), sharp scissors, CD player
Curriculum supplies: Donut Forget CD ("Do What Is Good")

Before the children arrive, make a sample pair of lookout glasses. Loop the two chenille wires to form two "lenses." Twist the lenses together. Then attach two lengths of wire to use as ear pieces. (If you have a child-sized model in your home or neighborhood, you may want to make a pair of child-sized glasses ahead of time so you can measure and pre-cut the chenille wires.)

Read 1 Corinthians 10:24. Lead the children in repeating the verse, then explain that they'll be making lookout glasses to help you remember to look out for ways to help others.

Form three groups: the Twisters, the Framers, and the Spectacle Makers. Have the Twisters twist different-colored chenille wires together. Then have the Framers bend the twisted wires into "lenses." Finally, have the Spectacle Makers attach the ear pieces. Have the children make enough glasses for everyone in the class. As the children work, play "Do What Is Good" from the Donut Forget CD.

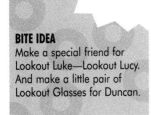

BITE IDEA
Make a special friend for
Lookout Luke—Lookout Lucy.
And make a little pair of
Lookout Glasses for Duncan.

When the children finish making all the glasses, praise them for the way they helped each other complete the project. Have each child put on a pair of glasses as you repeat the memory verse once more. Invite the children to wear their glasses to Gathering Time.

Center 3: Lookout Luke

Classroom supplies: pillows, old pillowcase, towels or baby blankets, child's long-sleeved shirt, child's pants, child's shoes, crayons or markers, scissors, construction paper, glue
Curriculum supplies: none

Before class, practice stuffing the child's clothing with towels, blankets and pillows until you can create a child's form.

Read 1 Corinthians 10:24. Lead the children in repeating the verse, then explain that they'll be making a special friend, Lookout Luke, who will remind you to look out for the good of others.

Form two groups. Have one group help you stuff the figure with blankets and pillows. Give the other group construction paper, markers, scissors, glue, and an old pillowcase. Help the children in this group work together to design Lookout Luke's head, hair, and facial features.

When the children finish, point out that without their help, Lookout Luke would still be in pieces on the floor. Encourage the children to use Lookout Luke as a reminder to help others while they are in class.

Help the children move Lookout Luke over to the Gathering Time area.

GATHERING TIME

Classroom supplies: lookout glasses from Center 2, Lookout Luke figure from Center 3
Curriculum supplies: none

Before class, think of several small service projects the children could do for your church—such as picking up trash outdoors, straightening hymnals, or washing windows. Plan a short walking route that will take you through potential project areas.

Have the children sit down in the Gathering Time area. Invite them to tell you about the things they made at their Learning Centers. Then say: **Wow! You've made a lot of really great things today—water chimes, lookout glasses, and our friend Lookout Luke. Today we're learning about looking out for ways we can help others. So let's all put on our lookout glasses.**

Distribute the lookout glasses to the children, then put a pair of glasses on Lookout Luke. Say: **For the next few weeks, we'll be looking for ways to help others. What are some ways you've helped others?**

Say: **We can help our friends in this class, we can help our families at home— we can even help people here at church. What are some ways we could help here at church?**

Let the children respond, then say: **Let's wear our lookout glasses on a walk around the church. If you see a way we could help, raise your hand and quietly say, "Look out!" Remember to say it quietly—we want to help others in our church by not disturbing their classes.**

Lead the children on a Lookout! walk and let them identify one or more simple service projects they can do as a class. Then lead them back to your classroom. When you return, say: **Jesus said that serving others is the greatest thing we can do. Later today we'll get to worship Jesus by helping others in some of the ways you named on our**

walk. **Right now, let's get ready to hear a Bible story about two of Jesus' friends who didn't understand about serving others.**

Collect the lookout glasses for use during Donut Forget Time.

BIBLE STORY TIME

Classroom supplies: Bible, CD player
Curriculum supplies: photocopies of the "Stop and Serve" stop sign (page 94), Donut Forget CD ("I Wanna Be Great")

Before class, enlarge and make photocopies of the "Stop and Serve" stop sign on colored paper. You'll need one copy for every two children in your class. Tape the copies to the floor.

Open your Bible to Mark 10:35-45 and show the passage to the children. Say: **Our Bible story today comes from the book of Mark. It's about two of Jesus' friends who both wanted to be really great.**

James and John were brothers. They loved following Jesus. They had seen Jesus quiet the storm, feed thousands of people, and make sick people well. They believed that Jesus was God's Son and they wanted to be with him in heaven someday. So they asked Jesus if they could be his two best followers.

Well, when Jesus' other followers heard this, they got angry. All Jesus' friends started fighting and quarreling about who was the best. Have you ever gotten into a fight with a friend about who was the best? What happened, and how did it make you feel?

Jesus told his friends to stop fighting. "You shouldn't fight about who's the best," Jesus said. "Whoever wants to be the best should serve like a servant."

Ask: **How do you feel when you do something to serve someone else? How is that different from the way you feel when you're trying to be the best?**

Say: **Jesus thinks we're all the best when we're serving others. Let's learn a song now to help us remember about that.**

Play "I Wanna Be Great." Let the children listen to the song once, then play it again and invite them to sing along.

Then say: **We're going to sing the song one more time. While we sing, I'll call out an action such as jumping, crawling, or skipping. Keep singing and doing that action until the music stops. When the music stops, go to one of the "Stop and Serve" stop signs and tell a friend one way you can serve others.**

Play "I Wanna Be Great" and stop the music several times. Each time you stop the music, have the children share ways they can serve others. After you finish the song, say: **That was fun! You thought of lots of great ways to serve others. Let's learn a Bible verse that will help us remember to put others first.**

SING-ALONG FUN TIME

Classroom supplies: Bible, water chimes from Center 1, CD player
Curriculum supplies: Donut Forget CD ("I Wanna Be Great," "Be a Helper")

Read 1 Corinthians 10:24. Then say: **Let's play a fun rhythm game to help us remember this verse.**

Form pairs. Have partners sit back-to-back as you lead them in the following rhythm game. As you say the verse, emphasize the bold-faced words or syllables. As you speak the emphasized words, do the actions in parentheses.

No one should **try** (slap knees)
to **do** what will **help** (clap hands)
only (cross arms, hands on shoulders)
him**self** (slap knees).
(Clap hands twice.)

Have the children turn around and face their partners, then continue:
He (clap hands) should
try (clap right hands together) to
do (clap hands) what is
good (clap left hands together) for
others (clap hands).
(Clap partner's hands twice.)

Repeat the rhythm several times, then lead the children in singing "I Wanna Be Great" and "Be a Helper." Invite the children to play their water chimes as you sing. After you're through, put the chimes away where the water won't get spilled. Plan to use the water chimes again during other Sing-Along Fun Times.

DONUT FORGET TIME

Classroom supplies: cleaning supplies as needed for service project, CD player (optional)
Curriculum supplies: Donut Forget CD ("I Wanna Be Great")

Say: **One way we worship God is by doing what he wants us to do. So for our worship time today we're going to serve others in our church.** (Describe the project you've chosen.)

Help the children complete their service project. As they work, affirm them for the good job they're doing. Remind them that we help others because we love Jesus. If you won't be disturbing another class, play "I Wanna Be Great" or "Be a Helper" from the Donut Forget CD as the children work. When the children have finished, return to your room.

Have the children gather in a circle around the cleaning supplies you used for your service project. (If you picked up trash, set the trash bag in the center.) Distribute the lookout glasses.

Say: **Look at all the great work you did. Let's put on our lookout glasses and say our memory verse together one more time to remind us to keep looking for ways to help others this week.**

Lead the children in repeating the verse, then close in prayer.

LEARNING CENTERS

Set up the following activities for the children to do as they arrive. Assign an equal number of children and a teacher or helper to each activity.

At each Learning Center, welcome the children to your class. Make sure you know each child's name. Explain that today you'll be talking about different ways of helping others and learning that we help others because we love Jesus.

Center 1: Sand Blocks

Classroom supplies: wood scraps, sandpaper, scissors, glue, CD player
Curriculum supplies: Donut Forget CD ("Be a Helper")

Before the children arrive, sand any rough or splintery edges on the wood scraps.

Read 1 Corinthians 10:24. Explain that the children will be helping each other make sand blocks to use for singing and playing the memory verse clapping game.

Form pairs. Have partners work together to create sand blocks. One partner can hold the wood scraps while the other traces them onto the sandpaper. Partners can then cut out and glue the sandpaper to the wood scraps to create sand blocks. Play "Be a Helper" from the Donut Forget CD while the children work.

When the children have finished their sand blocks, play "Be a Helper" again and let them "clap" along with their blocks.

Center 2: Building Contest

Classroom supplies: interlocking building blocks, CD player
Curriculum supplies: Donut Forget CD ("I Wanna Be Great")

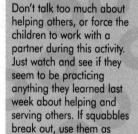

BITE IDEA
Don't talk too much about helping others, or force the children to work with a partner during this activity. Just watch and see if they seem to be practicing anything they learned last week about helping and serving others. If squabbles break out, use them as teachable moments to remind the children of what they've learned.

Before the children arrive, set up a table and chairs and put a small pile of blocks on the table in front of each chair.

Have the children work alone or with a partner to build the greatest creation they can think of. Announce that there will be a prize awarded to creator of the best creation. Play "I Wanna Be Great" as the children are building.

As the children work, talk with them about their creations. Ask them why they've chosen to work alone or with a partner. When the children have finished their creations, set them aside to be "judged" during Gathering Time.

Center 3: Lookout Luke

Classroom supplies: dress-up clothes (neckties, jackets, vests) and accessories (hats, watches, belts), Lookout Luke figure, CD player
Curriculum supplies: Donut Forget CD ("I Wanna Be Great")

Tell the children that Lookout Luke wants to be the best-dressed dummy around. Help the children put the different dress-up clothing items on the dummy. Let them take turns choosing which items to try. Let them enjoy dressing up Lookout Luke, but point out that Jesus isn't looking for the best-dressed people—he's looking for the best servants. As the children work, play "I Wanna Be Great" from the Donut Forget CD.

When the children finish dressing Lookout Luke, move him to the Gathering Time area.

GATHERING TIME

Classroom supplies: building block creations from Center 2, dressed-up Lookout Luke from Center 3, one large treat (such as a pan of brownies), CD player
Curriculum supplies: Donut Forget CD ("I Wanna Be Great")

Have the children who participated in Center 2 set their block creations where everyone can see them. Invite all the children to tell you what they did at their learning centers. Say: **Some of you made sand blocks that we'll get to hear later. If you made sand blocks, stand up and clap your hands, then sit down.**

Some of you dressed up Lookout Luke—doesn't he look fancy? If you dressed up Lookout Luke, say, "Luke, you're a stylin' dude."

The rest of you built creations. If you made a creation, come stand next to your creation now.

Help the children find their places near their creations. Then say: **Now, Lookout Luke is going to be our judge. With your help, he'll decide which block creation is the very greatest of all. When I name each person's creation, you show me with your applause which one you like the best. The creation that gets the most applause will win the prize—a special treat.**

Are you ready, everyone? (Let the children respond.) **Are you ready Lookout Luke?** (Nod the dummy's head.)

One at a time, announce the names of the children who have created structures. Let other children applaud their favorites. After you've applauded all the creations, thank the creators and have them join the rest of the group.

Say: **Thank you all for participating in the greatest block creation contest. I'll need to confer with Lookout Luke for a moment, then we'll announce the winners.**

Put your ear up to Lookout Luke's mouth as if you're listening to him. Say: **What? Well, I don't know. . . . You think so, huh? Well, okay. I guess you're right.**

Turn back to the children and say: **Well boys and girls, Lookout Luke has spoken. He says none of these block creations are the greatest. But I think I have an idea how we could still get the special treat.**

Motion the children to come close to you, as if you don't want the dummy to hear what you're saying. Say: **What if we took all the creations apart and helped each other make one big creation? Then we could all applaud together.**

Let the individual creators dismantle their block creations, then have the children work together to create one big structure. Set the structure near the dummy, then say: **Now let's applaud the greatest block creation.**

Lead the children in applauding the work they've done. Then say: **You did a great job working together and helping each other. No matter what Lookout Luke says, you all deserve a treat.**

Put your ear up to the dummy and say: **What's that, Luke? Oh, you agree. Well, of course they'll have to share the treat. But we have enough for everyone.**

Pass out treats and napkins. Let the children enjoy the treats as they listen to "I Wanna Be Great" from the Donut Forget CD. Have the children throw away their napkins, then return to their seats.

Say: **When we work together and help others, everyone is the greatest. Remember, helping others is a part of following Jesus. Let's take a few minutes now and review how James and John learned that lesson.**

BIBLE STORY TIME

Classroom supplies: Bible, water chimes from Lesson 1, sand blocks from Center 1
Curriculum supplies: none

Open your Bible to Mark 10:35-45 and show it to the children. Say: **Remember the story of James and John? It's found in our Bible in the book of Mark. Today we're going to do a fun rap version of the story.**

Pass out the water chimes and sand blocks. Help the children use the instruments to create a steady 1-2-3-4 rhythm.

Say: **Keep playing your instruments and repeat what I say.**

Speak the following rhyme in a rap-style rhythm. Pause after each line to allow the children to repeat it.

BITE IDEA
If you have mostly younger children, you may want to have half the children use the instruments and half repeat the words after you. Repeat the story twice so the children can experience both activities.

VERSE 1

Well, James and John followed Jesus' call.
So they didn't think he'd mind at all
When they asked him, "Hey, aren't we the best?
How 'bout puttin' us both at your right and left?"

CHORUS

Silly James, silly John—be kind!
Help a friend, be a servant—be kind!
Don't look out for yourself—be kind!
Silly James, silly John—be kind!

VERSE 2

"We wanna be the greatest," they fussed.
"We want the kingdom of God to belong to us."
When the other friends heard, they joined the fray
A-fussin' and a-fightin' both night and day.

REPEAT CHORUS

VERSE 3

Jesus broke up the fighting and said, "Listen up!
This quibbling and quarreling has got to stop.
God picks the seats on my left and my right,
And you won't get there chasing power and might!"

REPEAT CHORUS

VERSE 4

Old James and John, they had it all wrong,
Running after greatness all day long.
'Cause Jesus has something else in mind—
If you want to be great, then learn to be kind.

REPEAT CHORUS TWICE

SING-ALONG FUN TIME

Use the **Duncan** puppet and the script from the Donut Forget Songbook to talk about the memory verse, 1 Corinthians 10:24.

Classroom supplies: sand blocks and water chimes, CD player
Curriculum supplies: Donut Forget CD ("I Wanna Be Great," "Be a Helper," "Do What Is Good")

Lead the children in singing "I Wanna Be Great" with the Donut Forget CD. Each time you sing the word "great," have the children stand up, then sit down.

Lead the children in singing "Be a Helper" with the Donut Forget CD. As you sing, have the children play along on their water chimes and sand blocks.

After you sing the songs, lead the children in the memory verse chant you learned last week. First do the clapping game it as it appears on page 83, then repeat it using elbow claps instead of hand claps. If you have enough sand blocks, let the children use the sand blocks to clap.

After you finish the chant, sing "Do What Is Good" with the Donut Forget CD. Then say: **We help others because we love Jesus. Jesus has done so many things to help us. Remember to look for ways to show Jesus' love by helping others this week.**

DONUT FORGET TIME

Classroom supplies: Bible, construction-paper hearts, crayons or markers, tape, CD player
Curriculum supplies: Donut Forget CD ("Be a Helper," "With All My Heart" from Unit 3)

Before class, cut construction-paper hearts into halves. You'll need two heart halves for each child.

Form pairs. Open your Bible to John 15:13. Say: **In John 15:13 the Bible says: "The greatest love a person can show is to die for his friends." Jesus loves us so much that he died on the cross for us. And he wants us to be the kind of friends who show his love by helping others.**

Give each child two construction-paper heart halves and a crayon or marker. Say: **On one heart half write or draw a picture of one way that Jesus helps us. On the other heart half write or draw a picture of one way we can help others.**

Allow time for the children to finish their heart halves. While they work, play "Be a Helper" from the Donut Forget CD.

When the children finish, say: **Let's put our hearts into action. When we sing the words "be a helper" the first time, throw your helping others heart half up in the air and let it fall on the floor. Then each time we sing "be a helper," pick up another heart half—it doesn't have to be your own—and throw it up and let it fall.**

Sing the song and let the children pick up and toss the heart halves. After the song have the children keep the last helping others heart half they pick up. Then say: **Let's think about the ways Jesus has helped us. Because Jesus died for us, we can all be part of God's family. Let's sing "With All My Heart," to thank Jesus for what he's done. Each time we sing "with all my heart" we can toss our Jesus heart halves.**

Lead the children in singing "With All My Heart" with the Donut Forget CD. After the song, have the children keep the last Jesus heart half they pick up. Help the children tape their heart halves together. Say: **You may not have the heart halves you started with, but that's okay. We can all share our great ideas about sharing Jesus' love by helping others. Remember, we help others because we love Jesus. Put your helping heart on your bathroom mirror or closet door at home to remind you to help others this week.**

LEARNING CENTERS

Set up the following activities for the children to do as they arrive. Assign an equal number of children and a teacher or helper to each activity.

At each Learning Center, welcome the children to your class. Make sure you know each child's name. Explain that today you'll be talking about different ways of helping others and learning that we help others because we love Jesus.

Center 1: Twangers

Classroom supplies: shoe boxes or other small, sturdy boxes, different-sized rubber bands, CD player

Curriculum supplies: Donut Forget CD ("Good Samaritan")

Form pairs. Give each pair two boxes and a handful of rubber bands. Help the children work together to stretch the rubber bands around the boxes to create "twangers." Encourage them to take turns stretching the rubber bands and testing the sounds they make. Play "Good Samaritan" from the Donut Forget CD while the children are working.

As the children work, point out the ways they're helping each other. Encourage them to tell you about times they've helped others as the Good Samaritan did. When the children finish their twangers, have them twang along with the song.

Set the finished twangers aside for use during Sing-Along Fun Time.

Center 2: Finger Puppets

Classroom supplies: crayons or markers, scissors, fabric and yarn scraps, glue, tape, CD player
Curriculum supplies: photocopies of "Good Samaritan Finger Puppets" (pages 88, 89), Donut Forget CD ("Good Samaritan")

Before class, photocopy the "Good Samaritan Finger Puppets." Cut out sets of puppets for the children who'll be working at other Learning Centers. If you have mostly younger children, you may want to cut out all the puppets. You'll need one set of puppets for each child in your class.

Set out crayons or markers, glue, scissors, and fabric and yarn scraps. Give each child a set of finger puppets. Help the children cut out and decorate their finger puppets. As they work, tell them a little bit about each puppet they're creating. When the children finish their puppets, show them how to put the puppets on their fingers. Play "Good Samaritan" from the Donut Forget CD and encourage the children to wiggle the appropriate puppets as they're mentioned in the song.

Set the finished finger puppets aside for use during Bible Story time.

Center 3: Lookout Luke

Classroom supplies: Lookout Luke figure, additional dress-up clothes
Curriculum supplies: none

Tell the children that in today's Bible story you'll learn about a man who helped someone else even though he didn't really like the person. Have the children use the dress-up clothes to turn Lookout Luke into a "nerd"—someone who might not be liked at school. Encourage them to dress Lookout Luke in unmatched clothes, mess up his hair, or even change his facial features.

When the children finish, move Lookout Luke to your Gathering Time area.

GATHERING TIME

Classroom supplies: Lookout Luke figure
Curriculum supplies: none

Invite all the children to tell you what they did at their Learning Centers. Say: **Some of you made twangers to twang along with a new song we'll be learning today. If you made a twanger, give a friend a high five and say "twang!"**

Some of you made finger puppets to help us tell our Bible story today. If you made finger puppets, hold up both hands and wiggle your fingers.

Some of you . . . well, some of you did something funny to Lookout Luke. I hardly even recognized him. He sure doesn't look like anyone else in our class! Does he look like anyone you've seen at school?

Let the children respond, then ask:

- **What would you do if someone dressed like Lookout Luke came up to you at school and asked to borrow your crayons?**
- **What would you do if you were using your crayons?**
- **What would you do if you were using your crayons for an assignment?**
- **What would you do if the person dressed like Lookout Luke wanted you to stay after school and help him color a picture?**
- **What would you do if he asked you to stay after, but you already got invited to a friend's birthday party?**

Say: **It's easy to help our friends or family members. But it's not always so easy to help people you don't like or people who are different from you. Our Bible story today is about a man who stopped to help, even though it wasn't easy to do. Let's hear that story now.**

BIBLE STORY TIME

Classroom supplies: Bible, finger puppets from Center 2, CD player
Curriculum supplies: Donut Forget CD ("Good Samaritan")

Make sure each child has a set of finger puppets. Children who didn't make puppets at Center 2 can have a plain set to decorate at home.

Open your Bible to Luke 10:25-37 and show it to the children. Say: **Our Bible story comes from the book of Luke. Today we're going to learn a song that tells this story. We'll wiggle our finger puppets while we listen to the song. Let's review the characters so we'll know which fingers to wiggle.**

Help the children identify their finger puppets as they place them on the following fingers: Thumb—man walking to Jericho; Pointer—robber; Middle—priest; Ring—Levite; Pinky—Good Samaritan.

Play "Good Samaritan" from the Donut Forget CD. Have the children wiggle their puppets as they listen. After the song, say: **The Samaritan really took care of the hurt man. But it wasn't easy for him to do. He had to delay his own trip to take the man to the inn. And he had to pay his own money for the innkeeper to take care of the man.**

Ask: **Would you do something like that to help a friend? Why or why not?**

Say: **The man on his way to Jericho was Jewish. And the Jewish people didn't like Samaritans. But the Samaritan in this story still helped him.**

Ask: **Would you help someone who didn't like you? Someone you didn't like? Why or why not?**

Say: **Jesus wants us to show his love by helping others, even when it's hard to do. Let's use our puppets to learn a finger play that will help us remember to be helpers as the Samaritan was.**

Lead the children in the following finger play. Have them wiggle the appropriate puppets as you read.

Five little travelers walking down the road,
The first one said, "I'm off to Jericho."
The second one said, "Hey, robbers, let's attack!"
A third walked by and turned his back.

Donut Forget™ Bible Story Lessons

A fourth man looked, but wouldn't lend a hand.
The fifth man stopped to help the hurt man.

Repeat the finger play if time allows, then collect the finger puppets.

SING-ALONG FUN TIME

Classroom supplies: twangers made in Center 1, water chimes and sand blocks from previous lessons, CD player
Curriculum supplies: Donut Forget CD ("Good Samaritan," "Do What Is Good," "Be a Helper")

Lead the children in singing "Good Samaritan" and "Do What Is Good" with the Donut Forget CD. Have them play along on their twangers and other instruments as they sing.

After you sing "Good Samaritan" and "Do What Is Good" once or twice, have the children set their instruments aside. Say: **We've been learning the song "Be a Helper" for a few weeks now. Today let's have some fun by making up motions to that song.**

Form pairs or trios. Assign each group of children a phrase from the song, such as "clean my room," "mow the lawn," or "haul the trash." If you have a very large class, assign some phrases to more than one group.

Allow up to 5 minutes for the children to come up with their motions. If you like, invite them to use props they can find in the room. After 5 minutes call the children back together and sing the song again with the motions they've created.

After the song, say: **Great job creating those motions. When we worked together, we covered the whole song in just a few minutes. Remember the motions you created and try to act them out in real life as you serve others this week.**

DONUT FORGET TIME

Classroom supplies: Bible, aluminum foil, ribbon, scissors
Curriculum supplies: photocopy of "Servant Gifts" (page 95)

Before class, cut apart the illustrations on the "Servant Gifts" page. Place the illustrations in four different places in your room. Set up a table or work station near each illustration with aluminum foil, ribbon, and scissors.

Say: **1 Peter 4:10 says that each one of us has received a gift we can use to serve others. If you have a gift for something, that means you enjoy it or you're good at it. God wants us to be good servants with the gifts he's given us. We're going to make servant gift medallions to remind us to use our gifts to serve others this week.**

Look around the room and you'll see four pictures. Choose a picture that represents something you enjoy doing or something you're good at. For example, you might choose the picture of books and drawing supplies if you enjoy reading, drawing, or coloring. If you're good at sports or enjoy playing outside you might choose the picture of the ball and slide. Choose the picture that represents your gift and go stand near it now.

After the children have chosen their pictures, have them talk with others in their group about their gifts. Help them brainstorm ways they can use their gifts to serve others. For example, a child who enjoys playing sports might offer to toss a ball around with a younger sibling. Or a child who likes to draw might draw pictures for the children in the hospital.

Have the children sculpt the aluminum foil into a shape that represents their gift. Help them poke a hole in their shape and thread a ribbon through it to create a Servant Helper medallion.

Have the children stand in a circle with their finished medallions. As you hold up each child's medallion, invite the child to tell you what the medallion's shape represents. Then place the medallion around the child's neck as you say: **(Name of child), be a good servant of God's gift. Be a helper.** When all the children are wearing their medallions, close by singing "Be a Helper."

LEARNING CENTERS

Set up the following activities for the children to do as they arrive. Assign an equal number of children and a teacher or helper to each activity.

At each Learning Center, welcome the children to your class. Make sure you know each child's name. Explain that today you'll be talking about different ways of helping others and learning that we help others because we love Jesus.

Center 1: Coin Instruments

Classroom supplies: quarters, nickels, and dimes; small glass or plastic containers with lids; metal pots and pans with lids
Curriculum supplies: Donut Forget CD ("Good Samaritan")

Set out the coins you've brought. Explain to the children that the Good Samaritan gave the innkeeper two silver coins to care for the hurt man. Ask the children to tell you what they could buy with two silver coins (any denomination). Point out that in the man's time, two silver coins were the equivalent of two days wages—probably close to $100 or more today.

Set out the containers and pots and pans. As you play "Good Samaritan" from the Donut Forget CD, invite the children to use the coins and the other items to create rhythms to go along with the song. For example, they might put several coins in a lidded container to create shakers. Or they might drop coins one at a time into a pot or swirl them around in a metal lid. Encourage the children to use the coins in as many ways as they can think of.

Center 2: Good Samaritans

Classroom supplies: adhesive bandages, fabric bandages, dolls or stuffed animals, CD player
Curriculum supplies: Donut Forget CD ("Good Samaritan")

Set out the dolls or stuffed animals and first aid supplies. Explain that the Good Samaritan bandaged the hurt man's wounds, then took him to an inn where he could rest and get better. Invite the children to practice bandaging the dolls and stuffed animals.

As the children bandage the animals, have them tell you about times they've been hurt and the people who helped them feel better. Talk with them about ways they can help others who are sick or hurt.

Center 3: Lookout Luke

Classroom supplies: Lookout Luke figure, scissors
Curriculum supplies: photocopy of "Would You Help?" (page 96)

Before class, photocopy the "Would You Help?" page and cut apart the pictures. Lay the pictures face down on a table.

Point out to the children that you've been learning about helping others for a few weeks. Explain that you're going to do an activity to see how they'd do in real-life helping situations.

Donut Forget™ Bible Story Lessons

Have the children take turns turning over the pictures on the table, then talking to Lookout Luke as if he were the person in the picture. For example, they might say to the toddler reaching for a toy, "Can I help you get that down? Let's play with it together." If you want, have Lookout Luke "respond" to the children. You can speak answers yourself, or put your ear to the figure's mouth to "hear" what he's saying.

Repeat the activity for the other three pictures.

When you finish, move Lookout Luke to your Gathering Time area.

GATHERING TIME

Classroom supplies: Lookout Luke figure
Curriculum supplies: none

Invite all the children to tell you what they did at their Learning Centers. Say: **Some of you made coin instruments, some of you practiced helping sick people, and some of you played a game with Lookout Luke called "Would You Help?" We're going to play another game with Lookout Luke right now. It's called Servant Seat, and it's played like "Duck, Duck, Goose."**

Have the children sit on the floor in a circle. Set Lookout Luke in the center of the circle. Prop him up with a few books if necessary until he's in a sitting position.

BITE IDEA
Don't put Lookout Luke on a chair. As more and more children join him in the Servant Seat they could break the chair or hurt each other.

Say: **I'll choose someone to be *It*. *It* will go around and gently tap people on the head. Instead of saying "duck, duck, goose," *It* will say our memory verse. Do you remember how it goes? Let's say it once together right now.**

Lead the children in repeating the verse, then continue: **That was great. As a matter of fact, we can all say it together as *It* is tapping our heads. The last person who is tapped will be the next *It*. The first *It* will name one way to look out for the good of others, then join Lookout Luke in the Servant Seat. The object of the game is to get everyone in the Servant Seat— because we all want to be showing Jesus' love by serving others!**

Play the game with the children until everyone—including you—is in the Servant Seat. Then have the children repeat the verse together once more. Say: **Good serving. Let's all get up from the Servant Seat now so we can hear about someone else who was a servant—the Good Samaritan.**

BIBLE STORY TIME

Classroom supplies: chairs, tables, Lookout Luke figure, CD player
Curriculum supplies: Donut Forget CD ("Good Samaritan")

Open your Bible to Luke 10:25-37 and show it to the children. Say: **Remember our story about the Good Samaritan that's found in the book of Luke? Well today we're going to have fun acting it out. The first thing we'll need to do is build a "road" to Jericho. We'll use chairs and other things in the room to mark a winding road.**

Help the children choose nonbreakable items to mark a winding road through the room. You may need to move some furniture out of the way.

After you've marked your road, say: **Now we'll need some actors. I'd like everyone to find a partner.** (Pause for the kids to find partners.) **Decide with your partner who will be the hurt man and who will be the Samaritan.**

Pause for the kids to decide, then continue: **Do you remember our Good Samaritan song? In the second part of the song, it talks about how the Good Samaritan**

helped the man who got hurt. When you hear that part of the song, Samaritans pretend you're helping your hurt partners.

In the first part of the song, it talks about the robbers who beat up the man on his way to Jericho. Since we don't want anyone really getting hurt on our road to Jericho, we'll have Lookout Luke be the man in the first part of the song. Anyone who wants to be a robber can have a turn "beating up" Lookout Luke during the first part of the song. But I want to see all you robbers turned into Samaritans and hurt travelers during the second part of the song! We'll just listen to it once so you can see what I mean.

Play the song through once and let the children listen as you point out when they'll be robbers and when they'll be Samaritans. Then move Lookout Luke onto your road. Play the song again and let the children act out their parts. Have robbers hide behind chairs or other obstacles and take turns punching the dummy as you walk him down the road. Then have the children spread out along the road to act out their Samaritan and injured traveler roles.

After you finish, Lookout Luke will probably be falling apart. Say: **Oh dear. Look at poor Lookout Luke. Well it's a good thing we've all learned a lot about looking out for others. Do you think we can remember to help others without Lookout Luke? I think we can. Let's give ourselves three cheers for all the ways we can help others. When I count to three, we'll say "Help! Help! Hooray!" three times together. Ready? One, two, three.** Lead the children in cheering three times loudly, then more and more softly as they return to the Gathering Time area. Leave the road in place for use during Donut Forget Time.

SING-ALONG FUN TIME

Classroom supplies: rhythm instruments made during this unit, CD player
Curriculum supplies: Donut Forget CD ("Good Samaritan," "Be a Helper," "I Wanna Be Great," "Do What Is Good")

Lead the children in singing all the songs you've learned during this unit. Let them choose which songs they like best and what instruments or motions they want to do with each song.

After you've sung all the songs, say: **Great singing! Keep singing those songs at home to remind you to keep helping others.**

DONUT FORGET TIME

Classroom supplies: colored construction paper, crayons or markers, masking tape, CD player
Curriculum supplies: Donut Forget CD ("Be a Helper")

Have the children return to the partners they had during Bible Story Time. Set out crayons or markers. Give each child two sheets of colored construction paper.

Say: **On one sheet of paper, write your name and draw a picture of yourself. On the other sheet of paper, write the name and draw a picture of someone you'll help this week. Tell your partner how you'll help that person.**

Allow time for the children to complete their drawings. As the children finish, tape the drawings to the floor along the road you created during Bible Story time. Put each child's pair of drawings together. Place partners' drawings next to each other.

When all the drawings have been placed on the road, say: **It's not always easy to help others. In fact, sometimes it's pretty hard—just as it was hard for the Samaritan to help the hurt traveler. But helping others is something Jesus wants us to do, and he'll help us do it if we ask him.**

Donut Forget™ Bible Story Lessons

93

Go with your partner and stand by your drawings. Take a few minutes and pray that Jesus will help your partner help the person in his drawing. You don't have to pray a fancy prayer. Just say, "Jesus, please help my partner help his friend." If you want to, you can use the names of your partner and the person he wants to help.

Play "Be a Helper" as you help the children find their drawings and encourage them to say brief prayers for their partners. When they finish praying, have them sit down near their drawings.

Close by singing "Be a Helper" together. Then pray that God will help all the children as they serve others this week.

Servant Gifts

Would You Help?

Donut Forget to Do Good

BY THE END OF THIS UNIT, LEARNERS WILL

Know Name ways to do good.

Feel Feel ready to do what's right.

Do Do something good for another person.

MEMORY VERSE

"Never become tired of doing good" (2 Thessalonians 3:13).

By returning to say thank-you, one leper did what was right. He honored Jesus by showing his gratitude. A simple thank-you honors the one to whom thanks is due. A simple thank-you recognizes the value of a person whom God has created. Jesus taught that words are an important part of doing what is right. Words can show others that they are valuable to us and to God. Helping others recognize their value to God is one way to do what's right.

Four- to eight-year-olds love to talk, yet they tend to be shy when adults speak to them. They feel honored when others—especially adults—take the time to honor them and speak to them. This unit will lead the children to do what is right by speaking politely to those who have spoken to them, by prayerfully responding to those who hurt them, and by praising God.

	LESSON 1	**LESSON 2**	**LESSON 3**	**LESSON 4**
Center 1	thank-you letters	washer chimes	wire figures	salty snacks
Center 2	ten lepers	megaphones	worship signs	flashlight code
Center 3	do good wagon train	wagon train deliveries	wagon train hearts	wagon train tunnel
Gathering Time	memory verse song	memory verse echo	do-good situations	secret message
Bible Story Time	Luke 17, story letters	Luke 17, in the story	Matthew 7, picnic	Matthew 7, tent story
Sing-Along Fun Time	finger cymbals	do-good words	helping hearts	memory verse taps
Donut Forget Time	thank-you tickets	doing good, being polite	praying for each other	riding the train

Donut forget™ Bible Story Lessons

LEARNING CENTERS

Set up the following activities for the children to do as they arrive. Assign an equal number of children and a teacher or helper to each activity.

At each Learning Center, welcome the children to your class. Make sure you know each child's name. Thank each child for coming. Explain that today you'll talk about the importance of saying thank-you.

Center 1: Thank-You Letters

Classroom supplies: eight 9-by-12-inch sheets of tagboard or heavy construction paper, buttons, material scraps, ribbon, lace, glue, scissors, CD player
Curriculum supplies: Donut Forget CD ("Don't Forget to Say Thanks")

BITE IDEA
If you have fewer than eight children at this Center, assign the remaining key words to other children just before you tell the Bible story. Each child should have only one letter.

Before class, outline the letters of the phrase "thank you" on separate sheets of tagboard. Make large block letters using stencil patterns or draw the letters freehand.

Set out the block letters and the craft items you've provided. Help the children arrange the letters to spell out "thank you." Invite a child who can read to tell you what the letters spell. Talk with the children about why and when we say thank-you.

Then have the children select the material scraps, lace, and buttons they want to use and arrange them inside the outline of the letters. As the children work, play the song "Don't Forget to Say Thanks." When the children have completed their arrangements, have them glue the items in place.

Assign each child one of the following key words for her letter. Explain that you'll use the letters and the key words to help tell the Bible story later.

T is for *ten.*	H is for *help.*
A is for *answer.*	N is for *new.*
K is for *kneel.*	Y is for *yell.*
O is for *one.*	U is for *unkind.*

Set letters aside to dry for use during the Bible Story Time.

Center 2: Ten Lepers

Classroom supplies: butcher paper, markers or crayons, pictures of Bible-times clothing, CD player
Curriculum supplies: Donut Forget CD ("Don't Forget to Say Thanks")

Before class, cut ten 4-foot-long sections of butcher paper.

Explain that today's Bible story is about ten men who had a very bad skin disease called leprosy. Tell the children that they'll draw ten leper figures to use later in the lesson.

Have each child lie on a sheet of butcher paper so you can draw his outline. If you have fewer than ten children, outline some of them more than once. After you've outlined the figures, have the children use markers to add features and Bible-times clothing. (Have pictures of Bible-times clothing available for reference.) Explain that leprosy was a skin disease and that lepers wore strips of cloth for bandages. Encourage the children to draw bandages on the figures. As the children work, play "Don't Forget to Say Thanks" from the Donut Forget CD.

Remind the children that these lepers were real people with names and families. Have the children help you list Bible names such as Jonah, Stephen, Jacob, Aaron, or Peter. Then encourage the children to give each figure a name. Write the name below each figure. Hang the finished figures on the wall near the Bible Story area.

Center 3: Do Good Wagon Train

Classroom supplies: butcher paper; marker; one child's wagon for every two or three children; party decorations such as crepe paper and balloons; construction paper; cellophane tape; crayons; scissors; CD player

Curriculum supplies: photocopies of "Thank-You Tickets" (page 114), Donut Forget CD ("Never Become Tired of Doing Good")

BITE IDEA

If wagons aren't available, substitute large boxes or sturdy laundry baskets. The number needed will depend on the size of the boxes or baskets. A variety of sizes will make the train more interesting. Provide enough boxes or baskets so that each child has a seat. During train riding sections of this unit, have the children pretend that the train is moving.

Before class, letter the following phrase on a long length of butcher paper: "Do Good Wagon Train." If you have mostly younger children in your class, you may want to cut the Thank-You Tickets apart ahead of time.

Discuss with the children the importance of saying thank-you. Have them share times they've said thank-you to someone. Point out the wagons and explain that the words "thank-you" will be their ticket to ride the Do Good Wagon Train. Tell them that they'll hear more about the Do Good Wagon Train in a few minutes.

Form groups of two or three—one group for each wagon. Instruct the children to use the materials provided to decorate the wagons. Then have each group cut apart a sheet of Thank-You Tickets and tape them to its wagon. If time allows, help the children decorate the sign for the "Do Good Wagon Train." (If the children are too busy decorating the wagons, decorate the sign yourself while they're working.)

As the children work, play "Never Become Tired of Doing Good" from the Donut Forget CD.

GATHERING TIME

Classroom supplies: ten leper figures from Center 2, CD player
Curriculum supplies: Donut Forget CD ("Never Become Tired of Doing Good")

Have the children sit down in the Gathering Time area. Ask: **Have any of you said the words "thank-you" today? Why did you say thank-you?**

Let the children respond, then continue: **Saying thank-you is important. That's why the members of Center 1 decorated the words "thank you." If you were part of Center 1, say, "Thank you." Center 3 decorated our Do Good Wagon Train. If you helped decorate the train, say, "Whew! Whew! Thank you." Center 2 drew ten men. If you drew one of these ten men, say the name of the man you drew.**

Today we're going to find out how many of these ten men and how many of you will ride the Do Good Wagon Train. Our memory verse says, "Never become tired of doing good." We're going to hear a Bible story in a few minutes that tells about one important way we can do good. But first, let's learn our memory verse song. Listen to the words, and each time you hear the word "never," stand up, then sit down.

Play "Never Become Tired of Doing Good" from the Donut Forget CD. Join the children in standing each time the song says "never." After the song, say: **Whew! We might get tired of standing and sitting. I'm tired, aren't you? But I hope we never get too tired to do the good things Jesus wants us to do. One of those good things is saying thank-you. "Thank-you" will be our ticket for riding the Do Good Wagon Train today. Anyone who says thank-you will get to ride. Before we find out which of you gets to ride, let's find out which of these ten men gets to ride. For that we will need help from Center 1.**

99

BIBLE STORY TIME

Classroom supplies: Bible, Thank-You letters made at Center 1
Curriculum supplies: one Thank-You Ticket (page 114)

Open your Bible to Luke 17:12-19 and show it to the children. Say: **Our Bible story today is from the book of Luke. In this story, we will meet ten men who had leprosy. Center 2 has made ten figures to represent the ten men.**

Point out the figures, then continue: **Leprosy is a skin disease. In Bible times, people with leprosy had to live away from their families and friends. They lived with other people with leprosy in groups called leper colonies. Doctors and medicines could not cure leprosy, but Jesus could! These ten men with leprosy knew that Jesus was going to pass by their leper colony. Let's find out what happened when Jesus came by that day.**

Have members of Center 1 hold up their letters to spell the word "thank-you." If fewer than eight children participated in this Center, select additional children to hold letters. Whisper the corresponding word in each additional child's ear. Have each child in turn speak the key word for her letter. After each child speaks, read the teacher's part.

Child: **T is for *ten*.**

Teacher: **Ten lepers stood at the side of the road and called to Jesus.**

Child: **H is for *help*.**

Teacher: **"Help us, Jesus. Heal us of our leprosy," begged the ten lepers.**

Child: **A is for *answer*.**

Teacher: **Jesus answered the ten lepers, "Go show yourselves to the priests."**

Child: **N is for *new*.**

Teacher: **As the ten lepers were on their way to see the priests, they were healed. Their leprosy was gone. Their skin became new.**

Child: **K is for *kneel*.**

Teacher: **When one of the lepers saw that his leprosy was gone, he returned and kneeled at Jesus' feet.**

Child: **Y is for *yell*.**

Teacher: **This one leper was so happy, he yelled, "Praise God. Thank you, Jesus, for healing me!"**

Child: **O is for *one*.**

Teacher: **Only one leper out of the ten returned to tell Jesus thank-you. "Where are the other nine?" Jesus asked.**

Child: **U is for *unkind*.**

Teacher: **Nine lepers were unkind because they did not say thank-you to Jesus for making them well.**

Ask: **Which one of these lepers was one who said, "Thank you, Jesus"?** Have the children pick one leper figure from the ten figures made by Center 2. Attach the Thank-You Ticket to the one chosen.

Say: **This thankful leper has purchased a ticket to ride the Do Good Wagon Train.**

Ask:

■ **Which leper are you like?**

■ **Do you say thank-you to those who help you and who do kind things for you? Tell me about a time you thanked someone.**

Say: **We do good when we thank others for what they do for us. When we thank them, we honor them, and we honor Jesus, too.**

SING-ALONG FUN TIME

Classroom supplies: epoxy or other strong glue, 1/4-inch wide elastic, two fenders (1/4-inch center by 2 1/2-inch diameter) for each child (Note: Fenders look like large flat washers and can be purchased at local hardware stores for about ten cents each. This unit calls for a total of six fenders per child.)

Curriculum supplies: Donut Forget CD ("Don't Forget to Say Thanks," "Never Become Tired of Doing Good")

BITE IDEA
If time allows, have the children decorate their finger cymbals with glitter glue at the end of today's session. They will need several hours to dry.

Before class, make one set of finger cymbals for each child. Each finger cymbal uses two 2 1/2-inch fenders and a 1 1/4-inch length of 1/4-inch wide elastic. Fold the ends of the elastic under and glue along opposite edges of the center hole in the fender.

Lead the children in singing "Don't Forget to Say Thanks!" Each time the phrase "thank-you" or the word "thanks" is sung, have the children turn to another child, shake hands, and sing thank-you.

Open your Bible to 2 Thessalonians 3:13 and show it to the children. Say: **Whenever we say thank-you we do something good. We honor the person we thank. When we honor others, we honor God. We should never become tired of doing good. We should never become tired of saying thank-you.**

Let's say the verse together: "Never become tired of doing good, 2 Thessalonians 3:13." Now let's sing our memory verse song to help us remember 2 Thessalonians 3:13.

Distribute the finger cymbals. Have each child place one cymbal on the tips of his index finger and thumb on the same hand. When the children bring their fingers together, the cymbals will sound. Give the children a minute to practice with the cymbals. Then invite the children to play their finger cymbals as they sing "Never Become Tired of Doing Good." Encourage the children to sound the cymbals on each syllable of the word "never."

After the song, gather the cymbals to use again during other Sing-Along Fun Times.

DONUT FORGET TIME

Classroom supplies: chosen leper from the Bible Story, Do Good Wagon Train from Center 3, crayons, scissors, paper hole punch, CD player

Curriculum supplies: copies of "Thank-You Tickets" (page 114), Donut Forget CD ("Never Become Tired of Doing Good")

BITE IDEA
If your train is long, you may want to ask for volunteer "conductors" to push from the back as you pull it.

Ask: **Do you remember what kind of ticket we need to purchase in order to ride the Do Good Wagon Train? How can we purchase a Thank-You Ticket?**

Let the children suggest ideas, then continue: **We can purchase a ticket by saying thank-you. Which leper purchased a ticket to ride the Do Good Wagon Train? Yes, (name of leper) was the only leper to say thank-you to Jesus.** Take the leper drawing off the wall and put it in the wagon train. Say: **Now it's your turn to earn a ticket to ride the Do Good Wagon Train.**

Ask:

■ **Who can you honor by telling them thank-you?**

■ **Why do you want to tell (name of person) thank-you?**

If the children don't have ideas of their own, suggest people such as teachers, pastors, bus drivers, custodians, and so on.

Donut Forget™ Bible Story Lessons

Distribute the Thank-You Tickets and crayons or markers. Have the children color their Thank-You Tickets. Help the children write the names of the people they are thanking on the back of the tickets. (Children who are just learning to write can trace over names that you lightly write in pencil.) Have the children make as many tickets as time will allow. Make sure the children also put their names on the tickets. As they work, remind them that they are doing good and honoring these people by saying thank-you.

When the children finish, decide how the tickets will be delivered. If possible, have the children personally hand-deliver the Thank-You Tickets. Make arrangements to mail those tickets that cannot be hand-delivered.

Say: **Hold up the Thank-You Tickets that you made so I can see them. Wow! I see that we've done a lot of thanking today. You've done something good by telling another person thank-you. You have honored others. I think that each one of you has paid the purchase price for a ride on the Do Good Wagon Train. This train is covered with tickets. Pull one off and hop on the train.**

Shout: **All aboard the Do Good Wagon Train!**

As the children board the train, punch a hole in each of their tickets. Join the wagons by having the child in the back of the front wagon hold the handle of the second wagon. The child in the back of the second wagon holds the handle of the third wagon, and so on. Pull the wagon train around the room. While pulling the train, lead the children in chanting "Whew! Whew! Thank-you!" Then lead them in singing "Never Become Tired of Doing Good" with the Donut Forget CD. Pull the train into the station and close in prayer.

LEARNING CENTERS

Set up the following activities for the children to do as they arrive. Assign an equal number of children and a teacher or helper to each activity.

At each Learning Center, welcome the children to your class. Make sure you know each child's name. Thank each child for coming. Explain that today you'll talk about the importance of saying kind things to others.

Center 1: Chimes

Classroom supplies: two stainless steel fenders (1/4-inch center by 2 1/2-inch diameter) for each child, colorful ribbon, scissors, rulers, CD player
Curriculum supplies: Donut Forget CD ("Don't Forget to Say Thanks")

Have the children use the rulers to cut the ribbon into 12-inch lengths. Then have the children thread a length of ribbon through the opening in each fender, pulling the ribbon together so that it is even. Help the children tie the ribbons together in a single knot at the top. Make a set of two chimes for each child in the class. Show the children how to play the chimes by holding the ribbon and chiming the two fenders together. Hands should not touch the fenders—this will deaden the sound.

When the chimes are completed, play "Don't Forget to Say Thanks" as the children chime along. Have the children place the chimes in the Do Good Wagon Train when the Center 3 children bring it to their group.

Center 2: Megaphones

Classroom supplies: scissors, colored card stock, cellophane tape, markers, alphabet stickers
Curriculum supplies: none

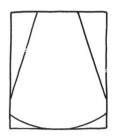

Set out the card stock, scissors, tape, markers, and alphabet stickers. Show the children how to roll a sheet of card stock into a megaphone and tape the ends together. Older children may want to use scissors to trim the corners off their papers as shown. Have the children use the alphabet stickers to put their names on the megaphones. As they work, talk about kind and polite things they can say to others. Use the alphabet stickers to add the polite words to the megaphones. Have the children make enough megaphones for everyone in the class.

When the megaphones are complete, invite the children to take turns saying polite words through their megaphones. Then have them use the megaphones to say the memory verse together.

Have the children place the megaphones in the Do Good Wagon Train when the Center 3 children bring it to their group.

Center 3: Do Good Wagon Train

Classroom supplies: Do Good Wagon Train, strips of cloth or elastic bandages, hat for each child at this Center, large index cards, markers, construction paper, crepe paper, scissors, cellophane tape, CD player

BITE IDEA
If the children need help thinking of do-good words, suggest the following: Hello; How are you?; Pardon me; Excuse me; Please; May I?; Yes, Sir; Yes, Ma'am; Thank you; You're welcome; I'm sorry; I forgive you; Good-bye.

Curriculum supplies: Donut Forget CD ("How Great You Are")

Before class, put the strips of cloth and elastic bandages in one section of the train. You'll need enough for each child in the class to have two or three. Reserve places on the train for the chimes from Center 1, the megaphones from Center 2, and the hats from this center.

Explain that today the Do Good Wagon Train will make some deliveries. Point out the cloths and bandages on the train. Tell the children that they'll also be picking up "cargo" from other Learning Centers.

Set out the hats. Explain to the children that they may decorate these "Do Good Delivery Hats" any way they would like. The only requirement is that each hat must have a different do-good word on it. Play "How Great You Are" as the children decorate their hats.

As the children work, remind them that God wants us to use our words to do good and help others feel special. When the hats are completed, have the children put them on and take the Do Good Wagon Train to pick up its cargo from Centers 1 and 2.

GATHERING TIME

Classroom supplies: Do Good Wagon Train with cargo, CD player
Curriculum supplies: Donut Forget CD ("Never Become Tired of Doing Good")

Have the children sit down in the Gathering Time area. Say: **Wow! All of you have been very busy in your Learning Centers. The children at the Do Good Wagon Train have prepared to be delivery children today. If you made a hat to wear while making deliveries, say "Chugga, chugga, we deliver."**

I also heard some chimes chiming. If you made chimes, sing, "Chime, chime, chime." I saw the rest of you making some megaphones. Those megaphones should be arriving any minute on the Do Good Wagon Train.

Have members of Center 3 pull the train to the Gathering Time area. Say: **Ah, here they are. Would those of you who made megaphones lead us in saying our memory verse?**

Have members of Center 2 pass out the megaphones so that each child has one. Have the children say the verse through their megaphones. Then have the children form two lines facing each other. Have Line 1 say the verse and line 2 echo it. Then quickly form six groups. Have each group say one word of the verse, then have everyone say the reference together.

Say: **I hope that none of you will ever get tired of doing good. We do good when we make others feel special. We make others feel special when we speak good words to them. We'll find out what some of those words are and when to use them in today's lesson. But first, let's all do a good thing and put our megaphones and hats into the Do Good Wagon Train. Let's see if we can get everything into the train before the end of our memory verse song.**

Play "Never Become Tired of Doing Good" as the children put their items into the train.

BIBLE STORY TIME

Classroom supplies: Do Good Wagon Train with cargo, an envelope with a letter that reads "Jesus is coming today," CD player
Curriculum supplies: Donut Forget CD ("Don't Forget to Give Thanks")

Open your Bible to Luke 17:12-19 and show it to the children. Say: **Remember our story from last week about the ten men with leprosy? Leprosy is a skin disease. In Bible times, doctors and medicines could not cure leprosy, but Jesus could!**

These lepers probably had cloth bandages wrapped around the places where the leprosy hurt them. That reminds me, I ordered some bandages for us to use in today's lesson. I'm expecting them to arrive any minute by the Do Good Wagon Train.

Have the Center 3 children remove the bandages from the Train and distribute them among the class. Then say: **Let's take these bandages and pretend that we are the ten lepers.**

Help the children as needed to wrap an arm, leg, hand, or foot. Use a bandage yourself. When everyone is bandaged, continue: **We are sad because we have leprosy. Let me see your sad faces. We are sad because we can't live with our families. We don't want our families to get leprosy. We are also very sad because the doctors can not cure our leprosy.**

Look! I have a letter from my family. I wonder what it says. Shall we read it? Read the letter: **"Jesus is coming today."**

Wow! Jesus is coming! What can Jesus do? Jesus can cure leprosy. What should we do? Take suggestions from the children. Then say: **Yes, yes, let's go see Jesus. Let's ask him to cure our leprosy. Remember, we must stay far away from Jesus. We'll have to yell.**

Lead the children around the room and back to your story area. Then say: **Look, there's Jesus. Let's ask Jesus to help us. Jesus, Master, please help us!**

What did Jesus say? Wait for the children to answer. Then say: **Jesus said, "Go show yourselves to the priests." Yes, Jesus, we will go see the priests.**

Lead the children across the classroom. Stop and say: **My leprosy is gone. It's gone! I'm cured!** Hug each child. Lead the children in cheering: **We're cured! Jesus can heal leprosy! Let's take off these bandages.**

When the celebration has died down, invite the children to tell you how the story ends. Only one leper returned to say thank-you to Jesus. Say: **Let's pretend we're the one leper who came back to thank Jesus for healing his leprosy. As we listen to "Don't Forget to**

Say Thanks," we'll dance around and wave our bandages to show our thanks to Jesus for helping us be well again.

Play "Don't Forget to Say Thanks" and encourage the children to wave their bandages on the "thank-you" choruses.

SING-ALONG FUN TIME

Classroom supplies: Do Good Wagon Train cargo, CD player
Curriculum supplies: Donut Forget CD ("Don't Forget to Say Thanks," "Never Become Tired of Doing Good," "How Great You Are")

Ask: **What do-good words did one leper use? Are these the only do-good words? What other do-good words do you know?**

Let the children respond, then say: **Our Do Good Wagon Train delivery children will remind us what some other do-good words are.**

Use the **Duncan** puppet and the script from the Donut Forget Songbook to talk about the memory verse, 2 Thessalonians 3:13.

Have Center 3 children put on their hats. Point to each child as you read the words from his hat. Point to each child as the class says the word written on that hat.

Lead the children in singing "Don't Forget to Say Thanks." Each time the word "thanks" or "thank-you" is used, replace it with one of the words from the hats. Tell the class which word to use by pointing to the child wearing that hat. Sing through the song twice.

Distribute the megaphones. Form two groups and have the groups face each other. Tell the children to use their megaphones to sing the word "never" in the memory verse song. Explain that you will point to their group when they are to sing the word "never." They are not to sing it unless you are pointing to them. As the children sing the song, direct them to banter back and forth singing the word "never." When finished, have the Center 3 children gather the megaphones and put them back in the Train.

Distribute the chimes from Center 1 and have children chime along as you sing "How Great You Are." Point out that words of praise to God are do-good words, too.

Collect the chimes for use in future Sing-Along Fun Times.

DONUT FORGET TIME

Classroom supplies: Do Good Wagon Train with cargo, CD player
Curriculum supplies: Donut Forget CD ("Never Become Tired of Doing Good")

Say: **We've learned a lot of do-good words today. Why do we need to know these words? When could we use them?**

Let the children respond, then say: **When we use these words, we are being polite to the people we speak to. We do good when we speak politely to others, especially when they have spoken to us first. Have any of you ever felt shy when someone has spoken to you? Instead of answering, maybe you hid behind your mom or dad. When we speak back to the person who has spoken to us, then we do something good. We treat the person who spoke to us with value. That person is valuable to God, so we should treat them with value by answering. What are some words we can use when someone speaks to us?**

Let the children respond, then say: **Let's practice some of those words now.** Put on the hat labeled *Hello.* **When someone says hello to you, how should you answer?**

105

Say hello to a child and wait for the child to answer back. Do this with several children. Then put on the hat labeled *Thank-You*. Say: **When someone compliments the way you look, how should you answer?**

Give specific compliments to several children and allow them to respond. Then put on the hat labeled *Yes, Sir* or *Yes, Ma'am*. Say: **When someone gives you instructions, how should you answer?**

BITE IDEA
If you don't want the children to share the hats, have them remove the words from the hats and pass those around instead.

Give directions to several children and allow them to respond. Continue putting on hats and letting the children practice responses until you've used all the hats. Then say: **Very good. Now it's your turn.**

Form groups of three. Give each group one hat. Instruct the children in each group to take turns wearing the hat. The child with the hat is the speaker; the other two children will respond with good words to the things he says. Rotate the hats between groups until each child has worn a hat.

Then say: **We practiced doing good today. We do good when we use polite words to speak to others. We show people they are valuable when we speak to those who have spoken to us. Our memory verse tells us that we should never grow tired of doing good. Let's say it together.**

Lead the children in repeating the verse, then say: **Look! Here comes the Do Good Wagon Train! It is full of megaphones. Take one and hop aboard. All aboard the Do Good Wagon Train!** Pull the train while the children sing "Never Become Tired of Doing Good" through the megaphones. Close with prayer.

LEARNING CENTERS

Set up the following activities for the children to do as they arrive. Assign an equal number of children and a teacher or helper to each activity.

At each Learning Center, welcome the children to your class. Make sure you know each child's name. Thank each child for coming. Explain that today you'll be talking about what Jesus said about doing good.

Center 1: Wire Figures

Classroom supplies: chenille wire, yarn, sequins, glue, scissors
Curriculum supplies: Donut Forget CD ("The Golden Rule")

Give each child two chenille wires. Help the children form the two wires into a people figure. Have the children make one chenille wire figure for each child in the class. If time permits, invite them to use sequins and yarn to dress the figures.

As the children work, play "The Golden Rule" from the Donut Forget CD. Place the chenille figures in the Do Good Wagon Train for use during Gathering Time.

Center 2: Worship Signs

Classroom supplies: CD player
Curriculum supplies: Donut Forget CD ("How Great You Are")

Explain to the children that worshiping God is an important way to do good. Tell them that you're going to learn the signs for some good words they can say to God. One at a time, demonstrate how to make the signs for *great, good, think,* and *worship* (see illustrations).

Have the children practice signing as you slowly read each word. Repeat the words until the children are comfortable making the signs themselves. Then let them make the signs with the song "How Great You Are."

great

Center 3: Do Good Wagon Train

Classroom supplies: various edging scissors, double-stick tape, construction paper, pencils, Do Good Wagon Train
Curriculum supplies: Donut Forget CD ("Never Become Tired of Doing Good")

Before class, make a variety of heart patterns from sturdy paper. If you have mostly younger children, you may want to trace and cut out some hearts before class. You'll need four hearts for each child in your class.

Set out the supplies and help the children trace the heart patterns onto construction paper. When the hearts are cut out, invite the children to decorate the hearts. They may use edging scissors to give the hearts a special edge. Or they could tape small hearts inside larger hearts.

good

Remind the children that we show love for others when we do good for them. Point out that 2 Thessalonians 3:13 encourages us to never become tired of doing good.

When the children finish decorating the hearts, apply a piece of double-stick tape to the back of each heart. Play "Never Become Tired of Doing Good" from the Donut Forget CD as the children decorate the Do Good Wagon Train with the hearts. Have the children attach all the hearts to the Train.

GATHERING TIME

Classroom supplies: Do Good Wagon Train with chenille wire figures from Center 1
Curriculum supplies: none

think

Have the children sit down in the Gathering Time area. Invite them to tell you about the things they did at their Learning Centers. Have a helper bring the Do Good Wagon Train to the Gathering Area. Say: **Doesn't the train look LOVE-ly today? If you decorated the Train with all of these hearts, say, "LOVE-ly." If you worked at Center 2 stand up and sign the word *great*. If you worked at Center 1 and made chenille wire figures, stand up and hop on one foot.**

Have the Center 1 children take the wire figures from the Train and pass them out to the class. When everyone has a figure, divide the class into pairs. If there is an uneven number of children, have one group of three or pair yourself with one child.

worship

Read the following situations to the group and have each pair act them out using the chenille figures. Pause after you read each situation to allow time for the children to act it out.

1. The two of you are playing with your favorite toys. You want the toy that your friend is playing with. You grab it out of your friend's hands. What happens next? Act it out.

2. The two of you are playing at the playground. You decide to play on the slide. Just as you arrive at the steps to the slide, your friend pushes you out of the way and climbs the stairs first. What happens next? Act it out.

3. The two of you are talking about who is the fastest runner. You think that you are and your friend thinks that he is. So you decide to race. Your friend wins the race and turns to you and says, "Nah-nah, nah-nah, nah-nah!" What happens next? Act it out.

After the children have acted out the situations, say: **If you've had one of these situations happen to you, hold up your chenille figure. Wow, I've had these things happen to me, too!**

Ask:

■ **How did you feel when these things happened to you?**

Donut Forget™ Bible Story Lessons

■ **What did you say? What did you do?**

Let the children respond, then continue: **When things like that happen to me, I feel hurt and angry, too. I've said some mean words in those situations. Today, we're going to find out what Jesus said about doing good in times like these. But first, let's put our figures back on the Do Good Wagon Train.**

Collect the figures, then have the children gather in the Bible Story Time area. Set the Do Good Wagon Train aside for use later in the lesson.

BIBLE STORY TIME

Classroom supplies: Bible, blankets, picnic basket, picture of praying hands, napkins, plates, forks, spoons, cups, pitcher of water, snack
Curriculum supplies: Donut Forget CD ("The Golden Rule")

Before class, obtain a picture of praying hands. If you can't find one, trace and cut out an outline of your own hands. Put the praying hands, Bible, napkins, plates, forks, spoons, cups, pitcher of water, and the snack in the picnic basket.

Show the children the blankets and picnic basket. Say: **We're going to have a picnic today as we learn what Jesus said about doing good. Let's spread these blankets out so that we have a place to sit.**

When blankets are spread out, have the children sit down on them. Open the picnic basket and take out the Bible. Open it to Matthew 7:12 and show the passage to the children. Say: **The book of Matthew tells us an important thing Jesus said about doing good. Jesus said, "Do for other people the same things you want them to do for you."**

Many people were gathered to listen to Jesus. They were sitting on the side of a hill. Some of the people probably sat on blankets or coats. Maybe some of the people brought their lunches with them. The people listened to Jesus tell them how to do good. Jesus taught them to do for other people the same things they wanted others to do for them.

Let's look and see what we have for our picnic today. Open the picnic basket and take out the praying hands. Say: **We need to pray on our do-good picnic.**

Lead the children in a prayer for the picnic and for help to do good. Then ask:

■ **How can we use prayer to do good?**
■ **Tell about a time you prayed for someone.**
■ **Tell about a time someone else prayed for you.**

Let the children respond, then continue: **We do good when we pray for others. It's easy to pray for people we like. But Jesus also told us that doing good means praying for people we don't like. Doing good means praying for people who hurt us and who are mean to us.**

Take the napkins, forks, spoons, and plates out of the picnic basket and have the children make their own table setting. Ask: **How can we use these things to do good?**

Let the children respond, then continue: **Are these all things you would want someone else to do for you? We can use these items in many ways to do good for others. Jesus said that we should always share what we have. If someone wants to borrow something from us, we should let that person borrow it. When we share our things with others, we do good.**

Take the cups and the pitcher of water from the picnic basket. Distribute the cups to the children. Wait until snack time to pour the water. Ask: **How can we use water to do good?**

Let the children respond, then continue: **If you were thirsty, would you want someone to give you a drink of water? Jesus said that when we give others a drink of water, we do something good.**

Take the snack out of the picnic basket. Ask: **How can we use food to do for others what we want them to do for us?**

Let the children respond, then continue: **If you were hungry, would you want someone to give you some food? Jesus said that when we feed those who are hungry, we do something good. I wanted to do something good for you so I brought you this snack.**

Distribute the snack and pour cups of water. Play "The Golden Rule" as the children eat the snack.

SING-ALONG FUN TIME

Classroom supplies: Do Good Wagon Train with hearts from Center 3
Curriculum supplies: Donut Forget CD ("How Great You Are," "The Golden Rule")

Have the children from Center 2 teach the signs they learned. Play the song "How Great You Are" as the Center 2 children lead the class in singing and signing. After the song, say: **Because we have such a great God, we want to show his love to those around us. God gives us the power to do good things. When we do good things for others, we honor them and we show God's love to them. We do for them the same things that we want them to do for us.**

Have a helper bring the Do Good Wagon Train to the Sing-Along Fun Time area. Play "The Golden Rule" and invite the children to take a heart from the train and stick it on a classmate every time the phrase "love others" is sung. Be ready with extra double-stick tape!

Have the children keep the hearts on during Donut Forget Time.

DONUT FORGET TIME

Classroom supplies: chenille wire figures from Center 1, Do Good Wagon Train, CD player
Curriculum supplies: Donut Forget CD ("Never Become Tired of Doing Good")

Ask: **What does Jesus tell us to do when others treat us badly?**

Let the children respond, then continue: **Jesus told us to do for other people the same things that we want them to do for us. Jesus said we should pray for people who treat us badly instead of using angry words.**

Say: **Let's act out the Gathering Time stories again. This time, when your friend hurts you, instead of saying angry words, pray for her.**

Distribute the wire figures and repeat the Gathering Time situations. Then remind the children that in order for us to do good, we must treat others the way we want to be treated.

Say: **We treat others the way we want to be treated when we pray for those who hurt us. Instead of saying angry words to the people who hurt us, Jesus tells us to pray for them. When we pray for them, we honor them. We do good!**

If you think you can remember to pray for someone who hurts you instead of using angry words with them, take off one of your hearts and stick it on the Do Good Wagon Train.

When everyone has attached a heart to the train, say: **All aboard the Do Good Wagon Train!**

BITE IDEA
Every child will need a flashlight with fresh batteries for Lesson 4. Send a note home with the children today and give them a reminder call the day before the next session. Gather flashlights yourself for children who may forget and for those who weren't here today.

When the children are situated, say: **The Do Good Wagon Train needs your help to get the engine started. Let's say our memory verse as loud as we can.**

After leading the children in reciting the verse, play "Never Become Tired of Doing Good" from the Donut Forget CD and pull the train around the room.

LEARNING CENTERS

Set up the following activities for the children to do as they arrive. Assign an equal number of children and a teacher or helper to each activity.

At each Learning Center, welcome the children to your class. Make sure you know each child's name. Thank each child for coming. Explain that today you'll learn what Jesus said about how our words can be like salt and light.

Center 1: Salty Snacks

Classroom supplies: electric popcorn popper, unpopped popcorn, oil (if needed), salt, salted and unsalted crackers, salted and unsalted pretzels, low sodium and high sodium beverage, bowls, cups, CD player
Curriculum supplies: Donut Forget CD ("The Golden Rule")

Have the children pop enough popcorn for the group. Divide the popcorn in half and place in two separate bowls. Add salt to one bowl and leave the second bowl plain. Let the children sample both.

Have this group set up a snack table with the salted and unsalted or low sodium foods. As the children work, play "The Golden Rule" from the Donut Forget CD. Point out that they are doing something for others that they like having done for them—making a snack!

Center 2: Flashlight Code

Classroom supplies: flashlight for each child
Curriculum supplies: copies of the "Flashlight Code" (page 113)

Give each child a copy of the Flashlight Code and a flashlight. Show the children how to shine their flashlights on a wall or ceiling and wiggle the flashlights to form each of the code letters. Have the children practice using the flashlight code to spell the phrase "do good." (If possible, have this group meet in a darkened area of the room.)

Explain that today you'll be learning how we can light up others' lives with our do-good words and actions. Tell the children that they'll get to present their Flashlight Code words to the class during Gathering Time.

Center 3: Do Good Wagon Train

Classroom supplies: materials to make a tunnel, Do Good Wagon Train, blankets, strips of paper, tape, markers, CD player
Curriculum supplies: Donut Forget CD ("Never Become Tired of Doing Good")

Before class, use a pencil to lightly write the following words on separate strips of paper: *polite, prayerful, praise.* Repeat the words as necessary so you'll have one word for each child in the class. Gather rolling blackboards, tall easels, empty bookshelves, or four-sided tables for the children to use in making their tunnel.

110

Tell the children that they will be making a tunnel from the materials you have provided. Help them set up the tunnel "walls," then cover the tunnel with blankets. Make the tunnel as dark as possible. Make sure the Do Good Wagon Train and passengers can pass through the tunnel.

When the tunnel is completed, invite the children to trace the words on the strips of paper and decorate them. Then have the children tape the words inside the tunnel. As the children work, play "Never Become Tired of Doing Good" from the Donut Forget CD.

BITE IDEA
If your building has a hallway that can be darkened, use it for the tunnel. This tunnel can also be used for the tent during Bible Story Time.

GATHERING TIME

Classroom supplies: flashlights from Center 2
Curriculum supplies: copies of "Flashlight Code" (page 113)

Before class, make several copies of the Flashlight Code for the children to share.

Have the children sit down in the Gathering Time area. Invite them to tell you about the things they did at their Learning Centers. Say: **You have been very busy working on projects to help us learn how to do good. If you were a part of the group who did something good by making us a snack, jump up and down like popcorn when it pops! If you prepared the flashlight words, turn on your flashlights and wave the light in the air. If you made a tunnel for the Do Good Wagon Train, say "Chugga, chugga, whew! whew! whew!"**

Invite the children from Center 2 to come forward. Distribute copies of the "Flashlight Code." Say: **We have a secret message to decode. The message only has three letters in it: D, G, and O. Look at the code key and watch the flashlights. Match the flashlight pattern with the pattern on your paper. Let's find out what the message is.**

Turn the lights down so the flashlight code will be easier to see. Help the children decode the phrase "do good," then say: **Jesus gave us some important instructions about using our words to do good. He also told us how our good words could be lights for other people. Let's hear more about that now.**

Have the Center 2 children keep their flashlights to use during Bible Story Time. Remind them that the flashlights are only to be used as you direct. Collect the children's flashlights if they're too distracting.

BIBLE STORY TIME

Classroom supplies: tent, flashlight for each child, snacks from Center 1
Curriculum supplies: none

Before class, set up a tent or make one using blankets and tables. Or use the tunnel created in Center 3. Set the extra flashlights inside the tent.

Open your Bible to Matthew 7:12 and show it to the children. Say: **These are the words of Jesus. Let's say this verse together. We have sung this verse in the song "The Golden Rule." Follow me when you know the verse.**

Stand up and lead the children in a march to the words of Matthew 7:12: "Do for other people the same things you want them to do for you." Lead the group into the tent.

Leave a tent flap open so that the tent has light. When all the children are settled, say: **When Jesus taught about doing good, he used salt and light to help people understand how important it is for his followers to do good.**

Donut Forget™
Bible Story Lessons

111

Have any of you ever been in a dark room? Tell me about it. What was it like? Are any of you afraid of the dark?

Let the children respond, then say: **I'm going to close the tent flap now and make it dark in our tent. What can we do in this tent without any light? That's right. We can't do very much. How does the darkness feel? It makes me feel sad.**

Let the children respond, then continue: **We could use a little light.** Ask a child from Center 2 to turn on a flashlight, then say: **Even a little bit of light helps us feel better.**

One at a time, distribute flashlights to the children. As you hand each child a flashlight, have that child turn on the flashlight. Continue until all the children have their flashlights on. Say: **Isn't all this light wonderful! We all feel better now because we have light instead of darkness. When we speak do-good words, we spread a little light. We help people feel better. The more do-good words we speak, the more light we spread. Jesus said our words should be like lights in the darkness. Now let's follow the light out of the tent.**

Use a flashlight to lead the children out of the tent to the Center 1 snack table. Say: **Here is a table of yummy snacks. We're going to have a taste test.**

Form four groups. Give each group one salted and one unsalted snack. Say: **One of your snacks has salt; the other snack doesn't. Work with your group to decide which has salt and which tastes better.**

When the children have completed their task, ask them to share the results. Point out that salt makes foods taste better. Say: **Our words should be good like salt. We can make the world better with our words. When we speak do-good words, we spread a little salt. We help people feel better. The more do-good words we speak, the more salt we spread. Jesus said our words should be like salt.**

DONUT REPAIR OPPORTUNITY

Jesus sent his Holy Spirit to help us do good.

SING–ALONG FUN TIME

Classroom supplies: flashlights, 1/4-inch wide elastic, fenders (1/4-inch center by 2 1/2-inch diameter), safety pins

Curriculum supplies: Donut Forget CD ("The Golden Rule," "Never Become Tired of Doing Good")

Before class, make two taps for each child. Thread a 6- or 7-inch length of elastic through the center of each fender. Overlap the elastic and secure the ends with a safety pin. The size of the taps may be adjusted by the amount of elastic that is overlapped and pinned together.

Ask: **What does our memory verse say about doing good?** Let the children respond, then distribute the shoe taps. Have the children pull the taps on over their shoes and fit them around the widest part of their feet. The taps should be situated on the ball of the foot. Play "Never Become Tired of Doing Good" from the Donut Forget CD and let the children tap as they sing along with the song.

Collect the taps and distribute the flashlights. Have the children turn their lights on and off each time the words "love others" are sung in the song "The Golden Rule."

If time allows, let the children request other unit songs or favorite songs from previous units. Let them use the flashlights, taps, finger cymbals, and chimes as they sing. Point out that God is pleased by the do-good sounds and lights of their praise singing.

BITE IDEA
If your classroom floor is carpeted, take the children to a uncarpeted area in the building. (Be sure you won't be disturbing another class.) Or if the weather permits, have the children tap outside on the sidewalk.

112

DONUT FORGET TIME

Classroom supplies: flashlights, Do Good Wagon Train, tunnel from Center 3, CD player
Curriculum supplies: Donut Forget CD ("How Great You Are")

Say: **When we worship and praise God, we use do-good words. Listen for the do-good words in "How Great You Are."**

Give each child a flashlight and ask the children to sit down. Turn the lights down or off and have the children shine the flashlights around the room as they sing. When you finish the song, ask: **What do-good words did you hear in this song?**

Let the children respond, then continue: **Let's take a ride on the Do Good Wagon Train and think about some more do-good words. All aboard the Do Good Wagon Train!**

When the children have boarded, pull the Wagon Train through the tunnel made by Center 3. In the middle of the tunnel, stop the Train. Invite the children to use their flashlights to find one of the following words written in the tunnel: *polite, prayerful, praise.* Ask the children to freeze their flashlights on the words they find. Read each word and ask the child whose flashlight shines on it to name a do-good word of that kind.

Pull the Wagon Train out of the tunnel and back to the classroom if needed. Ask the children to get out of the Train and kneel beside it. Close with a prayer of praise.

Collect any flashlights that you brought in. Return other flashlights to their owners. Let the children take home the taps, chimes, and finger cymbals if they want. Save any extra instruments for use in other Sing-Along Fun Times.

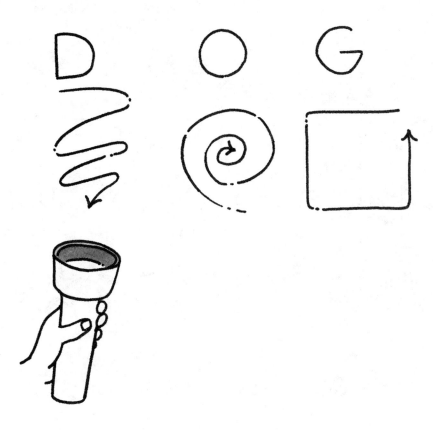

"Never become tired of doing good"
(1 Thessalonians 3:13).

THANK YOU

Do Good
Train

Do Good Wagon Train Co.

"Never become tired of doing good"
(1 Thessalonians 3:13).

THANK YOU

Do Good
Train

Do Good Wagon Train Co.

"Never become tired of doing good"
(1 Thessalonians 3:13).

THANK YOU

Do Good
Train

Do Good Wagon Train Co.

"Never become tired of doing good"
(1 Thessalonians 3:13).

THANK YOU

Do Good
Train

Do Good Wagon Train Co.

Donut Forget to Believe in Jesus

BY THE END OF THIS UNIT, LEARNERS WILL

Know   Tell about two miracles Jesus did.

Feel   Feel amazed at Jesus' power.

Do   Believe that Jesus is the Son of God.

MEMORY VERSE:

"Jesus did many other miracles . . . But these are written so that you can believe that Jesus is the Christ, the Son of God" (John 20:30, 31).

When Jesus walked on this earth, he was just like us. He looked like us. He talked like us. He was a man. He was also God. The God who made the world out of nothing by only the power of his word is the same Jesus who stopped the storm. People in Jesus' time knew Jesus was not an ordinary man because of the awesome miracles they saw him do. Even now, people still come to believe Jesus is God by reading about the miracles that are recorded in Scripture.

To young children, grown-ups are powerful. Grown-ups can do things—such as driving cars and purchasing toys—that kids can't do. And if the things parents and teachers can do amaze children, imagine the wonder Jesus' miracles will inspire! The children will be amazed to hear how Jesus stilled a storm and fed more than five thousand people with a little boy's lunch. These lessons will teach the children that Jesus could do these amazing miracles because he's God's Son.

	LESSON 1	LESSON 2	LESSON 3	LESSON 4
Center 1	bubble painting	storm sounds	basket lunch	puppet show
Center 2	wind chimes	sign language	fish shaker	cheerleaders
Center 3	shoebox boats	posters & pom-poms	fish & bread posters	more fish & bread
Gathering Time	walnut shell boats	memory verse rhythm	talk a walk	decorate lunch sacks
Bible Story Time	Matthew 8, acting groups	Matthew 8, in the boat	John 6, lunch for all	John 6, story bloopers
Sing-Along Fun Time	memory verse song	singing & cheering	outdoor singing fun	practice the show
Donut Forget Time	sailing fears	storm sounds	nature items	Marvelous Miracle Show

LEARNING CENTERS

Set up the following activities for the children to do as they arrive. Assign an equal number of children and a teacher or helper to each activity.

At each Learning Center, welcome the children to your class. Make sure you know each child's name. Explain that today you'll be talking about the amazing miracles Jesus did.

Center 1: Bubble Painting

Classroom supplies: drawing paper, crayons, liquid dishwashing detergent, water, blue tempera paint, drinking straw for each child, CD player
Curriculum supplies: Donut Forget CD ("What Kind of Man Is This?")

Before the children arrive, mix 2 tablespoons of liquid dishwashing detergent, 1/4 cup water, and 1 teaspoon blue tempera paint in a small jar.

Give each child a sheet of paper and a straw. Set out crayons and have the children draw boats in the centers of their papers. Tell the children not to draw the water yet. As the children work, briefly tell them how Jesus calmed the storm.

Have the children set their papers aside and listen as you play "What Kind of Man Is This?" from the Donut Forget CD. When you hear the words "he spoke to the rain," insert your straw in the paint mixture and blow bubbles. Each time you hear the words "he spoke to the . . . (rain, wind, waves)," let a child blow bubbles in the paint. Continue until the paint bubbles rise above the jar. Then stop the CD and have the children take turns dabbing their pictures on the bubbles. Their boats will sail on a sea of paint bubbles.

Set the finished pictures aside to dry.

BITE IDEA
Each week the children working at Center 3 will prepare various portions of a "Marvelous Miracle Variety Show" to be put on for parents at the end of the unit. To assure that each child will play an active role in the show, form three groups at the beginning of this unit. In Lessons 1-3, assign a different group to Center 3 each week. In Lesson 4 the children will spend their Learning Center time with their show groups practicing their "acts."

Center 2: Wind Chimes

Classroom supplies: electric fan, poster board, markers, scissors, glue, paper hole punch, colored yarn, small beads, CD player
Curriculum supplies: Donut Forget CD ("What Kind of Man is This?")

Before class, cut the poster board into 4-inch circles. You'll need a poster board circle for each child. Cut colored yarn into 2-foot lengths.

Tell the children they'll be making wind chimes to help them remember how Jesus calmed the wind. Give each child a poster board circle. Help the children punch 12 evenly-spaced holes around the edges of their circles. Let the children choose 12 lengths of colored yarn, then help them tie all the lengths together on one end.

Show the children how to thread lengths of yarn through the holes. Help them anchor each length of yarn by tying it around its hole. Then let the children thread beads onto the dangling yarn lengths. Help them tie a large knot at the bottom of each yarn length to keep the beads from falling off. As the children work, play "What Kind of Man Is This?"

When the children finish their chimes, turn on the fan and listen to the chimes. Have the children ring their chimes as you sing "What Kind of Man Is This?" with the Donut Forget CD.

Set the finished chimes aside for use during Sing-Along Fun Time.

Center 3: Finger Puppets & Shoebox Boats

Classroom supplies: empty shoebox (or other box of similar size without a lid) for each child; scissors, markers, paper hole punch, chenille wire

Optional classroom supplies: brown and white construction paper, glue, craft sticks or wooden skewers

Curriculum supplies: photocopies of finger puppets (page 131)

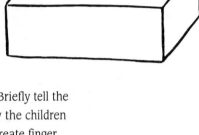

BITE IDEA
If time allows, let the children cover their "boats" with brown construction paper "planks." They could also add sails using white construction paper and craft sticks or wooden skewers.

Before class, cut out a sample set of puppets. Punch out the marked holes. Thread pieces of chenille wire through the holes in each puppet, then twist the ends together to create a loop that slips over your finger. If you have mostly younger children, you may want to cut out all the puppets ahead of time. The children can decorate the puppets and attach the chenille wire loops.

In the bottom of each shoebox, cut four finger puppet-sized holes, as shown in the illustration.

Tell the children that today you'll be learning how Jesus calmed a stormy sea. Briefly tell the story, then give each child a sheet of finger puppets to decorate and cut out. Show the children how to punch out the holes and thread the chenille wire through the puppets to create finger loops.

Distribute the shoeboxes. Have each child put a Jesus finger puppet on one hand and the three disciple puppets on his other hand. (It doesn't matter which fingers the children use for the puppets.) Show the children how to put the Jesus puppet through the single hole on one end of the boat. Have them put the three disciple puppets through the holes on the other end.

Read the Bible story from Matthew 8:23-27 and let the children act it out with their puppets. If time allows, play "What Kind of Man Is This?" from the Donut Forget CD and let the children "dance" their disciple puppets on the "decks" of their boats.

Have the children put their names on their shoeboxes and set their finished puppets inside. Explain that in a few weeks they'll get to use the puppets to put on a Miracle Puppet Play for parents.

Set the puppets and shoebox boats aside for use later in the lesson.

GATHERING TIME

Classroom supplies: empty walnut shell half for each child; dishpan of water, large towel, CD player

Curriculum supplies: Donut Forget CD ("What Kind of Man Is This?")

Have the children sit down in the Gathering Time area. Invite them to tell you about the things they did in their Learning Centers. Say: **If you painted a bubbly sea, touch your hands over your head and say, "Pop!" If you made wind chimes, wave your arms back and forth and make a "whoosh" noise like the wind. If you made finger puppets and shoebox boats, wave your fingers in front of your face and say, "It's a miracle!"**

Let the children respond, then ask:

■ **What do you know about miracles?**
■ **Can you tell about any of the miracles Jesus did?**

Let the children respond, then say: **A miracle is an amazing thing that only God can do. The Bible tells about many miracles Jesus did. He made sick people well, he made blind people see, and he even made a dead man come alive again. When Jesus did miracles, people knew he was really God's Son. In fact, the Bible tells**

us that's one reason why Jesus did miracles—so people would believe in him. Listen to what our memory verse says about that.

Read John 20:30, 31. Have the children repeat the verse with you. Then say: **Today we're going to hear how Jesus calmed a storm. To help us get ready for that story, I've brought some little boats.**

Give each child a walnut shell half "boat." Lay down a towel and set a dishpan of water on it. Have the children set their boats in the water, then gather around the dishpan.

While the water settles down, ask if anyone has been in a boat. Invite those children to tell what it was like. Then say: **When you're in a boat and the water is calm, like our water is now, it's very peaceful. The boat just rocks gently from side to side. Rock, rock, rock, rock. Pretend you're rocking gently in your boat. The gentle rocking might even lull you to sleep.**

Say: **Sometimes, when the wind picks up, the water gets a little bit choppy. If you're not used to being in a boat, the choppy feeling can make you a little uneasy. But if you're in a sailboat, you need the wind to move your boat across the water. Let's see how much wind we can create for our boats.**

Let the children blow the boats. Encourage them to blow as hard as they can. Then have the children create "waves" by splashing gently in the water.

As the "storm" rages, say: **Sometimes when the wind picks up, it means a storm is coming. The wind blows harder and harder, and the waves get bigger and bigger. Sometimes it rains, too. The rain pounds the boat, and great big waves splash onto the deck. The boat sways back and forth and up and down. Sometimes big waves stand the boat straight up in the water.**

It's very scary to be on a boat during a storm. Even experienced sailors can be thrown overboard and drown in a storm. You know, I don't think I like this storm. I'm feeling wet and sick and scared. I want to get off the boat. I want this storm to stop. When I count to three, let's all say together, "Stop, storm!" We'll take our hands out of the water and then maybe the storm will stop.

Lead the children in saying, "Stop, storm!" Then have them remove their hands from the water. Ask:

■ **Did the storm stop?**

■ **Why couldn't we stop the storm?**

Say: **If we stopped blowing and left our little storm alone long enough, eventually it would stop. But we couldn't stop it just by saying stop. And we surely couldn't stop a real storm at sea. But Jesus could. Let's hear about that now.**

Move the dishpan to a table where it won't distract the children.

BIBLE STORY TIME

Classroom supplies: Bible, large blue blanket (or several large towels), CD player
Curriculum supplies: Donut Forget CD ("What Kind of Man Is This?")

Form three groups: the sea, the boat, and the disciples. Have the boat group link elbows and form a "boat" around the disciples. (You may need to make the boat group larger than the sea group to accomplish this.) Give the sea group the blanket.

Say: **As I read our story from Matthew 8:23-27, please act out your parts. Disciples, enjoy your trip, then look and act scared during the storm. Boat, sail the disciples steadily around the room, then rock back and forth during the**

storm. **Sea, sail around with the boat. When the storm comes, toss the blanket water onto the people in the boat. I'll join you in the boat as Jesus.**

Join the children in the boat, then read the Bible story aloud. Repeat once or twice to allow the children to switch roles.

Then say: **The disciples were amazed that Jesus could stop the storm. They knew no regular man could have done what Jesus did. Because of Jesus' amazing miracle, they knew for sure that he was the Son of God.**

Disciples, let's pretend we're amazed. Boat and sea, sail us around the room as we sing our song about what the disciples asked, "What Kind of Man Is This?"

Have the boat "sail" around the room as you sing "What Kind of Man is This?" with the Donut Forget CD. When the song ends, "sail" to your Sing-Along Fun Time area, then collect the blanket and "disassemble" the boat.

SING-ALONG FUN TIME

Classroom supplies: chimes from Center 2, puppets and shoebox boats from Learning Center 3, CD player
Curriculum supplies: Donut Forget CD ("The Miracle Song," "What Kind of Man Is This?")

Open your Bible to John 20:30, 31 and show it to the children. Say: **Jesus did many miracles while he lived on the earth. John 20:30, 31 tells us why he did these special acts. It says: "Jesus did many other miracles . . . But these are written so that you can believe that Jesus is the Christ, the Son of God." Let's learn a song to help us remember this verse.**

Lead the children in singing "The Miracle Song" with the Donut Forget CD. Repeat the song and encourage the children to make up motions for the verses. For example, when the children sing "gave sight to the blind," they might cover their eyes, then uncover them with surprised looks on their faces.

Invite the children who made finger puppets and shoebox boats to lead the class in singing "What Kind of Man Is This?"

Then say: **Jesus isn't just a man—he's the Son of God. And he is stronger than storms and all the other things that scare us. Let's talk about some of those things now.**

DONUT FORGET TIME

Classroom supplies: empty walnut shell halves used in Gathering Time, modeling dough, toothpicks, removable sticky notes, markers, blanket used in Bible Story Time, CD player
Curriculum supplies: Donut Forget CD ("The Miracle Song")

Set the dishpan with the floating walnut shell boats on a table nearby. Next to the dishpan, set the toothpicks, sticky notes, and a lump of modeling dough.

Say: **When the storm came up, the disciples were really scared. We may not be in a boat on a stormy sea, but there are plenty of other "storms" in our lives that scare us. Turn to a partner and tell that person one thing that scares you.**

Let the children respond, then invite pairs to share their responses with the class. Say: **Jesus can calm those fears, just as he calmed the stormy sea. If we trust Jesus, he'll be with us in every scary situation. Let's give our fears to Jesus as we close our lesson today.**

Give each child a toothpick, a sticky note, and a pen or pencil. Have the children write or draw their fears on the sticky notes. Then have them attach the note to the toothpick and roll the sticky portion around the toothpick to create a sail.

Have the children mount their sails in a piece of modeling dough and set them in their boats. While the children work, lay the blanket in an open area. Have the children gather with their finished boats around the blanket.

When everyone has joined you, say: **Our Bible verse reminds us that we can believe that Jesus is God's Son. And we can trust him to take care of our fears, just as he took care of his disciples in the boat. As we listen to "The Miracle Song," pray silently about the fears you put on your sail. Then, when you're ready, give your fears to Jesus by setting your boat on our calm blanket sea. After everyone's boat is on the sea, I'll say a prayer for all our fears.**

Play "The Miracle Song." Encourage an attitude of quiet prayer as the children place their boats on the blanket. When all the boats are on the blanket, pray for the children's fears.

LEARNING CENTERS

Set up the following activities for the children to do as they arrive. Assign an equal number of children and a teacher or helper to each activity.

At each Learning Center, welcome the children to your class. Make sure you know each child's name. Explain that today you'll be talking about the amazing miracles Jesus did.

Center 1: Storm Sounds

Classroom supplies: cassette recorder; blank cassette; cookie sheets; wooden spoons; rice; clean, empty aluminum cans
Curriculum supplies: none

Review how Jesus calmed the storm. Then help the children use the supplies you've provided to record storm sounds on a blank cassette. For example, the children could make rumbling thunder by shaking the cookie sheets and beating them with wooden spoons. They could make rain sounds by shaking rice in the aluminum cans. Encourage the children to experiment with different sounds and to use other items in the room if they want.

Let the children practice making different sounds, then record their favorites on the blank cassette. If possible, have the children record at least 5 minutes of sounds. (This will be more than you need, but it will keep your storm from "stopping" itself during the Bible story.) Explain that you'll use the storm sounds later in the lesson.

Center 2: Sign Language

Classroom supplies: CD player
Curriculum supplies: photocopy of sign language (page 132), Donut Forget CD ("The Miracle Song")

Read or summarize the story of Jesus healing the deaf man (Mark 7:32-35.) Talk with the children about what it would be like not to be able to hear. Remind them that Jesus' power to help the deaf man came from God.

Read John 20:30, 31. Tell the children that they're going to learn to say this verse in the language of people who can't hear. Then read the verse again. As you read, pause and demonstrate the American Sign Language signs for the following words. (If you're teaching younger children, teach only the signs for *Jesus, God, written, and believe.*)

Have the children practice signing as you slowly read the verse. Repeat the verse until the children are comfortable making the signs themselves. Then let them make the signs with "The Miracle Song."

Center 3: Posters & Pom-poms

Classroom supplies: poster board, markers, large sequins, glitter glue, empty bathroom tissue or paper towel tubes, various colors of crepe paper, tape, CD player
Curriculum supplies: Donut Forget CD ("Aha! lelujah")

Before class, cut poster board into five 12-inch squares. If you have mostly younger children in your class, letter the syllables of "A-ha-le-lu-jah" onto the poster board in large block lettering. Put one syllable on each square.

Play "Aha! lelujah." Talk about how this song reminds us to praise God for all the amazing miracles he's done. Then explain that you'll be making cheerleading signs and pom-poms to go along with this song.

Form two groups. Give one group the poster board squares, markers, sequins, and glitter glue. Give the other group the cardboard tubes, crepe paper, and tape. Have the poster board group letter (if you haven't already done this) and decorate the syllables of *Aha! lelujah.* Children can work alone or in pairs or trios, depending on the size of your class.

Have the cardboard tube group make cheerleader pom-poms for the rest of the class to use. Help the children cut the colored crepe paper into 12-inch strips, then tape the strips to the cardboard tubes. Let the children make as many pom-poms as time allows—your show audience will enjoy waving any extras.

Set the finished posters and pom-poms aside for later use.

GATHERING TIME

Classroom supplies: CD player
Curriculum supplies: Donut Forget CD ("The Miracle Song," "What Kind of Man Is This?")

Have the children sit down in the Gathering Time area. Invite them to tell you about the things they did in their Learning Centers. Say: **If you recorded storm sounds for us to use with our Bible story, pat your hands on your knees like rain. If you made cheerleading posters or pom-poms, shout, "Aha! lelujah!" If you learned another way to say our memory verse, please join me at the front.**

Let the children respond. Then continue: **Our friends from Center 2 heard about another miracle Jesus did. Can someone from Center 2 tell us about that?**

Invite the children to tell the story of Jesus healing the deaf man. Then say: **When the deaf man realized he could hear, he knew Jesus was God's Son. Our memory verse says that Jesus' miracles can help us believe in him. Center 2, will you show us a new way to say our memory verse?**

Let the children demonstrate the signs as you read the verse. Then invite everyone to join them in doing the signs as you sing "The Miracle Song."

Then say: **That was a fun, new way to do that song—and to remember our verse. Let's have some more fun with another one of our unit songs.**

Form pairs and have partners sit on the floor facing each other. Teach the children the following clapping rhythm to do with "What Kind of Man Is This?" Begin by speaking the words as the children learn the claps. Then sing the song slowly without the CD. When the children have mastered the clapping rhythm, add the recorded music.

121

What (slap legs)

kind (clap hands)

of (clap partner's right hand)

man (clap hands)

is (clap partner's left hand)

this (clap hands once, then clap partner's hands twice)

He (slap legs)

spoke (clap hands)

to the (clap partner's right hand)

rain (clap hands)

and the (clap partner's left hand)

rain (clap hands)

stopped falling (clap partner's hands twice)

(Use the same motions for "He spoke to the wind . . ." and "He spoke to the waves . . .")

If the children enjoy the activity, stop the CD and encourage them to try singing and doing the rhythm faster and faster. Then say: **All these claps and slaps are reminding me of claps of thunder and pounding raindrops. Let's review how Jesus calmed the storm in our Bible story.**

BIBLE STORY TIME

Classroom supplies: Bible, inflatable raft or masking tape, electric fan, spray bottle filled with water, cassette player, cassette with storm sounds recorded in Center 1, towels
Curriculum supplies: none

Before class, blow up an inflatable raft. If you don't have one, use masking tape to outline a boat on the floor of your classroom.

Open your Bible to Matthew 8:23-27 and show it to the children. Say: **Our Bible story today is found in the book of Matthew. Matthew was one of Jesus' disciples, and he may have been in the boat with Jesus. Let's all climb into the boat and join the disciples.**

Have the children climb into the boat, then continue: **Whew! It's been a long day. All those people following us, listening to Jesus all day long. It will be nice to get across the lake where we can have a little peace and quiet.**

Begin rocking the boat with all of the children in it. If you don't have an actual boat, have the children rock from side to side. **Oh look, Jesus is asleep.** Pretend to point to Jesus, then put your head on your hands and make snoring sounds. Encourage the children to imitate you.

Then have a helper begin playing the storm sounds on the CD. Put your hand to your ear. Say: **Listen! Does anyone hear thunder? What's that over there? It looks like lightning to me. What do you think? Hmm. I wonder if we should turn back.**

Have a helper turn the fan on high and aim it at the children.

Well, no. We've seen storms like this before when we've been fishing. Maybe it will pass. I hope. But it looks pretty windy—yikes!

Mist the children with the spray bottle. **Oh no! The waves are crashing over the sides of the boat. Now I'm cold and wet. And Jesus is still sleeping. Do you think we should wake him up?**

Pause the tape, but have helpers continue to blow the fan and squirt the spray bottle as you encourage the children to debate this question. Point out that Jesus has had a long day of preaching and teaching. Tell the children that since Jesus isn't a fisherman or a sailor he probably wouldn't know what to do anyway. Continue until the children have convinced you to wake up Jesus.

Start the tape again, then continue: **Okay, okay, let's wake him up! Jesus, Jesus, wake up! We're afraid we'll drown!**

Well, when Jesus saw how frightened we were, he said to the water, "Peace, be still." And it was. What a miracle!

Stop the CD, the fan, and the squirt bottle. Snap your fingers and say: **Just like that, the storm was gone. The waves were calm and we sailed the boat across the lake. Jesus is amazing! There's no one else like him, that's for sure.**

BITE IDEA
If someone in your church is familiar with square dance steps, invite that person to design a simple square dance for the children to do as they sing, "What Kind of Man Is This?" If the children enjoy the dance, they can teach it to parents as part of your Marvelous Miracle Variety Show.

Help the children out of the boat. Let them dry off with towels if necessary, then move on to Sing-Along Fun Time.

SING-ALONG FUN TIME

Classroom supplies: "Aha! lelujah" posters and pompoms from Center 3, CD player
Curriculum supplies: Donut Forget CD ("The Miracle Song," "Aha! lelujah")
Sing "The Miracle Song" with the Donut Forget CD as you sign the symbols the children learned earlier. Repeat the song to allow the children to become familiar with the sign language.

Then invite the Center 3 group to help you introduce the song "Aha! lelujah." Tell the children that they'll get to perform this song at the Marvelous Miracle Variety Show. Have other children listen to the song as the Center 3 group cheers with their posters and pom-poms. Then have everyone join in the singing and cheering.

Use the **Duncan** puppet and the script from the Donut Forget Songbook to talk about the memory verse, John 20: 30, 31.

DONUT FORGET TIME

Classroom supplies: plain white paper, pencils, megaphone (optional), CD player
Curriculum supplies: Donut Forget CD ("What Kind of Man Is This?")
Give each child a blank sheet of white paper and a pencil. Have the children quickly write or draw a fear on their papers.

Say: **Last week we talked about how our fears can be like scary storms in our lives. Let's use our fear papers to make storm sounds.**

Have the children shake their papers. Then have them fold the papers in half and rub the halves together. Next, have them crumple their papers and push and pull the ends. Then form three groups and assign each group a different action to do with the papers. Let the children enjoy the paper noises for a few moments, then call for them to stop.

Say: **That's one noisy, scary storm you've made. But God is stronger than the storms, and he's more powerful than our fears. To remind us of that, I'm going to read some Bible verses about God's power and faithfulness. You can keep making your storm sounds, and I'll read in a loud voice. That will remind us that even when the storms are going on, God is still with us. When I finish reading, stop the storm.**

As the children make their "storm," read the following Scripture verses in a loud voice. If you have a large class, you may choose to use a megaphone.

"Lord God of heaven's armies, who is like you? Lord, you are powerful and completely to be trusted. You rule the mighty sea. You calm the stormy waves" (Psalm 89:8, 9).

"Lord, the seas rise up. The seas raise their voice. The seas lift up their pounding waves. The sound of the water is loud. The ocean waves are powerful. But the Lord above is much greater" (Psalm 93:3, 4).

"Let the sea and everything in it shout. Let the world and everyone on it sing. Let the rivers clap their hands. Let the mountains sing together for joy. Let them sing before the Lord" (Psalm 98:7-9).

Close by singing "What Kind of Man Is This?"

LEARNING CENTERS

Set up the following activities for the children to do as they arrive. Assign an equal number of children and a teacher or helper to each activity.

At each Learning Center, welcome the children to your class. Make sure you know each child's name. Explain that today you'll be talking about the amazing miracles Jesus did.

Center 1: Basket Lunch

Classroom supplies: juice boxes, sliced bread, fish cookie cutters, tuna fish salad, plastic knives, paper plate, picnic basket, CD player
Curriculum supplies: Donut Forget CD ("One Basket")

Explain that today you'll hear how Jesus fed more than 5,000 people with one little boy's lunch. Review the story by having the children listen to "One Basket" from the Donut Forget CD.

Then tell the children that they'll be making a lunch of fish and bread for everyone to enjoy during the Bible story. Form two groups: the Bread Cutters and the Tuna Spreaders. Give the Bread Cutters the fish cookie cutters and have them cut fish shapes out of the bread. Remind them that they'll need an even number of fish shapes to make sandwiches.

Set out the tuna fish salad and have the Tuna Spreaders spread it on the fish-shaped bread pieces. As the children finish making the sandwiches, stack them on a paper plate. Place the plate in a picnic basket. Have a helper add the juice boxes, then take the basket to the location you've chosen for your Bible story.

Center 2: Fish Shaker

Classroom supplies: small paper plates, colored construction paper, scissors, markers, barley, stapler, glue, CD player
Curriculum supplies: Donut Forget CD ("One Basket")

Before class, prepare a sample fish shaker according to the directions below.

Tell the children that today they'll learn how Jesus fed more than 5,000 people with just two fish and five loaves of barley bread. Let the children listen to "One Basket" to introduce them to this Bible story.

Set out the markers, construction paper, stapler, glue, and barley. Give each child two paper plates. Show the children the sample fish shaker you've made. Explain that it's filled with barley. Have the children draw a fish face and fins on the bottoms of their paper plates. Then help them

124

cut out construction-paper fish tails. Show the children how to attach the tails to the edge of one of their plates.

Place a small amount of barley on each child's fish tail plate. Have the children glue their other plates on top of their fish tail plates. While the glue is drying, let the children sing along with "One Basket" from the Donut Forget CD.

Set the finished fish shakers aside for use later in the lesson.

Center 3: Fish & Bread

Classroom supplies: cardboard; scissors; craft knife (optional); blue, green, brown, and tan tissue paper; blue, green, and brown construction paper; small bowls; glue; unsharpened pencils with erasers; markers; large and small resealable bags; stapler; CD player
Curriculum supplies: Donut Forget CD ("One Basket")

BITE IDEA
Some four- and five-year-olds may lack the fine motor skills to manage the tissue wrapping and dipping in this activity. If you have a mixed-age class, assign younger children to make the extra "miracle" fish and loaves while older children work on the cutouts. If you have a class of younger children, you may want to have them glue flat layers of tissue paper to the cutouts. You'll still get a neat mosaic effect on your finished fish and bread props.

Before class, draw two large fish shapes on stiff cardboard. Cut out the fish shapes using scissors or a craft knife. Then draw a group of five round loaves of bread. Cut out the loaves of bread. (Do not cut the loaves apart.) On the back of each fish shape, staple a small resealable bag with its opening near the bottom of the cutout. On the back of the loaves, staple a large resealable bag with its opening near the bottom of the cutout. Open the bags when you attach them to the cutouts. Don't staple through the bags so you can open them later. Cut the tissue paper and construction paper into 2-inch squares. Cut some of the blue and green construction paper squares into triangles.

Explain to the children that they'll be learning how Jesus fed over 5,000 people with just two fish and five little loaves of bread. Introduce the story by having the children listen to "One Basket."

Set out the tissue and construction paper squares, bowls of glue, unsharpened pencils, and the fish and bread shapes you've prepared. Tell the children they'll be making 3-D fish and bread props to use in the Marvelous Miracle Variety Show. Show the children how to wrap and hold a tissue paper square around an unsharpened pencil eraser, dip the tissue paper in the glue, and stick it on the fish or bread cutout. Explain that the children will need to fill the cutout shapes with the tissues.

Form several groups. Assign two groups of children to work on the fish cutouts and one group to work on the bread cutout. Have another group of children make extra "miracle" fish and loaves. They can make fish by gluing construction paper triangle "tails" to construction paper diamond (tilted squares) "fish." They can make loaves by tearing brown construction paper into small (about the size of two fingers) loaf shapes.

Encourage the children to fill the fish and loaf cutouts with as much tissue paper as they can. Explain that if they don't finish today, they can work on the cutouts again next week. (If the children are far from finished, you may want to fill in some more paper yourself before your next class time.)

Place the finished "miracle" fish and loaves in the resealable bags on the backs of the cutouts. Set the cutouts aside for use next week.

Donut Forget™ Bible Story Lessons

GATHERING TIME

Classroom supplies: picnic basket with sandwiches prepared in Center 1, juice boxes, blanket or tablecloth
Curriculum supplies: none

Before class, choose a location away from your room where you'll tell the Bible story. If the weather's warm enough, try to select a spot outdoors. Otherwise choose an out-of-the-way hallway or empty classroom in your church building.

Have the children sit down in the Gathering Time area. Invite them to tell you about the things they did in their Learning Centers. Affirm each group's work.

Say: **You've all been doing activities to help us learn about Jesus' miracles. What is a miracle? A miracle is a wonderful thing that only God can do. Miracles show us how powerful God is. Jesus did miracles so that we can believe he is God's Son. That's what our memory verse says. Today we are going find out how a little boy helped Jesus do a miracle.**

Have the children line up at the door. Say: **The little boy journeyed a long way to see Jesus. Let's take our own journey now to see what that was like.**

Lead the children on a roundabout route to your chosen location. Have a helper go on ahead of you and hide the picnic lunch.

As you lead the children, encourage them to hurry along. Say things like, "Keep going, kids. We don't want to miss Jesus." or "Oh, there's a flock of sheep in the road. We'll have to go a different way." Use your entire Gathering Time to reach your destination so the children will be tired when you get there. When you reach your destination, spread out your blanket and have the children sit down.

BIBLE STORY TIME

Classroom supplies: Bible, picnic lunch packed in Center 1, CD player
Curriculum supplies: Donut Forget CD ("One Basket")

Say: **Boy, I'm tired. Aren't you? That was a long walk. I wish I had something to eat. But I didn't bring anything with me. Does anyone else have something to eat? Check your pockets. Surely somebody must have something. How about a granola bar? A piece of candy? Not even a stick of chewing gum?**

Let the children look for food items, then continue: **It's going to be pretty hard to listen to Jesus on an empty stomach. If only I had packed a lunch. I'd have a turkey sandwich with Swiss cheese and no mayonnaise. And maybe a crisp, juicy red apple and some chips to go with it. An ice cold soda to drink, and of course, a chocolate chip cookie for dessert. What would you pack in your lunches?**

Invite the children to describe their favorite lunch items. Then say: **Oh, all this talk about food is making me so hungry. Fortunately, our Center 1 group did pack a lunch for us. We'll enjoy it in a few minutes, but first let's hear how Jesus satisfied the hunger of the crowds who came to listen to him teach.**

Open your Bible to John 6 and show it to the children. Say: **The book of John tells us that more than 5,000 people had gathered to listen to Jesus. That would be like more than 250 school classes getting together in one place. Let's imagine what all those hungry people must have sounded like as they waited for Jesus to start teaching. Turn to someone sitting near you and tell them how hungry you are. Now tell someone else. Tell one more person.**

Let the children respond, then continue: **Now let me hear your hungry tummies make growling noises.**

Let the children growl, then have them stop and listen. Say: **Jesus' disciples saw the hungry crowd, and they started to get nervous. Jesus wanted to know where they could buy bread to feed all the people, and they didn't know! There were no grocery stores or convenience stores or bakeries. And besides, they'd have to work for months and months to make enough money to pay for all that food.**

But then Andrew, one of Jesus' disciples, found a boy who remembered to bring his lunch! It was only a small lunch—two fish and five loaves of barley bread. The fish were small, and the loaves of bread were probably only as big as our dinner rolls. But the boy was happy to share it with Jesus.

Jesus told all the people to sit down. Then he thanked God for the food, and started passing out pieces of fish and bread.

Have the children sit in rows. Then bring out the picnic lunch. Say a brief prayer of thanks, then start passing out the sandwiches. Give a sandwich to the child at the end of each row and say, "Pass it down." Continue until you've passed out all the sandwiches. Distribute the juice boxes the same way.

When you've distributed all the food, say: **Well, all of our food is gone. I'm glad the Center 1 group made enough sandwiches for everyone. But Jesus made more than enough food. When Jesus finished passing out the food, there were leftovers. Even after all those people had eaten, 12 baskets of food were left. What a miracle!**

Let the children enjoy the sandwiches as they review the story by listening to "One Basket" from the Donut Forget CD. If possible, stay in your outdoor location for Sing-Along Fun Time.

SING-ALONG FUN TIME

Classroom supplies: CD player, fish shakers from Center 2
Curriculum supplies: Donut Forget CD ("Aha! lelujah," "One Basket")

If you're outdoors, help the children make up large-motor movements to go along with "Aha! lelujah" and "One Basket." For example, they might roll or tumble down a hill as they sing the chorus of "Aha! lelujah." They can also stomp and shout (as loud as they please) as the song directs. For "One Basket," they might link elbows to create one large "basket," then walk around in a circle. Encourage the children to be creative with their motions.

If you're indoors, have the children shake their fish shakers as you sing "One Basket." Have the children use the "Aha! lelujah" cheering posters and pom-poms as you sing that song.

DONUT FORGET TIME

Classroom supplies: nature items, CD player
Curriculum supplies: Donut Forget CD ("Aha! lelujah")

If possible, do this activity outdoors and allow the children to search for their own nature items. If you'll be indoors, you'll need to gather a variety of nature items before class. Set the items on a table and have the children gather around it.

Say: **Jesus did miracles so people would believe he was God's Son. He wanted people to praise God and give God glory for his amazing miracles. Our song "Aha! lelujah" talks about the trees, oceans, mountains, and birds praising God. The Bible tells us that God's miraculous power can be seen in the marvelous world he created. Just look at all the miracle people God made. We all have hearts that beat, minds that think, lungs that breathe, and much, much more. Find a miracle person partner right now.**

Help the children find partners, then continue: **Partners, as I play "Aha! lelujah," work together to find an object that reminds you of God's miraculous power. Maybe you'll find a twig from a tree covered with protective bark; or maybe you'll find a flower with perfectly shaped petals or a pine cone with perfectly shaped spikes. When the music stops, bring your nature items back to our circle.**

Play "Aha! lelujah" as the children look for their nature items. When the music stops, call everyone back together. Have partners take turns telling about their items. Close by reading Psalm 148:7-13.

As the children leave, remind them to invite their parents to join you for the last 20 minutes of next week's class. You may also want to call parents during the week with an additional reminder.

BITE IDEA
As parents drop their children off, remind them to return for the Marvelous Miracle Variety Show. Tell parents about what time your show will start.

BITE IDEA
Be creative in your use of time and supplies during today's Learning Center time. If you only have one CD player, let the Center 2 group use it first, since they don't have any additional props to prepare. Next, let Center 1 use it, then Center 3. If Center 1 finishes early, they can help make posters or, if necessary, they can help Center 3 finish up the fish and bread cutouts.

LEARNING CENTERS

Set up the following activities for the children to do as they arrive. Assign an equal number of children and a teacher or helper to each activity. **NOTE:** For today's Learning Center time, have the children work with their project groups from earlier lessons.

At each Learning Center, welcome the children to your class. Make sure you know each child's name. Explain that today you'll be talking about the amazing miracles Jesus did, and celebrating Jesus' miracles with a fun musical show.

Center 1: Puppet Show

Classroom supplies: finger puppets and boats from Lesson 1, table, large blanket, CD player

Curriculum supplies: Donut Forget CD ("What Kind of Man Is This?")

Help the children tip a table on its side, then cover it with a blanket to create a "sea" for their shoebox boats. Briefly review how Jesus calmed the storm. Play "What Kind of Man Is This?" from the Donut Forget CD and let the children practice moving their puppets with the music.

Center 2: Cheerleaders

Classroom supplies: cheering posters and pom-poms from Lesson 2, poster board, markers, poster putty, tape or thumb tacks, CD player
Curriculum supplies: Donut Forget CD ("Aha! lelujah")

Give the children the cheering posters and pom-poms they made during Lesson 2. Play "Aha! lelujah" and have the children practice their cheers. Remind the children that even nature acknowledges God's miraculous power.

If time allows, have the children create posters announcing your show. Help the children with lettering as necessary. Hang the posters on the outside of your classroom door and in nearby hallways.

Center 3: Fish & Bread

Classroom supplies: fish and bread cutouts from Lesson 3 (including extra supplies if the children haven't finished the cutouts yet), CD player

Curriculum supplies: Donut Forget CD ("One Basket")

Have the children finish attaching wrapped tissues to the fish and bread cutouts. If the children need to make additional "miracle" fish and loaves, have them also do that now. As the children work, review details from the Bible story.

When the children finish, assign one or two children to handle each fish cutout and two or more children to handle the bread cutout. Explain that the children will switch roles each time the song's chorus is sung. Children who aren't holding a cutout will be singers. Encourage the singers to add actions to the verses as they sing.

Practice moving the cutouts as you sing "One Basket" with the Donut Forget CD. Show the children how to open the resealable bags and release the "miracle" loaves and fish as you sing the last chorus, "one basket, two thousand fish and five thousand loaves of barley bread."

Have the children gather the miracle fish and loaves and return them to the resealable bags. Make sure the children understand how to do this. If they don't get it the first time, let them practice again with just a few fish and loaves in each resealable bag. Explain that they won't release the miracle fish and loaves during the practice show due to the time required for cleanup.

Set the finished cutouts aside for use later in the lesson.

GATHERING TIME

Classroom supplies: paper lunch sacks, unpopped popcorn, popcorn popper, oil (if your popcorn popper requires it), butter and salt (optional), markers, CD player

Curriculum supplies: Donut Forget CD

Have the children sit down in the Gathering Time area. Say: **You've all been practicing for our Marvelous Miracle Variety Show. We'll have fabulous finger puppets, creative cheerleaders, and lovely loaves and fish cutouts. It will be great fun to use these things to share what we've learned with our parents. Let's review our stories now.**

Invite the children to tell you their favorite parts of the miracle accounts you've heard. Then say: **Jesus is amazing! And the Bible is full of other miracle stories just like the ones we've heard. Our memory verse song talks about some of those. Jesus turned water into wine, healed sick people, made blind people see again, and even made a dead man come back to life. When people saw one of Jesus' miracles, they knew he was God's Son. We can know and believe that, too.**

Distribute the lunch sacks and markers. Say: **On your sack, draw or write something from one of our miracle lessons. For example, you might draw the stormy sea on one side and the calm sea on the other side. You could draw loaves and fish, or write the words to our memory verse. These will be our Marvelous Miracle Variety Snack Sacks, and when we're finished decorating them we'll fill them with popcorn for parents to enjoy during the show.**

Help the children think of ideas to decorate their sacks. As they work, play the unit songs from the Donut Forget CD. Have a helper pop popcorn. When the children finish, help them fill the sacks. Set the filled sacks aside.

BIBLE STORY TIME

Classroom supplies: Bible, CD player
Curriculum supplies: Donut Forget CD ("One Basket")

Open your Bible to John 6 and show it to the children. Say: **Let's quickly review how Jesus fed more than 5,000 people. Since we've already heard this story once, I know you know it pretty well. Listen carefully as I tell the story. If you hear me say something that's not part of the story, stand up.**

Read the following story. Pause for the children to stand as you read the italicized "bloopers."

Crowds of people had been following Jesus *all night* (all day). Some people had come from a long way away, and everyone was feeling tired and hungry. Jesus asked his disciples where they could buy some *hamburgers* (bread) for the people to eat.

The disciples told Jesus it would take *days* (months) to earn enough money to buy enough *hot dogs* (bread) for all those people. But a little *girl* (boy) offered to share his small lunch. The disciples didn't think that two *chickens* (fish) and five *packages of potato chips* (loaves) would feed all those people. Boy, were they in for a big surprise!

Jesus prayed for the food, then the disciples started passing it out. Jesus fed over *50* (5,000) people with the boy's lunch. When everyone had eaten as many *cookies* (pieces of bread) as they wanted, the disciples gathered up *2* (12) baskets of leftovers. Everyone was amazed, and they knew Jesus must be God's Son.

Applaud the children for their participation in the story. Say: **It's a good thing you were listening. I made a lot of mistakes, didn't I! Let's sing "One Basket" to remind ourselves how the story really goes.**

Lead the children in singing "One Basket" with the Donut Forget CD.

SING-ALONG FUN TIME

Classroom supplies: miracle puppets and shoebox boats, "Aha! lelujah" cheering posters and pom-poms, fish and bread cutouts, Bible, CD player
Curriculum supplies: Donut Forget CD (all unit songs)

Have the children help you choose a staging area and set up chairs to face the stage. Then rehearse their acts in the following order (children who aren't participating in an act can sing along as the choir).

■ Miracle puppets and shoebox boats with "What Kind of Man Is This?"
■ Fish and bread cutouts with "One Basket" (don't let the children drop the miracle loaves and fish)
■ Cheering posters and pom-poms with "Aha! lelujah"
■ Sign language with the chorus of "The Miracle Song"

Before each group presents their act, give a brief introduction to the song they'll be using. Read John 20:30, 31 before the children do their sign language with "The Miracle Song."

DONUT FORGET TIME

Classroom supplies: filled snack sacks, miracle puppets and shoebox boats, "Aha! lelujah"
cheering posters and pom-poms, fish and bread cutouts, Bible, CD player
Curriculum supplies: Donut Forget CD (all unit songs)

As parents arrive, welcome them to your room and offer them Marvelous Miracle Variety Snack Sacks. When you're ready to begin, invite parents to take their seats, then introduce the show. Say: **We've been learning that Jesus did amazing miracles so people would believe he is the Son of God. We believe, and after you see and hear our Marvelous Miracle Variety Show, we think you will, too.**

Introduce each act by telling a little bit about the song or Bible story the children will be presenting. Applaud each act. End the show by reading John 20:30, 31, then joining the children in signing the words with the song "The Miracle Song."

After the song, say: **We hope you've enjoyed our Marvelous Miracle Variety Show. Let's all give a thundering round of applause to our God. He's the real Marvelous Miracle Maker!**

Lead the children and parents in applause, then close in prayer.

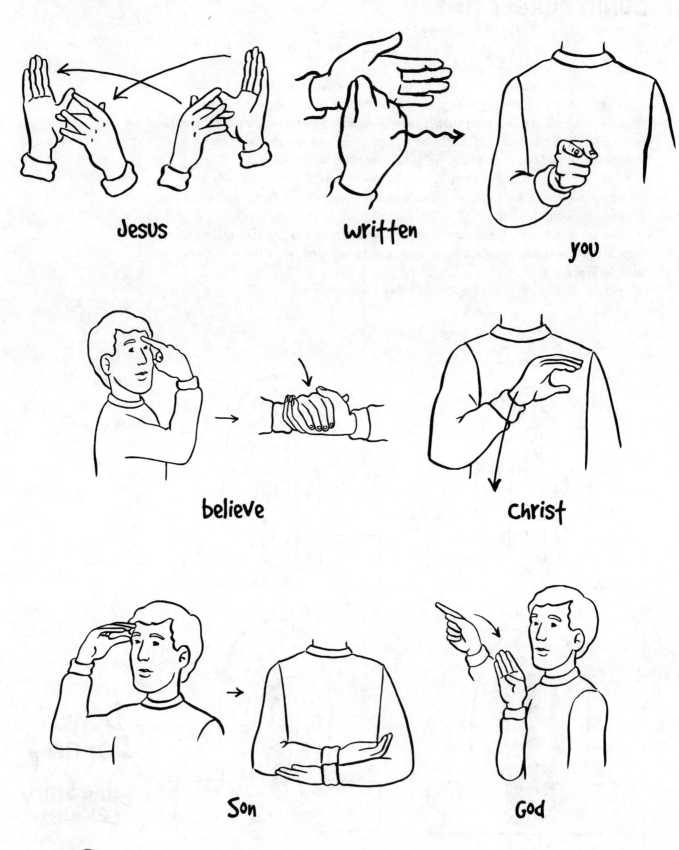

Jesus

written

you

believe

Christ

Son

God

132

Donut Forget to Believe the Good News

BY THE END OF THIS UNIT, LEARNERS WILL

Know   Tell the most special thing Jesus did.
Feel   Feel excited that Jesus died and rose from death.
Do   Believe the Good News about Jesus.

MEMORY VERSE

"And this was the most important: that Christ died for our sins, as the Scriptures say; that he was buried and was raised to life on the third day" (1 Corinthians 15:3, 4).

The death of someone special is never on anyone's list of "good news." But Jesus' death was different because of its powerful purpose. Jesus died because he loves us and wants to redeem us. Best of all, God's power raised him back to life! Jesus' death and resurrection prove that God our Father loves us without limit. This is something to celebrate! Jesus' death and resurrection *is* good news.

Believing in Jesus comes easily for most four- to eight-year-olds. They never tire of hearing and telling others that Jesus loves them. This unit will lead the children to praise God with voices, bodies, and hearts as they celebrate Jesus' love as seen in his death and resurrection.

	LESSON 1	LESSON 2	LESSON 3	LESSON 4
Center 1	heart snack	good news eggs	megaphones	good news decals
Center 2	glad-sad shakers	palm branches	Thomas puppets	sign language
Center 3	banner, people	banner, cross	banner, tomb	banner, assembly
Gathering Time	heart halves	story eggs	opposites game	song signs
Bible Story Time	Luke 23, 24, glad-sad faces	Luke 23, 24, Simon's story	John 20, puppets	John 20, story actions
Sing-Along Fun Time	memory verse song	palm branches, shakers	megaphone songs	practice processional
Donut Forget Time	heart message	forgiving others	heart medallions	worship procession

Donut forget™ Bible Story Lessons

LEARNING CENTERS

Set up the following activities for the children to do as they arrive. Assign an equal number of children and a teacher or helper to each activity.

At each Learning Center, welcome the children to your class. Make sure you know each child's name. Explain that today you'll be talking about how Jesus showed God's love by dying and living again.

Center 1: Heart Snack

Classroom supplies: brownie mix, heart-shaped cookie cutters, canned frosting, plastic knives or craft sticks, paper plates, mini-M&Ms or other candies, colored sprinkles, a tray or serving plate, CD player
Curriculum supplies: Donut Forget CD ("Christ Died for Our Sins")

Before class, make a pan of brownies and let it cool. Use heart-shaped cookie cutters to cut the brownies into heart shapes. You'll need one brownie heart for each child in your class.

Give each child a paper plate with some frosting on it and a plastic knife. Help the children spread the frosting on the brownies, then decorate the brownies with the mini-M&Ms and sprinkles.

As the children work, play "Christ Died for Our Sins." Tell the children that today they'll learn that Jesus showed God's love by dying and living again. Explain that the snacks will be shared with everyone later to celebrate God's love.

Set the snacks aside on a tray for Donut Forget Time.

Center 2: Glad-Sad Shakers

Classroom supplies: sturdy paper plates, dried beans or peas, stapler, staples, markers, CD player
Curriculum supplies: Donut Forget CD ("Christ Died for Our Sins")

Give each child two paper plates. Have the children draw a happy face on the back of one plate and a sad face on the back of the second plate. Show them how to staple the edges of the plates together, leaving about a 4-inch opening unstapled. Help them put a small handful of dried beans through the opening, then staple it shut.

As the children work, play "Christ Died for Our Sins." Explain that they will be hearing a story about Jesus today that has both happy and sad parts and that they'll use their glad-sad shakers to help tell the story.

Set the shakers aside to use during Bible Story Time.

Center 3: Good News Banner

Classroom supplies: poster board, white card stock, fabric paint or glitter glue, large poster-size marker, scissors, markers, glue, fabric scraps, yarn, other items such as lace or ribbon, CD player
Curriculum supplies: photocopies of page 147, Donut Forget CD ("Christ Died for Our Sins")

Before class, cut the poster board into three 20-inch squares. (See page 148 for an illustration of the finished banner. You may need to make the squares larger if you have more than eight children working at the Center each week.) Photocopy the figure on page 147 onto white card stock. You'll need one figure for each child at the Center. If you have mostly younger children, cut out the figures ahead of time.

BITE IDEA
Each week at Center 3, the children will work on a banner declaring their belief that Jesus died for us and rose again. Before starting this unit, arrange for permission to display the completed banner in your church's worship center. If possible, arrange for the children to deliver the banner in a procession to the worship center and sing one or two songs for the congregation.

BITE IDEA
For extra impact, use one large piece of banner felt instead of poster board squares. Decide where each week's items will go before gluing any items down. Use fabric paint to print the words directly on the banner. Consider using a glue gun to glue the items to the banner.

Explain to the children that today they'll be learning about how Jesus showed God's love. Tell them that over the next few weeks, they will be preparing a banner that will be used to tell others that they believe in Jesus.

Give each child a figure shape. Help the children use the fabric scraps and other supplies to add clothing details to their people. Have them glue pieces of yarn on for hair, then use the markers to add facial features. As the children work, play "Christ Died for Our Sins."

Help the children arrange the finished figures on the bottom two-thirds of one of the poster board squares. Use the large marker to write the words "We Believe" in the space above the figures. Then glue the figures down. Let the children decorate the letters with dots of fabric paint or glitter glue.

Set the finished poster near the Gathering Time area.

GATHERING TIME

Classroom supplies: banner piece from Center 3, construction paper, scissors, grocery bag or basket, safety pins
Curriculum supplies: none

Before class, cut heart shapes out of different colors of construction paper. Then cut the hearts in half lengthwise. You'll need one heart half per child. Put the heart pieces in a paper bag or basket.

Have the children sit down in the Gathering Time area. Invite them to tell you about the things they did at their Learning Centers. Then say: **You all did different things, but you were all learning that Jesus showed God's love by dying and living again. If you made a heart snack for all of us to eat later, stand up and rub your tummy, then sit down. If you made glad-sad shakers, smile and wave your hands in the air. If you worked on a special banner to tell others about Jesus, come stand by me now.**

Have the children from Center 3 help you hold up the banner piece and explain it to the children. Then say: **Over the next few weeks we'll be making a banner to hang in the church worship center. It will have three pieces to it. This first piece says, "We Believe." These figures represent all of us.**

Have the children sit down and ask: **What are some things you believe about God?**

Give the children time to respond. Then say: **Our banner will tell people some things we believe about God: that Jesus died for our sins, he was buried, and he was raised to life.**

Set the banner aside. Hold out the bag of half-heart shapes and have each child choose one. Say: **You each have half a heart. These heart pieces represent love and friendship. God showed us his love by sending Jesus to us. Find the friend that has the matching half to your heart. When you find your partner, come and sit down together.**

When the children have found their partners say: **Hold your heart pieces together to form one heart and tell your partner, "Jesus loves you."** Pause. **You'll be working with your friend later during Sing-Along Fun Time. Let's get ready to hear our Bible story now. It's the greatest story of love ever told!**

Pin children's heart halves to their shirts.

BIBLE STORY TIME

Classroom supplies: Bible, glad-sad shakers from Center 2, washable marker, CD player
Curriculum supplies: Donut Forget CD ("Jesus Showed Us God's Love")

Have the children from Center 2 bring their glad-sad shakers to the Bible story area.

Open your Bible to Luke 23 and 24 and show it to the children. Say: **Our Bible story comes from the book of Luke. I need your help telling the story today. Some of you made glad-sad shakers. Shake those now so we can see how they sound. That's a happy sound! When we get to happy parts in our story, shake your shakers and hold up the glad side. When we get to a sad part, hold up the sad side and don't shake them.**

Those of you who don't have a shaker can help, too. I'll draw a glad face on the front of your hand and a sad face on the back of your hand. You can hold up the side of your hand that goes with our story.

Use the washable marker to draw happy and sad faces on children's hands who don't have shakers. Then say: **Jesus was healing people, forgiving them for wrong things they had done, and telling them he was God's Son.** (glad) **Many people listened to Jesus' teaching and believed in him.** (glad) **They were so happy to see Jesus coming into town that they lined the streets with palm branches and shouted, "Hosanna!"** (glad)

But some people didn't like what Jesus was teaching. (sad) **They didn't like being told to stop doing bad things.** (sad) **They decided to get rid of Jesus.** (sad) **Jesus was arrested** (sad) **and nailed to a cross to die.** (sad) **His friends buried him in a tomb.** (sad) **But after three days something wonderful happened.** (glad) **Jesus came back to life!** (glad) **He rose from the dead** (glad) **and proved he was God's Son.** (glad) **Death was not strong enough to keep Jesus in the grave.** (glad)

Let's listen to a song called "Jesus Showed Us God's Love." Listen to the story and use your hands and shakers when you hear the glad and sad parts.

Play the song "Jesus Showed Us God's Love" and let the children hold up their glad and sad faces as they listen. Then play the song again and encourage the children to sing along.

SING-ALONG FUN TIME

Classroom supplies: CD player
Curriculum supplies: Donut Forget CD ("Christ Died for Our Sins," "Jesus Showed Us God's Love," "Aha! lelujah" from Unit 7)

Have the children find their "heart" partner from Gathering Time. Say: **Our memory verse is from 1 Corinthians 15:3, 4. Listen as I read it, then repeat it with me.**

Read the verse, then have the children repeat it together. Say: **We're going to learn a song for this verse. But first, I'll whisper a word to you that's in the song. You and your partner decide on an action for the word. Then we'll sing the song and put our actions to it.**

Whisper one of the following words to each pair of children: *important, died, sins, Scriptures, buried, raised*. It's okay if you give the same word to more than one pair of children.

After a few minutes, invite pairs to tell their words and show their motions. Then lead the group in saying the memory verse, having the pairs do their motions at the appropriate time.

Lead the children in singing "Christ Died for Our Sins." Encourage them to use all the motions they just created.

Play "Jesus Showed Us God's Love" and have any children who didn't use the shakers during Bible story time do so now.

If you have enough shakers, have the children toss the shakers back and forth to their partners in time to the music as you sing "Aha! lelujah." If you don't have enough shakers, have the children form two lines facing each other and toss the shakers back and forth.

DONUT FORGET TIME

Classroom supplies: construction paper, scissors, marker, heart snacks from Center 1, napkins
Curriculum supplies: none

Before class, cut a large heart out of construction paper and write the word *Forever* across it. Cut it in half lengthwise. Hide the two pieces somewhere in the classroom.

Say: **John 3:16 says that God loved us so much that he sent his only Son to die for us. Jesus became our sin. Jesus truly loves us and wants us to believe in him. Somewhere in the room I've hidden two heart pieces. One represents us and the other represents Jesus. See if you and your partner can find the pieces.**

Wait while the children find the pieces, then have them sit down around you. Say: **This heart has a message.** (Hold up one half.) **This half represents Jesus and** (hold up other half) **this half represents us.** (Put the pieces together.) **Because Jesus died and rose again, we can be together forever! The word on the heart says, "Forever." Let's celebrate God's "forever love" by sharing a special snack. Before you take a snack, share one thing you believe about Jesus. For example, you might say "I believe Jesus loves me!" or "I believe Jesus is God's Son!" or "I believe Jesus died for me!"**

Have Center 1 children carry the tray of heart brownies to the center of the group. After everyone has said an "I believe" statement, say a brief prayer thanking Jesus for showing us God's love by dying and living again. Eat and enjoy!

LEARNING CENTERS

Set up the following activities for the children to do as they arrive. Assign an equal number of children and a teacher or helper to assist with each activity.

At each Learning Center, welcome the children to your class. Make sure you know each child's name. Explain that today you'll be talking about how Jesus showed God's love by dying and living again.

Center 1: Good News Eggs

Classroom supplies: medium-sized plastic eggs, pebbles or small stones, small nails, Bible stickers, seeds, bowls, CD player
Curriculum supplies: Donut Forget CD ("Christ Died for Our Sins")

Before class, put the pebbles, nails, Bible stickers, and seeds in small bowls. You'll need at least three seeds and one pebble, nail, and sticker for each child in the class. If you can't find stickers showing a Bible or book, write the word "Bible" on small pieces of paper.

Have the children put one pebble, one nail, one sticker, and three seeds inside each plastic egg. Fill enough eggs so that every child in class will have one during Gathering Time.

137

As the children work, tell them that the Good News Eggs they're making will help everyone learn the memory verse. Demonstrate: (Hold up an egg, then open it.) **And this was the most important:** (hold up the small nail) **that Christ died for our sins,** (hold up the Bible sticker) **as the Scriptures say;** (hold up the pebble) **that he was buried** (hold up seed) **and was raised to life on the third day."** (Count out the seeds "1, 2, 3.")

Put the objects back in the egg. Play "Christ Died for Our Sins" and encourage the children to practice using their Good News Eggs as they sing. Explain that they'll share the egg story later with the other children.

Center 2: Palm Branches

Classroom supplies: Bible, construction paper, pencil, scissors, glue, paint-stirring sticks (available in hardware or paint stores) or craft sticks, CD player
Curriculum supplies: Donut Forget CD ("Shout Hosanna")

Read John 12:12-15. Explain what palm branches are and tell the children that they'll make a different kind of palm branch for Gathering Time today.

Trace children's hands on construction paper and have them cut out the hand shapes. Help them glue the paper hands to a stirring stick. As the children work, listen to "Shout Hosanna" and have them wave their palm branches in the air when they come to that part of the song. If time allows, have the children make extra palm branches for everyone in the class.

Set the palm branches aside for use later in the lesson.

Center 3: Good News Banner

Classroom supplies: one of the poster board squares prepared for Lesson 1, fabric paint or glitter glue, large poster-size marker, scissors, sandpaper, stapler, craft sticks, chenille wire, small twigs, twist ties, CD player
Curriculum supplies: Donut Forget CD ("Jesus Showed Us God's Love")

Before class, cut a variety of grits of sandpaper into an equal number of 4-inch and 6-inch lengths, about 1 inch wide. Cut chenille wire into 6-inch lengths. Gather a collection of 4- and 6-inch-long sticks. Make a sample of each of the following crosses: To make a sandpaper cross, staple a 4-inch strip to a 6-inch one. To make a craft stick cross, place two craft sticks in a cross shape and wrap chenille wire around them in an "x" pattern. To make a twig cross, wrap twist ties or chenille wire around two twigs in a cross shape.

Set out the sample crosses and the materials. Allow the children to make one or two crosses of their choice. As they work, play "Jesus Showed Us God's Love." Tell the children that the crosses remind us that Jesus showed us God's love by dying and living again.

Help the children arrange the finished crosses on a poster board square. Write the words, "Jesus died for our sins" on the poster with a large poster marker. Glue the crosses in place. Let the children decorate the words with dots of fabric paint or glitter glue.

Set the poster aside to dry near the Gathering Time area.

GATHERING TIME

Classroom supplies: Good News Eggs from Center 1, CD Player
Curriculum supplies: Donut Forget CD ("Christ Died for Our Sins")

Have the children sit down in the Gathering Time area. Invite them to tell you about the things they did at their Learning Centers. Then say: **Today we've experimented with different ways to tell the good news of Jesus. Center 2 made palm branches. People in the Bible used palm branches to shout the good news that Jesus was coming to Jerusalem. If you made palm branches, wave your palms in the air and**

shout "Hosanna!" Center 3 believes in the good news—tell us what your poster says. Hold up the banner piece and have Center 3 say, "Jesus died for our sins." **Center 1 has a special way for us to learn our memory verse. If you worked at that center, come and stand near me now.**

Hand the Good News Eggs to Center 1 children. Lead them in saying the memory verse while showing their story eggs.

Pass out eggs to the remainder of the group. Have the children sing "Christ Died for Our Sins" and use the eggs as they sing.

BIBLE STORY TIME

Classroom supplies: Bible, CD player
Curriculum supplies: copy of "Simon's Story" (page 149), Donut Forget CD ("Jesus Showed Us God's Love")

Before class, arrange to have someone dress up as Simon and come into the classroom to tell the story. Give him a copy of "Simon's Story" (page 149).

Open your Bible to Luke 23 and 24 and show it to the children. Say: **Our Bible story comes from the book of Luke. But today we're going to hear the story from someone who took a walk with Jesus one day. Let's listen to Simon's story.**

Have your actor enter and tell Simon's story. After the story, encourage the children to tell him what they believe about Jesus. If time allows, let the children use the Good News Eggs to tell Simon the memory verse. Then lead the children in singing "Jesus Showed Us God's Love."

SING-ALONG FUN TIME

Classroom supplies: Bible, palm branches from Center 2, glad-sad shakers from Lesson 1, CD player
Curriculum supplies: Donut Forget CD ("Christ Died for Our Sins," "Shout Hosanna")

Have the children stand in a circle. Say: **Let's pass on the good news, the Bible, to each other in a game as we sing our memory verse song.**

Play "Christ Died for Our Sins" as you pass a Bible around the circle. Stop the music at intervals. When the music stops, have the child holding the Bible say the memory verse. If a child needs help, have everyone say it with her. Repeat several times.

Use the **Duncan** puppet and the script from the Donut Forget Songbook to talk about the memory verse, 1 Corinthians 15:3, 4.

Pass out the palm branches and the glad-sad shakers from Lesson 1. Play "Shout Hosanna." Have the children jump up and wave their palm branches or glad-sad shakers each time the song says "jumping up and down." Next, have the children lay the palm branches and glad-sad shakers on the floor, spaced about 3 feet apart. Have the children form a single-file line. Each time the song says "jumping up and down" or "Jesus is alive," have the children jump over one of the palm branches or shakers. Collect the palm branches for use in future lessons.

Donut Forget™ Bible Story Lessons

DONUT FORGET TIME

Classroom supplies: hand mirror, CD player
Curriculum supplies: Donut Forget CD ("Jesus Showed Us God's Love")

Say: **Our Bible friend Simon asked us if we could forgive others the way Jesus did. Do you remember that Jesus forgave those men who did mean things to him? We can't always forgive on our own, but with God's help we can.**

Play the song "Jesus Showed Us God's Love" quietly in the background while you say: **Close your eyes and think about someone who has hurt you. It might be a friend or someone in your family. It might be someone in this room.** (Pause.) **Now silently ask Jesus to help you forgive that person.**

Have the children sit up and open their eyes. Show them the hand mirror and say: **Let's practice forgiving like Jesus did.** Look in the mirror and say: **Jesus, you forgive** (say your name). **Help me to forgive others.**

Have the children take turns holding the mirror and saying the prayer using their names. Then pray: **Thank you, Father, for forgiving me for the wrong things I've done. Help me forgive those who hurt me. Thank you for the good news that Jesus died for our sins and then rose again!**

LEARNING CENTERS

Set up the following activities for the children to do as they arrive. Assign an equal number of children and a teacher or helper to each activity.

At each Learning Center, welcome the children to your class. Make sure you know each child's name. Explain that today you'll be talking about how Jesus showed God's love by dying and living again.

Center 1: Megaphones

Classroom supplies: construction paper, tape, markers, CD player
Curriculum supplies: Donut Forget CD ("Shout Hosanna")

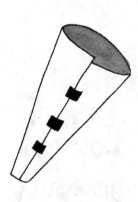

Before class, make a few extra megaphones according to the instructions below. Children who don't make a megaphone or a Thomas puppet (Center 2) will use the extra megaphones during Bible Story time.

Give each child a sheet of construction paper. Have the children decorate their papers with designs that remind them of things Jesus has done. If they need help, suggest such things as crosses, hearts, or happy faces. When the children finish their designs, show them how to roll their papers into megaphones. Help them tape the edges in place.

Explain that megaphones make sounds louder. Play the song "Shout Hosanna" and have the children use the megaphones to shout the words "hosanna" and "Jesus is alive."

Set the megaphones aside for use later in the lesson.

Center 2: Thomas Puppets

Classroom supplies: paint-stirring sticks or craft sticks, different colors of yarn, small self-adhesive wiggly craft eyes, glue, markers, chenille wire, CD player

Curriculum supplies: Donut Forget CD ("Jesus Showed Us God's Love")

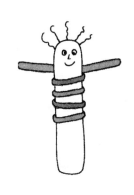

Tell the children that today they'll learn about someone named Thomas who didn't believe that Jesus rose from the dead. Give each child a stirring stick. Help the children attach craft eyes to the sticks to make Thomas puppets. Have them draw facial features and clothes with markers. Help the children glue on short lengths of yarn for hair. Then show them how to wrap a chenille wire around the body of the stick, leaving two ends sticking out for arms.

As the children work, play "Jesus Showed Us God's Love." When the puppets are finished, set them aside to use during the Bible story.

Center 3: Good News Banner

Classroom supplies: one of the poster board squares prepared for Lesson 1, fabric paint or glitter glue, large poster-size marker, small pebbles, aluminum foil, glue, CD player

Curriculum supplies: Donut Forget CD ("Christ Died for Our Sins")

Before class, write the words "He was raised to life" on the last banner piece with a large poster-size marker. Use a pencil to lightly outline a tomb shape, as shown here. Make the tomb big enough to fill most of the poster board.

Explain to the children that today they'll make the last part of the banner and that next week they'll put all the pieces together. Remind them that everyone who sees the banner will know that they believe Jesus died for their sins and was raised to life on the third day.

Read Luke 23:50-53 from an easy-to-read children's Bible. Explain that Jesus' tomb was cut out of a wall of rock. Have the children glue small pebbles onto the tomb shape, leaving the doorway without any stones. (If pebbles seem too heavy for your banner, have the children crumple small bits of aluminum foil into "pebbles" and glue them to the tomb.)

When the tomb is covered, have a child crumple a ball of aluminum foil about the size of the tomb door opening. Glue the foil stone to the poster board next to the tomb. Then have the children decorate the words with dots of fabric paint or glitter glue.

As the children work, play "Christ Died for Our Sins."

GATHERING TIME

Classroom supplies: megaphones from Center 1

Curriculum supplies: none

Have several children from Center 1 use their megaphones to call everyone to the Gathering Time area. Have the children sit down and invite them to tell you about the things they did at their Learning Centers. Then say: **Some of you made these great megaphones for us to use later. If you made a megaphone, put your hands around your mouth and say, "Hosanna!" Good job! Some of you made Thomas puppets for our Bible story. If you made a puppet, wave at me.** Hold up the third banner piece. Say: **If you helped make our banner piece, come stand near me now.**

Have the children explain about the empty tomb on the banner piece and then sit down. Say: **You all have done a lot to help us learn that Jesus showed us God's love by dying and living again. Let's play a word game of opposites to help us get ready for our Bible story. We'll start with one that reminds me of some good news about Jesus. For example, if I say "dead," you say—**(pause)—**yes, "alive." Good job! Jesus isn't dead, he's alive! If you know an opposite for my word, stand up.**

Donut Forget™ Bible Story Lessons

Say words with obvious opposites such as: go (stop), on (off), obey (disobey), lies (truth), up (down), in (out), and so on. After the children stand, let a volunteer say the opposite word into a megaphone.

Say: **Tell me a word for the opposite of "believe."** Children may suggest several words other than "doubt." Affirm anything close, then say: **There's a word we use when we're not sure about something. It's called "doubt." Sometimes we say, "I doubt it!" when we don't believe something. The opposite of "believe" is "disbelieve" or "doubt."**

There is a person named Thomas in our Bible story today who doubted Jesus. Let's hear how Thomas doubted him.

BIBLE STORY TIME

Classroom supplies: Bible, Thomas puppets from Center 2, megaphones, CD player
Curriculum supplies: Donut Forget CD ("I've Got No Doubt")

Open your Bible to John 20:24-29 and show it to the children. Say: **Our Bible story today comes from the Gospel of John. It's about one of Jesus' followers named Thomas. You can help me tell our Bible story.**

Pass out the Thomas puppets and megaphones. Say: **Whenever you hear me say Thomas's name, hold up the Thomas puppet or your megaphone and say, "I doubt it!" Ready? Let's begin.**

A man named *Thomas* followed Jesus as he taught about God and healed sick people. *Thomas* had seen Jesus arrested. He saw him die on the cross. But *Thomas* didn't see Jesus after he rose from the dead.

Jesus wanted to comfort his friends so he went to see them. But *Thomas* wasn't there. Everyone was so happy and excited. They told *Thomas*, "We have seen the Lord!" But instead of being happy, *Thomas* said, "I won't believe it until I see it." *Thomas* doubted their word.

One week later something happened that changed *Thomas's* mind! *Thomas* and his friends were meeting in a house with all the doors locked. But suddenly Jesus was in the room with them! Who do you think Jesus came to talk to?

Yes, *Thomas*! Jesus said to him, "Put your finger here; see my hands. Reach out your hand and put it into my side. Stop doubting and believe."

***Thomas* said, "My Lord and my God!" which was his way of saying, "I believe you, Jesus." *Thomas* changed from a doubter to a believer. Let's sing now about *Thomas*.**

Sing "I've Got No Doubt." Have the children wave the Thomas puppets when they hear Thomas's name and use the megaphones to sing the echo parts.

After the song, say: **After Thomas believed, Jesus told him something about you and me! Jesus said to Thomas, "Because you have seen me, you have believed. Blessed are those who have not seen and yet have believed." That's you and me! We believe even though we never saw Jesus' body or touched his wounds. That makes God happy!**

SING ALONG FUN TIME

Classroom supplies: palm branches from Lesson 2, megaphones, broom(s) or mop(s), CD player
Curriculum supplies: Donut Forget CD ("Shout Hosanna," "I've Got No Doubt")

Hand out the megaphones. Give the broom to a child and tell him to pretend it's the donkey Jesus rode on. If you brought more than one broom, more than one child can be Jesus riding the donkey.

Lead the children in singing "Shout Hosanna." Have them do actions such as jumping up and down, riding pretend donkeys (or brooms) around the room, waving the palm branches, and shouting "hosanna" into the megaphones. Sing the song again and have the children trade items so everyone gets a turn with a broom, megaphone, or palm branch.

Ask the children to tell you things they believe about Jesus such as "God loves me" or "Jesus is alive" or "Jesus is God's Son." Sing the song "I've Got No Doubt" and have the children sing their belief statements each time there's an echo at the chorus. Children can shout the words into the megaphones.

DONUT FORGET TIME

Classroom supplies: Bible, two nails for each child, felt, scissors, yarn, heart stickers, masking tape
Curriculum supplies: Donut Forget CD ("Christ Died for Our Sins")

BITE IDEA
If your class will present the banner in the adult worship session next week, make sure you know what time you'll need to be there. If you won't be participating in the adult worship, consider inviting parents to join you for the banner hanging at the end of next week's class.

Before class, cut a felt heart for each child. If you have mostly younger children, you may want to clip the slits for the nails ahead of time.

Say: **Thomas refused to believe in Jesus until he had seen the nail scars in Jesus' hands. We can't see and touch Jesus' hands as Thomas did, but we can still believe in him. We'll use nails to make Believing Heart medallions to remind us what we believe about Jesus.**

Give each child a felt heart and two nails. Help the children clip tiny slits in the hearts, as shown on this page. Show the children how to slip the nails through the slits to form a cross. Have the children place a small piece of masking tape on the back side of their hearts to hold the nails in place. Cut another slit in the top of each heart and thread a length of yarn through it. Measure the yarn around each child's neck, then cut and tie it.

Collect the finished Believing Heart medallions, then have the children stand in a circle. Read 1 Corinthians 15:3, 4. Then have the children sing along with "Christ Died for Our Sins." As they sing, go around the circle and place a Believing Heart medallion around each child's neck.

After the song, say: **If you believe in your heart that Jesus died for your sins like our memory verse says, come up and get a heart sticker and place it on your cross.**

Help the children attach the heart stickers to their medallions. Close by praying: **Jesus, thank you for loving us. Even though we haven't seen you, we believe that you came to earth, died for our sins, and are waiting to meet us in heaven. Amen.**

LESSON FOUR

LEARNING CENTERS

Set up the following activities for the children to do as they arrive. Assign an equal number of children and a teacher or helper to each activity.

At each Learning Center, welcome the children to your class. Make sure you know each child's name. Explain that today you'll be talking about how Jesus showed God's love by dying and living again.

Center 1: Good News Decals

Classroom supplies: colored glue, wax paper, tape, CD player
Curriculum supplies: photocopies of page 150, Donut Forget CD ("Jesus Showed Us God's Love")

Before class, photocopy the handout on page 150. You'll need one copy for each child at the Center. You'll need at least two different colors of glue, preferably in several bottles, so the children don't have to wait to use the glue.

At each child's place, tape a handout covered with a sheet of wax paper to the table. Make a sample decal so you'll know how much glue to apply and how long the decals will take to dry (at least 24 hours).

Tell the children that they'll make special window decals to remind them that Jesus loves and forgives us. Show the children the decal designs. Point out how they show through the wax paper. Help each child outline one of the designs with the colored glue. Show the children how to fill in the outlines with contrasting colored glue. Make sure that no gaps are left. Encourage the children to make extra shapes so that each child in your class will have one to take home (or make extras yourself ahead of time). As the children work, play "Jesus Showed Us God's Love."

Set the decals aside to dry. Explain to the children that the decals take about 24 hours to dry, so they'll get to take them home at the next class time.

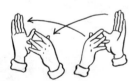

Jesus

God

Center 2: Sign Language

Classroom supplies: CD player
Curriculum supplies: Donut Forget CD ("Jesus Showed Us God's Love")

Before class, practice the signs on pages 144 and 145 until you can do them from memory.

Explain to the children that they will learn a special way to tell others the good news of Jesus. Using the illustrations shown, teach the children the signs for *Jesus, God, love, Father, forgive,* and *world.*

Listen to "Jesus Showed Us God's Love." Encourage the children to do the signs when they hear the key words. Practice the song several times.

Center 3: Good News Banner

Classroom supplies: banner pieces from previous lessons; 5 yards of 3- to 5-inch-wide ribbon; thin ribbon or curling ribbon; 1/2-inch diameter dowel; stapler; glitter glue and fiberfill (optional); CD player
Curriculum supplies: Donut Forget CD ("Christ Died for Our Sins")

Before class, cut the wide ribbon into two 2 1/2-yard lengths. Cut the thin ribbon into six 36-inch lengths. Cut the dowel to a 30-inch length.

- Assemble the main part of the banner as follows:
- Fold one end of each ribbon over the dowel and staple in place to itself.
- Lay the dowel and ribbons flat on a table. Lay the first banner piece ("We Believe") 6 inches below the dowel. Lay the second piece ("Jesus died …") 3 inches below the first. Lay the third piece ("He was raised …") 3 inches below the second. Use the illustration on page 148 as a guide.
- When you have the pieces positioned, staple them in place onto the ribbons. Cut the bottom of the ribbon at angles as shown, leaving about a 12-inch length hanging below the bottom banner piece.

Show the children the assembled banner. Help them tie the lengths of thin ribbon to the ends of the dowel for extra decoration. If the banner needs additional glitter glue or fabric paint, apply them now. For example, you may want to add "glory rays" coming up from the tomb or a fiberfill cloud to the third banner piece. If possible, hang the banner temporarily on a wall near the Gathering Time area.

If the children finish early, have them join Center 2 in learning the signs for "Jesus Showed Us God's Love."

love

father

forgive

GATHERING TIME

Classroom supplies: completed banner, CD player
Curriculum supplies: Donut Forget CD ("Jesus Showed Us God's Love")

Have the children sit down in the Gathering Time area. Invite them to tell you about the things they did at their Learning Centers. Then say: **Some of you made special decals to stick on our mirrors at home. If you worked on the decals, stand up. Tell the class what the decals are for.**

Let the children respond, then continue: **Some of you worked on our banner. Let's look at that now.** Point out the completed banner and admire it with the children. Remind them that they will be having a procession later to deliver the banner to the Worship Center.

Say: **Some of you learned a special way to tell others the good news about Jesus. If you learned sign language for our song "Jesus Showed Us God's Love," come up and stand by me.**

Play "Jesus Showed Us God's Love" and have the Center 2 children demonstrate the sign language signs. Then have all the children practice the signs with the song. Say: **Good job! We'll use those signs later to tell our parents and other adults in our church what we believe about Jesus. Let's review what Thomas learned about Jesus.**

world

BIBLE STORY TIME

Classroom supplies: Bible, CD player
Curriculum supplies: Donut Forget CD ("I've Got No Doubt")

Open the Bible to John 20 and show it to the children. Say: **Our Bible story about Thomas comes from the Book of John. You can help me tell the Bible story today. Let's all stand. Do what I do and repeat after me.**

Hi, my name is Thomas. (Point to self.)
I followed Jesus when he was on the earth. (Walk in place.)
He did mighty miracles. (Stop walking. Throw hands up in the air.)
He healed lots of people. (Make a sweeping gesture with arm.)
Some people hated him. (Cross arms and make a mean face.)
But I kept following him. (Walk in place with a smile.)

One day some mean people arrested him. (Cross wrists in front.)

They nailed him to a cross and he died! (Make pounding motion, then hands out with palms up.)

My friends and I were so sad! (Look sad.)

He didn't deserve it! (Shake head no.)

I was mad and scared. (Cower.)

I ran away. (Run in place.)

Three days later, (Hold up three fingers.)

my friends came to tell me, (Point thumb to self.)

"We have seen the Lord!" (Cup hands around mouth.)

"I will not believe," I told them, (Cross arms at chest and shake head no.)

"unless I see." (Circle eyes with fingers.)

Well, listen to what happened next! (Hands up straight, palms out.)

A week later we were praying at my friend's house. (Praying hands.)

His doors were locked. (Make a locking motion.)

No one could get in. (Cross hands over one another.)

But suddenly Jesus was with us! (Point one finger to heaven.)

I guess he came just for me. (Meekly point to self.)

He told me to touch his side and hands. (Touch sides and hands.)

I cried. (Rub fists to eyes.)

How could I have been so foolish? (Shake head.)

"My Lord and my God!" I said. (Get down on one knee.)

From that time on, (Stand and shake a finger.)

no doubts for me! (Cross hands over and out emphatically.)

I became a true believer! (Hold hands out and up, face towards heaven.)

What will *you* be? (Point to the children.)

Ask: **How did Thomas feel after Jesus appeared to him? How does Jesus feel about us when we believe without seeing him?**

Say: **Jesus is happy when we believe him without seeing! Let's sing "I've Got No Doubt" and tell Jesus that we believe him with all of our hearts.**

Lead the children in singing "I've Got No Doubt."

SING-ALONG FUN TIME

Classroom supplies: completed banner, palm branches from Lesson 2, CD player

Curriculum supplies: Donut Forget CD ("Jesus Showed Us God's Love," "Christ Died for Our Sins")

Use this time to practice for your worship processional. Have the children form two lines side by side and hold the banner between them. Children who aren't carrying the banner can carry palm branches. Make sure each child is carrying something.

Lead the children in singing "Christ Died for Our Sins" while they walk around the room in a procession, pretending to go to the worship platform. When the song is over, hang up the banner.

Lead the children in repeating the memory verse, one phrase at a time. Explain that they'll say the phrases and the adults will repeat the phrases after them.

Practice signing and singing "Jesus Showed Us God's Love."

146

DONUT FORGET TIME

Classroom supplies: completed banner, palm branches from Lesson 2, CD player
Curriculum supplies: Donut Forget CD ("Christ Died for Our Sins," "Jesus Showed Us God's Love")

Have the children line up with the banner and palm branches and follow you to the worship center. Have the children sing "Christ Died for Our Sins" as they carry the banner to the spot where the banner will hang.

After the processional, say to the congregation: **The children in our class would like to share what we believe about Jesus. If you believe that Jesus died for our sins, then rose again as the Bible says, please join us in saying 1 Corinthians 15:3, 4. We'll say a phrase, then you say it after us.**

Lead the children in repeating 1 Corinthians 15:3, 4, one phrase at a time. Then have the children sign and sing "Jesus Showed Us God's Love."

After the song, lead the children back to your classroom. Congratulate them on a job well done.

Pray: **Jesus, we believe in you. Thank you for giving us a chance to share our belief with others. We love you, Jesus. Amen.**

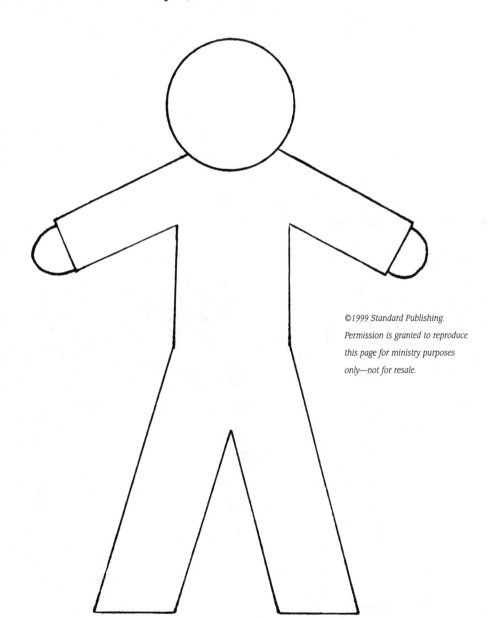

Donut Forget™ Bible Story Lessons

Good News Banner

Simon's Story

To the actor: Dress in Bible-time attire if possible. After the teacher introduces you, tell the children the following story.

My name is Simon. I want to tell you the story of how I met Jesus on a walk one day—a walk that wasn't for exercise and wasn't for fun. A walk that changed my life forever.

It happened right around the time of the Passover feast. On Sunday, there was a great ruckus in town because Jesus was coming. Crowds lined the streets to greet him. "Hosanna!" they shouted as he passed. Some people laid down their cloaks; others cut palm branches and laid them on the road. This Jesus was clearly someone important and special. It seemed like everyone in the city was rejoicing at his arrival.

That was on Sunday. A few days later, I was coming into the city from working in the fields when I was greeted roughly by a bunch of soldiers. They grabbed me and told me I had to help some criminal carry a heavy cross up a hill. I guess they thought I looked strong because I'm so tall. Anyway, they said this criminal was being punished for acting crazy and telling lies—something about being the Son of God.

So I picked up the cross and looked at this guy. It was Jesus! It was the same guy that everyone had welcomed with such great joy. One look at him told me he was no criminal—any fool could see that! His eyes were full of love and—and sadness, I guess. It's funny, but I felt like he knew all about me even though I just met him. And weirder still, I felt love coming from him. For me! Simon of Cyrene! I'm nobody special. Yet by the time we got to the top of the hill I knew without a doubt that I was special to him.

Well, you know the rest of the story. They nailed him to the cross and he died. It was horrible and unfair. Yet I heard him yell out to God before he died, "Father, forgive them, for they don't know what they are doing." Could you say that if they did those mean things to you? I don't think I could.

Just when I thought I couldn't stand it anymore, some women told me that he was the Christ, the Son of God, and that everything would be all right.

You know what? They were right! Three days later Jesus came back to life! He got up and came out of that big, old stone grave! Nothing could hold him down! Imagine that! I felt so happy I thought I'd burst! I knew that Jesus had died for me and for my sins! And even though this happened a long time ago, Jesus died for you too! *(Point to the children.)* If you could go for a walk with Jesus like I did, he'd tell you what he told me: that he loves you and died for you. Tell me, everybody, what do you believe about Jesus?

Let the children respond, then bid them farewell. As you leave, remind them to keep believing in Jesus.

Good News Decals

Donut Forget to Tell the Good News

BY THE END OF THIS UNIT, LEARNERS WILL

Know Describe how Paul told the good news about Jesus.

Feel Feel eager to tell others about Jesus.

Do Talk to a friend about Jesus' Good News.

MEMORY VERSE

"Go everywhere in the world. Tell the Good News to everyone" (Mark 16:15).

In the years immediately following Jesus' ascension, the good news about his death and resurrection spread quickly. The twelve disciples told everyone they knew, and those people told others. The news continued to spread until it reached a man named Saul. Saul didn't believe Jesus was the Messiah, and he persecuted anyone who did believe Jesus' claims.

While traveling to the city of Damascus, Saul encountered a blinding light, and heard the voice of Jesus. Right away, Saul/Paul changed his ways. Through the course of his missionary journeys, Paul was insulted, beaten, stoned, thrown in prison, put on trial and eventually shipwrecked on the island of Malta. Yet through it all, he continued to tell others the good news about Jesus.

Jesus' command to "tell the Good News to everyone" can seem overwhelming at times—even to adults. But when the children in your class discover that they can talk about Jesus to the people they know, they'll be eager to start telling the good news. In this unit, children will share the love of Jesus with people in their homes, schools, and community. Then they'll hear how missionaries are sharing Jesus' love in similar ways in countries around the world.

	LESSON 1	LESSON 2	LESSON 3	LESSON 4
Center 1	edible neighborhood	purple streamers	good news bags	salt dough map
Center 2	paper bag buildings	paper clip chains	good news socks	flags
Center 3	go everywhere quilt	quilt, people	quilt, places	quilt, countries
Gathering Time	loving actions	communication	build a wall	maps
Bible Story Time	Acts 9, Paul's Story	Acts 16, story walk	Acts 16, earthquake	Acts 18, in a tent
Sing-Along Fun Time	memory verse song	streamer motions	earthquake song & actions	waving flags
Donut Forget Time	good news cards	love soup	gift tags, gift bags	good news prayers

Donut forget™ Bible Story Lessons

151

LEARNING CENTERS

Set up the following activities for the children to do as they arrive. Assign an equal number of children and a teacher or helper to each activity.

At each Learning Center, welcome the children to your class. Make sure you know each child's name. Explain that today you'll be talking about telling others about Jesus.

Center 1: Edible Neighborhood

Classroom supplies: waxed paper, small square crackers, aerosol cheese spread, thin black licorice, pretzel sticks, milk, spreadable cream cheese, green food coloring, plastic knives, CD player
Curriculum supplies: Donut Forget CD ("Good News")

Before the children arrive, soften the spreadable cream cheese by mixing it with a little bit of milk. Mix in a few drops of green food coloring to create "grass" for the children to use in their landscapes.

Talk with the children about things that are delivered in their neighborhoods, such as mail or newspapers. Explain that Jesus wants us to deliver the good news about how much he loves us to everyone we meet.

Set out waxed paper squares, plastic knives, colored cream cheese, and other food items you've provided. Help the children use the food items to make mini-models of their neighborhoods. They can use the crackers and cheese spread to make houses and other buildings. They can use the licorice to outline streets and the colored cream cheese to create grassy "lawns" or parks. Pretzel sticks dipped in the cream cheese can represent trees. As the children work, play "Good News" from the Donut Forget CD.

When the children finish creating their neighborhoods, have them "walk" their fingers up to each house and say, "Good news! Jesus loves you!" Then let the children eat their creations.

Center 2: Paper Bag Buildings

Classroom supplies: small, medium, and large paper sacks; newspaper; markers; scissors; colored paper; glue; CD player
Curriculum supplies: Donut Forget CD ("Go Everywhere in the World")

Read Mark 16:15. Point out that Jesus wants us to tell people about him everywhere we go. Help the children list the places they've been this past week. Explain that they'll be making a paper bag city that includes all these places.

Let each child select two same-sized paper bags. Have the children use markers to draw a building on one of their bags. Encourage them to draw doors and windows, then add bricks or siding to their buildings. As the children work, play "Go Everywhere in the World" from the Donut Forget CD.

When the children finish drawing their buildings, have each child stuff his undecorated bag with newspaper, then slip the decorated building bag on top. If time allows, let the children cut out and glue colored-paper roofs to the tops of their buildings.

Set the finished buildings aside for use during Gathering Time.

BITE IDEA
In this unit children won't just learn about sharing Jesus' love—they'll practice doing it with hands-on service projects in your church and community. With a little advance planning, the service projects are easy to do. Here's an overview of the things you'll need to plan ahead for:
Lesson 1: Arrange for an adult "Paul" to visit your class. Give this person a copy of "Paul's Story" (page 169).
Lesson 2: Make arrangements for the children to prepare a meal for a family or individual in your church.
Lesson 3: Contact a local children's home and ask if the children can deliver "love bags" to the residents. Get a list of the children's names who will be receiving the bags.
Lesson 4: If you don't sew, arrange for a parent or other church member to sew the children's "Go Everywhere Quilt" squares onto a felt or fabric background.

BITE IDEA
Make sure each child in your class gets to visit Center 3 at least once during Lessons 1-3.

Center 3: Go Everywhere Quilt

Classroom supplies: 8- to 12-inch felt or solid-colored fabric squares (at least one per child), fabric paints, permanent markers, felt or fabric scraps, colored yarn, tacky glue, other craft items, CD player
Curriculum supplies: Donut Forget CD ("Go Everywhere in the World")

BITE IDEA
For easier quilt assembly (you'll do this before Lesson 4), use felt squares. The edges won't ravel and in a pinch they can even be glued to a background rather than sewn. If you want to use fabric, buy inexpensive fabric by the yard, or cut solid-colored bedsheets into squares of the desired size.

Before class, cut felt or fabric into squares of the desired size. Estimate how many children will visit this Center *during the unit*, and cut one or two squares for each child.

Read Mark 16:15. Explain that Jesus wants everyone to know how much he loves them. Invite the children to name people they could tell about Jesus, then invite them to identify places where they might encounter those people. Tell the children that they'll get to make squares for a class Go Everywhere Quilt to represent the people and places they've just named.

Set out the fabric squares and the other supplies you've provided.

Help the children design their squares as needed. For people, they might include names, birthdays (if known), or items that represent the person's interests. Encourage the children to do their people squares first, then, if time allows, have them design additional squares to represent school, church, neighborhood, or other community meeting places. As the children work, play "Go Everywhere in the World" from the Donut Forget CD.

Set the finished squares aside to add to the quilt.

GATHERING TIME

Classroom supplies: paper bag buildings from Center 2, small dolls or people figures, CD player
Curriculum supplies: Donut Forget CD ("Go Everywhere in the World")

Have the children sit down in the Gathering Time area. Invite them to tell you about the things they did at their Learning Centers. Say: **Some of you delivered "love-ly" news to houses in edible neighborhoods. If you made an edible neighborhood, say, "Mm-mm! Good news!"**

Some of you made the first squares for our Go Everywhere Quilt. Each of you will get a chance to add a square to this special quilt. When it's done, we'll hang it on our classroom wall to remind us of all the places and people who need to hear about Jesus. If you made a quilt square, say, "Go!"

Some of you made paper bag buildings to represent places in our community. If you made a paper bag building, come stand by me.

Invite the children to show and describe their paper bag buildings. Say: **Jesus wants us to share the good news about his love wherever we go—in all these places and many more. All around the world, people who love Jesus are sharing his love with the people around them. Sometimes we share Jesus' love by talking about him. Other times we share his love by treating people as Jesus would treat them—even if they've been mean to us.**

Ask:

■ **If you had to tell someone about Jesus who had never heard of him, what would you tell him?**

■ **What actions can we do to share Jesus' love?**

Say: **Good job thinking of words and actions. Let's practice using your ideas to share Jesus' love now.**

Form pairs or trios. Give each group one of the paper bag buildings and several people figures. Say: **I'm going to read some situations that might happen at any of your buildings. After I read each situation, use your people figures to act out what might have happened in your building and how you might share Jesus' love in that situation.**

Read the following situations. Pause after you read each one to allow time for the children to act it out in their groups. If time allows, invite groups to present their situations to the class.

- **You see someone at your building who's been mean to you.**
- **Someone at your building asks you, "Do you go to church? What do you do there?"**
- **Someone at your building has fallen down and gotten hurt.**
- **Someone at your building is crying alone in a corner.**

Say: **It's not always easy to tell people about Jesus. Sometimes people don't want to listen. Our Bible story today is about a man who didn't want to hear about Jesus at first. In fact, he went out of his way to keep Jesus' followers from telling others about Jesus. But when he met Jesus himself, he changed his mind. Let's find out what happened to him now.**

BIBLE STORY

Classroom supplies: Bible, bright flashlight or camera flash, CD player
Curriculum supplies: copies of "Paul's Story" (page 169), Donut Forget CD ("My Name Is Paul")

Before class, arrange for an adult to play Paul during today's Bible story. Give him a copy of the "Paul's Story" handout. Arrange for him to interrupt you as you're introducing the story. Give the flashlight or camera flash and a copy of "Paul's Story" to a helper. Have the helper flash the "blinding" light at Saul/Paul at the appropriate time.

Open your Bible to Acts 9 and show it to the children. Say: **Our Bible story today is from the book of Acts. It's about a man named Saul who spent all of his time doing mean things to Jesus' followers.**

Have your actor burst into the room and deliver his script. Have your helper flash the light at the appropriate time. When Paul asks the children to lead him into the city, help them lead Paul back to the Bible Story area.

After Paul leaves, say: **The Bible tells us that Saul later changed his name to Paul. After he met Jesus on the road that day, he was a changed man! Instead of doing mean things to Jesus' followers, he spent all of his time telling people the good news about Jesus. From town to town, he'd preach about all the things Jesus had done. He told about Jesus' miracles and how Jesus died and rose again. He told people that Jesus loved them and that they should believe in Jesus. We'll get to hear more exciting stories about Paul in the next few weeks. Right now, let's listen to a song that gives us a sneak preview of some of the things that Paul experienced.**

Play "My Name Is Paul." After the song, say: **Let's keep walking and talking about Jesus as we sing some more fun songs.**

SING-ALONG FUN TIME

Classroom supplies: paper bag buildings from Center 2, CD player
Curriculum supplies: Donut Forget CD ("Go Everywhere in the World," "My Name Is Paul")

Set the paper bag buildings around the room. Read Mark 16:15 and have the children repeat it with you. Then play "Go Everywhere in the World" and have the children sing along.

Play the song again and have the children move around the room as they sing. Stop the music several times. Each time you stop the music, have the children run to one of the paper bag buildings. Call on several children and have them tell you who they might tell the good news to in the place they've stopped.

Have the children march around the room as you listen to "My Name Is Paul" again. After they listen to the song, have them make up additional verses based on their own experience. For example, they might sing, "I've been to school, at the park, and I keep walking and I keep talking." Have them take turns inserting their names into the phrase, "That God is great and I am small, Jesus is Lord, my name is (name of child)." If the children want, let them take turns leading the line in marching and singing their new verses.

DONUT FORGET TIME

Classroom supplies: colored card stock, red or pink construction paper, scissors, tape, several colors or patterns of fabric ribbon, markers
Curriculum supplies: Donut Forget CD ("Go Everywhere in the World")

Before class, cut card stock into 1-inch strips along the long side. You'll need one full sheet and one 1-inch strip of card stock for each child. Cut a 24-inch length of ribbon for each child.

Set the card stock, construction paper, scissors, tape, and markers on a table or work area. Say: **Jesus wants everyone to know the good news that he's alive and he loves us very much. Let's make some special good news cards to give to people who don't know about Jesus. As I play "Go Everywhere in the World," take a moment to think of someone. When you've thought of someone, come join me at the table.**

Play "Go Everywhere in the World." After the song, show the children the supplies. Give each child a sheet of card stock. Help each child fold the card stock in half, then write the recipient's name on the front. Distribute the card stock strips. Show the children how to accordion-fold the strips, then cut out and attach a heart to the end, as shown on this page. Have the children open their cards and glue the accordion hearts to the center of the right inside panel. Above the heart, help the children write the word *Jesus*. Below the heart, help them write the word *you*.

Help the children tie their cards shut with the ribbons. When the recipient opens the card, the heart will pop up and remind them of Jesus' love.

Set the finished cards around the table. Have each child tell a little bit about the person who will receive her card. Close by praying: **Dear God, thank you for loving us. Thank you for sending Jesus to die for our sins. Help us to share Jesus' love with these friends this week. Amen.**

LEARNING CENTERS

Set up the following activities for the children to do as they arrive. Assign an equal number of children and a teacher or helper to each activity.

At each Learning Center, welcome the children to your class. Make sure you know each child's name. Explain that today you'll be talking about telling others about Jesus.

Center 1: Purple Streamers

Classroom supplies: purple crepe paper streamers, CD player
Curriculum supplies: Donut Forget CD ("Go Everywhere in the World")

Before class, cut purple crepe paper streamers into 4-foot lengths. You'll need two streamers for each child.

Explain that today they'll hear how Paul met a woman named Lydia who sold purple cloth. Tell the children that they'll use purple streamers to make up creative movements for the song "Go Everywhere in the World."

Give each child two of the long purple streamers. Let the children experiment with waving the streamers different ways. Then help them come up with streamer movements to go with "Go Everywhere in the World." Practice the movements a few times. Tell the children they'll get to teach the movements to the class during Sing-Along Fun Time.

Have a helper gently tape the streamers to the top of your classroom door for use during Bible Story Time.

Center 2: Paper Clip Chains

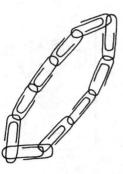

Classroom supplies: several boxes of large metal paper clips, CD player
Curriculum supplies: Donut Forget CD ("My Name Is Paul")

Explain to the children that today they'll hear how Paul and his friend Silas were put in prison for telling people about Jesus. Point out that they were freed after a big earthquake shook the jail and all the prisoners' chains fell off.

Set out the paper clips. Show the children how to hook them together to form chains. Let them decide if they want to make one long chain or short handcuff-style chains for each child. Handcuff chains require approximately six large paper clips per child. (You'll use the handcuff chains during the Bible story. If the children choose to make a long chain, simply unhook links of six paper clips for each child. Count the paper clips in the finished chain to make sure the chain is long enough to do this.)

As the children work, talk about what it might have been like to be in prison. Point out that Paul and Silas sang songs while they were in jail. Let the children put on the chains and sing "My Name Is Paul."

Set the finished chains aside for use during Bible Story Time.

Center 3: Go Everywhere Quilt

Classroom supplies: 8- to 12-inch felt or solid-colored fabric squares (at least one per child), fabric paints, permanent markers, felt or fabric scraps, colored yarn, tacky glue, other craft items, CD player
Curriculum supplies: Donut Forget CD ("Go Everywhere in the World")

Read Mark 16:15. Explain that Jesus wants everyone to know how much he loves them. Invite the children to name people they could tell about Jesus, then invite them to identify places where they might encounter those people. Tell the children that they'll get to make

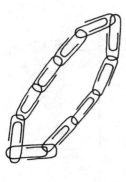

squares for the class Go Everywhere Quilt to represent the people and places they've just named.

Set out the fabric squares and the other supplies you've provided. Help the children design their squares as needed. For people, they might include names, birthdays (if known), or items that represent the person's interests. Encourage the children to do their people squares first, then if time allows, have them design additional squares to represent school, church, neighborhood, or other community meeting places. As the children work, play "Go Everywhere in the World" from the Donut Forget CD.

Set the finished squares aside to add to the quilt.

GATHERING TIME

Classroom supplies: at least three communication items (newspaper, magazine, portable radio, TV, toy or real telephone, computer, piece of mail), toy microphone or wooden spoon, CD player
Curriculum supplies: Donut Forget CD ("Good News")

Before class, hide the communication items in various locations around the room.

Have the children gather together and sit in a circle so they can see one another. Using your toy or wooden spoon microphone say: **I have some great news! It looks like you've all been working hard at your Learning Centers. I want to see what you've been doing, so I'm going to interview a few of you hard workers.**

Move around the circle and interview at least one child from each Learning Center.

Say: **I have a few more interview questions. Did anyone give away a Good News card this week?**

Invite the children who gave away their cards to raise their hands. With your microphone, ask the following questions to several children:

- **Who did you give your card to?**
- **What did the person say when he opened it?**
- **How did you feel after you saw the person's reaction?**

Then say: **Good news travels fast! The Good News card is one way to spread the good news about Jesus. Let's listen to our song "Good News" as we scout around the room for other ways good news can spread.**

As you listen to "Good News," lead the children around the room to the communication items you've brought. At each item, stop the music and invite the children to share ways that item could be used to spread the good news about Jesus. After the song, lead the children back to your Gathering Time area.

Say: **Which of these things do you think our Bible friend Paul used to tell people about Jesus? Did he call people on the phone? Did he appear on television? No, he had to talk to people face to face. Let's find out what happened when Paul and his friend Silas tried to share the good news.**

BIBLE STORY TIME

Classroom supplies: Bible, purple streamers from Center 1, paper clip chains from Center 2, basement or closet, CD player
Curriculum supplies: Donut Forget CD ("Aha! lelujah" from Unit 7, "Shout Hosanna" from Unit 8)

Before class, select a prison location you'll take the children to as you tell the Bible story. Look for a basement or large closet (be prepared to move a few things out of the way), or cover a table with blankets.

Open your Bible to Acts 16 and show it to the children. Say: **The book of Acts tells us about the many people Paul talked to about Jesus. One woman, Lydia, sold purple cloth for a living. When Paul told Lydia about Jesus, she invited Paul and his friends to stay at her house. Let's go through the purple doorway and pretend we're in Lydia's house now.**

Lead the children through the purple streamers and out into the hallway. Have them sit down. Say: **A river flowed near the town where Lydia lived, and Lydia often went to the river to pray. While Paul and his friend Silas were staying with Lydia, they probably prayed there, too. It's great to pray together with friends who believe in Jesus. Let's thank God for our friends in this class.**

Lead the children in prayer, then continue: **One day when Paul and Silas were going down to the river to pray, they met a slave girl. The slave girl had a bad spirit in her. Because of the bad spirit, the slave girl could tell people what would happen in the future. Her owners used her to make lots of money for themselves. When the slave girl saw Paul and Silas, she followed them and shouted, "These men are servants of God. They are telling you how to be saved." Let's all say that together.**

Cup your hands around your mouth and lead the children in repeating the slave girl's call several times. Then say: **The slave girl kept following Paul and Silas and shouting. Finally, Paul turned around and said, "In the name of Jesus, come out of her!" As soon as he said this, the bad spirit left the slave girl!**

Do you think that the owners of the girl were happy that she was better? No way! They were very angry, because they couldn't make money from her anymore. So they grabbed Paul and Silas and dragged them into the marketplace. They yelled and told lies about them.

The man in charge of the city took Paul and Silas and had them beaten. Then he threw them into prison. The jailer put them in a cell and chained them up.

Take the children to the prison you've selected. Bring the paper clip chains, the Donut Forget CD, and a CD player with you. Distribute the paper clip chains. As you help the children chain each other's hands, talk about what it might be like to be in prison.

Then say: **A prison is a horrible place to be. It was probably dark and cold in the cell where Paul and Silas were. But Paul and Silas didn't complain. No! Instead of complaining, they prayed and sang songs to God. Let's sing some songs to God from our prison now.**

Lead the children in singing "Aha! lelujah" or "Shout Hosanna." After the songs, say: **Do you think that Paul and Silas stayed in jail? Did they just keep singing and singing, or did they get tired of singing and just sit there? Did they get to tell any more people about Jesus? Next week we'll find out what happened to them.**

Collect the paper clip chains, then lead the children back to your classroom.

SING-ALONG FUN TIME

Classroom supplies: Bible, purple streamers from Center 1, paper clip chains from Center 2, CD player

Curriculum supplies: Donut Forget CD ("Good News," "Go Everywhere in the World," "My Name Is Paul")

As the children gather, say: **It's not always easy to tell others about Jesus. Some people would rather keep doing bad things than to follow Jesus and do the things he wants them to do. In John 16:33, Jesus told his disciples, "In this**

Use the **Duncan** puppet and the script from the Donut Forget Songbook to talk about the memory verse, Mark 16:15.

world you will have trouble. But take heart! I have overcome the world." The apostle Paul faced all kinds of troubles when he traveled around telling the good news about Jesus. Sometimes we may face trouble too, but Jesus is always with us to help us. And he wants everybody to hear the good news about his love! Let's sing about sharing that good news now.

Give the Center 1 group the purple streamers. Have them demonstrate their creative movements and lead in singing "Go Everywhere in the World."

Distribute the individual paper clip chains and let the children shake them each time they sing the words *good news* in the song "Good News." Then join all the chains together and have the children hold on in a single-file line. Let the children march around holding the chain as they sing "My Name Is Paul."

Collect the purple streamers for use in future lessons.

DONUT FORGET TIME

Classroom supplies: small heart cookie cutters (the smaller the better); 1 red pepper; 1 yellow squash; 1 zucchini; canned or frozen sliced carrots; two 14 1/2-ounce cans of beef, chicken or vegetable broth; small uncooked pasta shapes; 1 cup cooked ground beef (optional); kitchen knife; 1/2-cup measuring cup; can opener; medium-sized pot; wooden spoon; stove; large thermos or tightly-lidded plastic bowl; paper; markers

Curriculum supplies: none

BITE IDEA
For extra impact, challenge the children to bring cans of food each week for the rest of this unit. Donate the food to your church or other local food pantry.

Before class, quarter and remove the seeds from the red pepper. Cut thick slices of skin and flesh from the yellow squash and zucchini. Defrost the frozen carrots if necessary. Cook and drain the ground beef, if using.

If possible, arrange to use your church kitchen to prepare your "love soup." If you can't cook the soup during class, provide resealable bags for the children to store the vegetables and pasta. Deliver the vegetables, pasta, and cans of broth with cooking instructions.

Say: **Some people, like Lydia in our Bible story, are ready to hear about Jesus. Other people may be too hungry, too thirsty, or too sick to hear about Jesus right away. They need us to help them get food and drink and rest first. Taking care of people's physical needs is one way to share Jesus' love. Missionaries in other countries spend a lot of time making sure people have food, clean water, and medicine. Today we're going to share Jesus' love by making a meal for a family in our church.**

Lead the children to the church kitchen or other food preparation area. Explain that you'll be making "love soup" to share. Set out the pepper quarters, squash and zucchini skins, and carrots. Have the children pass the heart cookie cutters down an assembly line and take turns cutting out vegetable hearts. Then have them help you open the cans of broth and pour the broth into the pot. Add a little water if the broth's flavor is too strong.

Bring the broth to a boil. Stir in the pasta shapes and cook for about 5 minutes. Add the heart-shaped vegetables and cook until the vegetables and pasta are tender, about 5 minutes more. Let the soup cool slightly, then pour into a thermos or tightly-lidded plastic bowl.

While the soup is cooking, have the children dictate a letter to the family or individual who will receive the soup. Encourage them to tell how they made the soup and that the heart-shaped vegetables represent Jesus' love. Close the letter by telling the recipients that Jesus loves

them. Have the children sign their names on the letter. Close by thanking God for each child's willingness to share Jesus' love.

Deliver the soup and the letter as planned.

LEARNING CENTERS

Set up the following activities for the children to do as they arrive. Assign an equal number of children and a teacher or helper to each activity.

At each Learning Center, welcome the children to your class. Make sure you know each child's name. Explain that today you'll be talking about telling others about Jesus.

Center 1: Good News Bags

Classroom supplies: paper lunch sacks, decorative-edged and regular scissors, ribbon, markers, heart stickers (optional), CD player
Curriculum supplies: Donut Forget CD ("Good News")

Before class, cut paper lunch sacks in half and discard the top halves. You'll need one half-sack for each gift recipient.

Explain to the children that they'll be making gift bags to hold the good news slipper socks being made at Center 2. Tell the children that the slipper socks will have good news messages on the soles and will be given to children who need to hear about Jesus.

Set out the markers and (optional) heart stickers and let the children decorate the bags. Show the children how to use the decorative-edged scissors to cut a pretty edge on the top of the decorated bags. Then help them snip small slits all around the bag, 1 inch below the top. Cut a length of ribbon for each child, then show them how to thread the ribbon through the slits. As the children work, play "Good News" from the Donut Forget CD.

Set the finished gift bags aside for use later in the lesson.

Center 2: Good News Socks

Classroom supplies: child-sized cotton socks, poster board or cardboard, pencil scissors, fabric paint, CD player
Curriculum supplies: Donut Forget CD ("Good News")

Before class, purchase a pair of cotton socks for each child's gift bag. (Discount and wholesale stores may offer socks in packages of 12 pairs or more.) Wash and dry the socks according to the fabric paint directions. Cut poster board or cardboard into 12-inch squares. You'll need one cardboard square for each child.

Read Romans 10:15b to the children: "How beautiful is the person who comes to bring good news." Explain that they're going to make good news slipper socks to help the good news about Jesus travel to some children in your community.

BITE IDEA
Before class, contact a local children's home and ask if the children can deliver "love bags" to the residents. Explain that each hand-decorated bag will contain a pair of slipper socks with a message about Jesus' love. If possible, get a list of the first names of the children who will be receiving the bags. Try to include the same number of children as you have in your class.

If you can't make arrangements to deliver the gifts through a single organization, have the children give them individually to friends who don't know about Jesus.

BITE IDEA
If you prefer to emphasize world missions, contact a missionary who would distribute the socks. Ask for a picture of the kids wearing their Good News Socks.

Give each child a pair of socks and a cardboard square. Help the children trace and cut out their shoe prints. Have the children slip one shoe print cutout into each sock. This will keep the socks flat while the children decorate them.

Set out the fabric paints and help the children decorate the socks with pictures or words about Jesus' love. Younger children may just cover the sock bottoms with small hearts or crosses. Older children may want to include words. As the children work, play "Good News" from the Donut Forget CD.

Leave the cardboard in the socks while the paint dries. Set the socks aside for use later in the lesson.

Center 3: Go Everywhere Quilt

Classroom supplies: 8- to 12-inch felt or solid-colored fabric squares (at least one per child), fabric paints, permanent markers, felt or fabric scraps, colored yarn, tacky glue, other craft items, CD player
Curriculum supplies: Donut Forget CD ("Go Everywhere in the World")

BITE IDEA
If the children haven't yet made a square for your "Go Everywhere" quilt, have them make one today. Remind them that you'll be assembling the quilt before your next meeting time.

Read Mark 16:15. Explain that Jesus wants everyone to know how much he loves them. Invite the children to name people they could tell about Jesus, then invite them to identify places where they might encounter those people. Tell the children that they'll get to make squares for the class Go Everywhere Quilt to represent the people and places they've just named.

Set out the fabric squares and the other supplies you've provided. Help the children design their squares as needed. For people, they might include names, birthdays (if known), or items that represent the person's interests. Encourage the children to do their people squares first, then if time allows, have them design additional squares to represent school, church, neighborhood, or other community meeting places. As the children work, play "Go Everywhere in the World" from the Donut Forget CD.

Set the finished squares aside to add to the quilt.

GATHERING TIME

Classroom supplies: empty cereal boxes, shoe boxes, and grocery store boxes; blanket or sheet
Curriculum supplies: none

Lay a blanket or sheet on the floor near the Gathering Time area. Line up a few boxes on the sheet. Set the rest of the boxes nearby.

Gather the children together and invite them to tell you about the things they did at their Learning Centers. Say: **Some of you added squares to our Go Everywhere Quilt. If you added a square, say the name of the person or place on your square. Some of you decorated good news slipper socks to take the good news about Jesus to other children in our community. If you worked on slipper socks, wiggle your feet and say, "Good news!" Some of you made good news gift bags to hold the slipper socks. If you decorated a gift bag, cover your face with your hands, then uncover it and say, "Surprise!"**

Let the children respond, then continue: **Great job on your quilt squares, gift bags, and slipper socks!**

Say: **There are lots of ways to tell people about Jesus. We can read Bible verses or Bible stories to them, we can sing songs about Jesus, or we can show them things we've made in this class and explain how they remind us of Jesus' love. With so many ways to tell about Jesus, I wonder why so many people don't know about him.**

Ask: **What things keep us from talking to people about Jesus?**

Let the children respond. If they need help with ideas, suggest some of the following: too busy; friends and family who already know Jesus; scared of how people will respond; don't know what to say.

Point out the boxes and say: **Even though we're free to talk to people about Jesus, we don't always do it. Sometimes our worries about how people will respond are like prison walls that keep the good news about Jesus from getting out. When I point to you, name a reason why it's hard for you to tell people about Jesus, then add a box "brick" to our prison wall.**

Encourage each child to name a reason and add a box to the wall. It's okay if the children repeat the same reasons more than once. Continue until you've added all the boxes. Let the children choose whether to make one thick prison wall, or a four-walled prison "cell."

When you've used all the boxes, say: **It may seem impossible to get past our fears and share the good news about Jesus, but if we ask God to help us we can do it! Let's find out how God helped Paul and Silas out of a real prison.**

BIBLE STORY TIME

Classroom supplies: Bible, prison wall from Gathering Time, CD player
Curriculum supplies: Donut Forget CD ("Earthquake")

Have the children sit around the edges of the sheet with the prison wall on it. Open your Bible to Acts 16:16-40 and show the passage to the children. Say: **Our story about Paul and Silas comes from the book of Acts in the Bible. Who can remember what happened to Paul and Silas in our story last week?**

Help the children review details from last week's Bible story, then continue: **Even though they hadn't done anything wrong, Paul and Silas were thrown in jail. How do you think they responded when the jailer locked them up? Raise your hand when you think you hear what Paul and Silas might have said.**

Read the following statements as indicated. Pause after you read each one to allow time for the children to respond.

(In a regretful voice) **Oh boy, now we've done it. I knew we shouldn't have told so many people about Jesus. We're never going to get out of here.**

(In an angry voice) **Ooh. When we get out of here, we're going to get that slave girl's owner. He'll pay for this. If he hadn't dragged us to the city leaders, we'd never have been thrown in jail.**

(In a fearful voice) **Yikes. It's really dark and creepy in here. This cell is cold and damp. What if we catch cold and get sick and die? And those other prisoners look mean. If they start a fight, we won't stand a chance. We'll never make it out of here alive.**

(In a quietly confident voice) **Hmm. I never thought we'd end up in jail for telling others about Jesus. I guess we won't be preaching in the marketplace tomorrow. But maybe we could share the good news about Jesus with some other prisoners while we're here in jail.**

162

Acknowledge the children's responses, then say: **Paul and Silas weren't angry or bitter. They knew God would take care of them. Paul believed in Jesus, and he knew that God would make good things happen even when he and Silas were in jail.**

All night long, Paul and Silas sat in jail and sang praise songs to God while the other prisoners listened. They were still singing at midnight when suddenly, the earth started to shake. Show me how your body would shake if the ground underneath you was moving.

Have the children shake themselves, then continue: **The walls of the jail started to tremble and the prisoners' chains rattled together. The doors popped open and all the prisoners' chains fell off. Let's hear a song about that awesome earthquake as we shake down the "bricks" in our prison wall.**

Play "Earthquake." Have the children grab the edges of the sheet and shake it slowly at first, then faster until all the blocks fall over. Say: **Wow! The walls fell down! What a great chance to escape! But do you think Paul and Silas ran away? No, they stayed and so did all the other prisoners!**

When the jailer woke up and saw the jail all crumbled, he was scared because he thought everyone was gone. He knew he'd get in big trouble if all the prisoners escaped. But Paul said, "We're all still here." The jailer was very surprised! He asked Paul to tell him about Jesus. So Paul and Silas went to the jailer's house and told the jailer and his whole family the good news about Jesus' love. The jailer and all his family believed in Jesus and were baptized.

Even though the earthquake was scary, God made something good come out of it—the jailer and his family heard the good news and believed in Jesus. God can help us knock down the walls of our fears, too. Let's pray and ask God to help us be brave in telling the good news about Jesus.

Invite the children to pray if they want to, then close in prayer.

SING-ALONG FUN TIME

Classroom supplies: purple streamers from Lesson 2, yardstick, CD player
Curriculum supplies: Donut Forget CD ("Earthquake," "Good News," "Go Everywhere in the World")

Before class, tape the purple streamers to the yardstick. Space the streamers about 2 inches apart.

Let the children listen to the song "Earthquake." Form three groups: the Rockers, the Rollers, and the Poppers. Help groups decide what actions they'll do during the song. For example, Rockers might do a dance in pairs. Rollers could wheel their arms while doing a side step. And Poppers could squat down, then leap up in the air. Let the children practice rocking, rolling, and popping actions, then do the actions as they sing "Earthquake."

Bring out the yardstick with the streamers attached. Have an adult helper help you hold the yardstick level above the children's head height. Play "Good News" from the Donut Forget CD and let the children run through the streamers each time you sing the words "good news." Then carefully remove the streamers and distribute them to the children. Let the children do the creative movements from Lesson 2 as you sing "Go Everywhere in the World."

Donut Forget™ Bible Story Lessons

DONUT FORGET TIME

Classroom supplies: gift bags from Center 1, Good News Socks from Center 2, construction paper, scissors, ribbon, markers, tissue paper, paper hole punch
Curriculum supplies: Donut Forget CD ("Good News," "Go Everywhere in the World")

BITE IDEA
Instruct the recipients to wait three days before warm-water washing and air-drying the slipper socks. If your delivery time is more than three days away, you may want to wash and dry them yourself. If the children will give them away to friends, wash and dry the slipper socks, then redistribute them to the children next week.

Assign each child the name of a gift bag recipient. Set out the construction paper, scissors, and markers. Help the children design gift tags to attach to their gift bags. Each gift tag should include the recipient's name, the child's name, and a brief message about Jesus' love. If you have mostly younger children, have them draw a cross to represent *Jesus,* a heart to represent *loves,* and a capital letter *U* to represent *you.* As the children work on the gift tags, play "Good News" from the Donut Forget CD.

Punch a hole in each finished gift tag, then help each child thread a ribbon through the hole and attach the gift tag to the ribbon on his gift bag. Help the children line the gift bags with tissue paper, then set a pair of Good News Socks near each gift bag. Don't put the socks in the bags yet, since the fabric paint won't be completely dry.

Gather the children around the finished bags and lead them in praying specifically for each bag's recipient. Close by singing "Go Everywhere in the World."

When the socks dry, put them in the bags and deliver as planned.

LEARNING CENTERS

Set up the following activities for the children to do as they arrive. Assign an equal number of children and a teacher or helper to each activity.

At each Learning Center, welcome the children to your class. Make sure you know each child's name. Explain that today you'll be talking about telling others about Jesus.

Center 1: Salt Dough Map

Classroom supplies: Bible, salt, flour, water, measuring cups and spoons, large bowl, mixing spoon, large piece of cardboard, aluminum foil, toothpicks, construction paper, transparent tape, CD player
Curriculum supplies: enlarged photocopy of the world map (page 170), Donut Forget CD ("Go Everywhere in the World")

BITE IDEA
Before class, arrange the Go Everywhere Quilt squares. Include blank squares for the children to decorate this week as they learn about world missions. Decide whether the children will design a large globe illustration or individual country squares. For a globe, put blank squares in a block in the center of the quilt. For individual country squares, scatter blank squares throughout the design. Cut a piece of felt or fabric that's large enough for all the decorated and blank squares. Sew or glue all the squares to this background.

Before class, photocopy and enlarge the world map. The copy should be at least 11 by 17 inches. Cover a large piece of cardboard with aluminum foil. Tape the handout to the covered cardboard. Cut construction paper into 2-inch squares. Find out a little bit about the missionaries your church supports and note the countries where they're serving.

Read Acts 1:8b. Point out that Jesus wants us to take the good news everywhere—even to far away places at "the ends of the earth." Show the children the map you've taped to the cardboard. Explain that they'll make a 3-D map that represents all the places people can take the good news about Jesus.

Help the children measure out 1 1/2 cups flour, 1 1/2 cups salt, and 1 cup plus 2 tablespoons of water. Mix the salt and flour together in a large bowl, then slowly add the water until a smooth dough is formed.

Help the children fill in the land areas of the map with the salt dough. Play "Go Everywhere" as they work. Encourage the children to add mountains, hills, canyons, and valleys to their land shapes. Then help them tape construction paper squares to toothpicks to create flags. Place the flags on the salt dough map to indicate the locations of your church's missionaries.

Set the salt dough map aside to use during Gathering Time.

Center 2: Flags

Classroom supplies: reference source with information about flags; colored construction paper or felt; scissors; glue; wooden skewers; transparent tape; CD Player
Curriculum supplies: Donut Forget CD ("Go Everywhere in the World")

Before class, obtain color illustrations of various national flags (check encyclopedias, world atlases, or the Internet). Include flags of countries where missionaries supported by your church are serving, if possible. If you have mostly younger children, you may want to cut out stars or other intricate shapes used in the flag designs before class. If time allows, have the children make extra flags for the rest of the class. If not, make extra solid-colored flags before class.

Set out the construction paper, scissors, and glue. Read Matthew 28:19. Explain that Jesus wants us to take the good news about his love to all the nations of the world.

Show the children the flag illustrations. Tell them that each flag represents a nation of people who need to hear the good news about Jesus. Let each child choose a flag to reproduce. Help the children cut out shapes and assemble their flags. As they work, play "Go Everywhere in the World."

Tape the finished flags to wooden skewers. Set the flags aside for use later in the lesson.

Center 3: Go Everywhere Quilt

Classroom supplies: Go Everywhere Quilt assembled in Lessons 1-3, fabric paints, permanent markers, felt or fabric scraps, colored yarn, tacky glue, other craft items, CD player
Curriculum supplies: Donut Forget CD ("Go Everywhere in the World")

Show the children the assembled Go Everywhere Quilt. Remind them that the decorated squares represent people they know who need to hear about Jesus. Point out the blank squares and tell the children they'll decorate these squares to represent people in other countries who need to know about Jesus' love.

Set out the supplies you've provided and help the children decorate a large globe or individual country squares. (If you choose to do individual country squares, you may want to choose countries where your church supports missionaries.) As the children work, play "Go Everywhere in the World."

Set the finished quilt aside for use later in the lesson.

GATHERING TIME

Classroom supplies: salt dough map from Center 1; floor plan map or picture of your church; city, state, and national maps
Curriculum supplies: none

Donut
forget™
Bible Story
Lessons

Gather the children together and invite them to tell you about the things they did at their Learning Centers. Say: **Some of you made colorful flags, some of you made a salt dough map, and some of you finished decorating our Go Everywhere Quilt. You were all learning that Jesus wants us to take the good news everywhere in the world. We can start right here in our classroom. Let's see how quickly I can tell everyone in our class "Jesus loves you."**

Run around to each child and say, "Jesus loves you." Then continue: **Anyone else want to try? There's lots more good news about Jesus. Who would like to tell everyone, "Jesus died for you"?**

Choose a child to tell everyone, "Jesus died for you." Invite the children to suggest other good news phrases to tell each other, such as "Jesus is God's Son," or "Jesus wants us to be with him in heaven." After you've called on several volunteers, hold up the floor plan or picture of your church. Say: **Now, what would happen if I picked someone to share the good news with everyone in our church?**

Let the children respond. Then hold up the city map. Say: **This is a map of our city. Do you think one or two of us could share the good news about Jesus with everyone in town?**

Let the children respond, then show them the state map. Ask: **How could we share the good news with everyone in our state?** Hold up the national map. Ask: **What about everyone in our country? I'm sure there are an awful lot of people in our country who'd like to hear about Jesus.**

Help the children discuss ways to reach your city, state, and nation with the good news about Jesus. Then bring out the salt dough map from Center 1. Say: **I'm sure you can tell by now that one or two of us—or even our whole class—wouldn't be able to tell the good news about Jesus to everyone in the world! It's our responsibility to do our part by telling the people we know.**

But in some cities and states and countries, no one knows about Jesus yet. How can the people in those countries hear about Jesus if no one is there to tell them?

Missionaries are people who go to other places to tell people about Jesus. Some missionaries go far away to other countries. Some missionaries go to cities closer to home. Sometimes missionaries travel around to lots of different places, like Paul did. Our Bible story today is about two people who helped Paul tell the good news. Let's hear about them now.

BIBLE STORY TIME

Classroom supplies: Bible, tent or blankets and a table, CD player
Curriculum supplies: Donut Forget CD ("My Name Is Paul")

Before class, set up a tent in your classroom or other location. If a tent isn't available, drape a blanket over a table. (If your group is large, use more than one blanket and push several tables together.)

Open your Bible to Acts 18 and show it to the children. Say: **Remember where Paul's story comes from? It's from the book of Acts in the Bible. After Paul got out of jail, guess where he went? To Lydia's house. Then they left and went on to a new place to tell more people about Jesus. Paul and his friend Silas just kept walking and talking about Jesus everywhere they went. Let's sing our song "My Name Is Paul" to remind us of some of the things that happened to them on the way.**

Lead the children in marching around the room as you sing "My Name Is Paul." Encourage

166

the children to act out the things that happened to Paul as they sing about them. Continue the march until you come to the door of the tent.

Say: **Some missionaries today are also doctors or teachers or language translators. Besides being a missionary, Paul was a tentmaker. In Bible times, many people lived in tents. So making tents provided lots of opportunities for Paul to meet people and talk to them about Jesus. When Paul was in a city called Corinth, he met two friends who were also tentmakers. Their names were Priscilla and Aquila. Come into the tent and I'll tell you more about them.**

Lead the children into the tent. Then continue: **While we hear about Paul and Priscilla and Aquila, let's work on fixing up this tent. I think the stitching is coming loose. Everyone find a spot on the tent, take out your needle and thread, and keep sewing as I talk.**

Encourage the children to "sew" the tent as you tell the story. Say: **Paul stayed with Priscilla and Aquila for more than a year. Every week the three friends worked together making tents. Stitch, stitch, stitch.**

Every Saturday Paul and Priscilla and Aquila went into town and talked to people about Jesus. After a while, Paul was ready to go tell people in other cities about Jesus. Priscilla and Aquila decided to come along, too. So they all got on a boat and sailed away to the big city of Ephesus. Put down your needles and help me row this boat up to the shore.

Have the children pretend to row, then say: **When they got to Ephesus, Paul stayed a little while and went on to another city. Who do you think told the people in the city of Ephesus about Jesus? Yes, Priscilla and Aquila!**

After Paul left, Priscilla and Aquila met a man named Apollos. Apollos knew a little bit about Jesus, but he was eager to learn more. So Priscilla and Aquila invited him to their tent to talk more about Jesus. Then Priscilla and Aquila stayed in Ephesus while Apollos went on to tell people 'about Jesus in a different city.

The Bible doesn't tell us the names of the people Apollos talked to, but it does say that he was a great help to the people in the new city. If it weren't for Paul, Priscilla and Aquila, Apollos, and other missionaries, the good news about Jesus could never have spread so far.

Lead the children out of the tent and over to your singing area.

SING-ALONG FUN TIME

Classroom supplies: flags from Center 2, Go Everywhere Quilt, CD player
Curriculum supplies: Donut Forget CD ("Good News," "Go Everywhere in the World," "My Name Is Paul")

Distribute the flags and lead the children in singing "Good News." Have them wave the flags each time they sing the words "Good News."

Have the children carry the flags and the Go Everywhere Quilt on a march through your church hallways, or if the weather is good, around the perimeter of your church or up a nearby street. Lead the children in singing "Go Everywhere in the World" as they march.

If time allows, have the children crawl back into the tent and sing "My Name Is Paul." Encourage them to pretend that they're Paul telling his friends all the things that have happened on his journeys.

DONUT FORGET TIME

Classroom supplies: tent, flags from Center 2, modeling dough, Go Everywhere Quilt, CD player
Curriculum supplies: Donut Forget CD ("Go Everywhere in the World")

Before class, find out if your church-supported missionaries regularly provide newsletters listing specific prayer requests. Bring any requests you find with you to class.

Say: **We've learned lots of great ways to share the good news about Jesus. We can talk about Jesus to people we know, share Jesus' love by meeting people's needs, and support missionaries who tell people about Jesus in other places. Some of you may even decide to become missionaries in other countries some day. But right now, one of the best ways you can support missionaries is by praying for them. Praying is something each one of us can do every day. Let's pray for our missionaries right now.**

Have the children "stake" the flags around the tent. If you're meeting in a grassy area, they can poke the flags into the ground. If you're meeting indoors or in a paved area, have the children stand the flags in pieces of modeling dough. If possible, drape the Go Everywhere Quilt over the entrance to the tent.

Have the children gather around each flag and briefly pray that the people in that country would hear and accept the good news about Jesus. (If you have a large class, you may not have time to have all the children pray at every flag. Form small groups and assign each group several flags to pray around. Assign an adult helper to each group.) If you have specific prayer requests from missionaries in that country, include those as well. Encourage the children to pray if they want to.

After all the countries have been prayed for, have the children join hands around the tent and the flags. Close by singing "Go Everywhere in the World."

Hang the Go Everywhere Quilt in your classroom. Let the children take their flags home as reminders to pray for missionaries in other countries.

PAUL'S STORY

To the actor: Dress in Bible-time attire if possible. When you see the teacher showing the children the Bible, burst into the room and deliver the following monologue. Feel free to paraphrase it in your own words.

(Sounding gruff) **Are you Christians? Do you believe in Jesus? I thought so! You're just like all the rest of them. "Disciples" they call themselves. Followers of this Jesus character. You know what I think about Jesus? I think he's a big fake. He'd have to be God to do the things his followers are claiming he's done. Rise from the dead? Please. We all know that's impossible. Have any of you seen him walking around here lately? Didn't think so. Forgive sins? Even a fool knows that only God can forgive sins—not this Jesus. What a bunch of phony-baloney!**

(Continue ranting and raving about Jesus for several minutes. As you speak, encourage the children to try to convince you that Jesus is who he claims to be. After several children have attempted to persuade you, continue:)

All right. That's it. I've had it with you "Christians." I'm rounding you up and taking you in. The authorities in Jerusalem will deal with you.

(Begin gathering the children in a group. Pretend to tie them up with ropes. Lead them away from the story area. Continue until a volunteer shines a bright light in your direction. Then fall to the ground and cover your eyes.)

Hey, all you Christians I just herded up. Did you hear that voice? It said, "Saul, Saul, why do you persecute me?" Didn't anyone else hear it?

Who's there? I can't see. The light's too bright. Who are you?

(Pause for a moment, then slowly sit up and continue.)

Wow. Incredible. Amazing. You must have heard that. The voice said, "I am Jesus, whom you are persecuting." It told me to go into the city. Wow. I can't see a thing. Maybe it really was Jesus. That was one powerful light. Can you please help me find my way back to the city? I'd like to find out more about what's happened to me.

(Allow the children to lead you back to the story area. Then continue.)

Thanks. I can make it from here. I just need to take some time and think about all that's happened.

(Lie down and pretend to go to sleep. Sit up and pray, then lie down again. Then sit up and put your hand to your ear as if you hear a knock on the door.)

Yes. Yes, who's knocking? Come in. You must be Ananias. I've been praying that you'd come. The Lord sent me a vision about you. Please, come closer. Touch me so I can see.

(Rub your eyes and blink a few times. Squint and look at the children.)

Oh, hello, Christians. Are you still here? I'm glad. Have I got a story to tell you! You know the man they call Jesus? Well, he's real. He is God's Son. And he really did die on the cross and come back to life again. You know how I know? I saw him! I'd love to tell you the whole story, but I gotta go. There are so many people in the world who need to hear about Jesus! Gotta start telling them the good news about his love. Good-bye!

(Leave the room.)

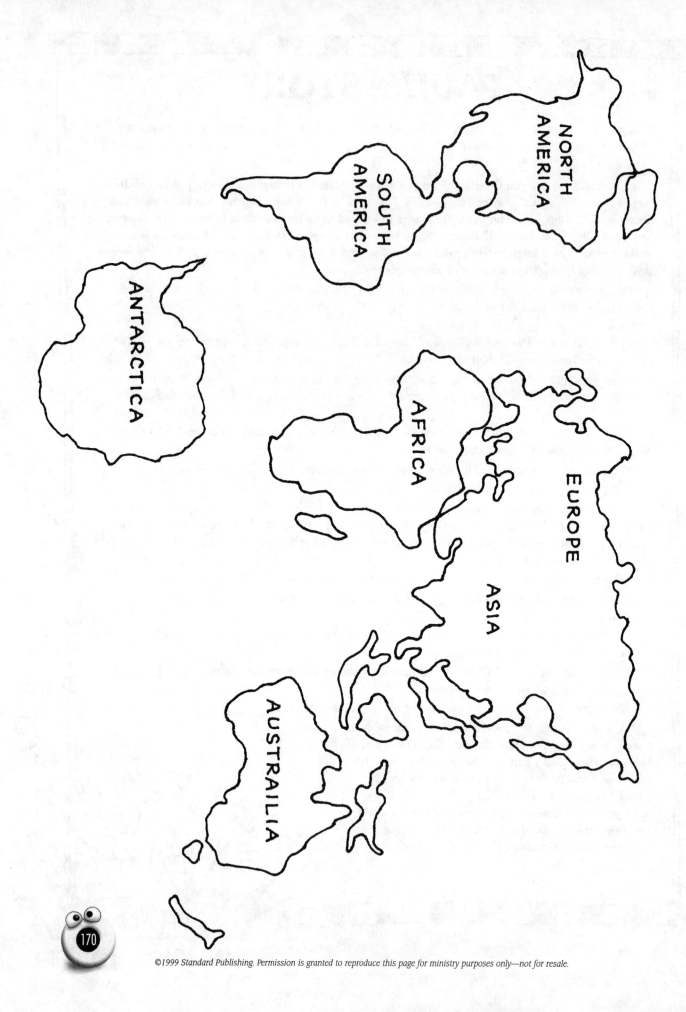

NORTH AMERICA

SOUTH AMERICA

ANTARCTICA

AFRICA

EUROPE

ASIA

AUSTRAILIA

170

Donut Forget We Can Live in Heaven

BY THE END OF THIS UNIT, LEARNERS WILL

Know Describe how wonderful heaven will be.

Feel Feel thankful that Jesus promised us a home in heaven.

Do Look forward to living with Jesus in heaven.

MEMORY VERSE

"We will be taken up in the clouds to meet the Lord in the air. And we will be with the Lord forever" (1 Thessalonians 4:17).

The disciples were sad when they realized Jesus would be leaving them. But Jesus comforted and assured them that he would prepare a place for them and they would live with him forever. The description that John paints of heaven in Revelation is glorious and beautiful, better than any of us can even imagine. Jesus' promise to us is that we will live with him forever.

Heaven is a place four- to eight-year-olds easily believe in. They are still at an age that responds wholeheartedly to truths in the Bible. This unit will help the children understand that heaven is a very special place because God is there. They will learn that we get to heaven by trusting in Jesus and that we can live with him there forever.

	LESSON 1	LESSON 2	LESSON 3	LESSON 4
Center 1	beautiful places collage	song motions	cloud pudding pictures	heavenly dessert
Center 2	cloud tambourines	cracker houses	heavenly harps	numbers 1s
Center 3	model of heaven	people in heaven	angels in heaven	jewels in heaven
Gathering Time	all kinds of rooms	crumbling cracker houses	heavenly game	model of heaven
Bible Story Time	John 14, waving	John 14, story rhyme	Revelation, story song	Revelation 21, story rap
Sing-Along Fun Time	partner motions	song motions	cloud game & song	sing about number 1
Donut Forget Time	imagine heaven	prayers to be with Jesus	angel wings	heavenly dessert, pray

Donut forget™ Bible Story Lessons

LEARNING CENTERS

Set up the following activities for the children to do as they arrive. Assign an equal number of children and a teacher or helper to each activity.

At each Learning Center, welcome the children to your class. Make sure you know each child's name. Explain that today you'll be talking about a special place called heaven where we can live with Jesus forever.

Center 1: Beautiful Places Collage

Classroom supplies: butcher paper, old magazines, scissors, markers, glue, CD player
Curriculum supplies: Donut Forget CD ("Jesus Showed Us God's Love" from Unit 8)

Before class, gather an assortment of old decorating magazines that have pictures of homes and beautiful rooms.

Set out a large sheet of butcher paper, the magazines, scissors, and glue. Have the children cut out pictures of homes and rooms they think are beautiful and glue them to the poster.

As the children work, play the song "Jesus Showed Us God's Love." Encourage the children to talk about what they think heaven will be like. Read or paraphrase the descriptions of heaven found in Revelation 21. Tell the children that today they'll hear how Jesus is preparing a place for us in heaven.

Set the poster aside to use during Bible Story Time.

Center 2: Cloud Tambourine

Classroom supplies: sturdy paper plates, unpopped popcorn, cotton balls or fiberfill batting, angel or nature stickers (optional), stapler, crepe paper, CD player
Curriculum supplies: Donut Forget CD ("Up in the Clouds")

Before class, cut several colors of crepe paper into 5-inch lengths. Assemble a sample tambourine as directed below.

Set out paper plates and a bowl of unpopped popcorn. Have each child put a handful of unpopped popcorn on a paper plate. Help each child cover the popcorn by stapling a second plate over it. Have the children shake the tambourines a few times to make sure no popcorn gets out.

Have the children decorate one side of the tambourines with markers and stickers. Have them glue fiberfill batting "clouds" to the center of the other side. Help the children tape or staple crepe paper streamers to the edges of their tambourines.

As the children work, listen to "Up in the Clouds." Tell them that the Bible says that one day Jesus will come and take us with him to heaven. Point out that the stickers and clouds on their tambourine shakers remind us that heaven is a good place because God is there.

Set the tambourine shakers aside to use during Sing-Along Fun Time.

Center 3: Model of Heaven

Classroom supplies: an assortment of small empty boxes; a large square piece of cardboard or poster board; aluminum foil; gold gift wrap; tape; glitter; glue; markers; CD player
Curriculum supplies: Donut Forget CD ("Up in the Clouds")

Before class, gather a collection of small empty boxes such as pudding or gelatin boxes, jewelry gift boxes, and different-sized shoe boxes. Cover a large piece of cardboard (cut the side out of a large cardboard box) or poster board with gold gift wrap for the base of the model. The cardboard square should be large enough to arrange a small box city on top of it.

Explain to the children that the Bible says we can live in heaven with Jesus when we die. Tell them that no one knows exactly what heaven looks like but that they'll use their imaginations and the descriptions of heaven in the Bible to make a model of what it might be.

Have the children decorate some of the boxes (open end down) with markers and glitter. Help them wrap other boxes with the gift wrap and aluminum foil. Encourage them to pretend that they're making their rooms or homes in heaven. Some children might want to tape several boxes together to form buildings with different rooms.

As the children work, play "Up in the Clouds." When the buildings are finished, arrange them on the piece of covered cardboard to build a model of a heavenly city. Encourage creativity and allow the children to set up the homes and buildings the way they want. The buildings don't need to be secured to the base. This will allow the children to arrange and rearrange the model.

Compliment the children on their "heavenly" artwork.

GATHERING TIME

Classroom supplies: heaven model from Center 3
Curriculum supplies: none

Have the children sit down in the Gathering Time area. Invite them to share with you about the things they made at their Learning Centers. Then say: **You all did different things today. If you made a collage of beautiful places to live, say, "Home, sweet home." If you made a cloud tambourine, clap your hands two times. If you worked on a model to represent heaven, come up and stand by me.**

Have the children describe the heaven model and point out each building they made. Say: **Great job! Thanks for making us a model of heaven. We'll be adding other things to it in the next few weeks.**

Have the children who worked on the model of heaven join the rest of the class. Say: **Houses have all kinds of rooms. Some houses have big rooms, some have small, some have many rooms, and others have just a few. What's your favorite room at your house?** Have a few children share about their favorite room.

Quickly form groups of three or four. Say: **I'm going to whisper the name of a room in a house to your group. Decide together how to act out what you do in that room, then you can act it out and we'll guess what room it is.**

Whisper a room to each group. Mention things such as dining room, living room, attic, kitchen, basement, bedroom, garage, and family room. Give the children a few minutes to plan, then have the groups act out their room activities while the others guess.

When everyone has guessed the rooms say: **Good acting, everyone! Let's get ready for our Bible story now and find out what Jesus said about the rooms we'll have in heaven.**

BIBLE STORY TIME

Classroom supplies: Bible, house collage made in Center 1, CD player
Curriculum supplies: Donut Forget CD ("I'm Going to Prepare a Place")

Hold up the collage made in Center 1. Have one or two of the children that worked on the collage tell what their favorite room on the poster is and why they like it. Then say: **Use your imagination now and tell me what your house would look like if you could have the most beautiful house in the world.**

Give the children time to respond. Then say: **Those sound so beautiful! Today we're going to learn that God's home for us in heaven will be even more beautiful than anything we can think of. The Bible says Jesus is getting a place ready for us!**

Open your Bible to John 14 and show the passage to the children. Say: **Our story is from the book of John. Listen carefully and find out what our story has to do with rooms. Wave at me when you hear the words *rooms* or *house*.**

One day Jesus was talking to his closest friends. He knew he was going to die on the cross soon, but his friends didn't know. Jesus wanted to tell them about heaven so they wouldn't worry when he was gone.

Jesus said, "Don't worry. Trust in God and trust in me. There are many *rooms* in my Father's *house*; I wouldn't tell you this if it weren't true. I'm going there to prepare a place for you. After I go and prepare a place for you, I'll come back and take you to be with me. You know the way to the place I'm going."

But one of the friends named Thomas said, "But we don't know where you are going. How can we know the way?"

Jesus said, "I am the way, the truth, and the life. The only way to the Father is through me."

Ask:

■ **What did Jesus say about rooms and a house?**
■ **Why did Jesus tell his friends about heaven?**
■ **How do we get to heaven?**

Say: **Jesus promises that he's getting a place ready for you in heaven! There's room for everyone in his Father's house! We get there by following Jesus. Let's learn a song about that called "I'm Going to Prepare a Place."**

Play the song and have kids make the sounds mentioned. When the song is over, say: **That's a great song! Let's get ready to sing this song again with our tambourine shakers.**

SING-ALONG FUN TIME

Classroom supplies: cloud tambourines from Center 2, CD player
Curriculum supplies: Donut Forget CD ("I'm Going to Prepare a Place," "Good News" from Unit 9, "Shout Hosanna" from Unit 8)

Pass out the cloud tambourines and have the children use them while you sing "I'm Going to Prepare a Place" one more time. Encourage the children with tambourines to play them up high in the air, down low on the ground, and swaying back and forth.

Have the children pass the tambourines to others who haven't had a turn, then sing the song "Good News."

Lead the children in singing "Shout Hosanna" while they play the following game. Have the children form pairs and stand facing each other. Let the shorter child in each pair be the leader. As the children sing, have each leader make up actions for her partner to copy. Play the song again and have the children switch roles.

174

DONUT FORGET TIME

Classroom supplies: Bible, drawing paper, markers, construction paper or card stock, a three-hole punch, ribbon, CD player

Curriculum supplies: Donut Forget CD ("Up in the Clouds," "I'm Going to Prepare a Place")

BITE IDEA
If you have time, briefly write the children's descriptions under their artwork.

Say: **All that singing and dancing made me tired! Let's lie down on the floor and relax for a few minutes. Listen while I read our new memory verse.**

Open your Bible to 1 Thessalonians 4:17 and say: **Our memory verse is from a book called 1 Thessalonians. This is what it says, "We will be taken up in the clouds to meet the Lord in the air. And we will be with the Lord forever." Close your eyes now while we listen to "Up in the Clouds." As you listen, think about God and about living with Jesus in heaven. Try to imagine what it will be like.**

Play the song as the children imagine what it will be like to live in heaven. Then play the song again. Pass out paper and markers to each child. Have the children draw pictures of what they think heaven will be like while the song plays in the background. They may want to include things they'll do with Jesus in heaven. If the children need more time to finish their drawings, play "I'm Going to Prepare a Place."

When the pictures are finished, invite several children to describe what they've drawn.

Use a three-hole punch to punch holes in each picture. Punch holes in two sheets of construction paper or card stock for the front and back covers. Use ribbon to bind the pages together through the punched holes, forming a book. Have a child who can write print the word "Heaven" on the cover.

Say: **This is a wonderful book. We can use it to help us remember that we can live with Jesus in heaven.**

Pray: **Thank you, God, for loving us so much that you sent Jesus to help us get to heaven. We want to live with you in heaven forever. We love you, Jesus. Amen.**

LEARNING CENTERS

Set up the following activities for the children to do as they arrive. Assign an equal number of children and a teacher or helper to each activity.

At each Learning Center, welcome the children to your class. Make sure you know each child's name. Explain that today you'll be talking about a special place called heaven where we can live with Jesus forever.

Center 1: Song Motions

Classroom supplies: book of heaven drawings from Lesson 1, CD player
Curriculum supplies: Donut Forget CD ("I'm Going to Prepare a Place")

Set out the book of heaven drawings made last week and enjoy the drawings together. Remind the children that Jesus told his friends he is preparing a place for us in heaven and that he wants us to live with him forever.

Play the song "I'm Going to Prepare a Place." Have the children work together to make up motions or think up ways to act out the song. If differing ideas emerge, form two or more small groups. Tell the children that they will get to perform the song later for the rest of the class.

175

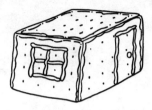

Center 2: Cracker Houses

Classroom supplies: box of graham crackers, frosting, resealable snack bags, scissors, paper plates, CD player

Curriculum supplies: Donut Forget CD ("I'm Going to Prepare a Place")

Before class, snip off one corner of each resealable snack bag. (The opening should be about 1/4-inch wide.) You'll need one bag for each child at the Center. Put about 2 tablespoons of frosting in each bag, then zip the bags closed. Carefully break the graham crackers into squares.

Remind the children that Jesus was a carpenter and that he learned to build many things while he worked with his father.

Give each child a paper plate to use as a working surface. Show the children how to squeeze the bags so that the frosting comes out the hole. Help them build houses and rooms by applying the frosting to the edges of the crackers and sticking them together. If they want, they can draw windows and doors on their houses with the frosting. Set the finished houses in the center of the table. Tell them they will be sharing the houses later in class.

As the children work, play "I'm Going to Prepare a Place." Keep the houses and some extra crackers and frosting at the table to use during Gathering Time.

Center 3: Model of Heaven

Classroom supplies: non-clip clothespins, chenille wire, markers, scissors, model of heaven made last week, CD player

Curriculum supplies: Donut Forget CD ("Up in the Clouds")

Set the model of heaven made in last week's lesson near the work area.

Have child draw a face and hair on the "ball" part of a clothespin using markers. Show the children how to use a chenille wire to make a shirt and arms by laying the clothespin in the middle of the chenille wire, then wrapping it around and up the clothespin, ending near the top. Let the ends of the chenille wire stick out for arms. Have the children make enough figures for every child in class to have one.

While the children are working, play "Up in the Clouds." Remind them that the Bible says we can live with Jesus in heaven. Explain that their clothespin figures represent themselves. Have them walk their figures around heaven! Allow them to rearrange the heavenly city if they want.

Set all the figures aside to use during Donut Forget Time.

GATHERING TIME

Classroom supplies: graham cracker houses made in Center 2, graham crackers, frosting
Curriculum supplies: none

Have the children sit down in the Gathering Time area. Invite them to tell you about the things that they made at their Learning Centers. Say: **Some of you made up motions to one of our songs to teach us later. If you did this, stand up and take a bow, then sit down. Some of you made figures of yourselves to add to our model of heaven. If you made a figure, shout "Hosanna!" Some of you built houses with crackers. Let's go over to the table, and without touching anything, let's look at what you built.**

BITE IDEA
If your mansion doesn't topple over, that's OK. Just end the activity by pointing out that our mansion is small and crumbly compared to God's and that his mansion will never be destroyed.

Have everyone gather around the table. Say: **Good job making houses! In the song "I'm Going to Prepare a Place" it says, "I'm going to build you a mansion, too." A mansion is a huge house with lots of rooms. Let's take these houses now and stack them up to make a mansion!**

Stack the houses one on top of the other, or connect them in any other manner the children might suggest. Use extra crackers and frosting if you need them. Keep stacking the houses until they topple over.

Say: **What happened! Our big beautiful house couldn't stand by itself anymore! Too many rooms! But God's house in heaven isn't like that. There's enough room for everyone and it will never crumble! Let's clean up this mess by eating it! Then we'll get ready to hear our Bible story.**

BIBLE STORY TIME

Classroom supplies: Bible, CD player
Curriculum supplies: Donut Forget CD ("I'm Going to Prepare a Place")

Gather the children in the Bible story area. Open your Bible to John 14 and show it to the children. Say: **Our Bible story comes from the book of John. Last week we learned that Jesus told his friends he was going to prepare a place for them in heaven. Thomas asked how they would know where heaven is. What did Jesus tell them? That's right—knowing him was the way to get to heaven. Let's tell our story in a rhyme today. You can help me by repeating each line after me.**

Read the following rhyme. Pause after each line to allow the children to repeat it.

Jesus told his friends one day
That he was going to go away,
Back to heaven and there to stay.
Here's what Jesus to them did say:

"Don't be unhappy; don't be sad!
I have news to make you glad!
My Father's house has many rooms.
Someday you will come there soon.

"I go to prepare a place for you,
A wonderful, extra-special place, too.
I want to take you up with me—
Heaven is a place you'll want to see."

Thomas said, "Jesus, we don't know—
Where's the place you're going to go?
And then how can we know the way—
Jesus, Jesus, what can you say?"

And Jesus told him, "I am the way.
You'll be with me in heaven some day.
I am the truth, I'm the life, too—
There's a place in heaven just for you!"

Say: **Good job, everyone! Let's sing our Bible story song "I'm Going to Prepare a Place."**

Lead the children in singing the song. Then ask:

■ **If we try to be good and go to church, will that get us to heaven?**

■ **How did Jesus say we get to heaven?**

177

Say: **There's only one way to get to heaven. That is to follow Jesus. We can be as good as we want, but if we don't believe in Jesus, we won't be going to heaven.**

SING-ALONG FUN TIME

Classroom supplies: CD player
Curriculum supplies: Donut Forget CD ("I'm Going to Prepare a Place," "Up in the Clouds")

Say: **Some of you made up motions during Center 1 for our song "I'm Going to Prepare a Place." Come stand near me now if you worked at that Center and teach us the motions you made up.**

Play the song "I'm Going to Prepare a Place" and have the children teach the class their motions.

Then say: **I like those actions! Good job, everyone! In a minute we're going to sing "Up in the Clouds" and we'll make up some motions for that too. But first let's say the verse together. "We will be taken up in the clouds to meet the Lord in the air. And we will be with the Lord forever" (1 Thessalonians 4:17).**

Repeat the verse a few times, then play "Up in the Clouds" and have the children make up motions for it as they sing. If they want to perform for one another, form two groups and have each group make up its own actions.

Use the **Duncan** puppet and the script from the Donut Forget Songbook to talk about the memory verse, 1 Thessalonians 4:17.

DONUT FORGET TIME

Classroom supplies: Bible, clothespin figures from Center 3, modeling dough or clay, CD player
Curriculum supplies: Donut Forget CD ("Up in the Clouds," "The Lord Listens When I Pray" from Unit 3)

Set the model of heaven in the center of the children. Pass out a clothespin figure to each child and keep one for yourself. Say: **Our clothespin figures represent us. We've been learning that Jesus wants us to be in heaven with him. How do we get there?**

Give the children time to answer. Say: **We follow Jesus because Jesus is the way to heaven! Let's take turns saying a short prayer to Jesus, telling him that we want to follow him. Then we'll put our figures in our model of heaven. When it's your turn you can say, "I want to follow you, Jesus." Then put a little of this modeling dough on the feet of your figure and stand it up in our model of heaven. The rest of us will answer, "There's room for you." I'll start.**

Say the prayer and have the children answer you. Repeat the activity until each child has had an opportunity to pray and put her figure in the model of heaven. Play the "Up in the Clouds" or "The Lord Listens When I Pray" quietly in the background during this activity.

Pray: **Thank you, Jesus, that you made a way for us to get to heaven. We love you, Jesus, and want to be with you forever. Amen.**

BITE IDEA
In the next two lessons the children will be adding more items to the model of heaven. There will be a lot of pieces, so you may want to glue the buildings to the base before the next lesson.

LEARNING CENTERS

Set up the following activities for the children to do as they arrive. Assign an equal number of children and a teacher or helper to each activity.

At each Learning Center, welcome the children to your class. Make sure you know each child's name. Explain that today you'll be talking about a special place called heaven where we can live with Jesus forever.

Center 1: Cloud Pudding Pictures

Classroom supplies: vanilla pudding or whipped cream, waxed paper, powdered flavored gelatin, CD player

Curriculum supplies: Donut Forget CD ("Up in the Clouds")

Before class, cover the table with waxed paper and tape the edges down.

Have the children wash their hands. Put several spoonfuls of pudding or whipped cream in front of each child on the wax paper. Encourage the children to use their fingers in the pudding "finger paint" to draw clouds, angels, or any things that make them think of heaven.

Set out small bowls or shakers of one or two flavors of powdered gelatin. Have the children sprinkle the gelatin on their clouds. Have them swirl their clouds again, then eat the results.

Lead the children in singing "Up in the Clouds" as they work. Remind the children that God is getting a place ready for them in heaven. Tell them that today's Bible story is about a man who got to see heaven.

When everyone has finished drawing and eating, clean up the mess by rolling up the wax paper and throwing it away.

Center 2: Heavenly Harps

Classroom supplies: recording of Handel's "Messiah" or other worshipful music; small heavy-duty paper plates, markers, scissors, rubber bands, 8-inch lengths of gold or silver curling ribbon, tape, CD or cassette player

Curriculum supplies: none

BITE IDEA
If the paper plates bend when you add the rubber bands, have the children use two plates. The double thickness will support the rubber bands better.

Before class, check out Handel's "Messiah" from the public library or select other worship music to use for this activity. Select music that is majestic and full. If you can find harp music, the children would learn what actual harps sound like.

Cut 3-inch diameter holes in the centers of heavy-duty paper plates. You'll need one cut-out plate for each child at the Center. (Make sure there's enough of an edge left on the plate to support the stretching of the rubber bands. You may need to adjust the size of the hole.)

Make 1/4-inch deep slits at the top and bottom edges of the plates, as shown on this page. The rubber bands will be strung through the slits to hold them in place. Make one of the harps before class so you'll know exact sizes and quantities of materials you'll need.

Tell the children that today's Bible story is about a man who got to see heaven. Explain that John saw people and angels singing to God and heard trumpets and harps (Revelation 5:8). Play the "Hallelujah Chorus" and encourage the children to imagine heaven with everyone praising God.

Give each child a paper prepared plate. Have the children decorate the plates with markers. Show them how to string the rubber bands over the plate. Use different sizes of rubber bands to get different sounds.

Donut forget™ Bible Story Lessons

When the rubber bands are strung, help the children tape lengths of gold or silver curling ribbon to hang like streamers from the bottom of their harps.

As the children work, continue playing the music you brought to class. Have the children strum along as they finish their harps.

Center 3: Model of Heaven

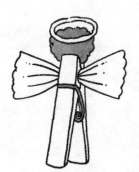

Classroom supplies: the model of heaven, clothespins, white or colored pom-poms, gold glitter chenille wire, scissors, basket coffee filters, glitter glue or markers, glue, CD player
Curriculum supplies: Donut Forget CD ("Up in the Clouds")

Tell the children that today's Bible story is about a man who got to see heaven. Explain that John saw people and angels worshiping God in heaven.

Show the children how to form wings by cinching a coffee filter together in the center and clipping a clothespin to it. Glue a pom-pom to the top of the clothespin for a head. Show the children how to make halos for their angels by cutting small pieces of chenille wire and forming them into circles. Help the children glue the halos to their pom-poms with a small amount of glue. Have the children decorate a few of the angel bodies with glitter glue.

As the children work, sing "Up in the Clouds." Have the children make extra angels (without glitter glue) so that every child in class will have one. Encourage the children to play with their finished angels in the model of heaven.

Set the angels with glitter glue on them in the model of heaven. Set the others aside to use during the Donut Forget Time.

GATHERING TIME

Classroom supplies: Handel's "Messiah" or other music from Center 2, masking tape, white sheet or blanket, CD player or cassette player
Curriculum supplies: none

Before class, put small pieces of masking tape on the floor throughout the room. You'll need one piece of tape for each child in your class. Set the white sheet or blanket near you.

Have the children sit down in the Gathering Time area. Invite them to share with you about the things they made at their Learning Centers. Then say: **You all did heavenly things at your Learning Centers today! Some of you made creamy clouds and ate them. Some of you made angels to share with everyone later. And some of you made harps and heard heavenly music. In our Bible story, we're going to learn about a man named John who got to see heaven. He heard the beautiful music of people and angels singing.**

Let's hear some beautiful music and play a heavenly game while we listen. Go find a piece of masking tape on the floor and stand on it. When the music plays, move around the room. When the music stops, stand on a piece of tape. If you're left without a piece of tape, you get to come stand near me in heaven.

Unfold the blanket or sheet and stand or sit on it. Say: **Remember, our memory verse says that we'll be taken up in the clouds to meet the Lord. We'll pretend this white sheet is a cloud of heaven. Are you ready?**

Play the music, then turn it off. Everyone should be on a piece of tape the first time. Remove one piece of tape and play the music again. Continue to stop the music and remove tape pieces until one person is left. Invite the last person to join you in "heaven."

Say: **Good job playing our heavenly game! Let's get ready to hear our Bible story now.**

BIBLE STORY TIME

Classroom supplies: Bible, white sheet or blanket, CD player
Curriculum supplies: Donut Forget CD ("Tell Me, John")

Have all the children sit with you on the sheet or blanket. Open your Bible to the book of Revelation and show it to the children. Say: **Our Bible story comes from the book of Revelation. John was one of Jesus' closest friends on earth. Long after Jesus had died, risen, and gone back to heaven, John was sent away to a prison on an island called Patmos. He was sent to Patmos because he wouldn't stop telling people about Jesus. By this time John was an old, old man.**

But Jesus didn't forget John! No! Jesus appeared to John and let John see heaven. Jesus told John to tell everyone what he saw—that in heaven Jesus is King and all evil and sadness are gone. John wrote the book of Revelation in the Bible so everyone would know and believe in Jesus.

Our new Bible story song tells us more about what John saw in heaven. As we play the song, listen carefully and see if you can tell me at least two things that John saw and heard.

Play the song "Tell Me, John." Have the children listen to the verses, but sing along on the chorus.

When the song is over, prompt the children to tell you things John saw and heard such as Jesus the Lamb, a beautiful chair, millions of angels, no more badness, people bowing, people worshiping, singing, trumpets, a loud voice.

Say: **Heaven will be a wonderful place! Let's sing some more songs to celebrate heaven now.**

SING-ALONG FUN TIME

Classroom supplies: white bed sheet, wooden building blocks or wood scraps, CD player
Curriculum supplies: Donut Forget CD ("Up in the Clouds," "I'm Going to Prepare a Place," "Only One")

Unfold the sheet and say: **We just heard a beautiful song about someone who saw heaven. Let's imagine that we get to go there now. We're going to pretend our sheet is a cloud. I need four children to hold up our cloud by the corners. Everyone else should get in a line and hold hands.**

Choose four children to hold up the sheet and help the others get in line. The child at the front of the line is the leader. Turn on the CD player and sing "Up in the Clouds." As you sing, have the line leader lead the children in and out under the sheet by going around each corner child.

When the line leader gets back to the first corner child, have him take hold of the corner. Have the original corner child join the end of the line. Then have the new leader lead the line in and out until it gets back to the second corner holder. Have the line leader take the second corner and the corner holder join the line as before. Continue moving in and out of the cloud this way, trading places, until the song is over.

BITE IDEA
If you have a large class, have eight children hold up the sheet (one at each corner and one at each side). This will increase the number of ins and outs the children will do—and it'll increase the fun!

Pass out two wooden building blocks or wood scraps to each child. Sing the song "I'm Going to Prepare a Place." Tell the children to pretend that one of their blocks is a hammer, the other a piece of wood. Have the children tap out rhythms as they sing the song. If you have time, have the children take turns being the "head carpenter" and let them tap on things around the room such as a bookcase, counter, chair, or door.

Donut Forget™ Bible Story Lessons

181

Say: **Great singing, everybody! We have a new song to learn called "Only One." Are there any guesses about what "Only One" means? How smart you are! Jesus is the only Son of God and the only way to heaven.**

Have the children use their rhythm blocks to keep the beat. Lead the children in singing "Only One."

DONUT FORGET TIME

Classroom supplies: Bible, harps from Center 2, tambourines from Lesson 1, white crepe paper, tape, CD player
Curriculum supplies: Donut Forget CD ("Tell Me, John")

Before class, cut white crepe paper into about 24-inch lengths. You'll need six streamers for each child.

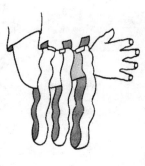

Say: **We've learned that one day we will be taken up to meet Jesus in the clouds. We'll be with him forever. Listen to what John wrote in Revelation 21:3, 4: "God himself will be with them and will be their God. He will wipe away every tear from their eyes. There will be no more death, sadness, crying, or pain."**

Ask: **How does that verse make you feel?**

Give the children time to respond, then say: **It makes me happy to know there will be no more badness in the world. Let's worship God now and sing to him like the angels in heaven. We'll use the heavenly harps and cloud tambourines some of you made earlier. We'll get some angel wings to move around the room with as we worship Jesus.**

Give each child six streamers. Have the children help each other tape three streamers to each of their arms. Have them tape one at each wrist, one below each elbow, and one midway up their forearms. Show them how to wrap and tape the streamers as shown on this page. These will be their angel wings.

Pass out the harps and tambourines. Lead the children in singing "Tell Me, John" and "Only One." Trade instruments midway through the songs so each child gets a chance to use an instrument. Encourage the children to move around the room as they sing, but don't let them get too silly with their angel wings. Remind them that even angels worship God respectfully.

When you've finished the songs, have the children sit down. Pass out the angels made during Center 3. Say: **These angels are for you to take home today. Put them somewhere special so that whenever you look at them, you'll remember that Jesus is waiting in heaven for you.**

Pray: **Father God, thank you so much for sending Jesus to show us the way to heaven. We love you and worship you. We want to be with you forever in heaven. Amen.**

LEARNING CENTERS

Set up the following for the children to do as they arrive. Assign an equal number of children and a teacher or helper to each activity.

At each Learning Center, welcome the children to your class. Make sure you know each child's name. Explain that today you'll be talking about a special place called heaven where we can live with Jesus forever.

Center 1: Heavenly Dessert

Classroom supplies: small paper plates, spoons, angel food cake, vanilla pudding, whipped cream, bowls, water or juice
Curriculum supplies: none

Encourage the children to try singing "Up in the Clouds" without the Donut Forget CD. Praise them for singing "like angels." Explain that they'll be making a heavenly treat to share with everyone later.

Have the children form an assembly line to create a "heavenly clouds" dessert. Have the first child pass paper plates to the second child, one at a time. Have the second child put a piece of angel food cake on each plate, then pass it on. The next child can add a spoonful of vanilla pudding beside the cake. The next child can spoon whipped cream on top of the cake, and the last child can set each plate of cake on a table (or on a tray if you're going to serve the dessert in the worship area). Have the children trade jobs after awhile. If you have more than five children at this Center, have other children set out napkins and cups of water or juice at each place setting.

Tell the children they will get to serve the heavenly dessert at Donut Forget Time.

Center 2: Number 1s

Classroom supplies: poster board strips, scissors, glitter and confetti, glitter glue, colored tissue paper, glue, CD player
Curriculum supplies: Donut Forget CD ("Only One")

Before class, cut out number 1 shapes from colored poster board. You'll need one number 1 for each child in your class. The shapes should be at least 10 to 12 inches tall and about 2 inches wide. Cut colored tissue paper into small squares.

Set out the number 1 shapes, glitter, confetti, glue, tissue paper squares, and glitter glue. Have the children decorate the shapes with the materials provided. Encourage the children to make enough for every child in class to have one. Explain that the shapes will be used during Sing-Along Fun Time.

Play the song "Only One" and have the children sing along as they work. Remind the children that Jesus is the only way to heaven.

Set the shapes aside for Sing-Along Fun Time.

Center 3: Model of Heaven

Classroom supplies: modeling dough or clay, craft sticks, glitter glue, small stones, glue, water, aluminum pie tins or empty yogurt containers, paint brushes or cotton swabs, different colors of glitter, small bowls, waxed paper, CD player
Curriculum supplies: Donut Forget CD ("Tell Me, John")

Before class, dilute glue with a small amount of water and pour it in a few pie tins or yogurt containers. Put different colors of glitter in small bowls.

Set out the model of heaven in the work area. Remind the children that Jesus let his friend John see heaven so he could tell us about it.

Read Revelation 21:12, 18-21 out loud to the children. Point out that the foundation stones in the heavenly city were made of jeweled stones. Tell the children that they'll make jewels for their model of heaven.

Show the children how to put dots of glitter glue on the craft sticks to represent jewels. Have them decorate at least twenty to thirty sticks. While the sticks dry, have the children paint the tops of the small stones with the diluted glue, then dip them into the glitter. Set them on a piece of waxed paper to dry.

While the stones and sticks dry, have the children help you make a line of modeling dough or clay around two or three sides of the model. Show them how to stand the sticks in the modeling dough next to each other to create walls and gates. Have the children set the stones around the model of heaven wherever they want.

As the children work, lead them in singing "Tell Me, John."

GATHERING TIME

Classroom supplies: none
Curriculum supplies: none

Have the children sit down in the Gathering Time area. Invite them to share with you about the things they made at their Learning Centers. Then say: **If you made a special dessert for us to eat later, stand up and say, "At your service!" then sit down. Thank you for making dessert! If you made a fancy number 1 for us to use during Sing-Along Fun Time, hold up one finger and wiggle it at me. What does the 1 stand for?**

Give the children time to respond. Say: **Good job making 1s! Some of you made something beautiful for our model of heaven. Let's go look at our finished model now.**

Gather the children around the model of heaven. Let the children who worked at Center 3 point out and explain what they added to the model.

When they're finished say: **John was the only one who got to see what heaven looked like. But we'll be there someday, too, and we'll live with Jesus. Let's get in a circle around our model of heaven now.**

I'm going to move around the circle and tap each of you on the head. If I say "jewel" when I tap you, don't do anything. But if I say "heaven," run over to the Bible story area. When everyone's in "heaven," we'll listen to our Bible story!

BIBLE STORY TIME

Classroom supplies: Bible, model of heaven from Center 3, CD player
Curriculum supplies: Donut Forget CD ("Tell Me, John")

Before class, practice the rap below so you can say it smoothly and enthusiastically with the children.

Open your Bible to Revelation 21 and show it to the children. Say: **Our Bible story comes from the book of Revelation. We learned last week that John was in prison but Jesus came to him and showed him heaven. What things can you remember that John saw or heard?**

Prompt the children to name such things as Jesus the Lamb, a beautiful chair, millions of angels, no more badness, people bowing, people worshiping, singing, trumpets, a loud voice.

184

Lead the children in singing "Tell Me, John."

When the song is over, ask:

- **Why did Jesus want John to tell us about heaven?**
- **How do we get to heaven?**

Say: **Jesus wanted John to tell us about heaven to give us hope. He wanted us to know that we can be with him forever in a wonderful place. In heaven there will be no more evil, no more sadness, and no more pain. But we must believe in Jesus to get there.**

Say the following rap and have the children repeat each line after you. Emphasize the italicized syllables and clap on those words. After saying the rap once, set the model of heaven on the floor and march around it while you say the rap a few more times.

One fine *day* John *saw a sight*—
He got a *view* of *heaven* so *bright.*
Where there's only *day,* there *is* no *night,*
For *God* him*self* is the *only light.*

John got to *see* the *Holy City,*
Full of *pearls* and *gold* so *pretty.*
Diamonds and *jewels* on *every wall,*
And *God* him*self* is *over all.*

Heaven is a *place* of *wonderful joy*—
For *every man,* woman, *girl,* and *boy.*
And *Jesus has* a *home* for *you*—
Can't you *see* he *wants* you, *too?*

After you repeat the rap the last time, lead the march to your Sing-Along Fun Time area.

SING-ALONG FUN TIME

Classroom supplies: number 1 shapes from Center 2, instruments made during this unit, wooden blocks used in Lesson 3, CD player

Curriculum supplies: Donut Forget CD ("Only One," "Up in the Clouds," "I'm Going to Prepare a Place," "Tell Me, John")

Pass out the number 1 shapes. Say: **Let's sing the song we learned last week called "Only One." Every time you hear the word *one*, hold up the shape. Listen carefully because the words come fast. Are you ready?**

Lead the children in singing "Only One" and have them hold up their shapes when they hear the word *one*.

Lead the children in singing the other songs you've learned during this unit. Let them choose which songs they like best and what instruments or motions they want to do with each song.

After you've sung all the songs, say: **Great singing! Keep singing these songs at home to help you remember that you can live with Jesus in heaven.**

DONUT FORGET TIME

Classroom supplies: dessert made at Center 1, colored sprinkles or mini-M&Ms
Curriculum supplies: Donut Forget CD ("Up in the Clouds")

Gather the children around you and say: **Jesus wanted John to tell us about heaven so we would want to go there. How do we get to heaven?**

Give the children time to respond, then say: **Believing in Jesus is the only way to get to heaven. Some of you might know people who don't know Jesus. In a few minutes we're going to celebrate that we get to go to heaven. But first, let's take time to pray for people who don't know Jesus. Tell me about someone you want to pray for, especially if that person is in your family.**

Provide time for the children to share about people to pray for. Say: **All these people need to know Jesus so they can be in heaven with us. We're going to pray for our friends and family. But first, let's go and sit around our dessert table. Find a place, but don't start eating until we pray.**

When everyone is seated at the table, say: **Center 1 prepared this heavenly dessert just for you.** Have the children who prepared the dessert explain how they created "heavenly clouds." Then continue: **John saw jewels everywhere in heaven! Let's add colored sprinkles to our desserts for jewels. When the shaker comes to you, pray for someone who doesn't know Jesus, then shake some sprinkles on your dessert and pass the shaker to the next person.**

When everyone has prayed and added sprinkles, pray: **Thank you, Jesus, that you want us all to be in heaven with you. Thank you that you showed us the way. We ask you to help the people we love believe in you and love you, too. Amen.**

While the children eat, play "Up in the Clouds." As the children leave, have them throw away their plates and spoons. Give them their rhythm instruments to take home.

186

Donut Forget to Be a Friend

BY THE END OF THIS UNIT, LEARNERS WILL

Know   Name two ways Jesus was a friend.

Feel   Feel willing to follow Jesus' example of being a friend.

Do   Be a friend to someone who needs a friend.

MEMORY VERSE

"You are my friends if you do what I command you" (John 15:14).

Jesus, the Son of God, calls us his friends. This amazing privilege is extended to every believer in God's family—man, woman, or child. When Jesus' disciples tried to keep the children away from him, Jesus rebuked them and welcomed the children with open arms and a loving heart. At a time in history when Jewish law forbade teachers to talk to women or Jews to talk to Samaritans, Jesus did both. He not only spoke to the Samaritan woman at the well, he challenged her, and changed her life forever. Jesus is a true friend to everyone.

Friends are a very important part of life for four- to eight-year-olds. They are busy with budding friendships at home, school, and church. They love to have friends over or to spend time at someone else's house, playing with different toys and different people. Use these lessons to help the children learn from Jesus how to be the best of friends.

	LESSON 1	LESSON 2	LESSON 3	LESSON 4
Center 1	friendly figures	finger friend puppets	heavy metal instrument	stone well
Center 2	shaker friends	friendly face snacks	crazy creations	funny bunny friends
Center 3	friendship necklaces	puzzle pairs	friendkerchiefs	heart bracelet
Gathering Time	special friends	obstacle course	favorite items	memory verse
Bible Story Time	Mark 10, shakers	Mark 10, finger puppets	John 4, story song	John 4, story script
Sing-Along Fun Time	song shakers	acting partners	follow the leader	favorite unit songs
Donut Forget Time	thank God for friends	bubbles & snacks	cupcake paper faces	serve each other

Donut forget™
Bible Story Lessons

LEARNING CENTERS

Set up the following activities for the children to do as they arrive. Assign an equal number of children and a teacher or helper to each activity.

At each Learning Center, welcome the children to your class. Make sure you know each child's name. Explain that today you'll be talking about being a good friend to others like Jesus is to us.

Center 1: Friendly Figures

Classroom supplies: two colored chenille wires for each child
Curriculum supplies: none

Help the children make chenille wire friends out of two different colors of wire. Form a loop for the head in the middle of one wire, then twist the ends around each other. Continue twisting down, stopping a few inches from the bottom of the wire ends. These untwisted ends are the legs. Next, lay the middle of the second chenille wire at the point where the twisting stops and the legs begin. Wrap the wire around the body and twist it up the body, stopping at the neck. Bend the ends down to form the arms.

Show the children how to pose their friends. As the children play with their friendship figures, point out that we are Jesus' friends when we love him and love others.

When the children are finished playing, link the figures' arms together by twisting them hand to hand. Hang the chain of friends on a wall to remind the children that Jesus wants us to love one another.

Center 2: Shaker Friends

Classroom supplies: one colored plastic egg for each child, rice, spoon, colored electrical tape, self-adhesive wiggly craft eyes, permanent markers, CD player
Curriculum supplies: Donut Forget CD ("This Is My Command")

Let each child choose a colored plastic egg. Have the children open the eggs and fill them with rice. Help the children put their eggs back together, then seal the crack with colored electrical tape. Let the children attach wiggly eyes to their shaker friends, then draw additional features with permanent markers.

As the children work, play "This Is My Command." Explain that Jesus wants us to love others just as he loves us. Remind them that they are Jesus' friends when they obey his command to love others.

Have the children make extra shakers, or make some ahead of time, so that each child in your class will have one. Set the finished shakers aside for use later in the lesson.

BITE IDEA
Each week at this Center, the children will do a simple activity to share with a special friend whom they will be assigned to during Gathering Time.

Center 3: Friendship Necklaces

Classroom supplies: small colored plastic beads, larger colored or specialty beads, bowls, ribbon or yarn small enough to insert through the beads, masking tape, small safety pins
Curriculum supplies: none

Before class, cut ribbon or yarn into 36-inch lengths, one for each child and adult. Make sure the ribbon is small enough to fit through the beads. Set out bowls of large and small beads along with the lengths of ribbon or yarn.

Let each child choose a piece of ribbon, a large, special bead, and two small beads. Show the children how to thread the ribbon through the beads, as shown on page 189. After the children have strung their beads, help them fold the ends of the ribbons in. Pin the folded ends to keep the ribbons from unraveling. (Don't tie the ribbons in a knot, because the children will

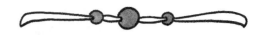

add new beads to their necklaces each week.) Attach a piece of masking tape with each child's name on it near his safety pin. Make additional necklaces for yourself and other adult workers.

Tell the children that they will get to wear their necklaces later during Gathering Time. Encourage them to make extras for other children. As the children work, praise them for their efforts. Remind them that by making extra necklaces for others they are being good friends.

GATHERING TIME

Classroom supplies: Bible, CD player, stickers, small basket, necklaces from Center 3
Curriculum supplies: Donut Forget CD ("This Is My Command")

BITE IDEA
Children love to claim their teacher as a friend. Be sure to participate in this activity by wearing a necklace. If you won't need to pair up with a child, then put a special bead on your necklace for each child in the class. Tell the children that you are a special friend to each of them.

Before class, place pairs of matching stickers in a small basket. You'll need enough stickers for each child in your class to have one.

Have the children sit down in the Gathering Time area. Invite them to tell you about the things they made at their Learning Centers. Then say: **You did lots of fun things today! Let's look at the figure friends some of you made.**

Point out the figure chain you hung on the wall, then say: **If you made a friendly figure, stand up so we can clap for you!** Hold up one of the shaker friends and say: **If you made a shaker friend, stand up and shake your body all over, then sit down.** Hold up the friendship necklaces and say: **If you helped make friendship necklaces, wave your hand at everyone. You all did such a good job. I have a sticker here for each of you. When you get your sticker, put it on your shirt so everyone can see it.**

Have each child choose a sticker from the basket and put it on her shirt. Then say: **Today we are going to learn about being friends. We're going to practice being good friends to each other. The stickers I just gave you are special. Only one other person in the room has exactly the same sticker as you! Find the person with the same sticker and stand next to her.**

Give the children time to match up their stickers. If you have an uneven number of children in your class, have an adult pair up with the extra child or encourage three children to form a "friendship trio."

Say: **The person with the same sticker as you is your special friend and partner for the day. Give a handshake to your special friend, then sit down.**

Hold up the necklaces made during Center 3. Explain: **These are the friendship necklaces some of you made earlier. Look at your partner now and decide which of you is taller. Taller partners, come up and find your friendship necklace now.**

Help taller partners locate their necklaces, then invite the shorter partners to do the same. When everyone has a necklace, say: **The special bead in the center represents your friend for today. Look at your partner and say, "You're special." For the next three weeks when you come to class, you'll get a new friend and a new bead to add to your necklace. We'll leave the necklaces here in class until our last day of learning about friends. Then you can take your necklaces home.**

Have the children sit down with their partners. Say: **Jesus teaches us how to be friends. He's our best friend.** Open the Bible to John 15:14 and show it to the children. Read the verse, then have the children repeat it with you. Say: **This verse tells us that we should do what Jesus says to do. Let's listen to a song about this. It's called "This Is My Command." Listen and see if you can find out what Jesus' command is.**

Donut Forget™ Bible Story Lessons

Play "This Is My Command" from the Donut Forget CD. After the song, ask:

- **What is Jesus' command?**
- **How does Jesus show his love for us?**

Say: **Jesus wants us to love others. If we do what he tells us, he says that we are his friends. Let's hear a Bible story about some children who spent some special time with their friend Jesus.**

BIBLE STORY TIME

Classroom supplies: Bible, shakers from Center 2
Curriculum supplies: none

Pass out the shakers from Center 2. Say: **Let's sit down with our shaker friends and get ready to hear a story about Jesus and the little children.**

Open the Bible to Mark 10:13-16 and show it to the children. Say: **Our Bible story today comes from the book of Mark. It's about Jesus and some little children. Many of them were just your age. But before I tell the Bible story, I was wondering if any of you would like to come up for a big hug or high five.**

Give hugs or high fives to any children who want them. Then ask: **How would you feel if you came to me for a hug or high five and I said, "Go away, I'm too busy?"** Let the children respond, then continue: **That would be sad, wouldn't it? Today's story is about what happened when some children wanted to see Jesus. You can help me tell the story. Whenever you hear me say the word *children*, shake your shaker friends at me. Let's try that—*children*. Good job! You're ready for the story!**

Read the following story. Pause each time you say *children* so the children can shake their shakers.

One day some people brought their little *children* to Jesus so he could touch them, hug them, and hold them. But Jesus' grown up friends saw the *children* coming. The *children* were happy and noisy and excited to see Jesus. But Jesus' friends told the parents to stop. They said the *children* couldn't go to Jesus. They said he was too busy for *children*.

But Jesus saw what was happening. He didn't like what his friends said to the *children*. He loved the *children*! He said to his friends, "Let the little *children* come to me. Don't stop them, because the kingdom of God belongs to people who are like these *children*."

Then Jesus took the *children* in his arms, put his hands on them, and blessed them.

Let's pretend I'm Jesus. Bring all your shaker friends and put them on my lap so I can hug them. You did a great job helping me tell the story today!

Ask:

- **How did the children feel when the grown-ups told them they couldn't see Jesus?**
- **What did Jesus do?**
- **How do you feel when you want to talk to your mom or dad and they're too busy?**

Say: **Jesus loves us so much! He's never too busy for us! He can be with us when our parents can't. He listens to us anytime we want to talk to him. He answers our prayers and helps us when we need it. He wants us to love each other. Let's learn some great songs about loving each other now.**

SING-ALONG FUN TIME

Classroom supplies: shakers from Center 2, CD player
Curriculum supplies: Donut Forget CD ("Become as a Child," "This Is My Command")

Distribute the shakers. Lead the children in singing "Become as a Child." Have the children shake the shakers at each echo: "You must (shake, shake), become (shake, shake) just like (shake, shake) a child (shake, shake)." When you sing "Let all the little children come to me," have the children put the shakers in your lap. On the words "I do not fancy that," return the shakers to the children as quickly as you can. Try to return the shakers before the chorus begins again. If you have time, let the children take turns having everyone put the shakers into their laps.

Lead the children in singing "This Is My Command." As you sing, have the children shake their shakers high in the air whenever they sing or shout the word *amen!*

Collect the shakers. Play the song again and have the children move around the room. Tell them that when you stop the music they should find their special friend and give that person a hug or high five. Repeat the game as time allows.

DONUT FORGET TIME

Classroom supplies: CD player
Curriculum supplies: Donut Forget CD ("This Is My Command")

Say: **One way we worship God is by doing what he wants us to do. Jesus said to love one another, so we're going to do just that!**

Have everyone stand up. Tell the children that when you stop the music, they should listen to your instructions and do what you say. Play the song "This Is My Command." Stop the CD player several times during the song and give the following instructions:

- Shake a friend's hand.
- Pat someone on the back and say, "You're a good friend."
- Tell someone, "I'm glad you're here today."
- Give someone a back rub.

As the song ends, gather the children in a circle and hold hands. When the song ends, say: **Good job showing love to one another! Let's thank God for giving us good friends. I'll start by saying "Thank you, God, for . . ." and I'll name the person on my right. Then we'll all go around the circle and thank God for the person next to us.** Thank God for the child on your right, then go around the circle and have the children thank God for the person next to them.

Close by praying: **Jesus, thank you for being our best friend. Help us to love one another the way you love us. We love you, Jesus. Amen.**

LEARNING CENTERS

Set up the following activities for the children to do as they arrive. Assign an equal number of children and a teacher or helper to each activity.

At each Learning Center, welcome the children to your class. Make sure you know each child's name. Explain that today you'll be talking about being a good friend to others like Jesus is to us.

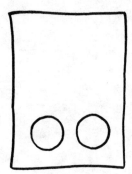

Center 1: Finger Friend Puppets

Classroom supplies: index cards, scissors, markers, CD player
Curriculum supplies: Donut Forget CD ("This Is My Command")

Before class, cut finger-sized holes in index cards as shown on this page. You'll need at least one index card for each child in your class.

Show the children how their fingers fit in the holes at the bottom of the cards. Explain that their fingers will be the legs of the puppet friends that they'll make. Set out markers and encourage the children to draw simple bodies above the finger holes. Have the children make extra finger friends for other children in the class.

As the children work, play "This Is My Command" from the Donut Forget CD. Remind the children that Jesus is their friend and that he wants to teach them how to be good friends to others.

Center 2: Friendly Face Snacks

Classroom supplies: peanut butter, plastic knives or craft sticks, English muffins, raisins and/or mini M&Ms, paper plates, napkins, CD player
Curriculum supplies: Donut Forget CD ("This Is My Command")

Give each child a paper plate. Show the children how to make English muffin friendly faces by spreading the peanut butter on the muffins, then adding raisins or mini M&Ms for facial features. Have the children make extras so there will be one for each child in the class.

As the children work, play "This Is My Command" from the Donut Forget CD. Point out that they are being good friends by making snacks for one another. Tell the children they'll get to eat the snacks later in class.

Center 3: Friendship Necklaces

Classroom supplies: small and large beads collected for Lesson 1 (see page 188), necklaces from Lesson 1, construction paper, old magazines, scissors, glue
Curriculum supplies: none

At one end of the table, set the bowls of special beads and small beads along with the necklaces the children made in Lesson 1. Have extra necklace materials on hand for any new children that may come to your class today.

Have each child choose one special bead and add it to her necklace. Remind the children that the special bead represents the new special friend they will get in class today. Make sure the children separate their special beads with a smaller bead. Have the children working at other centers add beads to their necklaces before Gathering Time.

At the other end of table, set out magazines, construction paper, scissors, and glue. Have the children cut out magazine pictures of friends doing something together. Help the children glue each picture to a sheet of construction paper. Cut the pictures in two pieces at different angles or in puzzle-type shapes, making each picture into a puzzle pair. Set the puzzle pairs aside to use during Gathering Time. You'll need one puzzle pair for every two children.

GATHERING TIME

Classroom supplies: puzzle pairs from Center 3, large grocery sack, gift box (wrapped or unwrapped) with candy treats inside, chairs, table, pillows, CD player
Curriculum supplies: Donut Forget CD ("This Is My Command")

Before class, set the box of treats at one end of the room. Use a table, chairs, pillows, or other items in your room to set up a simple obstacle course between the Gathering Time area and the box of treats.

Count the number of children in your class and put that many puzzle pieces in the grocery sack and mix them up. If you have an uneven number of children, cut one of the puzzles into three pieces instead of two.

Have the children sit down in the Gathering Time area. Distribute the friendship necklaces, then invite the children to tell you about the things they made at their Learning Centers. Say: **You did lots of great things today! Your friendship necklaces look good! Today we're learning about how to be a good friend like Jesus. It's time for us to find out who our special friend is for the day.**

Have each child draw a puzzle piece from the sack, then find the person who has the piece that matches it. Point out the box of treats and say: **I have some special treats for you and your friend today. Who likes treats? I do, too! But in order to get a treat, we have to link elbows with our partners and go through the obstacle course. You can get there any way you want. When you get to the treat box, sit and wait quietly until everyone gets there. Then we'll all get a treat.**

Invite the children to point out different ways they could go through the obstacle course, then let them make their way through it. As they go through the obstacle course, play "This Is My Command" from the Donut Forget CD. When everyone gets to the treat box, stop the music. Ask: **How would you feel if I said we don't have time for the treats? How would you feel if I said these treats are just for adults?**

Let the children respond, then pass out a treat to each child. Say: **That's how the children in our Bible story last week felt when they were told they couldn't see Jesus. Let's get ready to hear our Bible story today while you eat your treats.**

BIBLE STORY TIME

Classroom supplies: Bible, finger friend puppets made at Center 1, CD player
Curriculum supplies: Donut Forget CD ("This Is My Command")

Pass out the finger puppets made in Center 1 to each child.

Say: **While I tell the Bible story about Jesus and the children, you can act out parts of it with your finger puppets. Your puppet might be one of Jesus' friends, one of the children, or even Jesus—you decide.**

Open the Bible to Mark 10:13-16 and show it to the children. Say: **Our Bible story is from the book of Mark. One day some people brought their little children to Jesus so he could touch them, hug them, and hold them.**

Give your finger puppet a hug.

Jesus' grown-up friends saw the children coming. The children were happy and noisy and excited to see Jesus.

Show me happy, noisy finger puppets.

But Jesus' friends told the parents to stop.

Show me quiet finger puppets.

They said the children could not go to Jesus. They said he was too busy.

But Jesus saw what was happening. He wanted to see the children. He said to his friends, "Let the little children come to me. Don't stop them, because the kingdom of God belongs to people who are like these children. You must accept the kingdom of God as if you were a little child, or you will never enter it." Then Jesus took the children in his arms, put his hands on them, and blessed them. Put your hand on top of your puppet like you're giving a blessing.

Ask: **How did Jesus treat the children?**

193

Say: **Jesus showed us how to be a friend by the way he treated the children. He wants us to love each other, too. Let's show we're Jesus' friends by marching our friendly finger puppets as we sing "This Is My Command."**

Play "This Is My Command" and let the children march their puppets around your story area.

SING-ALONG FUN TIME

Classroom supplies: CD player
Curriculum supplies: Donut Forget CD ("Become as a Child," "Jesus Showed Us God's Love" from Unit 8, "This Is My Command")

Say: **Let's say our memory verse together. It's from John 15:14: "You are my friends if you do what I command you."** Have the children repeat the verse a few times.

Then lead the children in singing "This Is My Command." Say: **With your special friend, decide on a way friends show love and care to each other. Think of a way to act out your idea. Then you can act it out and the rest of us will guess what it is.**

Play the song in the background for a few minutes while the children work with their partners. Then play the song again, stopping the music at different spots and having the children quickly act out their situations. Encourage other children to guess how the acting partners are showing love. Invite them to tell about times they've shared love that way.

Have the children join hands in a circle as you lead them in singing "Become as a Child." As the children sing "You must become just like a child," have them take a step toward the center of the circle as they sing each word. As they sing "To enter the kingdom of God," have them move back out to their original starting place. On "Let the little children come to me," have the children skip around in the circle. Have them stop on "And don't you hold them back," then shake their heads no on "I do not fancy that."

If time allows, have the children also sing "Jesus Showed Us God's Love" from Unit 8. Encourage the children to move around the room as they sing the song.

> Use the **Duncan** puppet and the script from the Donut Forget Songbook to talk about the memory verse, John 15:14.

DONUT FORGET TIME

Classroom supplies: Bible, CD player, bubbles, snacks made in Center 2
Curriculum supplies: Donut Forget CD ("You Are My Friend")

Open your Bible to 1 John 5:1-3. Say: **In John 5:1-3 the Bible says, "Everyone who believes that Jesus is the Christ is God's child. The person who loves the Father also loves the Father's children. How do we know that we love God's children? We know because we love God and we obey his commands. Loving God means obeying his commands. And God's commands are not too hard for us."**

You've done many things with your friends in this class to show love. Let's do one more thing. Give your special friend a hug or a handshake and say, "You're special."

Have the children sit down and lead them in singing "You Are My Friend."

Play the song again, but this time play it quietly in the background. Blow bubbles gently into the group. As the children pop the bubbles, have them thank Jesus for a friend by praying something like, "Thank you, Jesus, for (name of child)." Make sure every child is named.

Put the bubbles away and have partners serve the friendly face snacks made during Center 2 to one another. When everyone is served, pray: **Jesus, thank you for calling us your friends. Help us to love each other the way you love us. Help us to be friends with God. We love you, Jesus. Amen.**

LEARNING CENTERS

Set up the following activities for the children to do as they arrive. Assign an equal number of children and a teacher or helper to each activity.

At each Learning Center, welcome the children to your class. Make sure you know each child's name. Explain that today you'll be talking about being a good friend to others like Jesus is a friend to us.

Center 1: Heavy Metal Instrument

Classroom supplies: metal household objects such as tongs, spatulas, colander, cheese grater, skewers, screwdrivers, empty aluminum cans or pie plates, pots and pans and/or lids; yardstick, heavy dowel or sturdy hanger; string or yarn; CD player
Curriculum supplies: Donut Forget CD ("Become as a Child")

Before class, cut the string into 24- to 36-inch lengths. You'll need a piece of string for each metal object. Set two adult-height chairs on the floor facing away from each other. Suspend the yardstick over the backs of the chairs. The kitchen gadgets will hang from the yardstick.

Explain to the children that they're going to make a special "heavy metal" instrument to use during Sing-Along Fun Time. Show the children how to hang the metal objects by tying them to the yardstick. Hang the objects at varying heights. You may need tape for some objects.

As the children work, play "Become as a Child" from the Donut Forget CD. Use a long metal object such as tongs or a screwdriver for a drumstick and let the children try out the pieces as they hang them. Tell them that they will get to use the instrument again during Sing-Along Fun Time.

Center 2: Crazy Creations

Classroom supplies: modeling dough, CD player
Curriculum supplies: Donut Forget CD ("Become as a Child")

Form pairs. Have partners stand together with arms around each other's waists. Each partner should have one free hand. Give each pair a lump of modeling dough and explain that they must work together with their partner-friend to make a crazy creation out of their modeling dough. Remind them that each partner can use only one hand. As the children work, play "Become as a Child."

When the children are finished, have them tell about their creations. Encourage both partners to share. Reinforce that when friends work together, good and fun things happen.

Center 3: Friendship Necklaces

Classroom supplies: beads and necklaces from previous lessons, white paper towels, water, food coloring, four shallow bowls
Curriculum supplies: none

Before class, put a little water in each of the four bowls and add a different color of food coloring to each one.

At one end of the table, set the bowls of special beads and small beads along with the necklaces the children made in Lesson 1. Have extra necklace materials on hand for any new children that may come to your class today.

Have each child choose one special bead and add it to her necklace. Remind the children that the special bead represents the new special friend they will get in class today. Make sure the children separate their special beads with a smaller bead. Have the children working at other centers add beads to their necklaces before Gathering Time.

At the other end of the table, set out the bowls of colored water and the paper towels. Show the children how to fold the paper towels into fourths or eighths. Then have them carefully dip each of the folded corners into the colored water. After the children have dipped all the corners, have them open up their paper towels and see the designs the colored water made. Call the finished colored towels "friendkerchiefs." Explain that after they're dry, the friendkerchiefs can be worn around a friend's arm or kept in a friend's pocket as a reminder of the children's friendship.

Set the finished friendkerchiefs aside to dry. When they're dry, help the children write the words *for (name of friend)* on them. Encourage the children to give their friendkerchiefs to a special friend at church or school.

GATHERING TIME

Classroom supplies: none
Curriculum supplies: none

Distribute the friendship necklaces, then invite the children to tell you about the things they made at their Learning Centers. Say: **You were busy today! Some of you made crazy creations out of modeling dough, some of you made a fun "heavy metal" instrument, and some of you made friendkerchiefs to give a friend. Let's play a game now to find out who our special friend for the day will be.**

As you call out each of the following choices, point to a corner of the room. Have the children move to the corner of the room that represents their choice.

- **My favorite dessert is: ice cream (corner 1), watermelon (corner 2), cake (corner 3), cookies (corner 4).**
- **My favorite room is: bedroom, living room, kitchen, bathroom.**
- **My favorite outdoor game is: tag, baseball, soccer, basketball.**

After the last set of choices, have the children tell others in their corner why they chose that favorite item. Then say: **Look around your group. Find someone that you haven't been special friends with yet and ask her to be your partner.**

Give the children time to find partners. Help guide their choices if necessary. Make sure everyone is with a new partner.

Say: **When you're friends with someone, you get to know what he likes and doesn't like. Ask your partner to tell you his favorite color and one other thing that is special about him. Remember what your friend tells you because you'll get to share it with the rest of us later.**

Allow time for the children to share, then continue with the lesson.

BIBLE STORY TIME

Classroom supplies: Bible, CD player
Curriculum supplies: Donut Forget CD ("If You're Thirsty")

Gather the children around you. Open your Bible to John 4:5-28 and show it to the children. Say: **Our Bible story comes from the book of John. One day when Jesus stopped at a well to get a drink, he met a Samaritan woman. In those days the Samaritans were considered bad people. Show me a bad face—you look so mean! Jesus was not supposed to talk to this woman. But Jesus loves everyone, so he talked to her anyway. She was surprised. Show me how you look when you're surprised. That's great!**

Jesus told the woman things about herself that no one else knew. They were her secrets. Pretend to tell the person next to you a secret. This woman had some bad secrets that made her sad, and Jesus knew that. How do you look when you're sad?

Jesus wanted the woman to be happy, so he told her that he would give her water from heaven. He wasn't talking about real water, but about life and all the good things she could have from God. What are some good things God gives us?

Let the children respond, then continue: **The woman was so surprised that Jesus knew her secrets. Show me another surprised look. She knew he must be someone special. Jesus told her he was God's Son. She went away and told everyone what happened to her.**

Ask:
- **How did Jesus show he was a friend?**
- **How can we be like Jesus to our friends?**

Say: **Jesus knew all about the woman, the good and the bad. And he still loved her. Jesus wants us to love our friends no matter what. Let's learn a song about this story.**

Lead the children in listening to and singing "If You're Thirsty." Then say: **Jesus knew all about the woman. He loved her like a true friend. During Gathering Time, your partners told you some special things about themselves. Let's introduce our friends now. Tell your friend's name, then tell us your friend's favorite color and something else that's special about your friend.**

Let the children take turns introducing their special friends. Prompt them if they need help thinking of special things to share. When everyone has been introduced, congratulate the children on learning new things about each other. Remind them that Jesus wants us love each other no matter what, just as he loved the woman at the well.

SING-ALONG FUN TIME

Classroom supplies: shakers made in Lesson 1, "heavy metal" instrument from Center 1, CD player

Curriculum supplies: Donut Forget CD ("Become as a Child," "If You're Thirsty," "This Is My Command")

Set out the heavy metal instrument and the shakers. Lead the children in singing "Become as a Child" and "If You're Thirsty." Encourage the children to take turns playing the instruments.

Have partners choose a leader and a follower. Have leaders do motions for the followers to imitate as you sing "This Is My Command." Encourage followers to imitate the leaders' motions as closely as possible. Then play the song again and have the children switch roles. Say: **Jesus wants us to imitate him just as we imitated our partners just now. We can imitate Jesus by loving our friends as Jesus loves us.**

DONUT FORGET TIME

Classroom supplies: poster board, markers, cupcake papers, glue sticks, CD player

Curriculum supplies: Donut Forget CD ("You Are My Friend")

Before class, draw a large heart shape on a sheet of poster board. Make the heart large enough to fit one cupcake paper per child inside it.

Say: **Jesus loved the Samaritan woman. He didn't tell anyone her secrets. Proverbs 11:13 says that a trustworthy person can keep secrets. Jesus is**

197

trustworthy. He knows all about us and he loves us. Let's sing a song to remind us how much Jesus loves us.

Lead the children in singing "You Are My Friend." Then say: **Now let's make something special to thank Jesus for being our friend.**

Set the poster board heart in the center of the circle. Give each child a cupcake paper and explain that the heart represents Jesus' love. Have the children draw faces inside the papers to represent themselves, then glue the cupcake papers on the heart. Have the children write their names near their cupcake paper faces. As the children work, play "You Are My Friend."

Set the glue and markers aside and say: **This poster reminds us that Jesus' love makes us all friends and family. Let's stand up and hold on to the poster while we pray. Jesus, thank you for being our friend and making us all one big family. Thank you for dying on the cross for us. You help us see how much the Father loves us. We love you more every day, Jesus. Amen.**

Let the children pray if they want. As they leave, remind them to be good friends this week.

LEARNING CENTERS

Set up the following activities for the children to do as they arrive. Assign an equal number of children and a teacher or helper to each activity.

At each Learning Center, welcome the children to your class. Make sure you know each child's name. Explain that today you'll be talking about being a good friend to others like Jesus is to us.

Center 1: Stone Well

Classroom supplies: fifty paper grocery sacks, newspapers, CD player
Curriculum supplies: Donut Forget CD ("If You're Thirsty")

Review the details of the story about the woman at the well. Explain to the children that they'll be making stones for a well you'll use during Bible Story Time.

Set out the paper grocery sacks and newspapers. Form pairs and give each pair an even number of grocery sacks and a stack of newspapers. Have the children work together to stuff half of the grocery sacks with newspapers. Then have them slip an empty bag over each of the stuffed bags. Encourage partners to work together—one partner can hold the stuffed bag while the other partner slips the empty bag on top.

As the children work, play "If You're Thirsty" from the Donut Forget CD. When the children finish, have them arrange the "stones" to form a well in your story area.

Center 2: Funny Bunny Friends

Classroom supplies: construction paper, markers or crayons, glue, chenille wires, CD player
Curriculum supplies: Donut Forget CD ("This Is My Command")

Before class, cut the chenille wires into 3-inch pieces. You'll need six to eight pieces for each child.

Remind the children that they've been learning about being good friends. Have each child choose a partner for this activity. Have the first partner form a fist, then raise her index and middle fingers as shown on page 199. Have the second partner trace around the first partner's fisted hand and fingers on a sheet of colored construction paper. Point out that the traced outline forms the shape of a funny bunny friend.

Then have the first partner trace the second partner's hand on the same sheet of paper. Have partners autograph their respective funny bunny friends. Set out the markers, glue, and chenille wires. Encourage the children to add eyes, noses, and chenille wire whiskers to their bunnies. As the children work, play "This Is My Command" from the Donut Forget CD.

Help the children write "Friends" at the top of their finished papers. Ask them to choose a spot in the room to hang the bunny friends so everyone can admire them. Or, if time allows, have partners make a second set of bunny friends so each partner can take one home.

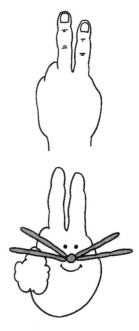

Center 3: Friendship Necklaces

Classroom supplies: beads and necklaces from previous lessons, photocopies of Friendship Hearts from page 202, card stock paper, markers, scissors, tape
Curriculum supplies: none

Before class, make photocopies of the bracelets from page 202 on card stock paper. You'll need one page (two bracelets) for each pair of children.

At one end of the table, set the bowls of special beads and small beads along with the necklaces the children made in Lesson 1. Have extra necklace materials on hand for any new children that may come to your class today.

Have each child choose one special bead and add it to his necklace. Remind the children that the special bead represents the new special friend they will get in class today. Make sure the children separate their special beads with a smaller bead. Have the children working at other centers add beads to their necklaces before Gathering Time.

When they've added their last beads, tell the children that today is the last day of the unit on friends and that their necklaces are complete. Praise them for being good friends to one another. Remove the safety pins and tie a knot in the ends of each child's necklace.

At the other end of the table, set out markers. Help the children find partners. Have partners sit across the table from one another. Set a heart bracelet handout on the table between each set of partners. Have the partners on each side of the table color the two rows of hearts that are closest to them. Then help the children cut the bracelets out and tape them around each other's wrists. As the children work, play "This Is My Command" from the Donut Forget CD.

GATHERING TIME

Classroom supplies: paper bag well from Center 1, CD player
Curriculum supplies: Donut Forget CD ("This Is My Command," "If You're Thirsty")

Invite all the children to tell you what they did at their Learning Centers. Say: **Some of you made funny bunny friends.** Point out some of the bunny pictures on the walls. **If you made funny bunny friends, make bunny ears on the top of your head with your hands and wiggle them at us. You're funny!**

Some of you made friendship bracelets. Wave your bracelet hands in the air so we can see them. Those are great bracelets! We have more bracelet papers for those of you who didn't get a chance to make them.

Touch the well, then say: **And what's this? Some of you have made a stone well for us to use during our Bible story. If you made stones for the well, rub your hands together and say, "Well, well, well."**

Have everyone stand and say: **Your friendship necklaces look great! They tell me you've all been good friends to one another! That's what Jesus wants us to be.**

Let's play a fun game with our friends. I need everyone to take off one shoe and put it in the well.

When everyone has added a shoe to the well, say: **Our shoes will help us find our special friends for the day. I'll pull out two shoes. The owners of those two shoes will be special friends today.**

Retrieve the shoes from the well two at a time. Make sure everyone has a partner, then encourage the children to help each other put their shoes back on. (Help younger children with tying if necessary.)

Say: **That was a fun way to use our well. Our well helped us meet our special friends. Now let's see if we can say our memory verse. Who remembers our memory verse about being Jesus' friends? Let's say it together.**

Have the children repeat the verse, then continue: **Now sit on your knees facing your partner. Join hands. Let's pretend we're pulling up buckets of water from our well. One partner will be the bucket, and the other partner will be the puller. Pullers, you'll lean back as you gently pull your partner's hands. When you've leaned all the way back, switch roles and let your partner pull you. Let's try that.**

Let partners practice pulling each other back and forth. Then say: **As we pull up our "water," we'll say the memory verse. Each time we say a word of the verse, partners will switch roles.**

Repeat the memory verse with the pulling motions, then let the children continue pulling each other as you sing "This Is My Command" with the Donut Forget CD. After the song, say: **Great singing! Now let's sing "If You're Thirsty." We have a special visitor coming today. Maybe our singing will attract her attention.**

Lead the children in singing "If You're Thirsty" until your woman at the well enters the room. Then stop the CD and move directly into Bible Story Time.

BIBLE STORY TIME

Classroom supplies: Bible
Curriculum supplies: none

Introduce your visitor and let her present the Bible story. Encourage her to comment on the children's singing, then sit near the paper bag well to tell her story. Follow along in the script on page 203. After the woman has said good-bye to the children, say: **Our Bible story came from the book of John.** Open your Bible to John 4 and show it to the children. Then ask:

- **How did Jesus show he was a good friend to the woman?**
- **What are some ways you can be like Jesus with your friends?**

Say: **Jesus wants us to be friends with everybody, even people that others don't like. When people told Jesus to stay away from certain people like the little children and the woman at the well, he didn't listen to them. Jesus is a friend to everyone. He wants you to be like that, too.**

SING-ALONG FUN TIME

Classroom supplies: instruments made during this unit, CD player, spray bottle filled with water, paper towels
Curriculum supplies: Donut Forget CD ("This Is My Command," "Become as a Child," "If You're Thirsty," "You Are My Friend")

Lead the children in singing the unit songs. Let them choose which songs they like best and what instruments or motions they want to use with each song.

Close by singing "Become as a Child." As the children sing the song, lead them in vigorous calisthenics. For example, they might do jumping jacks as they sing "You must become just like a child," then run in place on "To enter the kingdom of God." They could do toe touches on "Let all the little children come to me." Repeat the song and motions more than once if necessary, until the children begin to tire.

Then say: **Whew! That was tiring. We need to rest and be refreshed.**

Gently mist the children with water from the spray bottle. Offer them paper towels to dry off if they want. Say: **Sometimes we get tired and worked up about our problems or the wrong things we've done, just as you're tired right now. Being friends with Jesus is like having refreshing water after a tiring workout. We can always trust our friend Jesus to refresh us and help us do what's right. Let's thank him for that now.**

Pray: **Jesus, thank you for being our friend. Please help us trust you and obey your command to love each other as you have loved us. Amen.**

DONUT FORGET TIME

Classroom supplies: Bible, CD player, paper cups, pot filled with water
Curriculum supplies: Donut Forget CD ("You Are My Friend")

Have the children gather around the well. Set the paper cups and a pot of water on a table or sturdy chair nearby.

Open the Bible to 1 John 4:19-21 and say: **We've been learning from Jesus' example how to be a good friend. Listen to what the Bible says in 1 John 4:19-21.**

Read the verses, then ask:

■ **Why are we supposed to love each other?**

■ **What can you do when you don't feel love for someone?**

Say: **We're supposed to love each other because Jesus does. He died for each one of us. Sometimes we have people in our lives that are hard to love. But God promises to help us. He sent Jesus to be an example and to help us love one another.**

Fill a cup by dipping it into the pot of water. Hold it up and show it to the children. Say: **Let's encourage our special friends with Jesus' love now. As we listen to "You Are My Friend," come up and get a cup of cool water for your partner. Give your partner the water and say, "Jesus loves you."**

Play the song and let the children serve each other water. After everyone has been served, have the children sit with their eyes closed and listen to the song once more. Encourage them to worship God in their hearts as they listen to the words.

When the song is over, pray: **Jesus, thank you for coming to earth so we could know God's love. Thank you for helping us love each other. We ask you to keep teaching us how to be the best of friends. Amen.**

The Woman at the Well

Hello. I want to tell you about a very special friend I met one day at Jacob's well. I was surprised to see him sitting there—most people come to the well in the early morning, before the sun gets hot. That's why I go at noon. Nobody likes me very much, and when people see me they often say mean things about me. I'd rather bear the hot sun than those people's mean insults.

So when I saw this man sitting by the well, I figured he was going to hang around and insult me like everybody else. But instead, he asked me to give him a drink. *Me* give *him* a drink! He obviously didn't know who he was asking. He was Jewish, and I'm a Samaritan. Our people don't hang out together. Besides, no one would want a drink from a person like me.

Well this man, Jesus, told me he could give me living water. I didn't really know what he meant, so I asked him some questions. Jesus told me that if I drank his living water, I'd never be thirsty again. I didn't completely understand about the living water, but I knew one thing: Jesus cared about me, and he wanted to be my friend.

Before I met Jesus, I was lonely and sad because of all the bad things I'd done. But somehow Jesus knew about those things and he loved me anyway. Jesus' friendship changed my life. Ever since I met him, I've spent all my time telling people about what a wonderful friend he is. And now I'm telling you. I hope Jesus can be your friend, too. Good-bye!

203

Donut Forget these great resources!

The Donut Repair Club™ Happy Day® Books

Coloring & Activity Book — With THE DONUT man: and Duncan

Ages 4 to 7

Donut Forget!

22063

Coloring pages, games, and activities reinforce the unit themes covered in "Donut Forget Bible Story Lessons."

When The Donut Repair Club receives an invitation to help out with a nursing home picnic, everybody is thrilled; everybody except Drew. But when one of the residents, Mrs. Rollins, begins to tell Drew stories about her childhood, he realizes that people of all ages are valuable. The Donut Repair Club learns how important it is to help others.

A Happy Day® Book — With THE DONUT man:

The Donut Repair Club™ Helps Out

04285

Coloring & Activity Book — With THE DONUT man: and Duncan

Ages 4 to 7

Around the World

22064

The Donut Man®, Duncan, and the children of The Donut Repair Club travel around the world to tell children that God loves them. Features games, mazes, dot to dots, and more!

When their concert is cancelled, The Donut Repair Club decides to take their donuts to the circus to tell everybody there the greatest news on earth—that God sent his Son for them.

A Happy Day® Book — With THE DONUT man:

The Donut Repair Club™ Tells the Good News

04284

.... The Donut Man® coloring & Activity Books

Bean Sprouts

Growing Kids in God's Light™

www.standardpub.com

Donut Forget to Ask God for Forgiveness

BY THE END OF THIS UNIT, LEARNERS WILL

Know Tell why it is important to confess that we do wrong things.

Feel Feel sorry for doing wrong. Feel thankful for God's forgiveness.

Do Ask God to forgive the wrong things we have done.

MEMORY VERSE

"If we confess our sins, he will forgive our sins. . . . He will make us clean from all the wrongs we have done" (1 John 1:9).

In Jesus' story of the prodigal son, the boy returned home to find his father eager to forgive him. Truly sorry for the wrongs he'd done, he was overwhelmed at the welcome and forgiveness of his father. Likewise, because of Jesus' love and forgiveness, Zaccheus enthusiastically agreed to change his sinful ways. God's plan for forgiveness is the basis for our faith and the life we are called to live in Christ.

Most four- to eight-year-olds are painfully aware of the "bad" things they think or do. They know it's wrong to lie to a friend or disobey a parent. Sometimes it seems they can't help doing these things in spite of themselves. This unit teaches the children that God is ready to forgive them when they're sorry, just as the father forgave his prodigal son and Jesus forgave Zaccheus. Learning about God's forgiveness gives children hope in a troubled world.

	LESSON 1	LESSON 2	LESSON 3	LESSON 4
Center 1	butterflies	storytelling	celebration bells	pigs in a blanket
Center 2	kazoos	tree shakers	edible jewelry	party pinata
Center 3	tree mural	tree leaves	tree fruit	tree decorations
Gathering Time	cocoons & butterflies	washing hearts	good fruit	ready to party
Bible Story Time	Luke 19, puppet	Luke 19, story rhyme	Luke 15, story rhyme	Luke 15, story motions
Sing-Along Fun Time	play kazoos	washing hands	shuffle-hop dance	colored bubbles
Donut Forget Time	memory verse song	forgiveness prayers	eating jewelry	celebration

Donut Forget™ Bible Story Lessons

LEARNING CENTERS

Set up the following activities for the children to do as they arrive. Assign an equal number of children and a teacher or helper to each activity.

At each Learning Center, welcome the children to your class. Make sure you know each child's name. Explain that today you'll be talking about how God forgives us when we do wrong.

Centers 1: Butterflies

Classroom supplies: unused basket-style coffee filters, chenille wires, spring-type clothespins, markers

Curriculum supplies: none

Before class, make a sample butterfly following the instructions below.

Set out markers and show the children how to decorate the coffee filters with a variety of colors. Have each child choose a colored chenille wire. Help the children fold the wire in half around the filter, cinching the filter together in the center to form wings. Then have them form two antennae by twisting the wire together at the top and pulling the ends apart. Show the children how to clip a clothespin to the bottom of the wire for the body of the butterfly. Encourage them to add eyes and to decorate the clothespin bodies with spots, stripes, or other designs.

Have the children make enough butterflies for each child in the class to have one. Set them aside to use during Gathering Time.

As the children work, talk about how God made caterpillars to spin a cocoon and then change into beautiful butterflies. Explain that in today's Bible story they'll learn about how Jesus' love and forgiveness changed a man from bad to good.

Center 2: Kazoos

Classroom supplies: cardboard toilet paper or paper towel tubes, gift wrap, rubber bands, waxed paper, scissors, glue, CD player

Curriculum supplies: Donut Forget CD ("Zaccheus")

Before class, cut pieces of colorful gift wrap into 4 1/2-by-6-inch pieces (or the size of the tubes you use). Cut waxed paper into approximately 4-inch squares. You'll need a piece of gift wrap and a waxed paper square for each child. Make a sample kazoo to show the children.

Help the children make kazoos by gluing the gift wrap pieces to cardboard tubes. Show them how to cover one end of the tube with a piece of wax paper and hold it in place with a rubber band. Show the children how to hum into the other end of the kazoo. As the children work, play "Zaccheus" from the Donut Forget CD. When they finish, let them play their kazoos along with the song.

Have the children make extra kazoos so each child in the class will have one. Since this is a mouth instrument, write the children's names on their kazoos and explain that they should use only their own kazoos.

Set the kazoos aside for use during Gathering Time.

Center 3: Tree Mural

Classroom supplies: green construction paper, brown butcher paper or grocery sacks,
clear tape, stapler, scissors
Curriculum supplies: none

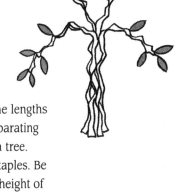

Before class, prepare a tree mural on a wall near the Gathering Time or Bible Story
Time area. Scrunch and twist 6- to 8-foot lengths of brown
butcher paper to form a tree trunk and branches. (If you don't
have brown butcher paper, use paper grocery sacks.)

Form the trunk of the tree by grouping the bottom half of the lengths
together and stapling or taping them. Form the branches by separating
the lengths of paper and spreading them out like branches on a tree.
Mount each length, or branch, to the wall using clear tape or staples. Be
sure to let some of the branches hang down at the level of the height of
your students. Set aside some of the paper for branches the children will
add later.

Point out the tree mural on the wall to the children and explain that they'll be using the tree
during the next several weeks to help tell the Bible stories for the day. Tell them that they'll also
use it to learn about how God forgives us when we do something wrong.

Have the children cut or tear leaf shapes from green construction paper, then tape or staple
the leaves to the branches. While the children work on the leaves, have some of them help you
add one or two more branches to the tree.

GATHERING TIME

Classroom supplies: butterflies from Center 1, kazoos from Center 2
Curriculum supplies: none

Before Gathering Time, tuck the sample butterfly into the sample kazoo that you made. Place
it near you in the Gathering Time area.

Gather everyone around the tree. Invite the children to share what they did at their Learning
Centers.

Say: **Some of you made butterflies. They will help us learn about forgiveness.
If you made a butterfly, flutter your arms like butterfly wings, then sit down.
Good job! If you helped build our beautiful tree, stand up and hold your arms up
tall like branches. Wave your "branches" in the air, then sit down. Great! Some
of you made kazoos. If you made a kazoo, come and help me pass out kazoos to
everyone.**

Give out the kazoos to the children whose names are on them.

Hold up the sample kazoo with the butterfly tucked inside. Hold it so the children can't see
the butterfly. Say: **This kazoo reminds me of a cocoon. What can you tell me about
cocoons?**

Give the children time to respond. Wiggle an index finger and say: **When a little
caterpillar builds a cocoon** (stick your finger inside the cardboard tube) **something
wonderful happens as it rests inside. God changes it into a beautiful butterfly!**

Pull out the butterfly and show it to the children. Straighten out its wings and say: **When
butterflies are newly hatched, they have to unfold their wings from the tight
little cocoon and stretch out before they're ready to fly.**

Show the butterfly to the children and say: **Now let's all try this. Those of you who
made butterflies at your Center can help me pass out a butterfly to everyone.**

When everyone has a butterfly, show them how to gently tuck the butterflies into their kazoos. Ask: **When you do something you're not supposed to do, how do you feel?** Give the children time to respond, then say: **When we do wrong things, it makes us feel bad. Maybe we'd like to be like this little caterpillar and hide inside a cocoon!**

Have the children put an index finger inside their kazoo cocoon, but tell them not to pull out their butterfly just yet. Continue: **When we say "I'm sorry" to God, he forgives us and makes us beautiful on the inside. Our butterflies remind us that he can change us, too!**

Have the children pull the butterflies out of their cocoons and straighten out their wings. Help them take turns clipping their butterflies to the tree with the clothespins. Set the kazoos aside to use during Sing-Along Fun Time.

When everyone is seated again, say: **Look at our beautiful tree! It's all dressed up with pretty green leaves and your beautiful butterflies! Today we're going to learn how Jesus changed a bad man named Zaccheus into a good guy. Let's find out what happened!**

BIBLE STORY TIME

Classroom supplies: Bible, tree from Center 3, CD player, paper bag, glue, scissors, crayons
Curriculum supplies: Donut Forget CD ("Zaccheus"), photocopy of Zaccheus puppet pieces (page 221)

Before class, make the paper bag puppet by gluing the top of Zaccheus' face to the bottom of the bag. Glue the bottom of his face below the fold.

Open your Bible to Luke 19:1-9 and show it to the children. Say: **Our Bible story comes from the book of Luke. One day Jesus was walking through a town where lots of people had gathered to see him. Among the crowd of people was a man named Zaccheus. He wanted to see Jesus. But he was so short he couldn't see above the heads of the people! So he climbed a tree to see better. When Jesus came by, he looked up in the tree and said, "Zaccheus, come down! I want to visit you at your house today!"**

Zaccheus was happy and excited. But he was nervous, too, because he had done some bad things. His job was to collect taxes from people, but he often took more money than he was supposed to. He kept the money for himself.

This made people angry. They couldn't understand why Jesus would want to see Zaccheus. But Jesus loved him. Zaccheus could see Jesus loved him, and he said, "I'm sorry for what I've done. I will repay everything I've taken." He was sorry and Jesus forgave him.

Hold up the Zaccheus puppet and say: **Let's listen to a fun song now that tells this story. As I hold the Zaccheus puppet in front of me, hold your hand in front of you, too. When I move Zaccheus, you move your hand, too and do what I do.**

Play "Zaccheus" from the Donut Forget CD. Hold the puppet in front of you as the story is told. On the chorus, hold the puppet near the tree and make it pretend to climb the tree. At the end of the story, lower the puppet to show the children that Zaccheus climbed out of the tree and followed Jesus.

When the song is over, put the puppet aside and ask: **What bad things did Zaccheus do? How did Zaccheus change after being with Jesus?**

Say: **Zaccheus changed like a caterpillar changes to a butterfly—he changed from doing bad to doing good. Jesus will change us, too, when we say we're sorry for the wrong things we do.**

SING-ALONG FUN TIME

Classroom supplies: kazoos made in Center 2, CD player
Curriculum supplies: Donut Forget CD ("Zaccheus," "A-ha! lelujah" from Unit 7, "Good News" from Unit 9)

Lead the children in singing the familiar song "A-ha! lelujah." Encourage them to clap and do other motions that the words suggest. Then pass out the kazoos to their owners and hum along as you play the song "Good News."

Form two groups. Play the song "Zaccheus." At the chorus, have the first group sing, "I've got to see Jesus." Have the second group sing, "I climbed up a tree." Then have both groups join together and shout, "My name is Zaccheus!"

Set the kazoos aside for the children to take home at the end of class.

DONUT FORGET TIME

Classroom supplies: Bible, several blankets, sheets, or bath towels, CD player
Curriculum supplies: Donut Forget CD ("If We Confess")

Have the children sit down around you and say: **We know that Zaccheus took money from people that didn't belong to him. That was wrong. The wrong things we do are called sins. What are some things we do that are wrong?**

Give the children time to respond. Be sure to tell something you have done for which you needed forgiveness.

BITE IDEA
Use a sponge and dip it in water to soak up **all** the water. Talk about how Jesus took our punishment.

Open up your Bible to 1 John 1:9 and say: **The Bible says in 1 John 1:9 that "if we confess our sins, he will forgive our sins. . . . He will make us clean from all the wrongs we have done."**

When Jesus forgives us, we are set free—just like our butterflies are set free after being inside that tight little cocoon. Let's close our eyes and listen to the song that has this verse in it. While you listen, silently tell God the things you've done wrong and thank him for his forgiveness.

Play "If We Confess" from the Donut Forget CD. When the song is over, have the children wrap themselves in the towels and blankets you brought. If you don't have enough for everyone, have the others pretend to be wrapped in a cocoon. Play the song again and have the children slowly emerge from their blanket cocoons as they sing along.

Repeat the game so everyone has a chance to use a blanket. Then say: **Pretend that now your blankets are butterfly wings and fly around the room. Say, "Thank you, Jesus, for forgiving me!" Then fly over to the door because it's time to go home!**

As the children leave, give them their kazoos to take home.

Donut Forget™ Bible Story Lessons

209

LEARNING CENTERS

Set up the following activities for the children to do as they arrive. Assign an equal number of children and a teacher or helper to each activity.

At each Learning Center, welcome the children to your class. Make sure you know each child's name. Explain that today you'll be talking about how God forgives us when we do wrong.

Center 1: Storytelling

Classroom supplies: children's story Bible with large colorful pictures
Curriculum supplies: none

Place the children's Bible on the floor or table where everyone can see it. Explain that after Zaccheus met Jesus and visited with him, Zaccheus changed. He was sorry for the wrong things he had done. Jesus forgave him and washed his heart clean.

Hold up the story Bible and open it to a picture of a familiar Bible story, such as the lost sheep. Tell the children that you're going to pretend to visit with Jesus like Zaccheus did.

Point at the picture and ask for a volunteer to tell the story to the others. (Young children often hear Bible stories but don't get a chance to tell them to others.) Then ask the children to think about what Jesus would want us to learn from the story if he were visiting with us. For example, he might want us to learn from the lost sheep that he loves us and cares for each one of us, just like the shepherd loved and cared for the sheep.

Repeat this exercise with several stories about Jesus. Look for themes of forgiveness wherever possible. Be prepared to explain the stories yourself if the children choose stories that aren't familiar to them.

Center 2: Tree Shakers

Classroom supplies: toilet paper or paper towel tubes, small paper plates, stapler, uncooked popcorn or rice, green construction paper, green markers or crayons, glue, clear tape, CD player
Curriculum supplies: Donut Forget CD ("Zaccheus")

Give each child a cardboard tube and a small paper plate. Show the children how to make tree-shaped shakers by pinching one end of their cardboard tubes closed. Then have them fold their paper plates in half and staple them to the pinched end of the tubes. The cardboard tube is the trunk of the tree and the plate is its top.

Put a tablespoon of uncooked popcorn or rice into the open end of each child's cardboard tube. Then pinch the open end in the direction perpendicular to the previously pinched end and staple it closed. (If both ends are stapled the same direction, the tube will be flat. If the ends are stapled in different directions, the tube forms a pocket for the popcorn to shake.)

Encourage the children to decorate their tree shakers by gluing small green paper leaves on them or coloring them with green markers.

As you work, help the children review the details of Zaccheus' story. Remind them that Jesus forgives them when they're sorry, just as he forgave Zaccheus. Play "Zaccheus" as the children finish their work and clean up.

Center 3: Tree Mural

Classroom supplies: brown construction paper, clear tape, CD player
Curriculum supplies: Donut Forget CD ("Zaccheus")

Have the children tear brown leaves from the construction paper, then crumple the leaves slightly. Tape the leaves to the branches of the tree mural. Listen to the song "Zaccheus" as you work.

When the leaves are all attached to the tree, ask the children to describe what the tree looks like. Point out that the tree looks scraggly and sick with all the shriveled brown leaves. Explain that when we do wrong things, our hearts get filled up with old, dead sin. Tell the children that in today's lesson, they'll find out how our heart gets washed clean when we tell God we're sorry for the bad things we've done.

GATHERING TIME

Classroom supplies: Bible, two heart shapes cut from white fabric or felt, permanent marker, tub of soapy water, CD player
Curriculum supplies: Donut Forget CD ("Bath Song")

Before class, cut two large hearts (about 6 to 8 inches) from white fabric or felt. Put one heart in your Bible to mark 1 John 1:9.

Have the children sit down in the Gathering Time area. Invite them to tell you about the things they made at their Learning Centers. Say: **Some of you pretended to visit with Jesus. If you helped tell each other stories about Jesus, say, "Jesus loves me!" Some of you helped make tree shakers. If you made a tree shaker, say, "Shake, shake, shake!" Some of you helped decorate our tree today. If you helped put leaves on the tree, wave your hands in the air.**

Say: **Good job at your Learning Centers! We're all learning about forgiveness today. We all need God's forgiveness, because we all do wrong things sometimes. The Bible calls the wrong things we do sin. When we do wrong things, our heart gets dirty with sin.**

Hold up one of the hearts. Tell about a wrong thing you've done, then make an "X" on the fabric heart with a dark marker. Then say: **I'm going to pass around the heart and marker. When it comes to you, think of something you've done wrong. If you want to share it with us, you can. Or you can keep it to yourself. Either way, make an X on the heart to represent the wrong thing you're thinking of. Then pass the heart to the next person.**

When everyone has marked on the heart, hold it up and say: **Oh dear. Our heart is all dirty with sin. Let's see if we can wash it clean.**

Set out the tub of soapy water and invite the children to help you scrub the heart clean. The permanent marker won't come out. Say: **Just as we couldn't get the marks out of this heart, we can't get rid of the sin in our hearts on our own. But if we tell God we're sorry for the wrong things we've done, something wonderful happens. Listen to what that is.**

Open your Bible to 1 John 1:9. Say: **Our memory verse from 1 John 1:9 says, "If we confess our sins, he will forgive our sins. . . . He will make us clean from all the wrongs we have done."**

BITE IDEA
If you feel it's appropriate for your class tell them that the "super soap" in the "Bath Song" is the blood of Jesus.

Pull out the clean heart and show it to the children. Say: **God's forgiveness makes us clean! Let's listen to a song about that. Then we'll hear how Zaccheus was forgiven for the wrong things he had done.**

Play "Bath Song" from the Donut Forget CD. Let the children listen and sing along if they want. Then continue with the lesson.

Donut Forget™
Bible Story Lessons

211

BIBLE STORY TIME

Classroom supplies: Bible
Curriculum supplies: none

Open your Bible to Luke 19 and show it to the children. Say: **Our story about Zaccheus comes from the book of Luke in the Bible. Today we're going to do a fun action rhyme to review that story.**

Have the children stand with you. As you say the following rhyme, encourage the children to imitate your motions and repeat your words.

(Cup hands around mouth.)
Here comes Jesus! Here comes Jesus!
That's the news they heard one day.

(Gesture as if calling someone to come here.)
Hurry, Zaccheus! Hurry, Zaccheus!
Come and see him pass your way.

(Pat your legs to make a running sound.)
Zaccheus ran and ran and ran,
But found he couldn't see.

(Use hands to pretend to climb up a tree, one over the other.)
So up and up and up he climbed
To peek out from a tree.

(Hold hand in front of you as if signaling someone to stop.)
Then Jesus stopped down on the road
And looked up at the man.

(Cup hands around mouth.)
He said, "Zaccheus, come on down
As quickly as you can!"

(Use hands to pretend to climb down a tree, one under the other.)
Down, down, down Zaccheus slid
Till on his feet he stood.

(Hold hands out, palms up, as if surrendering.)
He said, "I'm sorry for my sins.
From now on I'll be good!"

(Hold your hands over your heart.)
Then God forgave him of his sins
And washed his heart so clean.

(Reach out to shake the children's hands.)
Zaccheus lived an honest life
And was no longer mean.

212

Have the children sit down and ask: **What mean things did Zaccheus do before he met Jesus? How did his actions change after he met Jesus?** Let the children respond, then ask: **How can Jesus help us?**

Say: **Let's get ready now to sing some really great songs!**

SING-ALONG FUN TIME

Use the **Duncan** puppet and the script from the Donut Forget Songbook to talk about the memory verse, 1 John 1:9.

Classroom supplies: tree shakers from Center 2, tub filled with warm soapy water, potting soil, several towels, CD player
Curriculum supplies: Donut Forget CD ("Zaccheus," "Bath Song")

Let the children shake the tree shakers as you sing "Zaccheus." As the children sing the song, have them stand up and sit down alternately each time they sing the words "I" or "I'm" or "I've."

After the song, say: **Before Zaccheus met Jesus, he thought only about himself. But Jesus forgave him for being selfish. Then Zaccheus gave money to the poor and helped others. Our memory verse tells us that God "will make us clean from all the wrong we have done."** Let's review the song we learned earlier about God's forgiveness.

Play "The Bath Song" through once. Then set out a shallow pan of potting soil, a tub of soapy water, and several towels. Invite the children to rub their hands in the potting soil. Encourage them to get as dirty as they want (or as dirty as their church clothes will allow).

Talk about how sin makes our hearts dirty, but God's forgiveness can make us clean again. Have the children wash their hands in the soapy water as you sing "Bath Song" one more time.

DONUT FORGET TIME

Classroom supplies: Bible, brown leaves from tree mural, trash can, CD player
Curriculum supplies: Donut Forget CD ("If We Confess," "How Great You Are" from Unit 6)

Seat the children around the mural tree. Open your Bible to Psalm 86:5. Say: **In Psalm 86, King David prayed to God and said, "Lord, you are kind and forgiving. You have great love for those who call to you."**

Point to the tree and say: **Today we covered our tree with wrinkled, brown leaves. How does that make our tree look? It looks dull and kind of ugly, doesn't it? These leaves are like the wrong things we've done. When we tell God we're sorry, he forgives us.**

Remove a leaf from the tree. Play "If We Confess" quietly in the background as you say: **Let's take a minute now and think of wrong things we've said or done and tell God we're sorry.**

Give the children time to reflect as the song plays. Then encourage each child to pick a brown leaf off the tree. As the children pick their leaves, have them say, "Jesus, thank you for forgiving me."

Pray: **Dear God, we're sorry for the wrong things we've done. Thank you for forgiving us and making us clean on the inside.**

Pass around the trash can and have everyone throw away the brown leaves. Say: **Once we say we're sorry, we don't have to worry anymore, just like we don't have to look at these brown leaves anymore! Now look at our tree—all bright and green again! God's forgiveness is great!**

If time allows, close by singing "How Great You Are."

Donut Forget™ Bible Story Lessons

LEARNING CENTERS

Set up the following activities for the children to do as they arrive. Assign an equal number of children and a teacher or helper to each activity.

At each Learning Center, welcome the children to your class. Make sure you know each child's name. Explain that today you'll be talking about how God forgives us when we do wrong.

Center 1: Celebration Bells

Classroom supplies: Styrofoam drinking cups, chenille wire, jingle bells, small stickers, markers
Curriculum supplies: Donut Forget CD ("We're Gonna Have a Party")

Point out that when God forgives our sins, we feel happy and want to celebrate. Explain that today's Bible story is about a family who celebrated forgiveness. Tell the children they'll be making celebration bells to use during Sing-Along Fun Time.

Show the children how to attach a jingle bell to one end of a chenille wire. (Make sure to purchase bells that are large enough to jingle once the wire is in place.) Help the children twist or knot the chenille wire about 2 inches above the bell. Have the children turn their cups upside down. Then have them poke the wire up through the cup until the wire knot is at the bottom of the inside of the cup. Show the children how to loop the excess wire to make a handle on the outside of the cup.

Encourage the children to decorate the outside of the cups with small stickers and markers. Set the bells aside to use during Sing-Along Fun Time.

Center 2: Edible Jewelry

Classroom supplies: yarn, cereal and candy with holes in them, bowls
Curriculum supplies: none

Before class, cut yarn into a variety of lengths from 10 to 20 inches long. Put the cereal and candy in separate bowls.

Remind the children that God is ready and waiting to forgive us when we say we're sorry. Tell them that today's Bible story is about a father who celebrated his son returning home by giving him beautiful jewelry.

Set out the lengths of yarn and the cereal and candy. Help each child tie a piece of cereal to one end of a piece of yarn. (This will keep the other items from sliding off.) Then have the children string the cereal and candy on the yarn to make necklaces. When the necklaces are as long as they want, tie the ends together. Use shorter lengths for bracelets and rings.

Have the children make enough jewelry so that every child in the class has at least one piece. Set the jewelry aside and explain to the children that they'll get to eat the jewelry later in the lesson.

Center 3: Tree Mural

Classroom supplies: red and orange construction paper, small paper plate or large plastic lid, pencil, scissors, stapler, newsprint, basket
Curriculum supplies: none

Before class, use a pencil and a small paper plate to trace 6-inch red and orange construction paper circles. If you have mostly young children, you may want to cut out the circles. You'll need two red or orange circles for each child.

Set out the red and orange circles and several large sheets of newsprint. Help each child staple two red (apple) or two orange shapes together, leaving several inches open. Then have the children gently stuff the shapes with strips of newsprint and staple them closed. Have the

214

children make extras, so you'll have at least one piece of fruit for each child in your class.

Explain to the children that later in the lesson you'll use the fruit they are making to talk about God's forgiveness. Remind the children that God loves us and wants to forgive us when we say we're sorry for the wrong things we do.

Set the finished fruit in a basket near the tree mural.

GATHERING TIME

Classroom supplies: fruit from Center 3, stapler, tape
Curriculum supplies: none

Invite one volunteer from each Learning Center to stand and explain what they did at that Learning Center. After each volunteer shares with the class, have the children who participated in that Center also stand and have the rest of the class clap for them. Continue until all three Centers are explained and everyone has had a chance to be clapped for.

Distribute a piece of fruit made during Center 3 to each child. Say: **In the Bible, in Colossians 1:10, it says that if we live to please the Lord, we "will produce fruit in every good work." We've been learning that when we say "I'm sorry," God forgives us. That's good fruit! God's forgiveness makes me feel ready to do good things for him. I'm going to name some actions that are fruits in our lives. If you think what I say is a good fruit, hold your apple or orange up high. If you think the example is a bad fruit, keep your piece of fruit in your lap.**

Read the following examples, allowing time for the children to respond by either holding their fruit in the air or in their laps.

At game time you say, "Me first!"
You hold the door open for your friend.
You tell your brother or sister, "Get out of here!"
You help clean up a mess you made.
You say, "I'm sorry."
You tell your friend his clothes are ugly.
You say, "I forgive you."

Say: **In today's Bible story, we're going to learn about a son who told his father he was sorry for all the wrong things he'd done. He had lots of bad fruit. But when he said, "I'm sorry," that was good fruit. Let's attach our pieces of fruit to the tree mural and get ready to hear our Bible story.**

Help the children staple or tape their pieces of fruit to the tree mural.

BIBLE STORY TIME

Classroom supplies: Bible, two sheets of paper, markers, CD player
Curriculum supplies: Donut Forget CD ("We're Gonna Have a Party")

Before class, draw a happy face on one piece of paper and a frowning face on the other. Tape the faces on opposite walls in your classroom.

Gather the children in the center of the room. Point out the happy and frowning faces on the walls. Open your Bible to Luke 15:11-31 and show it to the children. Say: **Our Bible story comes from the book of Luke. I'm going to read a rhyme that tells this Bible story. When I pause, you decide if the people are happy or unhappy in that part of the story. If you think they're happy, run and stand next to the happy face. If you think the people are sad, stand next to the frowning face.**

Read the following rhyme. In between each stanza, pause and let the children move to the

215

wall of their choice. Don't worry if some of them stay at the same wall or if the children don't all agree.

Now once there was a dad
and he had two older boys.
Their house was filled with laughter
and a whole bunch of joy.

Pause while the children move to one of the walls.

But then one day the younger son
walked up and spoke to Pop.
He said, "Hey, give me half your gold—
you know it's quite a lot!"

Pause.

Now actually, in Bible times,
this was okay to do.
So Pop split all his stuff in half,
for young son number two.

Pause.

The younger son then ran away.
He ran right out the door.
He spent his money everywhere
and soon he had no more.

Pause.

Now the son was very sad;
his money was all gone.
He had no food! He had no coins!
He'd spent them one by one.

Pause.

One day while he was feeding pigs,
he realized he'd done wrong.
So off he ran, back home again.
It didn't take him long.

Pause.

Pop saw him coming down the road;
his heart filled up with joy.
Pop ran to him and hugged him tight.
"Welcome home, my boy!"

Pause.

The son said, "Wait! I'm sorry, Pop,
for all the stuff I've done."
And Pop said, "I forgive you, Son!
Let's celebrate—you're HOME!"

Let the children run to the happy or frowning faces, then have them return to the story area and sit down. Ask:

■ **What wrong things did the son do?**

■ **What did the father do when he saw the son coming back?**

Say: **The boy's father loved him so much he couldn't wait to forgive him! The Bible says he was so happy that he gave his son a robe, a ring, and a party. God's love for you and me is like that. No matter what we've done, God is always happy to forgive us. Let's sing a new song called "We're Gonna Have a Party" to celebrate God's love.**

Play "We're Gonna Have a Party." Stop the CD several times throughout the song and encourage the children to move to either the happy face or the frowning face.

At the end of the song, have all the children gather near the happy face. Say: **I'm so happy that God forgives us! Let's sing some more fun songs to celebrate God's forgiveness.**

SING-ALONG FUN TIME

Classroom supplies: celebration bells from Center 1, tree shakers from Lesson 2, CD player
Curriculum supplies: Donut Forget CD ("We're Gonna Have a Party," "Bath Song)

Distribute the celebration bells and tree shakers, then lead the children in singing "Bath Song" and "We're Gonna Have a Party." Remind the children that the Bible story about the father and son teaches us that God is ready to forgive us when we say we're sorry.

Set the instruments aside and have the children form a line. Have each child hold the waist of the child in front of her. Have the first child in the line grab your waist. Lead the children in a shuffle-hop dance around the room as you sing. Shuffle your feet as you sing the verses. When you sing the chorus, jump forward, back, then forward again as you sing "party, party, party." Encourage a festive atmosphere as you sing and dance with the children. God's forgiveness is something to celebrate!

If time allows, repeat the shuffle-hop and let the children take turns leading the line.

DONUT FORGET TIME

Classroom supplies: Bible, edible jewelry from Center 2, CD player
Curriculum supplies: Donut Forget CD ("If We Confess," "Only One" from Unit 10)

Open the Bible to Nehemiah 9:17 and show it to the children. Say: **In the book of Nehemiah it says, "You are a forgiving God. You are kind and full of mercy. You do not become angry quickly. And you have great love." That's a great promise for us. Even though sometimes we sin and do wrong things, God's not angry with us. He's happy with us! That makes me want to celebrate!**

Have the children who worked at Center 2 pass out a piece of edible jewelry to every child. While they pass out the jewelry and put it on, sing "If We Confess." Let the children eat their jewelry, if they want, until the song is finished.

Then say: **I'm so glad God forgives us. During Gathering Time we talked about good fruit in our lives. Another good fruit is to worship God and tell him we love him. Let's sing "Only One" and worship God for loving us and forgiving us.**

As you sing "Only One," encourage the children to hold up one finger and point to the sky each time you sing the phrases "only one" and "only him."

LEARNING CENTERS

Set up the following activities for the children to do as they arrive. Assign an equal number of children and a teacher or helper to each activity.

At each Learning Center, welcome the children to your class. Make sure you know each child's name. Explain that today you'll be talking about how God forgives us when we do wrong.

Center 1: Pigs in a Blanket

Classroom supplies: hot dogs, plastic knives, prepared biscuit dough, rolling pin, cookie sheet or toaster oven pan, oven or toaster oven, CD player
Curriculum supplies: Donut Forget CD ("We're Gonna Have a Party")

Before class, purchase or prepare biscuit dough. Arrange to use the oven in your church kitchen to bake the "pigs in a blanket." If your church doesn't have a kitchen you can use, arrange to bring in a toaster oven to bake the snacks.

Review the story of the prodigal son. Remind the children that when the son ran out of money, he got a job feeding pigs. Explain that they'll be making pigs-in-a-blanket snacks.

Form two groups. Have one group help you roll out the biscuit dough on a clean table. Have the other group use plastic knives to cut hot dogs into halves or thirds. Cut the biscuit dough into triangular pieces that are slightly larger than the hot dog pieces. Show the children how to wrap the dough around the hot dogs to create "blankets" for the "pigs." While the children are working, play "We're Gonna Have a Party" from the Donut Forget CD.

Have a helper bake the snacks while the children participate in the rest of the lesson.

Center 2: Party Piñata

Classroom supplies: large paper grocery bag, small resealable plastic bags (enough for each child in the classroom), treats such as candy or small toys, duct tape, markers, stickers
Curriculum supplies: none

Have some of the children fill the small plastic bags with equal amounts of candy or toys. Make sure the filled bags are completely sealed. Have other children decorate the grocery bag with markers and stickers. Explain that they'll be having a party today to celebrate God's forgiveness. Tell the children they're making a piñata for the party.

BITE IDEA
If you have a large class, fill some of the treat bags before class. You may need to make two piñatas to hold all the treats.

As the children work, help them think of other times in the Bible when God forgave people for their sins. Remind them that God is always ready to forgive them when they're sorry.

When the grocery bag is decorated, have the children put the individual treat bags inside it. Tape the bag closed and set it near the tree mural.

Center 3: Tree Mural

Classroom supplies: crepe paper, balloons, clear tape, curling ribbon, CD player
Curriculum supplies: Donut Forget CD ("We're Gonna Have a Party")

Let the children use crepe paper, curling ribbon, and balloons to decorate the tree mural and the area around it for your party. Hang crepe paper streamers from the tree branches, then blow up the balloons and use curling ribbon to tie them to the tree. Blow up and attach at least one balloon for each child.

Remind the children that in last week's Bible story, the father gave his son a party when the son said he was sorry. Tell them that God forgives us, too, and that today they'll have a party to celebrate God's forgiveness.

As you decorate, play the song, "We're Gonna Have a Party."

GATHERING TIME

Classroom supplies: classroom tree mural
Curriculum supplies: none

Invite all the children to sit on the floor near the tree mural. Say: **Today we're having a party! What are we going to celebrate?**

Give the children time to offer their suggestions, then say: **We're happy because we know that God forgives us when we do wrong. We're going to celebrate God's forgiveness. You helped us get ready for the party with the things you made and did at your Learning Centers. Tell us what you did.**

Have several children explain the things they did to get ready for the party. Then say: **You all worked hard to get ready for our party! Let's listen to our Bible story now and hear again about the son who told his father he was sorry.**

BIBLE STORY TIME

Classroom supplies: Bible, party hats and party horns for each child in the class, marker, crepe paper streamers, cups, napkins, pitcher of juice, snacks from Center 1, CD player
Curriculum supplies: Donut Forget CD ("We're Gonna Have a Party")

Before class, cut an 18-inch length of crepe paper for each child. Arrange for a helper to prepare a party area for the children. If the weather permits, you may want to have your party outdoors. If the weather isn't favorable, set up the party in the Learning Center area. Have the helper set out cups, napkins, a pitcher of juice, and the baked pigs-in-a-blanket snacks.

Distribute the party hats, horns, and streamers to the children. Write each child's name on her horn. Encourage the children to use only their own horns to prevent germs from spreading.

Open your Bible to Luke 15:11-31 and show it to the children. Say: **Our Bible story comes from the book of Luke. You can help me tell the story by using your hats, horns, and streamers. Copy my motions as I say this rhyme.**

The son asked the father to give him half his gold.
(Hold up a streamer.)

The father gave him half, as the story was told.
(Rip the streamers in half.)

The son ran away and tried to have a good time.
(Put your streamers down and swing your party hat in the air.)

He spent all his money till he didn't have a dime.
(Put your hat down and pretend to cry.)

He finally got a job feeding pods to the pigs.
(Use your horn "pig" to eat out of the hat "feeding trough.")

Then he ran back home 'cause his problems were so big!
(Put horn and hat down and pat your knees as if running.)

The father hugged his son, happy he was home.
(Put the hat on.)

The son said, "I'm sorry for everything I've done."
(Bow head as if sorry.)

The father then forgave him for making his mistakes.
(Wave both streamers in the air.)

They had a great big party to laugh and celebrate!
(Blow horn.)

219

When you finish the rhyme, sing "We're Gonna Have a Party." Encourage the children to play their party horns during the chorus.

When the song is finished, invite one or two children to tell the story in their own words. Then ask:

- **What did the son do that was wrong?**
- **What do the father's actions tell us about God?**

Say: **Jesus told this story because he wants us to know that whenever we say we're sorry for the wrong things we do, he is ready to forgive us. He loves you so much!**

SING-ALONG FUN TIME

Classroom supplies: instruments made during this unit, water, light corn syrup, liquid dish soap, food coloring, bubble wand, CD player
Curriculum supplies: Donut Forget CD ("Zaccheus," "Bath Song," "We're Gonna Have a Party," "If We Confess")

Before class, mix up a batch of colored bubbles. Mix 1/4 cup light corn syrup and 1/2 cup liquid dish soap with 5 cups of water. Add a few drops of food coloring.

Bring out the instruments the children have made during this unit. Lead the children in singing "Zaccheus" and "If We Confess." Encourage them to take turns playing the various instruments.

When you're ready to sing "Bath Song," bring out the colored bubbles. Say: **Here are some super-fun colored soap bubbles to remind us that Jesus washes us clean with the super soap of his forgiveness.** Blow bubbles at the children as they sing. Then let kids take turns blowing the bubbles.

Repeat the shuffle-hop dance from Lesson 3 as you sing "We're Gonna Have a Party." Let the children take turns leading the shuffle. On the last time through, lead the line to your party area.

BITE IDEA
If you have time and the weather permits, move the piñata outdoors and hang it from a rope on a swing set or jungle gym. Use a baseball bat and have blindfolded children take turns swatting at the piñata until it bursts open and the treats fall to the ground. Make sure each child gets an individual treat bag.

DONUT FORGET TIME

Classroom supplies: instruments made during this unit, snacks from Center 1, piñata from Center 2, pitcher of juice, cups, napkins, CD player
Curriculum supplies: Donut Forget CD ("We're Gonna Have a Party")

Have the children gather around the table your helper has set up. Say: **We're glad God forgives us. Let's take a moment to thank him before we start our celebration.**

Pray: **Thank you, God, for loving us and forgiving us. Help us remember to come to you when we've done something wrong. Help us to say we're sorry and to receive your forgiveness. Amen.**

Let the children help themselves to cups of juice and the pigs-in-a-blanket snacks. As they enjoy the snacks, play "We're Gonna Have a Party" or any other unit songs the children request. When the children finish their snacks, top off your celebration by opening the piñata and distributing the treats. Let the children choose an instrument to take home, as well as the butterflies and any other items from the tree they want. Encourage a happy atmosphere of celebration!

Give kids more than just morsels of wisdom.
Give them Donuts!

THE CELEBRATION HOUSE
In this fun-filled episode, The Donut Repair Club learns about working together and the joy of a servant's heart in an entertaining way. Your children will laugh along when Duncan gets dunked, and watch a moving live dramatization of Mary, Martha, and Jesus.
Code: IKV002

CAMP HARMONY
Join The Donut Repair Club as they go to Camp Harmony with exciting adventures, outdoor fun, and fireside story songs! Watch as the Repair Club learns how we can all get along.
Code: IKV007

THE RESURRECTION CELEBRATION
The Donut Repair Club learns the importance of Jesus' life as they prepare for a very special play at their church. From the playful puppet song "The Mustard Seed" to the poignant performance of "The Last Supper," your children will learn about the importance of the Resurrection.
Code: IKV006

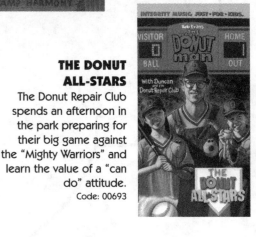

THE DONUT ALL-STARS
The Donut Repair Club spends an afternoon in the park preparing for their big game against the "Mighty Warriors" and learn the value of a "can do" attitude.
Code: 00693

ON THE AIR
Lights! Camera! Action! Join The Donut Man, The Donut Repair Club, and Duncan for an exciting live television broadcast on The Donut Satellite Network. Amid the fun, the kids and Duncan learn that Jesus is the real star of the show.
Code: 02963

AFTER SCHOOL
In this episode, The Donut Man, Duncan, and Mary teach troubled kids that God's love is greater than any wrong they could ever do.
Code: 10413

THE REPAIR SHOP
The Donut Man, Duncan, and The Donut Repair Club open The Repair Shop. The Club learns the basics of Salvation as they learn to fix broken toys and broken hearts.
Code: 09453

To locate the Christian bookstore nearest you,
call 1-800-991-7747.

www.integritymusic.com   www.donutman.net

© 1999 Integrity Incorporated

INTEGRITY MUSIC.
JUST FOR
kids

Donut Forget to Love Each Other

BY THE END OF THIS UNIT, LEARNERS WILL

Know Describe who the church is and what they do.

Feel Feel excited to be a part of the church.

Do Show love to someone in Jesus' church.

MEMORY VERSE

"If we love each other, God lives in us. If we love each other, God's love has reached its goal" (1 John 4:12).

Just before Jesus ascended to heaven, he promised to send a helper to be with his followers on earth. Even though the followers had the promise of the Holy Spirit, they must have been surprised when a loud rushing wind swept through their gathering and "tongues of fire" appeared. The excitement continued to grow as believers began speaking in different languages to spread the good news of Jesus to all who had gathered in Jerusalem. Three thousand members were added to the church that day, but many more were added later as Peter, Paul, and others traveled far and wide to spread the gospel.

Being a part of God's church is exciting! In these lessons, the children will discover that the church isn't just a place they come on Sundays. The church is filled with loving, caring, sharing people just like them. Teach the children the joy of being part of Jesus' church.

	LESSON 1	LESSON 2	LESSON 3	LESSON 4
Center 1	flame sponge prints	Donut Forget rhyme	prayer walk	church chain poster
Center 2	flame cupcakes	wind stick	pan flutes	fruit salad
Center 3	Barnabas project	project for teens	project for staff	story glove puppets
Gathering Time	heart bottles	people church	prayer walk	display church poster
Bible Story Time	Acts 2, sound effects	Acts 2, story rhyme	Acts 12, act it out	Acts 2, 12, story gloves
Sing-Along Fun Time	story song motions	sharing the wind stick	pan flutes & high fives	passing the wind stick
Donut Forget Time	church birthday party	deliver the project	prayer cards	project presentation

Donut Forget™ Bible Story Lessons

223

LEARNING CENTERS

Set up the following activities for the children to do as they arrive. Assign an equal number of children and a teacher or helper to each activity.

At each Learning Center, welcome the children to your class. Make sure you know each child's name. Explain that today you'll be learning how the church began.

Center 1: Flame Sponge Prints

Classroom supplies: orange tempera paint, pie pan, sponges, scissors, dish soap, light colored construction paper, markers, CD player

Curriculum supplies: Donut Forget CD ("They Had to Wait")

Before class, cut sponges into flame shapes. Mix orange tempera paint with a few drops of dish soap for easier cleanup.

Tell the children that today they'll hear how God sent his Holy Spirit to the believers in the early church. Have the children listen to "They Had to Wait." Explain that the "little tongues of fire" were God's way of showing people a visible sign of the invisible Holy Spirit.

BITE IDEA
Cut out the flame prints and attach each to a cardboard band to make headdresses for the kids to wear during Bible Story Time.

Set out the construction paper, flame sponges, and a pie pan of orange tempera paint. Have the children draw a line of people along the bottom of the paper. Then show them how to print flames over the people's heads. As the children work, play "They Had to Wait."

Set the finished flame print pictures aside to dry.

Center 2: Flame Cupcakes

Classroom supplies: cake mix, muffin tin, cupcake wrappers, prepared frosting, candy corns, orange sprinkles, birthday candles, CD player

Curriculum supplies: Donut Forget CD ("They Had to Wait")

Before class, bake a cupcake for every child in your class.

Explain to the children that today they'll hear about Pentecost, the birthday of the church. Tell them they'll be making special cupcakes to celebrate. Have the children listen to "They Had to Wait." Explain that the "little tongues of fire" were signs that God's Holy Spirit had come.

Set out the cupcakes, frosting, plastic knives, orange sprinkles, and candy corns. Have the children decorate the cupcakes with frosting, orange sprinkles, and candy corn "flames." Then have them stick a birthday candle into each cupcake.

Set the cupcakes aside to eat later in the lesson.

Center 3: Barnabas Project

Classroom supplies: several clean empty quart- or liter-sized plastic bottles, colored construction paper or craft foam, curling ribbon, chenille wire, scissors, red hot candies (heart-shaped if possible), colored electrical tape, CD player

Curriculum supplies: Donut Forget CD ("God Lives in Us")

Tell the children that during this unit they'll learn that people in the church love and encourage each other. Point out that a man named Barnabas was a great encourager to the people in the early church. Read Acts 11:23-26 to give the children a little more information about Barnabas. Tell the children that each week Center 3 will help prepare a special "Barnabas Project" to encourage a group of people in your church. Today's Barnabas Project will go to the babies in your church nursery.

Set out the empty bottles and other supplies. Help the children cut out two construction paper or craft foam hearts for each bottle. Show them how to roll up the hearts so they'll fit through the opening, then push the hearts into the bottle. Have other children cut 12-inch lengths of curling ribbon. Use scissors to curl the ribbon if desired. Have the children put a handful of ribbons into each bottle. As the children work, play "God Lives in Us."

Show the children how to wrap different colored chenille wires around their fingers to create spiral twists. Have the children put four to six twists in each bottle. Have the children add a heaping tablespoon of red hot candies in each bottle, then screw the lids on tightly. Seal the bottles by taping the lids with colored electrical tape.

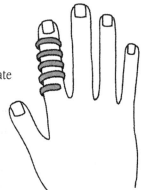

GATHERING TIME

Classroom supplies: heart rattle bottles from Center 3, blow dryer, CD player
Curriculum supplies: Donut Forget CD ("God Lives in Us")

Have the children sit down in the Gathering Time area. Invite them to tell you about the things they did at their Learning Centers. Say: **Some of you made flame print pictures and learned how God sent his Holy Spirit to the early church. If you made a flame print picture, hold your hands in a flame shape above your head. Some of you made flame cupcakes to celebrate the birthday of the church. If you decorated cupcakes, say, "Happy Birthday!"**

Some of you made heart bottle rattles to share with the babies in our church nursery. If you worked on the heart bottle rattles, come up and stand by me, then tell us what you learned about Barnabas.

Help the children explain that Barnabas encouraged the Christians in the early church. Say: **God wants all the people in his church to love and encourage each other. So each week, we'll do a Barnabas Project to encourage a different group of people in our church.**

This week, Center 3 has made heart bottle rattles for us to deliver to the babies in the nursery. The babies will enjoy shaking and banging the rattle bottles, and the nursery workers can point out the hearts in the bottles when they talk to babies about God's love. Let's listen to a new song about God's love now.

Play "God Lives in Us." After the song, ask:

■ **If we can't see God, how can we tell that God is living in us?**

■ **What are some ways we can show love to others in this class? In our church?**

Let the children respond, then say: **We can't see God, but we can see the smiles on others' faces when we treat them lovingly—the way God would treat them. Let's play a game now to remind us of the ways we can show God's love.**

Plug in the blow dryer and turn it on. Blow one of the heart bottles across the floor where the children can see it. Say: **We can't see the wind from this blow dryer, but we can see its effects when it blows things around the room. In the same way, we can't see God, but we can see the effects of his love when we love other people. Let's pretend one of these heart bottles is God's love. We'll take turns using the wind from the blow dryer to blow God's love to each person in our class.**

Choose a volunteer to go first. Have that child name a way to show God's love, then use the blow dryer to blow the heart bottle until it rolls into another child. Have the first child sit next to you (facing the group), then let the child who was "hit" by "God's love" take the next turn. Continue until all the children are sitting with you.

Say: **Well, I'd say God's love has reached its goal! We've all received God's love, and now we're sitting together here at church. I love having each one of you in this class—I'm so glad you're all part of the church. Let's find out how Jesus' wonderful church started.**

225

BIBLE STORY

Classroom supplies: Bible, paper, candle, matches, CD player
Curriculum supplies: Donut Forget CD ("They Had to Wait")

Open your Bible to Acts 2 and show it to the children. Say: **Our Bible story today is from the book of Acts. When Jesus was getting ready to go back to heaven, he gathered all his followers together. He wanted to tell them about a special gift he had for them. What do you think that special gift was?**

Let the children respond, then continue: **The special gift was the Holy Spirit! You've already learned a little bit about the Holy Spirit in some of your Learning Centers. Tell me what you've learned.**

Let the children respond, then continue: **The Holy Spirit is a special helper for everyone who believes in Jesus. We can't see the Holy Spirit, just like we can't see God, but the Holy Spirit is always with us. The Holy Spirit helps us do what's right. Jesus told his followers something else that the Holy Spirit would help them do. The Holy Spirit would help the followers tell others about Jesus!**

The followers stayed together in Jerusalem as they waited for the Holy Spirit to come. One day when they were together, they heard a loud noise. It sounded like a big, rushing wind. Let me hear you make a big wind sound. Whoosh! Whoosh! Whoosh!

Let the children make the sound, the give each child a sheet of paper. **Next, flames of fire appeared. Crinkle your paper to sound like fire crackling.**

Let the children crinkle their papers for a few moments, then collect them. Continue: **But the flames didn't burn anything up. Instead, they separated into "little tongues of fire" like we sang about in our song. And then something else amazing happened. All of the followers started speaking in different languages. Does anyone here know any words in another language?**

Encourage the children to share any foreign words they know, including "pig latin" words. Help each child think of a word—even if it's just his name spoken backwards. Say: **Now let's all say our foreign words at the same time. When I say go, keep saying your foreign word over and over until I say stop. Go.**

Have the children repeat their words for no more than thirty seconds, then tell them to stop. Say: **It gets pretty noisy with everyone speaking at the same time in so many different languages, doesn't it? When Jesus' followers spoke other languages, they didn't just say one or two words. They suddenly knew all the words they needed to tell the people who spoke the other languages about Jesus. All the followers were talking about Jesus in different languages, all at the same time!**

Pretty soon a crowd of people heard all the noise and came to see what was going on. The people in the crowd listened carefully. Even though the crowd was full of people from all different nations, they all heard and understood that the followers were talking about Jesus! The Holy Spirit was helping the followers tell people about Jesus, just as Jesus had promised.

Then Peter stood up and began to preach about Jesus. He told the crowd how Jesus died and rose again. He told them that Jesus loved them and wanted to forgive them for the wrong things they'd done. With the help of the Holy Spirit, 3,000 people heard the good news and believed in Jesus that day. They joined Jesus' followers and formed the first church.

Review the story by singing "They Had to Wait."

226

SING-ALONG FUN TIME

Classroom supplies: heart bottle rattles from Center 3, CD player
Curriculum supplies: Donut Forget CD ("God Lives in Us," "They Had to Wait")

Read 1 John 4:12, then have the children repeat it. Have the children sing along with "God Lives in Us." Then have the children sit down in two lines facing each other. Space the lines about 3 feet apart. Let the children roll the heart bottles back and forth as they sing "God Lives in Us" again.

Play "They Had to Wait" and have the children move around the room as they sing. Encourage them to use different movements as the song indicates. For example, they might tiptoe on "they had to wait," skip on "Joyfully, joyfully," or jump on "laughing and leaping."

After the song, take the children to the nursery to deliver the heart bottles. Explain that the children made the rattles because they wanted to encourage the people (workers and babies) involved in the nursery ministry. If time allows, have the children sing "God Lives in Us" for the workers and babies.

DONUT FORGET TIME

Classroom supplies: flame cupcakes prepared in Center 2, matches, water or juice (optional), CD player
Curriculum supplies: Donut Forget CD ("God Lives in Us")

Set the flame cupcakes on a table. Have the children sit in chairs around the table. Say: **In our story today we heard how the Holy Spirit helped Jesus' followers start the church. The day the Holy Spirit came is called Pentecost, and it's the birthday of the church. The church has been loving people and telling the good news about Jesus for hundreds of years. As long as people love each other and believe in Jesus, there will always be a church! Let's celebrate the church's birthday now.**

Play "God Lives in Us." As the song plays, help the children pass the flame by lighting each other's candles. Be very careful as you do this. Have the children place their hands under the table. Light one child's cupcake candle. Then place your hand over the child's hand and help the child pick up the cupcake and carefully light another child's candle. Have the child who is receiving the flame keep her hands under the table until the candle is lit. Continue until all the candles are lit. Then lead the children in singing "Happy Birthday" to the church. Eat and enjoy!

LEARNING CENTERS

Set up the following activities for the children to do as they arrive. Assign an equal number of children and a teacher or helper to each activity.

At each Learning Center, welcome the children to your class. Make sure you know each child's name. Explain that today you'll be talking about the people who make up God's church.

227

Center 1: Donut Forget Rhyme

Classroom supplies: Bible, construction paper, crayons, stickers (optional)
Curriculum supplies: Donut Forget CD ("More and More People")

BITE IDEA
It might be fun to use this rhyme when you deliver the pizza to the teenagers (Center 3). Include the Duncan puppet and let one of the kids practice using Duncan to say the rhyme with the group.

Before class, enlarge and copy the words "Donut Forget" on construction paper for each child in the class.

Read Acts 2:42-47 from an easy-to-understand translation. Explain that when the church was brand new, Jesus' followers did many things together. Being together helped them remember to be good followers of Jesus.

Give each child a Donut Forget sign. Read it together so everyone understands that it means "do not forget." Give the children time to color and decorate their signs. Then explain that the following rhyme talks about some of the things the church does. Ask the children to repeat each line after you.

Donut forget to meet together.	**Donut forget to worship God.**
Donut forget to share.	**Donut forget to pray.**
Donut forget to remember Jesus.	**Donut forget to tell about Jesus.**
Donut forget to care.	**Every single day! Hooray!**

Practice the rhyme several times. Set the signs aside to use during Bible Story Time.

Center 2: Wind Stick

Classroom supplies: 2-by-24-inch cardboard mailing tube with plastic caps, 1/2 pound of 2-inch nails, hammer or wooden block, dried beans or lentils, red or orange butcher paper, colored electrical tape, CD player
Curriculum supplies: Donut Forget CD ("They Had to Wait")

BITE IDEA
You can use any size mailing tube for this project. Just make sure the nails are the same length as the width of the tube. If you use a tube that's longer than 24 inches, you'll probably want to put in some of the nails before class.

Before class, wrap butcher paper around the cardboard tube. Cut a length that will wrap the tube twice. Set the butcher paper aside for use later in the lesson.

Remind the children that when God's Holy Spirit came, the followers heard a sound like a loud rushing wind. Explain that they'll make a wind stick to remind them of the day the Holy Spirit came.

Set out the cardboard tube and the nails. Help the children tap the nails into the cardboard tube. If you have mostly younger children, you may want to poke the nails through the cardboard yourself, then let the children push them in the rest of the way. Older children will enjoy using a lightweight hammer or wooden block to tap the nails into the tube. Make sure the nails are in straight so they don't poke through the tube.

Have the children space the nails about 1/8-inch apart, following the spiral seam of the mailing tube. To save time, have the children work from both ends of the tube and meet in the middle. As they work, play "They Had to Wait."

When the children finish putting in the nails, have them put about 1/2 cup of dried beans or lentils in the tube. Then secure the plastic caps on both ends with colored electrical tape.

Let the children enjoy shaking the wind stick as they listen to "They Had to Wait."

Center 3: Barnabas Project

Classroom supplies: pre-baked pizza shell, grated cheese, pizza sauce, pepperoni, plastic wrap, CD player
Curriculum supplies: Donut Forget CD ("More and More People")

Before class, make arrangements to deliver a pizza to your church's youth group. Decide whether you'll cook the pizza and eat it with the youth group or deliver it for teenagers to enjoy later.

Tell the children that during this unit they'll learn that people in the church love and encourage each other. Point out that a man named Barnabas was a great encourager to the people in the early church. Read Acts 11:23-26 to give the children a little more information about Barnabas. Tell the children that each week Center 3 will help prepare a special Barnabas Project to encourage a group of people in your church. Today's Barnabas Project will go to the teenagers in your church youth group.

Set out the pizza supplies. Have the children spread the sauce on the pizza shell, then sprinkle the cheese over it. Have the children arrange the pepperoni on top in a heart, cross, or church shape. If time allows, and if you have access to your church kitchen, have a helper bake the pizza while you continue with the lesson. If not, simply wrap the assembled pizza in plastic wrap for delivery.

GATHERING TIME

Classroom supplies: wind stick from Center 2, red or orange butcher paper to wrap the wind stick, clear packaging tape, CD player
Curriculum supplies: Donut Forget CD ("More and More People")

Have the children sit down in the Gathering Time area. Invite them to tell you about the things they did at their Learning Centers. Say: **Some of you learned a fun way to remember what the church does. If you learned a rhyme, say, "Donut Forget!" Some of you made a pizza to encourage the teenagers in our church. If you made pizza, say, "Pepperoni!" Some of you made a wind stick. The sound it makes reminds us of the rushing wind that Jesus' followers heard the day the Holy Spirit came. If you helped make the wind stick, say, "Whoosh."**

Hold up the wind stick and point out all the nails. Say: **Without each one of these nails, our wind stick wouldn't work. It needs each nail to form the inner maze that lets the beans fall through. The church is like that, too. Each person who believes in Jesus is an important part of the church. When we work together, we use our special gifts and talents to tell others about Jesus.**

When we think of the church, sometimes we think of our church building. But the church isn't a building—it's the people inside the building. To help us remember that the church is made up of people, let's use ourselves to "build" a church right here in our classroom.

Help the children "build" a church. Assign children to be doors, windows, pews, platforms, roofs, or steeples. Encourage them to be creative as they shape themselves into a church building. When they finish, say: **You see, it really did take all of us to make a church. One person couldn't have "built" a church like this all alone. And just as our church "building" needs all of us, our church family of people needs all of us, too. It also needs someone else.**

Hold up the wind stick and the red or orange butcher paper. Say: **Without something to hold these nails in place, they might fall out and stop doing their jobs.** Wrap the butcher paper around the tube and tape it in place. Then say: **The church needs the Holy Spirit to do its job of telling people about Jesus. The Holy Spirit is what "holds the church together." Let's find out more about the church now.**

Donut Forget™ Bible Story Lessons

229

BIBLE STORY

Classroom supplies: Bible, "Donut Forget" signs and rhyme from Center 1, CD player
Curriculum supplies: Donut Forget CD ("More and More People")

Open your Bible to Acts 2:42-47 and show it to the children. Say: **The beginning of the church was an exciting time! Thousands of people started following Jesus and became part of the church. They all wanted to know how to follow Jesus. They wanted to know what it meant to be part of Jesus' church.**

BITE IDEA
Ask the children to help you make up a motion for each line of the rhyme. For example, fold hands with fingers intertwined for "meet together," hands out and palms up for "share," sign language for "Jesus" for "remember Jesus," hug self for "care."

In Acts 2 where it tells about the beginning of the church, it also tells what the brand new followers of Jesus did. Read Acts 2:42-47 from an easy-to-read translation. Ask: **What kinds of things did the new church do to show they were following Jesus?**

Let the children respond, then say: **The new people in the church wanted to learn about Jesus. They wanted to meet together, share what they had with others, eat together, pray together, and remember what Jesus had done for them. And they were very happy!**

Give "Donut Forget" signs to each child in the class. Then ask the children from Center 1 to present the Donut Forget rhyme. Do it again, inviting all the children to repeat the lines after you.

Ask: **What did people who saw the new followers of Jesus think of the things they were doing?**

Let the children respond, then say: **The people who saw the followers sharing, meeting together, and praising God together thought, "I would like to be a part of that group." And more and more people were being saved every day. More and more people were becoming followers of Jesus.**

Play "More and More People," then collect the signs and have the children gather for Sing-Along Fun Time.

SING-ALONG FUN TIME

Classroom supplies: wind stick from Center 2, CD player
Curriculum supplies: Donut Forget CD ("They Had to Wait," "God Lives in Us")

Use the **Duncan** puppet and the script from the Donut Forget Songbook to talk about the memory verse, 1 John 4:12.

Have the children form a line. As they sing "God Lives in Us," have them pass the wind stick down the line. Point out that the sound of the wind stick is a reminder that God's Holy Spirit lives in each of us.

Play "They Had to Wait." Have the children lie down and "wait" on each chorus. Each time a verse begins, have them spring up and form the people church from Gathering Time. Have the children return to their places on the floor when the chorus begins again. Encourage them to sing along as they "wait" and "leap" into action.

Practice singing "More and More People" so you can sing it for the teenagers.

DONUT FORGET TIME

Classroom supplies: pizza assembled in Center 3, CD player
Curriculum supplies: Donut Forget CD ("More and More People")

Have the children deliver the pizza to the youth group. Say to the teenagers: **We've been learning that the church loves each other. We're glad you're part of our church, and we wanted to share our love by sharing a yummy pizza snack.**

Have the children point out that the pepperoni is laid out to form a church (or other related shape). If you've cooked the pizza, stay and enjoy it with the older kids. If the pizza will be baked later, set it aside.

Have the children present the "Donut Forget" rhyme for the teenagers. Then they can demonstrate the people church structure they made earlier during Gathering Time. Encourage the teenagers to join the people church. If you have enough teenagers, you might even be able to make a two-story church by having the teenagers hold the children on their shoulders.

When the expanded church (children and teenagers) is assembled, say: **Wow! Our people church has doubled in size. There's always room for more people in God's church. Let's thank God right now for sending the Holy Spirit to start the church that we're all part of.**

Pray: **Dear God, we're so glad to be part of your family, the church. Thank you for sending the Holy Spirit to start the church and help us tell others about Jesus. Amen.** Sing "More and More People" with the Donut Forget CD.

If the teenagers enjoy interacting with the children, invite them to join you for Donut Forget Time next week. Lead the children back to your room to meet their parents.

LEARNING CENTERS

Set up the following activities for the children to do as they arrive. Assign an equal number of children and a teacher or helper to each activity.

At each Learning Center, welcome the children to your class. Make sure you know each child's name. Explain that today you'll be learning that the church prays together.

Center 1: Prayer Walk

Classroom supplies: paper, clipboard, pen
Curriculum supplies: none

Before class, arrange for the children to visit several other classes to ask for prayer requests. If possible, also arrange to visit members of your church staff who may be in their offices.

Read Acts 2:42. Explain that God wants people in his church to pray for each other. Encourage the children to share any prayer requests they might have, then lead them on a prayer walk through your church. Stop at the classrooms you've arranged to visit and ask for prayer requests in each class. Carry paper and a clipboard with you. Write down the prayer requests yourself, or let older children take turns writing. After you've visited all your sites, return to your classroom.

Set the prayer requests aside to use during Gathering Time.

Center 2: Pan Flutes

Classroom supplies: five clear plastic drinking straws for each child, glue, paper plates, cotton swabs, permanent marker, CD player
Curriculum supplies: Donut Forget CD ("They Had to Wait")

Before class, cut the drinking straws into five different lengths. For example, you might have 4-, 5-, 6-, 7-, and 8-inch straws.

Donut Forget™ Bible Story Lessons

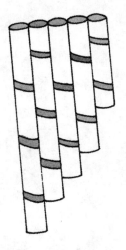

Remind the children that Jesus' followers heard a sound like a loud rushing wind when the Holy Spirit came. Explain that today they'll make an instrument that makes sound when the "wind" of their breath is blown through it.

Set out piles of different-sized straws, plates of glue, and cotton swabs. Have each child take one straw of each size. Help the children arrange their straws from shortest to tallest. Have the children use the cotton swabs to apply glue to the sides of the straws, then have them stick the straws together, as shown. Help the children not to get glue on the ends of the straws, since these will go in or near their mouths. If time allows, have the children make extra pan flutes for other children. Use a permanent marker to put each child's name on his pan flute.

Let the children try out their pan flutes as they listen to "They Had to Wait." Set the finished pan flutes aside for use during Sing-Along Fun Time.

Center 3: Barnabas Project

Classroom supplies: several unused self-stick notepads, round color-coding labels (primary or neon-colored), box of binder clips, box of ball-point pens, new unsharpened pencils, pencil sharpener (optional), colored chenille wires, small beads, craft foam, glue, small basket or box, CD player
Curriculum supplies: Donut Forget CD ("More and More People")

Tell the children that during this unit they'll learn that people in the church love and encourage each other. Point out that a man named Barnabas was a great encourager to the people in the early church. Read Acts 11:23-26 to give the children a little more information about Barnabas. Tell the children that each week Center 3 will help prepare a special Barnabas Project to encourage a group of people in your church. Today's Barnabas Project will go to members of your church staff.

Explain that the minister and other members of your church staff have to do a lot of office work to keep all the church's ministries organized. Tell the children they'll make special decorated office supplies to give to the staff.

Set out the supplies. Let the children choose whether they'll make a decorated notepad, a pen or pencil grip, a pen or pencil topper, or a decorated binder clip. Play "More and More People" as they work.

For notepads, have the children place a round color-coding sticker on each sheet of self-stick paper. Encourage them to draw happy faces, hearts, crosses, or church shapes on the stickers. They could also use the stickers as people faces and add bodies with a message such as "The church is people." Remind the children to leave enough space on the papers for the users to write.

For decorated binder clips, help the children cut out heart, cross, or church shapes from the craft foam. Glue the shapes to the black part of the binder clips. (Make sure the shapes don't hang over onto the clips or they'll get crushed when the clips are opened.)

For pen or pencil grips, have the children wrap colored chenille wires around a pen or pencil, near the bottom. (This is a good project for very young children.)

For heart pen or pencil toppers, have the children cut two identical heart shapes out of craft foam. Sandwich the pen or pencil between the two hearts, then staple the hearts together close to both sides of the pen or pencil.

For cross pen or pencil toppers, have the children cut two 6-inch lengths of chenille wire, then twist the wires together to form a cross. Have the children thread beads onto the vertical wire of the cross, leaving 3 inches of wire at the bottom of the cross to wrap around the pen or pencil. Have the children wrap the extra wire around the pen or pencil, then trim the horizontal wire as needed. Have the children thread beads onto the horizontal wire. Show them how to bend the ends of the wire around the last bead to keep the beads from sliding off the wire.

Attach the cross to the pen or pencil by placing a dab of craft glue at the top and bottom of the wrapped wire.

Place the finished items in a basket or box. Explain that they'll be delivered later.

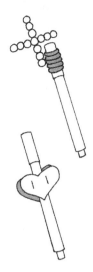

GATHERING TIME

Classroom supplies: prayer requests gathered in Center 1
Curriculum supplies: none

Before class, plan out a tour of your church building. Plan stops at the worship center, church office, minister's office, nursery, choir or music room, church kitchen, and various classrooms. You won't need to speak to anyone in these places—just be prepared to tell the children what goes on there.

Have the children sit down in the Gathering Time area. Invite them to tell you about the things they did at their Learning Centers. Say: **Some of you made pan flutes to use during Sing-Along Fun Time. Some of you decorated office supplies to encourage our church staff. We'll all get to do some more things to encourage the church staff later in our lesson. Some of you traveled around our church on a special prayer mission. If you went on the prayer walk, come stand by me.**

Invite the children to tell about the classes they visited and the prayer requests they gathered. Then say: **The last time we met, we talked about some of the things the church does. "Donut forget to pray" was one line of our rhyme. Today we're going to have a chance to pray for people in the church and learn more about what they do in our church.**

Lead the children on your planned tour. Stop at or near each place and briefly tell the children what goes on there. Answer any questions the children have, then pray for any requests associated with that place.

As you walk, if you meet people who aren't involved in classes or worship, invite them to tell you how they're involved in your church. Lead the tour back to your classroom, then say: **And in our classroom, we sing songs and do fun activities to learn about the Bible. Let's go in and hear our Bible story now.**

BIBLE STORY TIME

Classroom supplies: Bible
Curriculum supplies: none

Open your Bible to Acts 12 and show it to the children. Say: **Our Bible story today is again from the book of Acts. It's about a time the early church prayed together for their friend Peter. You can help me tell the story by acting it out.**

Form groups of three or four. Then say: **Listen as I read the story. Each time I stop reading, join with the members of your group to form a human statue scene that shows what's happening in the story.**

Read the following story, pausing as indicated. Encourage the children to pose as gates, bars, and other inanimate objects as well as people. Or the children could make sound effects that relate to the story.

Peter was preaching the good news about Jesus all over Jerusalem. Mean King Herod didn't like this, so he had Peter put him in jail. (pause) **The night before Peter's trial, Peter was sleeping between two soldiers, bound with two chains.** (pause) **Other soldiers were guarding the door of the jail.** (pause) **Suddenly, an angel appeared and woke Peter up.** (pause) **"Hurry! Get up!" the angel said.**

233

The chains fell off Peter's hands. (pause) **"Get dressed and put on your sandals,"** (pause) **the angel told Peter. Peter put on his sandals, then the angel said "Put on your coat** (pause) **and follow me." So Peter followed the angel out of the cell.** (pause)

They went past the first and second guards (pause) **and came to an iron gate. The gate opened by itself for them,** (pause) **and they went through it. After they had walked down one street,** (pause) **the angel left Peter.**

When Peter realized he was really free, he went straight to the house where the church was meeting. (pause) **Many people were gathered there to pray.** (pause) **Peter knocked on the door** (pause) **and a servant girl named Rhoda came to answer it.** (pause) **When she heard Peter's voice, she was so happy she forgot to open the door. She ran inside and told everyone, "Peter is at the door!"** (pause)

The other Christians said to Rhoda, **"You're crazy!"** (pause) **But Rhoda kept insisting Peter was at the door. Peter kept knocking,** (pause) **and they finally opened the door.** (pause) **Peter explained how the angel had led him out of jail, then he went on to tell the good news about Jesus in another place.**

Applaud the children for their participation, then say: **All the time that Peter was in jail, the other people in the church were praying for him. God heard the prayers of the church and sent an angel to help Peter get out of jail. God hears our prayers, too, and he wants us to pray for people in our church. Let's sing and praise God now for hearing the prayers of the church.**

BITE IDEA
If you have a video or audio cassette recorder, tape the children singing and stepping forward to follow Jesus. Give a copy of the tape to your church staff along with the basket of office supplies.

SING-ALONG FUN TIME

Classroom supplies: pan flutes from Center 2, wind stick from Lesson 2, video camera or cassette recorder and blank video or audio cassette (optional), CD player
Curriculum supplies: Donut Forget CD ("They Had to Wait," "God Is Great," "More and More People")

Let the children listen to "God Is Great." Then play the song again and encourage them to jump up and give each other high fives each time the song says "God is great!"

Pass out the pan flutes and let the children play along as you sing "They Had to Wait." If some children don't have pan flutes, let them pass the wind stick back and forth.

Sing "More and More People" with the Donut Forget CD. Then sing it again without the CD and have the children insert their names in the chorus. Instead of singing "more and more people," sing the children's names. For example, you might sing "Ashley and Jason are becoming followers of Jesus." Continue singing until each child's name has been sung. Then have the children form a line. Sing the song again and have each child step forward as his name is sung.

DONUT FORGET TIME

Classroom supplies: construction paper, markers, scissors, box of decorated office supplies from Center 3, CD player
Curriculum supplies: Donut Forget CD ("More and More People")

If possible, arrange for the teenagers you met last week to assist you with this activity. Before class, obtain at least one prayer request from each of the following people: minister(s), church office staff, music/worship leader, Sunday school teacher(s), custodian, elder(s) or other ministry group leaders. Try to obtain one prayer request for every two or three children.

Form pairs or trios. Assign an adult or teenage helper to each group. Set out construction paper, markers, and scissors. Help each child trace one of her hands on a folded sheet of construction paper. Have the children cut out their "praying hands," being careful not to cut along the fold. Have adult or teenage helpers write the words "We prayed for you today" on each child's praying hands. Set the finished cards on a table.

After the children have completed the praying hands, say: **We've learned about a lot of different people in our church today. Now we're going to spend some time praying for those people. In 1 Thessalonians 5:17, the Bible tells us to pray all the time. Peter's friends kept praying for him until he was set free from jail. If we keep praying for others in our church, our prayers will be answered, too.**

We prayed for you today

Give each group a prayer request. Have adult or teenage helpers lead in prayer, then encourage the children to join in. Let the children add their own requests if they want. After groups have finished praying, have the children pick up and sign their praying hands cards. Have the children keep the signed cards with them in their groups. When all the cards have been picked up, you'll know everyone has finished praying.

Set out the box of office supplies. Say: **Without the people we just prayed for, a lot of people in our church wouldn't know about Jesus. Ministers, teachers, and other church leaders do a lot of work to keep our church programs running. Thanks to these people, more and more people can come to our church to hear about Jesus. I know they'll be encouraged by our prayers.**

Close by singing "More and More People." As you sing the song, have the children place their praying hands cards in the box of office supplies.

LESSON FOUR

LEARNING CENTERS

Set up the following activities for the children to do as they arrive. Assign an equal number of children and a teacher or helper to each activity.

At each Learning Center, welcome the children to your class. Make sure you know each child's name. Explain that today you'll be reviewing all the things you've learned about the church.

Center 1: Church Chain Poster

Classroom supplies: poster board, tempera paint or washable ink pads, liquid dish soap (if using tempera paint), construction paper, scissors, stapler, CD player
Curriculum supplies: Donut Forget CD ("God Lives in Us")

Before class, use the children chain pattern from Unit 1 (page 23) to cut out at least three people figures for each child. If you have mostly younger children, cut out additional figures yourself. Mix tempera paint with a few drops of liquid dish soap for easier clean up.

Set out a sheet of poster board and pans of tempera paint or washable ink pads. If desired, cut the poster board into the shape of a church building. Have the children use the paint or ink

Donut forget™ Bible Story Lessons

pads to make handprints around the edge of the poster board. Inside the handprints write "The Church Is People!" in large letters.

Tell the children that they'll be making a people chain that includes everyone in your church. Give each child two people figures. Have the children decorate one figure to look like themselves and one figure to look like someone else in your class. (If time allows, the children may decorate additional figures to look like other people they know in your church.) Play "God Lives in Us" as the children work.

As the children work on the figures, staple a construction paper pocket to the church poster. Place blank figures and one or two markers in the pocket. On the outside of the pocket write, "If you believe in Jesus and are part of this church, please add yourself to our church chain."

Collect the children's finished figures for use later in the lesson. Make sure you have a decorated figure for each child in the class.

Center 2: Fruit Salad

Classroom supplies: bananas, apples, oranges, and other seasonal fruit (as many kinds as possible); mixing spoon, large bowl, cutting knife, plastic knives
Curriculum supplies: Donut Forget CD ("God Is Great")

Set out the different kinds of fruit. Ask the children to tell you which fruits they like best. Point out that even though each kind of fruit tastes good, no one would make a fruit salad out of just one kind. Just as it takes all kinds of fruit to make a fruit salad, it takes all kinds of people to do the work of God's church.

Help the children cut up the fruit and mix it in a large bowl. As the children work, play "God Is Great!" Talk about all the great people God has placed in your classroom and in your church.

Set the finished fruit salad aside to eat during Gathering Time.

BITE IDEA
Child-sized work gloves are available for less than a dollar per pair at discount stores such as Wal-Mart. If child-sized gloves aren't in stock, you can substitute adult-sized gloves for about the same price.

Center 3: Story Glove Puppets

Classroom supplies: one pair of child-sized work gloves for every two children; orange, yellow, brown, black, and red craft foam; scissors; craft glue; CD player
Curriculum supplies: Donut Forget CD ("More and More People")

Before class, cut out five 1 1/4-inch brown or orange craft foam circles for each child in your class. Save any scraps you have left over. If possible, plan to have an additional adult helper at this Learning Center.

Tell the children that during this unit they'll learn that people in the church love and encourage each other. Point out that a man named Barnabas was a great encourager to the people in the early church. Read Acts 11:23-26 to give the children a little more information about Barnabas. Tell the children that each week Center 3 helps prepare a special Barnabas Project to encourage a group of people in your church. Today's Barnabas Project will go to the older adults in your church.

Give each child a pair of work gloves. Explain that they'll use the gloves and other materials you've provided to create story puppets to tell what they've learned about the church. Give each child ten orange or brown foam circles. Set out the scissors, craft foam, and craft glue. Help the children snip the foam scraps into hair for their finger puppet faces. Have the children glue the hair to the brown or orange foam circles. As the children work, play "More and More People." Point out that they are creating more and more puppet people to review the Bible story!

Help the children glue the finished faces onto the work gloves, one face on each finger. Don't draw facial features yet. Children will do this later in the lesson. Set the finished gloves aside to dry. It's important that the children complete a glove for each child in the class, since you'll use the gloves for your Barnabas Project during Donut Forget Time. Have adult helpers make extra gloves as the children work, or make extras yourself ahead of time.

GATHERING TIME

Classroom supplies: church poster and people figures from Center 1, poster putty, CD player
Curriculum supplies: Donut Forget CD ("God Lives in Us")

Before class, arrange to hang the church poster in a well-traveled hallway in your church.

Have the children sit down in the Gathering Time area. Invite them to tell you about the things they did at their Learning Centers. Say: **Some of you made story glove puppets to help us review what we've learned about the church. If you made puppets, stand up and wiggle your fingers, then sit down. Some of you fixed a yummy fruit salad for us to enjoy in a little while. If you made fruit salad, stand up and say the name of your favorite fruit, then sit down.**

Some of you made a church poster and people figures. If you worked on the church poster, come up and help me pass out the people figures.

Have the Center 1 children stand near you. Say: **We've learned that the church is more than just a building we come to each week. The church is a group of people who believe in Jesus. People in the church love each other and encourage each other to do the things Jesus wants us to do. When I call your name, tell us one thing you've learned about the church, then come up and get your person figure.**

Affirm the children's responses as you distribute the figures. When all the figures have been distributed, hold up the church poster. Say: **Each one of us is an important part of our church. But we're not the only important parts of this body! There are many other people to love and encourage in our church. We want everyone to feel loved and welcome at our church. So we've made some extra people figures. We'll put up our poster where everyone can see it, and when people come to our church they can add their own people figures to our church "family."**

Lead the children to the hallway where you'll hang the poster. Hang the poster, then have the children attach their people figures in a chain leading away from the poster. Use poster putty to stick the figures to the wall. As the children put up their figures, play "God Lives in Us."

BIBLE STORY

Classroom supplies: Bible, story glove puppets from Center 3, permanent markers
Curriculum supplies: none

Open your Bible to Acts and show it to the children. Say: **Our Bible story today is from the book of Acts. We'll use our story gloves to review all the things we've learned about the first church.**

Distribute the story glove puppets. Have the children use permanent markers to draw faces on the finger puppets. On the fingers, have them draw three male faces and one female face. On the thumb, have them draw a face to represent themselves.

After the children finish drawing their faces, collect the permanent markers. Have the children put on their gloves. Say: **Remember our Bible friend Peter? Wiggle one of your boy puppets to represent Peter. Peter stood up in front of a huge crowd of people to preach the good news about Jesus. After listening to Peter's sermon, over 3,000 people became part of God's church. Who preaches the good news about Jesus in our church?**

Let the children respond, then say: **Our minister preaches sermons to a big group of people, just like Peter did. But we don't have to have a big group of people to talk about Jesus. We can all do that anytime!**

The new followers of Jesus wanted to learn all about Jesus. They met together and learned from the men who had been with Jesus. Those men were called

Donut Forget™ Bible Story Lessons

237

apostles. **Wiggle a finger puppet for one of the apostles. The apostles taught about Jesus and helped the church be good followers. Who teaches about Jesus in our church?**

Let the children respond, then continue: **Sunday school teachers teach the children and adults about Jesus in classes. But we can teach about Jesus anywhere—just like the apostles did.**

Wiggle your girl puppet. Can you guess who it is? It's Rhoda, the slave girl who prayed for Peter while he was in prison. We can pray for people, too, that they would get to hear about Jesus. What are some other things people in our church can pray about?

Let the children respond, then continue: **We can pray for people who are sick, sad, or lonely. We can pray for ourselves, for our families, and for our church. It's really encouraging to know that other people in our church are praying for us.**

Wiggle another boy puppet. Who could it be? Someone who encouraged many people in the early church—Barnabas! In a little while, we're going to do our Barnabas Project and encourage the older adults by sharing what we've learned about the church.

Now wiggle your last puppet. Who is it? It's you! You're an important part of God's church! You can pray, encourage others, and tell people about Jesus!

Let's get ready to encourage the older adults in our church. I'm going to teach you a song to sing with your puppets. I'll sing a line, then you sing it after me. You can wiggle your puppets as you sing.

Teach the children the following song to the tune of "Frere Jacques." Pause after you sing each line for the children to repeat it. Have the children fill in their own names on the last verse. Practice the song several times.

**Peter, Peter
Preached God's Word.
Jesus Christ is risen.
He's our Lord.**

**Jesus' apostles
Met and taught
The good news of Jesus
Everywhere.**

**Rhoda prayed
The whole night through.
God heard Rhoda's prayer.
He hears ours, too.**

**Barnabas, Barnabas
Traveled 'round,
Encouraging and loving
All he found.**

**My name is (your name)
And I'm here to say:
I'm glad to be a part of
God's church today!**

238

SING-ALONG FUN TIME

Classroom supplies: wind stick from Lesson 2, CD player
Curriculum supplies: Donut Forget CD ("More and More People," "God Lives in Us," "God Is Great")

Have one child hold the wind stick as you play "More and More People." Each time the song says "more and more people," have two more children grab onto the wind stick. Continue until everyone is holding the stick. Let the children pass the stick back and forth as you sing "God Lives in Us" and "God Is Great." If time allows, let the children suggest favorite songs from other units. Encourage them to add their own motions and creative ways to "play" the wind stick.

DONUT FORGET TIME

Classroom supplies: "Donut Forget" rhyme from Lesson 2, story glove puppets from Center 3, fruit salad from Center 2, paper plates, plastic forks, napkins, CD player
Curriculum supplies: Donut Forget CD ("God Lives in Us")

Before class, arrange for the children to present their puppet song and the "Donut Forget" rhyme to a group of older adults.

Take the children to the classroom where the older adults are meeting. Bring the story gloves, fruit salad, plates, forks, and napkins with you. Say to the older adults: **We've been learning that people in the church love and encourage each other. I'm sure many of you have encouraged lots of children and adults in our church with your wisdom. You've probably shared countless Bible stories with your children and grandchildren. Today we'd like to encourage you by sharing a song and then a rhyme about the people in God's church. Please join us by echoing each phrase after us.**

Lead the children in singing the song they learned during Bible story time. Then help them present the "Donut Forget" rhyme. Have the children wiggle their puppets as they sing and recite. If possible, have each child sit next to an older adult.

After the presentation, have the children explain how the different fruits in the fruit salad remind us of all the different people in God's church. Have the children serve the fruit salad to the older adults. Encourage the children to visit with the older adults as they enjoy the snack. Close by praying: **Dear God, thank you for sending your Holy Spirit to start the church. Thank you for all the wonderful people you've brought to our church family. Please help us love and encourage each other always. In Jesus' name, amen.**

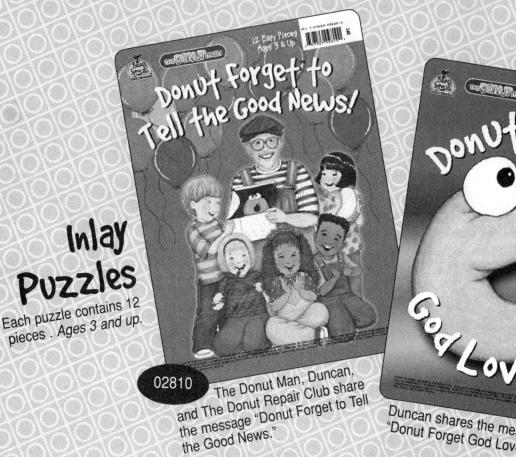

math expressions

DEVELOPING STUDENT THINKING
AND PROBLEM SOLVING THROUGH
COMMUNICATION

Dr. Cathy Marks Krpan

PEARSON

Feedback on this publication can be sent to editorialfeedback@pearsoned.com.
Pearson Canada Inc.
26 Prince Andrew Place
Don Mills, ON M3C 2T8
Customer Service: 1-800-361-6128

7 8 9 10 11 EBM 20 19 18 17 16
Printed and bound in the United States of America

Publisher: Mike Czukar
Research and Communications Manager: Craig Featherstone
Managing Editor: Joanne Close
Developmental Editor: Sarah Mawson
Project Editor: Lisa Dimson
Copy Editor: Kate Revington
Proofreader: Tilman Lewis
Indexer: Noeline Bridge
Permissions Editor: Christina Beamish
Production Coordinator: Susan Wong
Production Director, School, Print and Digital: Peggy Brown
Cover and Interior Design: Alex Li
Composition: David Cheung
Cover Image: Doug Ross/Stock Illustration Source
Manufacturing Coordinator: Karen Bradley
Vice-President, Publishing: Mark Cobham

PEARSON

ISBN: 978-0-32-175615-2

©P

Table of Contents

Acknowledgments

I have been fortunate to work with many fabulous people over the years who have enhanced my knowledge and understanding of the teaching and learning process. *Math Expressions* is a culmination of their wisdom.

I would like to thank Tony Krpan. I am indebted to you for your relentless inspiration and belief in my abilities. I would like to also thank Kay and Walter Marks for their encouragement and my family for their support, including the insightful and lively dinner conversations about education.

Sincere gratitude goes to my wonderful OISE colleagues David Booth, Larry Swartz, and Kathy Broad for their invaluable friendship and guidance. Your generosity and passion for teaching have always been a foundation for my learning and growth.

I would like to acknowledge Michael Czukar, publisher, and Craig Featherstone, research and communications manager. You believed in the concept of *Math Expressions* before a single word was ever written. Your ideas and input played a critical role in the development of this book. I would also like to acknowledge Sarah Mawson, developing editor. Your late-night emails, patience, and keen insight into the teaching/learning process enhanced this project immensely. You were instrumental in refining and organizing my ideas. Many thanks go to Lisa Dimson, project editor. Your ability to keep me organized and move everyone forward, while respecting the vision of this book was invaluable. I would also like to thank Joanne Close, managing editor. Your humour, dedication,

©P

expertise, and laughter always reassured me that things would work out. You were such an integral part of this book's success and my sanity.

I would like to recognize my esteemed colleagues from many school districts and OISE, as they have continually improved my research and practice, providing me with rich learning opportunities. Special mention goes to Carol Rolheiser for her continued support of field-based research. I would like also to acknowledge the following principals and teachers who invited me into their schools and classrooms to explore many of the strategies and research included in this book: Fred Albi, Luigi Bartucci, Jane Caswell, Janice Collins, Colin Daniel, Stefanie De Angelis, Sean Fullan, Jill Harrison, Stephanie Kearney, Sharma Madhu , Zohrin Mawji, Kaie Mclaughlin, Louanna Mootoo, Paul Roul, Ian Santiago, Sonal Sekhon, and Eric Williams.

Most importantly, I would like to honour the students whom I have taught over the years. Your mathematical expressions and insights continue to help me grow and learn. Your mathematical voices are the inspiration for this book.

A Culture of Mathematical Expression

Communication is a critical component of learning new concepts because through articulating their understanding of a concept, students often crystallize that understanding. Mathematical communication encompasses a range of skills: reading and creating pictures and text in a variety of formats, sharing ideas and discoveries through discussion, and listening to the ideas of others. Communication, combined with meaningful, guided inquiry, can help students reach their full mathematical potential.

Communication: The Critical Piece for Student Success

Many people believe that mathematics is a subject that consists only of formulas and right-or-wrong answers. They are of the opinion that it does not require discussion, debate, or exploration and that it offers little in the way of meaningful connection to their daily lives. These misconceptions are often due to how people experienced mathematics in social contexts or in school. By infusing a variety of learning experiences into our mathematics program, however, we can help students develop an understanding that mathematics has relevance in their lives.

- In a Grade 2 class, students were busy discussing a math problem that involved sharing 3 cookies between two people. One student stated: *"That is not fair! You cannot give 2 cookies to one person and only 1 to another. You need to share the extra cookie. Then each person can have 1 cookie and one-half of a cookie."* Her partner agreed: *"Yeah, OK. Let's cut this one up into two halves. We can also cut it up into 4 pieces and then each person can have two quarters, but that is too much work. Let me show you what I mean."*

- In a Grade 6 class, students were deciding how much each person would get if they had to share $1\frac{1}{2}$ pizzas between six people. The first student said: *"I don't understand. How much of a pizza does each person get if we divide the whole and the half into 6 pieces?"* His partner responded: *"One sixth and one twelfth, which is equal to three twelfths."* The other student replied: *"How do they equal three twelfths? Show me with the fraction pieces."*

In each context, I was intrigued by how the students explained their mathematical ideas to each other using sketches, manipulatives, and words. They were required to think carefully about their own understandings of fractions and then communicate them in a way that another person could understand. The students were comfortable discussing their ideas and exploring different solutions to a problem. They were not reciting what someone had told them as they had not formally learned the fraction concepts they were discussing. They were testing their own ideas and making connections in their learning based on their current mathematical knowledge. It was a rich exchange that allowed these students to explore their thinking and learn the essence of what it is to do mathematics (Stein, 2007).

The purpose of this resource is to provide you with practical ways to infuse opportunities for student communication into your mathematics program. In each chapter, you will find an overview of the background research that supports the specific communication approach and practical, how-to examples and activities that you can implement immediately in your mathematics program. The *Math Expressions* website contains links to professional resources, reproducible versions of all line masters in this book, and additional teaching tools you can use to engage your students in mathematical expression.

To view the *Math Expressions* website, go to www.pearsoncanada.ca/mathexpressions

Challenges That Face Math Educators

By integrating mathematical expression into your classroom, you can enable students to communicate their mathematical understanding in ways that will enhance their learning, enrich your mathematics program, and help you to meet the diverse learning needs of your students.

Becoming a Facilitator of Mathematical Expression

For resources about this topic, see the *Math Expressions* website: www.pearsoncanada.ca/mathexpressions

As we encourage our students to go deep in their thinking, many of us are taking similar risks in our own teaching (Cohen & Ball, 2001; Marks Krpan, 2001). To create a classroom culture in which our students express their mathematical thinking by sharing ideas and posing questions, we need to become *ambassadors of mathematical expression*. Rather than telling our students what to think and providing them with prescribed steps to solve problems, we need to become facilitators, effective listeners, and thoughtful readers. The process of shifting from a more traditional teaching approach to engaging students in expressing their thinking takes time, and for each teacher the change process is unique. This journey is about setting personal teaching goals and exploring new approaches with your students.

One teacher role is to pose questions that challenge students to explore and share their mathematical thinking and take risks in their work. Asking such questions is not easy. Students may share ideas with which you are unfamiliar or produce solutions to problems that require you to take more time to verify whether they are mathematically sound. When this happens, you may decide to keep the work, take a picture, or write down a point that students shared during a discussion. You thereby gain time to consider the ideas so you can address them the next day. What is more important, you can develop confidence in your teaching as you infuse more communication opportunities into your mathematics lessons.

Infusing Communication into Mathematics

Educators often wonder how they can include student communication in an already full mathematics program. Engaging students in sharing their thinking and exploring mathematical concepts does not require adding something *onto* our mathematics program, but making changes to *how* we teach. A balanced mathematics program engages students in making discoveries about mathematical concepts on an ongoing basis. Communication, which encompasses making conjectures through to recording, discussing, and explaining observations and results, is a natural part of this learning process. You can use mathematical investigations to introduce a concept or to explore what students already know about a topic. Investigations can be completed as a class, in small groups, or individually. They can also be modified to meet the needs of all your students, from those who struggle to those who excel.

Supporting Learners with Math Anxiety

We often hear adults and students admit freely that they are not "good" at mathematics. Yet many adults and students will not readily admit that they struggle with reading. It is often socially acceptable not to understand or like mathematics, but the opposite is true for reading or writing (Zaslavsky, 1999). In many cases, those who feel that they are not good at mathematics or who try to avoid it may suffer from some form of math anxiety. Math anxiety is defined as an inconceivable dread of mathematics that can interfere with manipulating numbers and solving math problems (Buckley & Ribordy, 1982). Stressful emotions such as math anxiety can change the chemical makeup of the body in negative ways, hindering a learner's ability to think (Wolfe, 2001). Learners can often feel helpless and overwhelmed by math. These emotions can lead to avoidance, a negative attitude toward math as a subject, and a lifelong lack of self-confidence in mathematics.

For resources about this topic, see the *Math Expressions* website: www.pearsoncanada.ca/mathexpressions

While it is true that parents' attitudes toward mathematics can have an impact on students' perception of the subject, how we teach mathematics can also influence students' attitudes. Teachers can do a lot to alleviate math anxiety by infusing cooperative group work, using diverse assessment practices, and providing many opportunities for students to communicate their ideas and justify their thinking (Furner & Duffy, 2002).

Supporting Learners Who Struggle in Mathematics

Students who struggle in mathematics do so for many reasons. These students are often reluctant to share their ideas or take risks in exploring new approaches. There are many ways we can support them, however. A supportive and collaborative classroom culture can make a significant difference for these students (Marks Krpan, 2011) (see Chapter 1). Providing learning experiences in which students who struggle can make meaningful connections to their own lives and encouraging students to explore different strategies can enable them to develop strong thinking skills (Allsopp, Kyger, & Lovin, 2007). Inviting students to share their thinking renders the learning process more transparent for all learners and communicates the important message that everyone's ideas are valued and that there can be different ways to think about and do mathematics.

Kenney (2005) points out that mathematics is a complex language full of nuances and multiple meanings but one that is learned almost entirely at school. She notes that there is a *double decoding* that students must perform when learning the language of mathematics. In the early stages, students need to decode spoken mathematics into everyday language and then translate it to the different context of mathematical usage. This double decoding also takes place when students encounter written mathematical numbers or symbols, which they must decode and then connect to a concept that may or may not exist in their prior knowledge.

It is crucial that we allow students to express their ideas in a way that works for them. When we engage learners who struggle in sharing their thinking, we need to differentiate the tasks so that they can fully participate and develop key communication skills. For example, students who may be unable to write out their ideas may experience success using graphic organizers or explaining their ideas verbally.

Supporting English Language Learners

Each chapter contains suggestions for assisting ELLs with the communication skill that is the focus of the chapter.

For resources about this topic, see the *Math Expressions* website: www.pearsoncanada.ca/ mathexpressions

Some people hold the misconception that mathematics involves only numbers and thus is easy for English Language Learners (ELLs) (Brown, 2005), but it is through language that we develop a deep understanding of mathematical concepts. For example, there is a rich collection of vocabulary we use to understand what the number 16 represents—*even, two-digit number, multiple of 8,* and so on. Mathematical vocabulary can be very confusing for students (Marks Krpan, 2008b; Rubenstein & Thompson, 2002). Some words are homonyms (*pi* and *pie*), others are used primarily in mathematics and are uncommon in everyday discourse (*isosceles; denominator*), and some have different meanings in mathematics than in everyday language (*translation* of languages vs. *translation* of a figure). It is important for us to consider these challenges not only for our ELLs, but also for our native speakers. Because mathematics requires knowledge of specific terms and vocabulary, all our students must have opportunities to discuss mathematics and use mathematical language.

Some teachers feel that because ELLs do not have command of the English language, it is better for them to do easier activities and work on their own or with other ELLs. However, through participating in cooperative mathematical activities with native speakers, ELLs develop a better knowledge of mathematical vocabulary and greater confidence in their mathematical abilities (Brenner, 1998). Even though ELLs may not be able to share their mathematical ideas in English, as they listen to their classmates or see their classmates' mathematical writing, they learn patterns of language and develop an understanding of how to communicate mathematical ideas in English and how specific vocabulary is used. It may be helpful for ELLs to write and speak in their native language as it is in their native language that their mathematical ideas are formed. If they do so, they may be able to bridge the mathematical understandings they developed in their homeland with the new learning and language they are acquiring (Cummins, 2001).

Educators should provide ELLs with rich, challenging mathematical work. Having lower expectations for ELLs can cause them to become passive and less motivated to participate in classroom activities (Brown, Cady, & Taylor, 2009). It is important to note that most ELLs possess extensive knowledge of mathematics that they have acquired in their homeland—they are capable of engaging in the same level of thinking that we expect from native speakers.

Not only are ELLs trying to learn a new language and culture, they are also trying to adapt to new teaching approaches. We need to keep in mind that teaching strategies such as collaborative learning, the communication of mathematical thinking, and the use of manipulatives may be very different from how ELLs learned mathematics in their homeland (Marks Krpan, 2009). In some cases, making mistakes can have negative consequences in other educational systems. These past experiences can discourage ELLs from contributing to classroom discussions as they may fear making a mistake. Creating a supportive classroom environment will help ELLs to learn and experience success.

Invite your ELLs to share the problem-solving approaches they know. Doing so can lead to rich discussions and sharing for all learners.

The Three-Part Problem-Solving Lesson: A Structure for Communication and Investigations

The three-part problem-solving lesson is an effective way to teach through problem solving and teach about problem solving as it provides opportunities for student investigations and mathematical communication. All the activities in this book can be incorporated in a three-part lesson, the key elements of which are described on the next page. As part of the planning process for a three-part lesson, it is critical that educators identify the objectives of the lesson—the specific mathematical concepts, ideas, and skills they want students to understand by the end of the lesson. This enables you to plan with the end in mind, selecting problems or explorations that are aligned with specific learning objectives that suit your students' needs. You need to thoroughly understand the problem and anticipate possible student responses and misconceptions that may arise.

Minds On/Getting Started

The first part of the lesson involves preparing the students for the investigation or problem. This can be done in a number of ways, depending on the needs of your students. You may decide to revisit a previous problem so students can make connections between the strategies they used previously and those they may need for the new problem. You may also review a concept related to the problem. The problem or investigation is also presented during this part of the activity. It is important that students understand both the activity and the indicators for success (see pages xvi–xvii). It is also critical to inform students how they will be sharing their ideas and solutions with the rest of the class—will they be sharing informally in small-group or whole-class discussion, or as part of a more structured process such as a gallery walk, math congress, or Bansho (see Chapter 2)?

Working on It/Action

The second part of the lesson involves students actively solving the problem by exploring a variety of strategies. Students work in small groups or pairs, which enables them to discuss their ideas and learn from each other. Instead of giving answers, the teacher circulates to facilitate learning by posing questions that promote deep mathematical thinking, illuminate misconceptions, and engage learners in reflecting on and explaining their ideas and solutions. You may need to scaffold questions in order to assist learners who may struggle. You also make notes and observations of students during this time to document learning and note themes and ideas you may wish to highlight when students share their ideas during the consolidation part of the lesson.

Consolidation/Reflecting and Connecting

Consolidation is an important but often missing piece that is a key component of strong teaching and learning. After students have had time to explore the problem, the teacher facilitates sharing in which students discuss their solutions and problem-solving strategies. This can be done through a whole-class sharing, a gallery walk, math congress, or Bansho.

As students complete their solutions on paper and/or using manipulatives, you may want to take pictures using a tablet and then share the images using an interactive whiteboard or a screen. This will allow you to document the learning and add any annotations directly to the image. You can also invite students to arrange manipulatives or place their written work under a document camera, take a picture, and annotate their thinking on the whiteboard. This documentation can then be used for future reference. Using technology does not replace your students' written work, but rather enhances the documenting/sharing process.

Regardless of how you decide to structure the consolidation process, students should have opportunities to share their ideas, pose questions of each other, and compare and analyze different solutions. It is through such experiences that students develop the abilities to identify effective strategies and reflect on their own mathematical understanding. The skills and mathematical concepts the teacher wanted the students to acquire (the objectives of the lesson) should be explicit to all. This may require additional clarification, modelling, and discussion. These discussions also provide you with rich insights into student learning and conceptual understanding of mathematics, around which further teaching can be planned.

Assessing Math Learning

It is critical that we use a wide variety of assessments to fairly document our students' progress. Inviting students to communicate their thinking in different ways enables educators to gain critical insight into what their students understand mathematically that may not be evident in a traditional test format. We need to create an equitable learning environment in which students can share what they know in authentic learning contexts and develop confidence as learners of mathematics.

For resources about this topic, see the *Math Expressions* website: www.pearsoncanada.ca/ mathexpressions

We can gather information about student progress using several kinds of assessment processes:

- Diagnostic assessment takes place before instruction and determines students' readiness to learn.

- Formative assessment is ongoing and enables educators and students to provide descriptive feedback for continued progress and set personal learning goals.

- Summative assessment usually occurs at the end of learning in which the educator assigns a value or mark to represent the level of learning.

Each of these approaches can be used to gather rich information about student learning. How the assessment data is to be used determines how we gather it (Harlen, 2006). This relationship is illustrated in the table on the next page, which is adapted from *Growing Success: Assessment, Evaluation, and Reporting in Ontario Schools* (Ontario Ministry of Education, 2010).

Summary of Assessment Approaches and Purposes

Assessment Approach	Purpose of Assessment	Use of Information
Diagnostic assessment	Assessment *for* learning: • Information about student progress is used to make decisions about programming. • Both teacher and student are involved in the decision making.	The information collected provides teachers with critical data about students' mathematical knowledge and areas in their learning they may need to improve. It enables teachers to plan instruction and assessments that meet the individual needs of students.
Formative assessment	Assessment *for* learning: • Information about student progress is used to make decisions about programming. • Both teacher and student are involved in the decision making.	The information collected is used by teachers to provide specific feedback on student progress to improve student achievement, scaffold next steps, and inform instruction to meet student needs.
	Assessment *as* learning: • Information enables students to self-assess and set personal learning goals. • This kind of assessment focuses on deepening students' understanding of their learning skills and knowledge in mathematics.	The information gathered is used by students to self-assess, set personal learning goals, make changes in their learning, reflect on their progress, provide feedback to their peers, and monitor their own progress.
Summative assessment	Assessment *of* learning: • Information is used to create statements or symbols about how well students are learning.	The information collected is used to assign a value that represents the students' quality of learning and to communicate information about achievement to parents, teachers, and students.

© Queen's Printer for Ontario, 2010. Adapted and reproduced with permission.

One piece of student work can be assessed for different purposes. For example, a written reflection on geometry can be used for assessment *as* learning by having students assess their writing skills based on a set of criteria. It can also be used as an assessment *for* learning in which the teacher provides feedback to guide students in improving their performance.

Regardless of the approach or purpose of assessment you choose, your students need to understand the criteria that define quality work.

Indicators of success can help you share the assessment information with your students. These are lists of performance criteria that describe what students need to do to successfully achieve a specific curriculum objective. They are written in student language and can be in the form of questions or statements. They are most effective when created in collaboration with students. These lists should be posted in the classroom so all students can refer to them when working on a task. Indicators of success enable students to self-monitor their own progress and to set

©P

learning goals. Many educators use them to provide students with meaningful descriptive feedback to help improve student learning. Indicators of success are revisited and refined during the learning process as students and teachers continually explore what constitutes a quality piece of work or performance (Greenan, 2011).

Sample indicators of success are provided in each chapter of this book. You may wish to modify the wording or content of these lists to suit your learners' needs. Take the time to develop and discuss the indicators with students. Provide examples of mathematical work that satisfies these goals. You could also provide examples that do not fit the indicators of success and discuss with your students how the work can be improved.

Using Descriptive Feedback to Promote Strong Communication and Problem-Solving Skills

Providing feedback for students as they communicate their thinking in mathematics is a key part of the assessment process. There are several kinds of feedback: *motivational*, *evaluative*, and *descriptive*. Each kind of feedback has a different goal. The goal of motivational feedback is to encourage students and make them feel good about themselves. The goal of evaluative feedback is to measure student achievement and summarize student learning. This kind of feedback does not provide any suggestions for further growth or improvement. On the other hand, descriptive feedback provides learners with suggestions on how they can move forward and engages them in thinking critically about their work. This type of feedback is most effective when based on indicators of success. Effective descriptive feedback also poses questions to learners to empower them to develop strong self-assessment strategies. In mathematical communication, descriptive feedback is critical to assist students in understanding the elements of effective communication and provide opportunities for students to become independent learners.

Examples of descriptive feedback are included with many of the student samples in this book. The feedback you provide needs to be individualized based on each student. You may choose to provide more or less feedback than is shown with the samples. You may also decide to give feedback verbally or in written form.

The following examples illustrate how you can provide different types of feedback on one piece of student work.

Types of Feedback

The student completes a problem and creates a poster on chart paper to share his strategies.

- Motivational feedback: "I like how you worked on this assignment."

- Evaluative feedback: Level 3, B+ (based on a rubric)

- Effective descriptive feedback: "The strategy you used to show the different pieces of the rug helps the reader to see how you arrived at the mathematical equation. What written piece could you include to explain why you chose the strategy you did? What other way can you calculate the area of the rug besides counting the squares? Is there a more efficient way you can do this?"

In a journal entry, the student shares what she likes about mathematics.

- Motivational feedback: "I like your enthusiasm."

- Effective descriptive feedback: "This entry is better than the last one, as you have taken the time to provide reasons why you like specific areas in mathematics. What other reasons could you add to convince those students who do not like mathematics that it is an important subject?"

Meaningful descriptive feedback can assist students in becoming metacognitive of their own communication skills. As students become more aware of how others understand and interpret their work, they learn which areas of their mathematical communication are effective and how they can improve other areas.

A Culture of Collaboration and Inquiry

Indicators of Success

In an effective collaborative mathematics classroom, students do the following:

- Students share their mathematical ideas clearly with one another, the class, and the teacher, using a variety of approaches such as manipulatives, writing, pictures, and discussion.

- Students listen attentively to each other and can clearly explain what they have heard in their own words.

- Students negotiate any differences in mathematical thinking in a collegial way.

- Students pose questions that promote and support further mathematical thinking.

- Students take turns and allow each member to speak and contribute to the group process.

- Students reflect on the strategies they use to work collaboratively with others.

For a reproducible version of these indicators of success, see the *Math Expressions* website: www.pearsoncanada.ca/ mathexpressions

What the Research Says About...
Cooperative Learning

For resources about cooperative learning, see the *Math Expressions* website: www.pearsoncanada.ca/mathexpressions

Cooperative learning is a teaching approach in which students collaborate in groups to complete specific activities. It can provide many opportunities for students to share their thinking and engage in mathematical discourse (Marks Krpan, 2009). Unlike group work where there is no collaborative structure, cooperative learning focuses on developing key collaborative skills and ensuring that all group members participate in each task. Discussions that take place during cooperative group activities in mathematics can improve students' understanding of the concepts they are learning and enable students to learn different approaches and strategies (Downey, 2000; Sousa, 2001).

Cooperative learning can assist the brain in retaining concepts and ideas efficiently and thus improve student achievement (Jensen, 2005; Johnson, Johnson, & Holubec, 2008). It can also play a key role in creating a safe learning environment for students (Bennett, Rolheiser, & Stevahn, 2001). Cooperative experiences create rich learning contexts in which students can express ideas and concepts using specific mathematical language. Because of these factors, cooperative experiences can help learners who struggle to develop key mathematical skills.

Some Key Benefits of Cooperative Learning

- Students can learn mathematical strategies from each other.

- Students can discuss and write about their mathematical thinking and receive feedback from their peers.

- Students can develop effective verbal, writing, and reading skills.

- Discussions or writing activities that arise from cooperative activities can help students consolidate their understanding of specific mathematical vocabulary or concepts.

- Students can share different ways to model a problem.

- The cooperative process can assist in developing collaborative learning skills that are critical to an effective mathematics classroom.

Elements of the Cooperative Learning Experience

All of the activities discussed in this book can be implemented as cooperative endeavours. The remainder of this chapter explores how to teach cooperative learning skills in mathematics and how to infuse cooperative learning structures into your mathematics program.

For cooperative learning to work effectively, students need to have the skills and knowledge to work with others. Even though cooperative skills may be taught in other subject areas, we need to explicitly teach these skills in mathematics, as cooperative math activities have challenges that do not exist in other subject areas. In mathematics, students often need to represent mathematical language and concepts in different ways. They can use manipulatives, numbers, pictures, and models to support their ideas and conjectures and communicate their thinking. Another challenge is that much of the language used by students in mathematics is not language they use in daily conversations.

According to Johnson and Johnson (1989, 2005), several key elements need to be part of a cooperative learning experience:

- exploration and teaching of the social processes of collaboration

- interdependence

- individual accountability

- a common goal

- face-to-face interactions

Teaching Social Processes: Equity for All Learners

Before students begin to work collaboratively on mathematical activities, we need to ensure that they develop an understanding of *group norms*, or behaviours that guide cooperative work. These group norms are important not only for cooperative group work, but also for the overall classroom environment. These behaviours can be introduced using the Cooperative Math Chart, a chart based on the work of Jeanne Gibbs. An example is provided as Line Master 1.1 (Cooperative Math Chart), though the chart can be modified to include different skills. Completing the chart encourages students to consider the different aspects of cooperative learning and what they look like, sound like, and feel like in mathematics. Using it as part of your teaching can improve cooperative behaviour in groups (Marks Krpan, 2009).

All line masters are provided in print format starting on page 133 of this book. They are also provided in a reproducible format on the *Math Expressions* website: www.pearsoncanada.ca/mathexpressions

Before introducing the Cooperative Math Chart, invite students to identify key cooperative behaviours that are necessary to work effectively as a group. You may choose to list the behaviours on the board and discuss why they are important. Then show the class the Cooperative Math Chart. Explain that to work collaboratively together, they need guidelines to follow. Record some of the skills on a Cooperative Math Chart.

You can fill out the Cooperative Math Chart as a whole-class activity in which students provide ideas and you record them under the appropriate headings. Invite students to share what each skill looks like, sounds like, and feels like. You may need to provide guidance, as students may be unused to describing behaviours in these terms. For example, suppose you are considering the skill disagreeing in a positive way. Under the heading "Looks Like," students should be thinking about what they would see a person doing if that person were following the group norm. They could describe what the person would be doing, such as nodding her head and

Sample Cooperative Math Chart Completed as a Whole-Class Activity

	Looks Like 👁	Sounds Like 👂	Feels Like ♥
Listening	• looking at the person who is speaking • sitting with good posture • raise your hand to share an idea • try not to fidget	• everyone is quiet • hear the voice of the speaker • raise our hand quietly	• feel and show respect • our brain is soaking up knowledge "I understand" • might feel confused + upset "I don't understand" embarrassed • calm, focussed on the speaker
Sharing my Thinking	• hand is raised • listening with their eyes • show your thinking using pictures, words, numbers, patterns, grids, shapes...	• person shares their ideas using words • those listening might ask questions	• the person is thinking and maybe learning new things • feel shy, nervous, confused • feel excited, happy • being curious · try something new • agree or disagree
Disagree in a positive way	• hand is raised • confused faces • the people who disagree should look at each other • show their work to prove their opinion	• laughter (bad thing) • "we have different answers" • that's okay! we are allowed to disagree. "good try" • positive words • voices might get too loud	• might feel sad, mad, cry, frustrated • might want to stop and give up • want to learn different ways • learn from our mistakes • always feel safe to disagree • always more than one way to do something

©P

looking at the group members' work. Under the heading "Sounds Like," students should be thinking about what kinds of things the person would be saying. They can use an adjective to describe the person's words, such as "encouraging" or "helpful," or provide phrases the person might say, for example, "I prefer a different way to do this," or "Can you think of another way?" Under the heading "Feels Like," students should describe how they think people in the group may feel when this specific norm is being used.

You can also invite your students to work in small groups to fill out the chart and then decide through a class discussion which ideas should be recorded on the large class chart. As students complete cooperative math activities, you can refer to the class chart to review expectations and provide guidance.

For students to improve their cooperative skills in mathematics, they need to consider which collaborative strategies they used effectively and which ones need improvement. They can do this in a debriefing, where you invite students to reflect on their cooperative skills. The reflection process can take place as a journal activity or as a discussion. I like to invite students to debrief in their groups and then have a class discussion about the cooperative process. However, if time is an issue, just take a few minutes and facilitate a class discussion on several key cooperative learning strategies. Some questions that you can pose to facilitate the debriefing are provided on the next page. You may need to modify the questions to suit the needs of your students.

Sample Cooperative Math Chart Completed by Students

Skill	Looks Like	Sounds Like	Feels Like
Listening to others	- eyes on speaker - serious - mouths are shut	- one person talking - quiet	- respect the speaker - being careful about your reactions
Sharing my thinking	- use expression when speaking - eye contact	- creative - pacing yourself - clear	- included - important
Disagreeing in a positive way	- no negative facial expressions - talking to each other - sharing ideas	- calm conversation - one person talking at a time	- understood by the other person
Including everyone in the process	- everybody has a job or is "doing" - everybody has a turn to talk - participation	- each group member expresses opinion w/o being interrupted	- everyone feels important and included
Posing good questions during presentations	- peers look curious - making eye contact with presenter - raising hand - waiting your turn	- not asking questions that you already know the answer to - one person talking at a time	- could feel impatient cause you want to ask your questions or present - at times you feel interested and other times you feel bored

- Did you have any disagreements in your group? If so, how did you resolve them?

- What are the different strengths of each group member? List them.

- How did you ensure that all members of your group participated?

- Did you encounter any challenges as you worked collaboratively on this activity? How did you overcome these challenges?

- Which cooperative learning skill do you feel your group executed effectively?

- How do you feel you can improve how you work in a group for the next activity?

- Can you provide me with an example of how you shared materials, listened effectively, or disagreed in a positive way? Please do so.

- What cooperative skill would you like to improve for next time? Which cooperative skill do you do well?

Valuing Cultural Diversity and Diverse Learning Styles

When filling out the Cooperative Math Chart, students and teachers need to be sensitive to the cultural diversity in their classrooms and the impact culture can have on group interactions. For example, active listening can look different in different cultures. In some cultures, it is insulting to have eye contact with the speaker. Crossing the arms may seem disengaging in North American cultures, but in other cultures listeners do this to communicate to the speaker that they are listening and their hands are still. We must ensure that our students are aware that there are many diverse ways to demonstrate effective group interactions. In some classrooms, this discussion may not arise naturally. However, as educators we must create opportunities for these kinds of discussions to take place. In addition, students of different cultures may not feel comfortable initiating a conversation on this topic. To ensure that the cooperative process is inclusive, we need to include a variety of examples so that all students feel respected and valued in the classroom.

In addition to cultural diversity, the chart should take into consideration the variety of learning approaches in our classrooms. For example, for the skill sharing mathematical ideas, it is important that students consider a variety of modes of communication. Beyond talking and writing on paper, students may use adaptive technology, manipulatives, models, or drawings to communicate their ideas. It is also important to ensure that English Language Learners are included in the examples. Some ELLs may prefer to write their ideas in a language other than English in order to process their thinking or organize their ideas. You may also have students who feel more comfortable speaking to each other in a different language when thinking through a problem. These are just a few examples to consider. As your students discuss what to include in the chart, ensure that the ideas and examples are inclusive and equitable for all learners.

Positive Interdependence and a Common Goal

Positive group interdependence is when the success of the task depends on the full contribution of all group members. If one group member does not contribute, the completion of the task is compromised. Providing the group with a common goal, such as solving a math problem or providing examples of a mathematical concept, ensures that all group members are striving for the same outcome. Here are some ways you can establish interdependence for cooperative learning in mathematics:

- Assign each group member a role. These roles need to be meaningful and helpful to the group process. See "Assigning Group Roles" on pages 8–10 in the Facilitating Cooperative Learning section for more information.

- Explain to your class that all group members need to understand the whole task and solution as you may call on any group member to explain the process, solution, or mathematical meaning.

- Include all learners by ensuring that the task you provide requires a diverse skill set and knowledge.

- Provide each group member with a different piece of information that needs to be shared with the whole group in order for the task to be completed. This information can be about the actual task or related to a problem that the group is to address.

Individual Accountability

Individual accountability takes place when each member of the group is responsible for sharing ideas and learning. This sharing can take many forms, including a written reflection, a presentation, or a summary to the group members of what was learned. Individual accountability encourages all members of the group to participate. By creating opportunities for individual accountability, you also provide more opportunities for assessment. Here are some ways to build in individual accountability:

- After a problem-solving activity, each member writes a journal reflection discussing why the group's solution was effective or not effective.

- At the end of a think-pair-share activity in which the students determine whether or not a non-standard algorithm makes sense, each member shares the ideas of her or his partner with the rest of the class.

- After a cooperative activity in which students create and name different triangles, students individually complete a small review in which they identify four different triangles.

- After exploring different ways to make 40 by combining the numbers 4, 7, 5, and 8, each group member explains two solutions to members of a different group.

Face-to-Face Interactions

When students are working collaboratively, it is important that they work in close proximity to each other. They can be seated in groups at desks or tables pushed together, or even seated on the floor separated from other groups. They should have easy access to the materials and be able to share ideas readily with one another.

Facilitating Cooperative Learning

Cooperative Groupings

In classrooms where students collaborate and share ideas, the classroom organization is often different than that of a traditional mathematics classroom. Students are organized in groupings that change based on the topics explored and the students' individual needs.

For cooperative learning to work well, be sure to consider the needs of your students and how they work with others when you are creating groups. You can create groupings based on abilities, interests, learning styles, or other criteria. Keep in mind that a student may be strong in one area of mathematics yet need more support in another. You can also invite students to create their own groups. Varying the groupings throughout your mathematics program will enable students to explore mathematical ideas and concepts with different learners. As well as varying the kinds of groupings, vary the size of the groups. Groups of 2, 3, or 4 students work best. I recommend that cooperative groups have no more than 5 students.

Assigning Group Roles

Assigning a specific role to each member in a cooperative group helps to ensure that everyone participates in the cooperative process. Group roles also promote equal distribution of responsibility in the group. A list of possible roles and responsibilities is shown in this table. You may decide to select from this list or use different roles depending on the needs of your students. Another option is to create cooperative roles collaboratively with your students and discuss the responsibilities of each.

Possible Group Roles and Responsibilities	
Role	**Responsibilities**
Timekeeper	• keeps the group on task and keeps track of the time • reminds the group members when they are halfway through the activity and again when time is almost up
Materials monitor	• collects and organizes the materials for the group • explains how materials are to be used • organizes the cleanup process for the group
Advice seeker	• asks any questions of the teacher on behalf of all other group members • ensures that no one in the group already knows the answer to the question before asking a question of the teacher • ensures that everyone in the group understands the teacher's answer
Recorder	• records information for the group • verifies that what is recorded is accurate by consulting group members
Checker	• continually checks to make sure that the group's ideas and answers make mathematical sense • ensures that everyone in the group understands the answers
Presenter	• presents the final answer to the class or other groups • verifies content to make sure that it accurately represents the group's ideas

Line Masters 1.2 and 1.3 (Cooperative Group Roles for Mathematics) provide descriptions of group roles for primary and junior/intermediate students. You may decide to post the descriptions in the classroom or provide a copy of the appropriate line master to each group.

You can assign these roles in a variety of ways: group members can number off from 1 to 5 and then you randomly assign a role to all the number 1s, 2s, and so on; you can outline the roles on index cards and invite students to draw cards to determine their roles; students can also discuss in their groups which role they would like to have.

It is important that throughout the school year, students have opportunities to take on different roles that they can handle. Students can thereby develop a variety of cooperative skills. It is also important to know the strengths of your students as you do not want a student who struggles in writing to feel pressured to take on the role of recorder if it would cause discomfort. However, this situation could be a great opportunity to invite the group to record the information in a different way such as a mind map, concept map, model, or picture. Always ensure that each role is needed and not assigned for the sake of everyone having one. I often post the expectations for each role in the classroom during the cooperative activities. Providing sample statements or questions that could be used by a person in each role is also very helpful. Doing this enables students to take part more fully and understand what each role requires.

In some cases, assigning the role of presenter before the group completes the activity is unwise. It can create a sense of complacency among the other group members because they know that someone else will be presenting the information. To avoid this, you can assign roles to all group members without assigning a presenter. Explain to the class that everyone should be ready to share: you will call on a different member to explain each group's ideas. Keep in mind that students should be able to share their group's ideas in a way that is conducive to their learning style and comfort level, using models, charts, analogies, or other structures. You can also invite each group member to explain their learning individually through a journal entry or brief reflection after the presentations are made.

Promoting Equity

Arranging students in cooperative groups does not mean that they will automatically practise or develop cooperative skills. Many power issues and inequities that need to be addressed in our teaching can arise in cooperative group activities. For example, students who are less mathematical may be made to feel incompetent by those who are strong in mathematics. Their attempts to contribute to the group may be ignored or dismissed. Students who have skills that others perceive as being superior may gain more status or power in the group. These kinds of inequities can prevent group members from participating, leading to less learning and achievement for all students (Cohen, 1994). It is critical that we broaden our students' perceptions of what it is to be smart and ensure that they understand that all students can make meaningful contributions to a task. You can facilitate this process by providing tasks that require a diverse set of skills to complete.

Assessing Cooperative Learning

Cooperative activities can be used effectively as an assessment *for* learning and *as* learning to strengthen student problem-solving, teach specific strategies, and enable students to assess their work and the work of others. Building in individual accountability in your cooperative activities will enable you to assess the progress of individual students more readily. It is challenging to assess a piece of work that was completed by four students when you are not sure of what each student contributed to the project.

The cooperative context can provide you with rich data about how students approach mathematical problems and explain their thinking to others. When students work on cooperative activities, I often circulate with a checklist to document their problem-solving approaches, mathematical discourse, and ideas. A sample is provided as Line Master 1.4 (Observation Checklist for Cooperative Work). This checklist can also be used when students share ideas with the rest of the class. Including an individual demonstration of learning as part of the cooperative process can provide you with assessment information about the individual progress of each student. This information could take many forms, including a journal reflection, summary, question sheet, or evidence of what each student contributed to the final product.

Cooperative Learning Structures

Cooperative learning structures provide the necessary organization and guidance for students as they work collaboratively in groups. There are more than 100 cooperative structures (Kagan & Kagan, 2009). In this section I will introduce a few of the structures that I have found to be helpful for teaching mathematics. These cooperative structures are meant to be used with any of the activities described in this book.

Think-Pair-Share

Think-pair-share is a cooperative structure that begins by inviting each student to think about a specific mathematics topic or question and then discuss his or her ideas with a partner. Once each pair has discussed their ideas, they can share their ideas with the whole class. This cooperative structure is very effective as you can infuse it into any learning experience, and it does not take up a lot of time. By inviting your students to think and then discuss an idea with another classmate, you ensure that all students have an opportunity to reflect on their knowledge, discuss their mathematical thinking, and learn from others.

materials
- none

Sample Implementation of Think-Pair-Share

1. THINK. Invite students to think about a specific mathematical question or topic. Allow at least 15 to 30 seconds.

2. PAIR. Invite students to face a partner.

3. SHARE. Prompt students to share their ideas with their partners.

You can also invite pairs to share their ideas with other pairs or in larger groups.

Extension: Think-Pair-Share-Write

Once the students have completed the sharing part of a think-pair-share activity, invite them to write independently about the topic just discussed.

Placemat

materials

- any materials specific to the assigned task

- a piece of chart paper for each group

- a marker for each group member

- painter's tape (optional for activity modification and extension)

Placemat is a cooperative structure that helps students to work together and share ideas in a group. It enables each group member to reflect on the task before sharing with others. In traditional group work, one student may take over and other group members may not participate. The placemat structure creates a high level of accountability as each group member is expected to fill in a section of the placemat and sign his or her name in the section. This practice allows you to document what each member contributed to the final response in the middle. The placemat structure enables students to write, draw, and/or arrange concrete materials to represent their ideas and communicate their thinking to others. Students also gain the opportunity to see how others organize their ideas and communicate mathematically.

You may want to provide students with some guidance on how to decide which ideas to include in the middle square. The group can base the decision on which ideas are most common among the group members or invite each member to provide one idea for the middle. The group can also decide which ideas make the most sense and include those in the middle square.

You can use the placemat structure in a variety of ways. In an agreed-upon placemat section, students can work with manipulatives or on a math problem and then share their solutions with the group. The final solution, such as the arrangement of the manipulatives, a reflection, or a response to a word problem, can be put in the central square.

Sample Implementation of Placemat

1. Each group draws a central square or oval in the middle of a piece of chart paper and divides the surrounding space into the same number of sections as the number of group members, as shown in these samples for groups of 3, 4, and 5 students. Each group member sits facing one of the spaces.

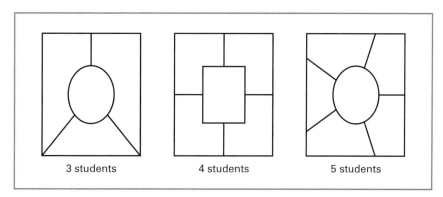

3 students   4 students   5 students

2. Provide the question or task to complete. Each student writes independently (in silence) in a designated space. Remind students to record their names in the appropriate placemat section. You will then be able to see at a glance what each person contributed to the final answer.

Each student can also have a different related topic or task to think about.

3. Each student shares ideas within the group. The group discusses the responses and decides on a collaborative response which they write in the middle space, incorporating the ideas from each member.

4. Each group shares its collaborative response with the whole class.

Modification and Extension of Placemat

This structure is similar to the placemat activity above, except each student begins working on the task on a separate sheet, then students come together in pairs to share.

1. Provide each student with a sheet of paper—tabloid size works well.

2. Assign students a task or problem to solve.

3. Students work on the task independently on their own sheet of paper.

4. Once students have completed the task, they pair up to share their ideas with another student. They attach their sheets of paper together with a blank sheet of paper between them. As they share, they record their collaborative response on the middle blank sheet. Painter's tape can be used to attach the sheets as it can be removed easily without harming the students' work. See the diagram on the next page.

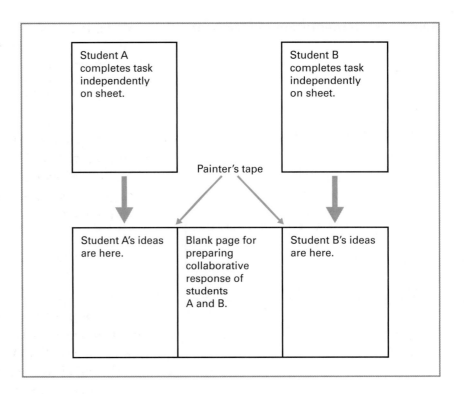

5. As an extension of this activity, each pair of students can take their collaborative response and work with another pair of students. Each pair removes the pages of individual work from the sides of their collaborative response. The two pairs of students then attach their collaborative pages together with a blank page between them. The two pairs share their ideas and write a final collaborative response on the blank page.

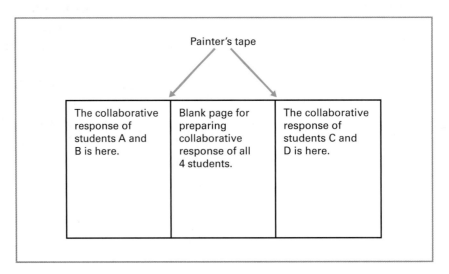

©P

Placemat

Groups of students were asked, "What are the differences between a triangle and a square?"

Left: The difference is a square has 4 sides and a triangle has 3 sides. If they were in 3D they would have a flat bottom.

Top: The difference between a triangle and a square is that a square has parallel sides and a triangle doesn't have parallel sides. A square has four sides and a triangle has three sides.

Right: The difference between a square and a triangle is a triangle has three corners and a square has four. And the square has parallel lines and the triangle doesn't have parallel lines. And a triangle looks like a pyramid and the square does not.

Bottom: The rectangle has four corners and the triangle has three corners. A triangle looks like a pyramid. A square looks like a…

Middle: The square has 4 corners and sides. The triangle has 3 sides and corners.

Each student wrote a different idea in his or her square. The students were able to provide a variety of examples of how the two shapes are different. In the middle, the group commented on the sides and corners, which was common to all four answers. To conclude the activity, each group shared its final answer with the class.

Sample Descriptive Feedback

I like how you have commented on the different numbers of corners and sides, which are key differences. What other differences from your group's ideas might you add to the centre? How could you show the differences using the images you have included?

Placemat

Grade 8

Groups of students were asked, "Which is larger, 1.7 or $1\frac{1}{2}$?"

Lower left: 1.7 is larger than $1\frac{1}{2}$. 1 whole $\frac{7}{10}$. If you convert $1\frac{7}{10}$ into a decimal, 1.7. 1 whole $\frac{5}{10}$. Convert to a decimal, 1.5. $1.7 > 1\frac{1}{2}$.

Upper left: 1.7 is larger than $1\frac{1}{2}$ because $\frac{1}{2}$ can be represented as 0.5 so $1\frac{1}{2}$ would (be) 1.5 so 1.7 is bigger because it is more than 1.5.

Upper right: 1.7 is larger than $1\frac{1}{2}$ because $1\frac{1}{2}$ can be represented as 1.5 so $1\frac{1}{2}$ would (be) 1.5 so 1.7 is bigger because it is more than 1.5.

Lower right: 1.7 is larger than $1\frac{1}{2}$ because $1\frac{1}{2}$ is 1.5 and the other number is 1.7 which is larger. There is a difference of 0.2 or $\frac{2}{10}$. $1.5 + .2 = 1.7$.

Middle: 1.7 is larger than $1\frac{1}{2}$. $1.5 < 1.7$. $1\frac{1}{2}$. $\frac{1}{2}$ is also 0.5 so it would be 1.5, and 1.7 is more than 1.5 so 1.7 is greater.

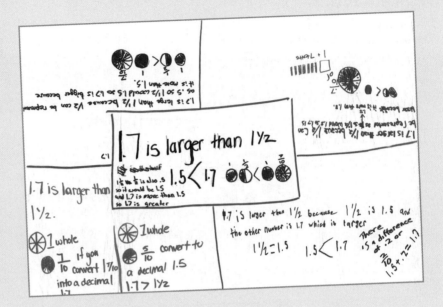

These students had already studied decimals and fractions. The teacher felt that this activity was a great way to explore what her students understood about these concepts, as students would demonstrate their ability to apply their knowledge in the context of proofs and mathematical arguments.

The students knew how to convert a fraction to a decimal to demonstrate the difference between two numbers. They understood that decimals and fractions can express the same quantity. They also used images effectively to represent the differences between the two numbers visually.

Sample Descriptive Feedback

In your final answer, you use images effectively to show that 1.7 is larger than $1\frac{1}{2}$. How could you use these images to show the reader how much larger 1.7 is than $1\frac{1}{2}$? I like how you converted $\frac{1}{2}$ into the decimal 0.5 so that you could compare the two numbers easily. This is an effective strategy to use in mathematics when numbers are written in different forms. What other visuals could you include to show that 1.7 is larger than $1\frac{1}{2}$?

Three Stay, One Stray

For this cooperative activity, students form groups of four, which are their *home* groups. The teacher provides the class with a math activity to complete. Examples of activities include a writing response, a word problem, modelling ideas with manipulatives, or mathematics brainstorming. Each group can complete the same activity or a different version of one activity.

Sample Implementation of Three Stay, One Stray

1. Provide each group with its activity and allow enough time for each group to complete it. This cooperative structure works best if students record their thinking on chart paper to make it easy to share.

2. Groups choose a spokesperson to share the work they have completed, or the teacher determines who will be the spokesperson. One good practice is to wait until the students have completed the activity to determine who will share. Doing so ensures that all group members realize that they must be knowledgeable about the group's work as they may be called upon to share.

3. When told to do so, the spokespeople each visit another group to share what their groups did.

4. The students who stay behind listen carefully to what the visiting spokesperson shares and take notes. The spokesperson can also take notes of comments and suggestions from the group to take back to the home group.

5. Once the spokespeople have shared, you can ask them to each visit another group or to return to their home groups.

6. When the spokespeople return to their home groups, they report on comments from the other group(s), and the home groups make changes to their original work as necessary.

materials
- any materials specific to the assigned task
- a piece of chart paper for each group
- a marker for each group

Gallery Walk

During this cooperative structure, students post their group work in the classroom. Students circulate, look at other groups' work, and provide feedback. As students examine the different work samples, they move around from piece to piece, which helps the brain learn more effectively. This activity also enables students to learn different mathematical strategies and gain immediate feedback on their work.

materials
- any materials specific to the assigned task
- a piece of chart paper for each group
- a marker for each group
- sticky notes for each group

Sample Implementation of Gallery Walk

1. Arrange your students in groups of 4 or 5.

2. Ask the groups to complete a math activity, perhaps a reflection, a drawing activity, a writing activity, or a problem-solving activity. Groups record their work on chart paper.

3. Once students have completed their work, invite groups to post their work on the wall in different parts of the classroom.

4. Provide each group with a pad of sticky notes. Invite each group to circulate to the other pieces of work posted in the classroom. They can circulate as a group or on their own. Ask the groups to examine each piece and write feedback on the sticky notes. They then post the sticky note on the piece of work.

5. Each group or individual in the group can write several sticky notes. The feedback can take many forms, including a compliment, a suggestion, a question, or a comment. It is helpful to explore with your students what constitutes effective descriptive feedback. Some sample descriptive feedback prompts are provided here. You may wish to post a list of prompts as a reference for students.

Sample Descriptive Feedback Prompts

- Can you think of another way to explain…?
- What you wrote is not clear to me because…
- Try to add more detail to…because…
- I do not understand…
- I like the way you…because…
- You need to explain…because…
- You forgot to add…
- The diagram that you created of…is very helpful because...
- I did not think of using this strategy. It is very effective because…
- The strategy you used does not make sense to me because…
- Your presentation is clear and easy to follow because…

6. Students sign their name to their comments. This requirement builds in individual accountability and allows you to identify which students have made comments.

7. Once the groups have had a chance to view and provide feedback on each piece of work, they return to their own piece of work and read the feedback.

8. The groups can make whatever changes they want to their work.

Extension of Gallery Walk

One way of extending this activity is to work with students to develop indicators of success for descriptive feedback. These ideas can help students when they are providing feedback on a gallery walk or on any other cooperative activity. Below are sample indicators you may wish to modify in wording or content to suit your learners' needs.

Sample Indicators of Success for Descriptive Feedback

❑ Do I use the indicators of success (for the material being assessed) as a guide?

❑ Do I provide suggestions and/or comments that can help the author(s) improve his/her/their work?

❑ Do I include examples from the work in my feedback?

❑ Do I point out what is good and why it is good?

❑ Do I explain what needs to be improved and why?

❑ Do I pose questions or make comments that can help the author(s) improve his/her/their mathematical thinking/ideas?

For a reproducible version of these sample indicators of success, see the *Math Expressions* website: www.pearsoncanada.ca/mathexpressions

Inside-Outside Circle

This activity engages students in discussing mathematical ideas with classmates with whom they may not work on a regular basis. Like gallery walk, this structure gets students moving, which helps the brain learn more effectively. It also engages all students in talking at once. You can invite students to answer previously prepared questions that review the previous day's lesson, to reflect on a math problem and discuss how they would solve it, to discuss one challenge or success that they had in mathematics that week, to explain different vocabulary words, or to review concepts before a test. The possibilities are endless! You can also provide students with a list of questions that they discuss with each new partner.

materials
• none

Sample Implementation of Inside-Outside Circle

1. Organize your students into two concentric circles with the same number of students in each.

2. Invite the students in the inside circle to face the student standing in front of them in the outside circle and vice versa. Every student should be facing a partner.

3. Provide students with a discussion topic as described on the previous page. Explain that when you say to begin, the person in the outside circle will begin to talk about the topic while the person in the inside circle listens for a specific timed duration, such as 30 seconds or one minute.

4. Invite students to change roles. The students standing in the inside circle talk about the topic with their partner in the outside circle.

5. Once they have completed the discussion, ask the students in the inside circle to move clockwise to face a new partner in the outside circle.

6. Students take turns again, sharing with their new partners. You may either provide another topic or have the students share what they discussed with their last partner and add to it.

Chapter 2

Mathematical Discourse

Indicators of Success

Goals for students include the following:

- Students are able to explain their thinking clearly.

- Students are able to build on what others contribute to mathematical discussions.

- Students are able to paraphrase or explain what others are saying.

- Students are able to modify their ideas when appropriate, as they listen to others.

- Students are able to provide helpful feedback to others.

- Students use appropriate mathematical vocabulary.

- Students are able to pose effective questions to elicit thinking from others.

- Students are able to describe models or diagrams and how they represent mathematical ideas.

For a reproducible version of these indicators of success, see the *Math Expressions* website: www.pearsoncanada.ca/mathexpressions

What the Research Says About...
Mathematical Discourse

For resources about mathematical discourse, see the *Math Expressions* website: www.pearsoncanada.ca/mathexpressions

While teaching a Grade 6 math class, I invited students to discuss how they completed a specific problem. Blank faces stared back at me. Finally, a student spoke up and said: "Sorry, miss, this is not language arts—it's math. Just tell us how to do it and that is all we need. We do not talk math." Too often, students perceive mathematics as a subject that requires no discussion or sharing of ideas—all that matters is the answer. They follow the rules and if they get stuck, they wait, as they know that someone will eventually rescue them with an answer (Marks Krpan, 2008a).

When students practise computational procedures without discussing the conceptual ideas that underlie the procedures, the computation method is often forgotten or learned incorrectly (Bransford, Brown, & Cocking, 1999; Fosnot & Dolk, 2001; Hiebert, 1999). This approach can leave students overly dependent on prescribed processes, limiting their ability to solve problems unless they have a strategy provided to them. When students experience learning in this way, they often develop a narrow view of mathematics and problem solving (Stein, 2007). The National Council of Teachers of Mathematics (NCTM) (2000) recommends that students explore different strategies to solve problems and understand how different approaches are used in different contexts. For this to occur, we need to allow time in our instruction for communication and reflection on those strategies. Instead of providing the answers and listing the steps to follow, we become facilitators and questioners, guiding discussions and helping students make meaning of the mathematics. Students need opportunities to reflect on, explore, and analyze different mathematical approaches. In this learning environment, their ideas are valued and serve as a rich context for learning (Knuth & Peressini, 2001; NCTM, 2000).

When we encourage students to talk about mathematics, we provide them with opportunities to rehearse their thinking and link ideas together (Marks Krpan, 2009; Zolkower & Shreyar, 2007). We also enable them to develop key critical thinking skills. Hiebert et al. (1997) stress that stopping to reflect on one's thinking is almost sure to result in increased understanding. Students learn to communicate and communicate to learn (NCTM, 2000). Student achievement and engagement are improved when students have opportunities to explain, compare, and justify their mathematical thinking (Fosnot & Dolk, 2006; Kazemi & Stipek, 2001; Turner & Meyer, 2004). As students strive to justify their solutions, especially to others who think differently, they will gain a better understanding of mathematics.

By infusing our classrooms with mathematical discourse, we can help both students and ourselves as teachers. We can assist students in deepening their personal understanding of current knowledge, in acquiring new ideas, and in strengthening problem-solving skills (Lambert, 1990;

Rigleman, 2007). At the same time, student discourse can provide insight into student learning and help us to identify any misconceptions that can be concealed by a correct answer (NCTM, 2000).

Furthermore, when students share their thinking and discuss mathematical ideas, their overall knowledge of mathematics improves. They have opportunities to use mathematical terms in meaningful contexts, which helps them to deepen their understanding of mathematical language. They also listen to others construct mathematical knowledge, an experience that can broaden and enhance their view of mathematics. Engaging students in meaningful problem solving and mathematical discussions about their thinking is critical to success in mathematics (Fosnot, 2005; Marks Krpan, 2011).

What Students Say...

The comments of these students reflect a recognition of the benefits of talking about mathematical ideas.

- *When I talk to my friends I can hear my thinking.* (Grade 2)

- *When I explain my ideas in math, I have to think a lot more.* (Grade 3)

- *When I talk about math, sometimes I discover that I did not understand an idea and now I do.* (Grade 4)

- *I like discussing ideas because I can learn new things from other students.* (Grade 7)

Assessing Mathematical Discourse

To make effective decisions about student learning, teachers need to collect assessment data from a variety of sources, including discourse and in-class activities. This approach will allow teachers to create a comprehensive picture of their students' learning and enable both teachers and students to set meaningful learning and teaching goals (NCTM, 2000).

Mathematical discourse can provide rich formative assessment that can inform your teaching and be used to support other kinds of assessments you use in your mathematics program. An observation checklist such as Line Master 2.1 (Student Discourse Observation Sheet) can help you gather data as you listen to your students share their thinking. As students make conjectures and debate mathematical ideas, they make connections in their learning.

Since mathematical talk is a dynamic part of the learning process, grading student discussions is ineffective. If students know that they may be penalized for making an incorrect conjecture or for sharing an incorrect idea, the benefits of mathematical discourse can be negated. Students may refrain from sharing their thinking or exploring ideas freely in this context. As they debate ideas in mathematics, students need to feel comfortable taking risks.

Student interviews are an effective way to gain insight into how students think mathematically. By creating a set of questions related to a specific topic, you can engage students in sharing their ideas or demonstrating their skills in a specific area of mathematics. You can invite a student to complete an activity in front of you and then discuss what the student did and why. Unlike group discussions or other assessment approaches, interviews enable you to assess student thinking in depth and pose follow-up questions for clarification or support. I often found one-on-one interviews to be extremely effective in learning about what my students knew mathematically. As they answered the questions or modelled an idea using manipulatives, I documented what they did and said on an interview sheet such as Line Master 2.2 (Interview Sheet).

As described in the introduction to this book, providing students with indicators of success can assist them in understanding your expectations. Sample indicators for discourse are shown below. You may wish to modify the wording or content of this list to suit your learners' needs.

For a reproducible version of these sample indicators of success, see the *Math Expressions* website: www.pearsoncanada.ca/mathexpressions

Sample Indicators of Success for Effective Mathematical Discourse
❑ Can I explain my ideas clearly so others understand what I mean?
❑ Do I use listening skills such as paraphrasing and posing questions?
❑ Do I use math words correctly when I explain my thinking?
❑ Can I explain other people's ideas in my own words?
❑ When others talk, do I ask questions to help them explain their thinking?

Facilitating Mathematical Discourse

When considering the elements of rich classroom discussions in mathematics, I often think of the dinner conversations I have with my colleagues. We create a warm environment in which our conversations can take place. We feel comfortable sharing our ideas as we know that they will be respected. We discuss what is meaningful to us. All of us follow certain social expectations. We do not interrupt, but listen carefully to build on each other's ideas or comments. If we do not understand, we ask questions—we feel safe to do so.

Creating a Culture of Meaningful Talk

The elements I just described are critical pieces that need to be in place for our students to discuss mathematics. The classroom needs to be a safe place in which educators create opportunities for students to share and debate ideas.

Mathematical discourse can take place in pair, small-group, or whole-class discussions. It is important to use all three approaches in your program so students can work and learn in different contexts. Some students may feel more comfortable sharing in pairs than in whole-class settings. While it may not be possible for all of your students to share during one lesson, try to ensure that all students can share their ideas over the course of a unit of study. Keep in mind the learning needs and personalities of your students and structure the discussions in a way that is inclusive and supportive.

Encouraging Complex Discourse

In the beginning, facilitating mathematical discussions with your students may feel awkward. You may not be used to this kind of interaction in your mathematics teaching or have experienced this approach as a student. To become more comfortable in facilitating student discussions, one group of teachers found it helpful to write several key questions on an index card and use them as a guide during discussions.

Your students may also feel awkward, as they may not be used to explaining their mathematical thinking. It often takes time before they feel confident enough to participate fully in sharing their ideas. We need to ensure that our students feel safe and understand that they will not be criticized for sharing an incorrect answer. Students also need to understand the purpose of mathematical discussions: through making conjectures and posing questions, everyone learns and builds a strong mathematical community. If students are unclear on why they are supposed to be sharing their ideas, they may be reluctant to do so.

The assessment table on the next page provides insight about the different levels of discourse that can take place in a classroom. It can assist you in setting goals to achieve more complex levels of discourse in your mathematics program. The table is adapted from Stein (2007), who, in turn, adapted Hufferd-Ackles, Fuson, and Sherin's (2004) work on levels of discourse in mathematics.

Levels of Discourse in Mathematics Classrooms	
Level	**Characteristics**
0	The teacher asks questions and affirms the accuracy of answers or introduces and explains mathematical ideas. Students listen and give short answers to the teacher's questions. Product is valued over process.
1	The teacher asks students direct questions about their thinking while other students listen. The teacher explains student strategies to the group, filling any gaps before continuing to present mathematical ideas. The teacher may ask one student to help another by showing how to do a problem. A few strategies are shared.
2	The teacher asks open-ended questions to elicit student thinking and prompts students to comment on one another's work. Students answer the questions posed to them and voluntarily provide additional information about their thinking. Various ideas are shared and discussed.
3	The teacher facilitates the discussion by encouraging students to ask questions of one another to clarify ideas. Ideas from the community build on one another as students thoroughly explain their thinking and listen to the explanations of others. Many strategies are considered, explored, and discussed.
4	Students readily discuss and share mathematical ideas in small and large groups, requiring limited facilitation from the teacher. Students pose questions of one another and are able to lead discussions about the mathematical topics they are learning. Students can explore different ways of thinking mathematically and present clear arguments to support their ideas and those of others.

Republished with permission of National Council of Teachers of Mathematics from *The Mathematics Teacher, Levels of Discourse in Mathematics, 10* (4), 2007.

Effective Questioning

Effective questioning is critical for encouraging deep, insightful mathematical discourse in your classroom. Try to pose questions that require students to explore mathematical ideas, learn new concepts, and gain insight into their own mathematical thinking. The table on the next page provides some suggestions on how to modify your questioning to promote mathematical discussion. You may choose to use this table as a guide when planning your lessons.

As you reflect on the concepts and skills you want your students to learn, develop questions that enable students to explore their understanding of these concepts. In addition, anticipate possible misunderstandings or misconceptions you think students may have and create questions that can address them. Doing so is helpful. In one instance, a teacher who was planning a lesson on perimeter anticipated that his students might confuse that concept with area, which they had studied earlier in the year. With this concern in mind, he posed this question in his lesson, using a think-pair-share cooperative structure (as described in Chapter 1): *"What are the key differences between area and perimeter?"* His students' answers revealed that they *did* confuse the two concepts, and this information enabled him to clarify these misunderstandings through further questioning and discussion.

Samples of Effective Questioning

Instead of saying	Say...
What answer did you get for...?	• Explain how you arrived at your answer. • Tell me what you were thinking when you arrived at this answer.
Do you understand what Andrew said?	• Please explain what Andrew just said in your own words.
Who arrived at the same answer as Sonal?	• Please share with Sonal the strategies that you used. • How are they the same or different?
Any other questions?	• Turn to your partner and share what you have learned today. List any questions you would like to ask before we begin the activity. • Can someone explain what I just said in their own words?
This answer is correct. That answer is not correct.	• Is this answer correct? Why? Why not? • Does this answer make sense? • Do you agree with Matthew? Explain to him why you do or do not. • Prove that your answer is correct. • Explain to Group 4 why you do not agree with their answer.
These are the same strategies.	• How are these strategies similar or different? • What do you notice about these strategies?
This is the best way to solve these kinds of questions.	• Let's compare the different strategies that were shared. Which do you feel is the most efficient? Why?
What is the formula for?	• Turn to your partner and explain how this formula works.
What formula did you use?	• Explain to us why you chose the formula you did for this problem.
The term...means...	• What does...mean? • Can you give me an example of...? What is it?

Chapin, O'Connor, and Anderson (2009) discuss the importance of facilitating productive talk in mathematics classrooms. They have outlined several practical questioning strategies that educators can use to promote student discourse in mathematics. They named their strategies "Talk Moves."

Talk Moves

Revoicing: This strategy involves clarifying for students what you think they are saying. (*So, are you saying...? Do you mean...?*)

Repeating: This strategy involves asking students to explain other students' thinking. (*Can you explain what Enza just said? Can you repeat what Tony said in your own words? Can you explain what Parvinder said in a different way? Please do so.*)

Adding On: In this strategy, students are invited to add to what another student said. (*Would anyone like to add on to what Matthew said?*)

Wait Time: This strategy involves allowing at least 5 seconds to elapse before choosing a student to answer a question.

Reasoning: This strategy involves inviting students to apply their own reasoning. (*Do you agree or disagree? Why?*)

Republished with permission of Math Solutions, *Classroom Discussions: Using Math Talk to Help Students Learn, Grades K–6*, Suzanne H. Chapin, Catherine O'Connor, and Nancy Canavan Anderson, 2009.

Supporting English Language Learners

For a resource of multilingual math words, see the *Math Expressions* website:
www.pearsoncanada.ca/mathexpressions

Some educators believe that English Language Learners (ELLs), who may have limited knowledge of English, cannot take part in mathematical discussions. They worry that ELLs may feel overwhelmed if they do not understand what other students are saying and lack experience explaining their mathematical thinking. Due to these concerns, some educators have ELLs complete other work or leave the class to receive direct language instruction while the rest of the class engages in mathematical discussions. When making such program decisions, you need to consider that listening to the target language enables students to establish patterns and acquire new vocabulary (Borgioli, 2008). By excluding ELLs from experiencing mathematical discourse, you may be limiting their opportunities to develop an understanding of how mathematical vocabulary is used in natural learning contexts.

The ideal learning context for ELLs in mathematics is explicit language instruction embedded in a meaningful learning context (Bresser, Melanese, & Sphar, 2009). Many of the strategies that help ELLs can also play a key role in native speakers' acquisition of mathematical language and concepts. *Word cards*, such as the samples shown in the margin, are index cards that have a mathematical word written in English and the same word written in the student's native language. They may also include sketches. Students can use these cards as references while working or as communication tools (by holding up a specific card). Word walls (see Chapter 3), Frayer models (see Chapter 4), and word cards can assist ELLs as they practise using mathematical vocabulary. Inviting your class to give verbal and visual examples of specific mathematical vocabulary during mathematics instruction can help both ELLs and native speakers to clarify what mathematical concepts mean.

With one class that had a high ELL population, we used *question lists*. These lists had key questions that were asked during most mathematics lessons translated into several native languages of the ELLs. Examples of key questions included these: *Do you agree or disagree? Why? Which strategy did you use? Can you do this another way? How?* When the teacher posed one of the questions, he would point to the corresponding question list. Even though the ELLs may not have understood all of the discussion, the question lists provided them with the context. They could thereby think mathematically about the question and perhaps contribute to the discussion. A sample for one question is shown in the margin.

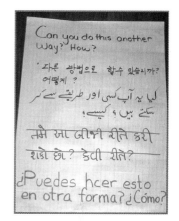

Another way to support ELLs is by appropriately structuring questions. By posing questions that support their learning, you can provide meaningful opportunities for ELLs to engage in mathematical discussions. Below, adapted from Montgomery County Public Schools (2004), is a list of questioning strategies that can support ELLs during mathematical discussions:

- Building the answer into the question supports ELLs. For example, ask: *Is this a triangle or a square?*

- Making a request that involves physically showing the correct answer enables ELLs to participate and make connections between visual examples and mathematical vocabulary. For example: *Point to the even number* or *Point to the answer that makes sense.*

- Posing yes-or-no questions allows ELL students to give a correct response without having to elaborate. For example: *Is this three hundred?* or *Is this cube larger than that cube?*

- When you pose yes-or-no questions, you can elicit responses by a show of hands or the thumbs-up sign for agreement. This approach can encourage participation by ELLs and other students who might be reluctant to volunteer verbal responses.

Wait Time

Appropriate wait time is critical in promoting mathematical discussions (Chapin, O'Connor, & Anderson, 2009). Providing a longer wait time can enable students to feel more at ease and creates a safe learning environment for students (Bennett, Rolheiser, & Stevahn, 2001). Increased wait time can also assist students who may need more time to process information or organize mathematical ideas before speaking.

A simple modification to our teaching in this area can have great results. The average time teachers wait before choosing a student to answer a question is approximately 1.5 seconds (Rowe, 1987). When wait time is increased to 3 seconds, the following improvements occur (Casteel & Stahl, 1973; Rowe, 1987; Stahl, 2009; Tobin, 1987):

- The length of student responses increases.

- The correctness of answers increases.

- The number of *I do not know* responses decreases.

- The number of student volunteers increases.

Stahl (1990) uses the term *think time* to describe the uninterrupted silence required by teachers and students to complete processing tasks, reflections, oral responses, and actions. He notes that while a 3 second wait time is effective, a 5 second wait time is even better. As Chapin, O'Connor, and Anderson (2009) caution, however, you will need to demonstrate to your students that you are willing to wait until someone answers. Once students realize that you are neither going to *rescue* them with an answer nor move on to the next part of the lesson, they will begin to participate. This approach can be used in large- and small-group discussions.

Mathematical Discourse: Skills and Structures

Conversational Skills

You may need to ensure that your students understand the social and behavioural expectations of mathematical conversations by teaching them the skills they need to share ideas effectively. The list of effective mathematical discourse skills below may be used to guide your practice. These skills are also essential for success in other subject areas and learning contexts. Using the Cooperative Math Chart format (see Chapter 1) as a means of establishing these class expectations can be very helpful. For example, you may decide to explore what attentive listening or effective paraphrasing *looks* like, *sounds* like, and *feels* like.

Student Skills for Effective Mathematical Discourse
• Sharing ideas and opinions
• Listening attentively
• Paraphrasing the words of others
• Summarizing what has been discussed
• Posing questions that elicit rich mathematical ideas and discussion
• Editing and modifying ideas based on new learning
• Responding to questions
• Waiting for others to complete their sharing before speaking

Talk Prompts

Students may sometimes be unsure of how to talk about mathematical ideas with others. Talk prompts such as those shown on the next page can help guide students as they engage in mathematical discussions. In one classroom, we posted a list of talk prompts to assist students. We noticed that students often referred to the prompts to guide their sharing and interactions. We also invited students to add other prompts that they felt would be useful. If a student or teacher thought a student shared an idea in a helpful way, we would add the prompt the student used to our list.

For a reproducible version of the talk prompts shown on the following page, see the *Math Expressions* website: www.pearsoncanada.ca/mathexpressions

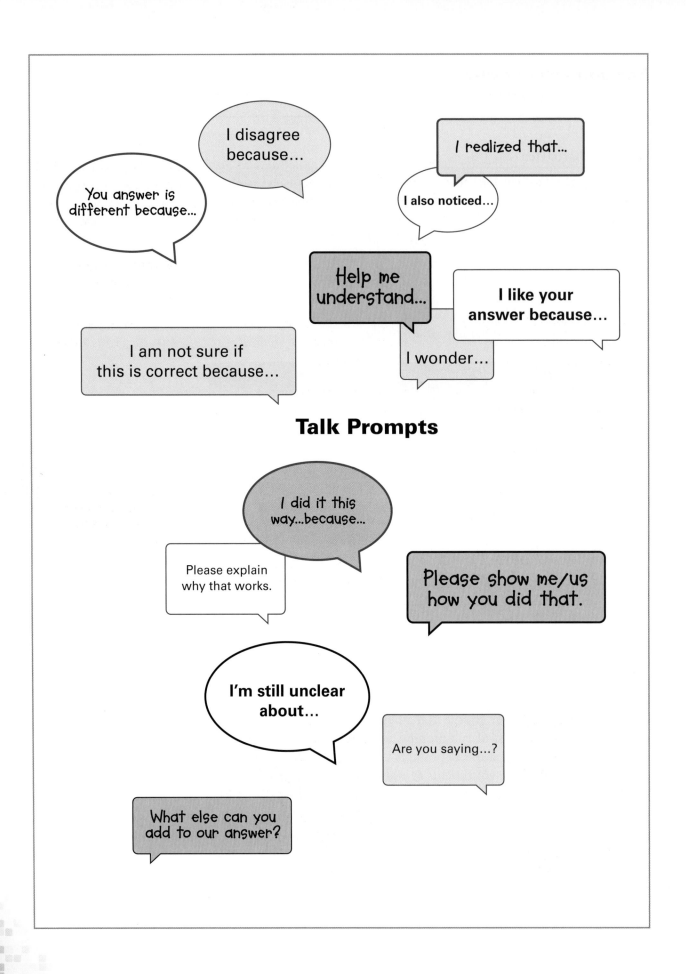

Talk Prompts

Teaching Strategies

Pattern Block Talk

People often consider geometry to be a visual strand that does not require much language. However, geometry is one of the most language-laden topics in mathematics. Pattern Block Talk can help students to learn geometrical language. The activity also exposes students to the challenges involved in communicating effectively and being aware of how others interpret what we say.

Sample Implementation of Pattern Block Talk

1. Organize your class in pairs. Have pairs sit so that each student cannot see what the other is doing. For example, pairs could sit back-to-back or have their work shielded from view with a binder or screen.

2. Give each pair more than enough Pattern Blocks to re-create the design they will receive. You could post pictures of the Pattern Blocks along with their names so that students are using the same vocabulary when describing the blocks.

3. Provide one student in each pair with a copy of the design enclosed in a file folder. The file folder allows students to look at the design and close the folder so that other students cannot see the picture.

4. Invite the students with file folders to describe the design to their partners so that the partners can re-create the design. The student who is providing the description cannot look at what the partner is doing. The partner cannot ask questions.

materials

- Pattern Blocks (plastic manipulatives shaped like hexagons, rhombi, squares, trapezoids, and triangles)

- two different designs created with Pattern Blocks (see samples below)

- building blocks or other manipulatives (optional for activity modification)

To view more pattern block designs, see the *Math Expressions* website: www.pearsoncanada.ca/mathexpressions

Sample Primary Design

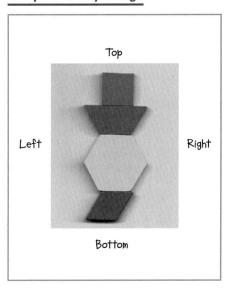

Sample Junior/Intermediate Design

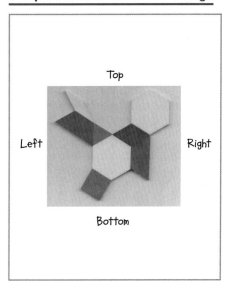

5. Allow enough time for students to complete the designs based on their partners' descriptions. They should complete designs even if they are not correct.

6. Once you feel that students have had enough time, invite pairs to look at the design made by the student using the blocks and the design in the folder.

7. Ask students to note similarities and differences between the two designs. Invite the students who were using the blocks to share with their partner which parts of the description were confusing and which were helpful. Take the opportunity to highlight that, when communicating an idea, we often need to add more details in order for others to understand what we are saying.

8. Facilitate a class discussion to allow the pairs to share and discuss the challenges of communicating effectively. It is a good idea to record specific comments, directions, or vocabulary the class found helpful.

9. After the debriefing, you can distribute a different design and invite the students to switch roles. The students can thereby apply what they learned from the first experience.

Modifications and Extensions for Pattern Block Talk

- Before beginning the activity, work together to create a list of key phrases and vocabulary that may be helpful when providing instructions to a partner. This preparation can support ELLs and those who may find the activity challenging.

- Modify the designs by increasing or decreasing the number of Pattern Blocks and the complexity of the design. You can also reduce the variety of Pattern Blocks in the design. For example, create a pattern that involves only triangles and hexagons.

- Instead of providing each pair with their own copy of the design, show an image of the design on a large screen. Each of the partners delivering instructions can face the screen while the partners using the blocks face the other direction.

- Provide different pairs with different designs in order to meet the diverse needs of your students.

- Invite students to build designs that other students can use for this activity. Students can use Pattern Blocks or other manipulatives such as building blocks. Take pictures of the designs, scan them into a computer, and print them on card stock.

Clipboard Walk and Talk

This activity is based on Milling to Music, which Jeanne Gibbs (2006) includes in her Tribes program. It works well for any mathematics question or problem. Clipboard Walk and Talk engages students in sharing ideas about a variety of mathematical topics. It also allows them to share their thinking using talk, writing, and pictures.

materials

- music that you can start and stop

- clipboards or other portable surfaces on which students can write

Sample Implementation of Clipboard Walk and Talk

1. Think of a question that describes a mathematical problem or activity for your students to answer. Here are some examples: *How would you measure the amount of water in a puddle? How many jelly beans do you think this jar can hold?* The question should not take longer than 5 to 10 minutes for students to resolve.

2. Pose the question to the class. You might also post the question in the classroom for reference during the activity. Depending on the question's complexity, allow 5 to 10 minutes for students to think and record their strategies and/or answers.

3. Invite your students to stand. Explain that you are going to play some music. While the music plays, students are to walk around the classroom silently. Once you stop the music, students are to stop walking and pair up with a person standing nearby.

4. Invite students to share their ideas with their partner. Allow enough time for each partner to share. Encourage students to pose questions of one another to clarify thinking.

5. Once students have shared, explain that when you start the music again, they are to repeat the process.

6. After students have shared with several partners, bring the class together. Discuss students' solutions to the initial problem or activity. Invite students to share with the class how they communicated their ideas. What worked? What did they find challenging?

Modifications and Extensions for Clipboard Walk and Talk

- This activity can be used for review of mathematical content or strategies. For example, I observed a Grade 3 teacher invite students to represent 3×4 in two different ways and a Grade 7 teacher invite her class to think of two different ways to measure the volume of the classroom. You can also differentiate this activity by giving different questions to different pairs of students. Students discuss each of their questions with the same partner.

- Provide students with three different questions and allow time for them to reflect on each one before they circulate. Each time they pair up with a different person, they discuss the next question.

- Once students have shared their ideas in pairs, invite them to circulate with their partner. When the music stops, they must find another pair to form a group of four. Once in a group of four, each member of the pair explains her or his partner's idea to the group.

It Is and It Isn't

materials
- none

Students discuss a mathematical concept by describing what it is and what it is not. This activity encourages students to develop critical thinking skills and to support their ideas with mathematical information. While the activity works best in pairs, you may choose to model it with the whole class first. Provide the class with a concept and invite them to share what the concept is and what it is not.

Sample Implementation of It Is and It Isn't

1. Organize students in pairs.

2. Provide students with a mathematical concept they are to discuss with their partners.

3. Explain that one student in each pair will share what the concept is and the other student will share what the concept is not. For each fact shared, the student should provide a mathematical explanation or justification.

4. Once students have had enough time to complete the activity, you may want to invite the class to discuss the ideas they shared in pairs. You can make a list of all the things the concept is and is not.

Modifications and Extensions for It Is and It Isn't

- For students who struggle or for English Language Learners, you may decide to invite pairs to share what the concept is and isn't without explaining their reasoning.

- You can conduct this activity using the Inside-Outside Circle structure described in Chapter 1. The students on the inside share what the concept is and the students on the outside share what the concept is not. Students share a different idea each time they change partners in the circle.

- Once students have discussed their concept, they can use a T-chart to record what they shared. You may want to draw a T-chart with the headings "It Is" and "It Isn't" on the board for students to copy.

It Is and It Isn't

Here are two sample discussions from It Is and It Isn't. Both discussions occurred after students had completed a unit of study involving the topics they discussed.

First student: *It is an even number because it can be evenly divided by 2.*

Second student: *It is not a prime number because it has more than 1 and itself as factors. It has 1, 22, 2, and 11.*

First student: *It is a palindrome because it reads the same forward and backward.*

Second student: *It is not a decimal because it does not have part that is less than 1.*

First student: *It is a whole number because there is no fraction or decimal part.*

Second student: *It is not an odd number because its last digit is a 2.*

First student: *It is a triangle because it has 3 sides.*

Second student: *It is not a square because it has only 3 angles.*

First student: *It is a polygon because it has no open sides.*

Second student: *It is not a circle because it is not round.*

First student: *It is a regular shape because all sides are the same length.*

Grade 6

Concept: Students were asked to describe the number 22.

Grade 2

Concept: Students were given a picture of an equilateral triangle.

Concept Attainment

Concept attainment is based on the work of Bruner, Goodnow, and Austin (1956). During a concept attainment activity, students determine the underlying concept that defines a group or category. They do this by comparing the attributes of items that are part of the group to those of items that are not included. This activity assists students in developing critical thinking skills and verbally sharing their thinking. The design of concept attainment also allows for continued scaffolding. Those who take longer to determine the concept are provided with more clues to guide their thinking. Sample sets of Yes and No example cards are provided on Line Masters 2.3 to 2.7: one set for shapes with line symmetry, one set for shapes with an area less than or equal to 6 square units, and one set for prime numbers. You may choose to use one of these concepts or select a concept of your own that suits the needs of your students.

materials

- a set of Yes and No example cards for your chosen concept (see Line Masters 2.3 to 2.7)

- a T-chart with one column labelled "Yes" and one column labelled "No"

- index cards with *Yes* on one side and *No* on the other (optional for modified activity)

Sample Implementation of Concept Attainment

1. Choose a concept that is suitable for your students, such as even numbers, shapes that are symmetrical, figures that have an area less than 10 cm², or mixed numbers.

2. Create a set of example cards that represent the concept (Yes cards) and a set of example cards that do not represent the concept (No cards). You can use words, numbers, pictures, or all three! Depending on the complexity of the concept, it is good to have between 5 and 10 of each type of card.

3. Create a T-chart with "Yes" on one side and "No" on the other. Do not announce the concept, but explain to students that examples that represent the concept will be placed in the "Yes" column and those that do not represent the concept will be placed in the "No" column. Their challenge will be to identify the concept. Begin by presenting two Yes examples and placing them in the "Yes" column. Ask students to think about what the two examples have in common. You may invite students to discuss their ideas with a partner.

4. Present a Yes or No example, and invite students to determine in which column it belongs. Once some students share their opinions, place the example in the correct column.

5. Keep presenting Yes and No examples for students to classify. Invite students to think about what the underlying characteristic of items in the Yes group is—this will become clearer the more Yes and No examples you present. The order in which you present the example cards can have an impact on how much thinking is required. It is best to leave the most helpful examples to the end. More thinking skills are required when students cannot immediately detect the underlying concept and are somewhat *misled* by the No examples.

6. Once you feel that some students have identified the concept, invite them to provide a Yes or No example of their own rather than asking them to share their answer. Doing this enables you to verify their thinking while still allowing those students who have not determined the concept to address the challenge further.

7. Students who have correctly identified the concept can help facilitate the activity by assessing whether examples that other students offer are correct.

Modifications and Extensions for Concept Attainment

- Present all of the examples at one time, alternating between Yes and No examples. As you show each example, identify whether it falls under the Yes or No category before placing it on the T-chart. When all of the examples are in place, invite students in small groups or pairs to discuss what they think the Yes examples have in common. Once students have had time to discuss their ideas, invite them to share with the class. You may test their conjectures by displaying an example card and asking where it should be placed.

- Provide students with index cards with the word *Yes* written on one side and the word *No* written on the other. When you present an example, students hold up their index cards, showing either the yes or no side. This approach avoids students calling out the answer and allows you to identify students who correctly classify the example cards and those who do not.

- Provide small groups of students with all of the Yes and No example cards for a given concept, but do not tell them which cards are which. Invite the groups to classify the example cards and identify the underlying concept.

- Instead of using visuals or symbols on the example cards, use fact statements. For example, here are two statements for triangles: *It has three sides* (Yes statement). *All sides must be the same length* (No statement).

- Invite students to create their own sets of Yes and No example cards based on a recent unit of study. Allow students to present their cards to the class.

Mathematical Clothesline

In this activity, students organize a group of concept cards in a particular order or grouping on a clothesline, as shown in the sample on the next page (a clothesline for whole numbers from 0 to 10). As students hang the cards, they need to consider both the cards they have and the cards that other groups have placed on the line. Working in small groups, students share their rationale about where they think the cards should be placed and arrive at a final group decision. The mathematical clothesline serves as a visual format for displaying mathematical concepts. It differs from a formal number line in that, in lieu of numbers, cards may have images of shapes, examples of solutions, or other material. Furthermore, when number cards are used, they are not placed in a measured and scaled sequence, but simply display a specific order. It is important to discuss these differences with your students.

materials

- a set of concept cards for your chosen concept

- a piece of string long enough and strong enough to hold the concept cards, and a method of hanging the string

- clothes pegs

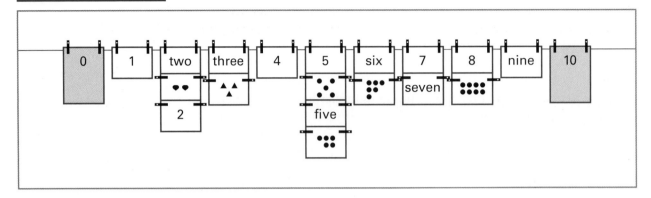

Sample Implementation of Mathematical Clothesline

Decide on a concept that is appropriate for your students. The implementation described here is for the concept of simple fractions.

1. Organize your students into groups of 4 or 5.

2. Hang a clothesline in the classroom, along with two or three reference cards. These cards will change depending on the concept and/or size of numbers used for the activity. For a clothesline about simple fractions, the numbers 0 and 1 can be used as references, with 0 placed at the left end of the clothesline and 1 at the right.

3. Give each group 5 or 6 cards on which numbers, pictures, and/ or words that describe or represent the chosen concept are written. Explain to your students that they will need to arrange the cards from least to greatest on the clothesline. If two cards represent the same concept, such as an image of three-quarters and the numerical representation $\frac{3}{4}$, ask students to hang one below the other on the clothesline, as shown in the margin.

4. Depending on the amount of discussion and difficulty of the concept, allow about 10 minutes or so for students in each group to determine the order of the group's cards.

5. Invite one group of students at a time to the clothesline to hang their cards. Explain that they may need to move cards placed by other groups to create room for theirs.

6. As groups hang their cards on the clothesline, remind seated students to observe where the cards are placed so they can provide feedback to the other groups at the end of the activity.

7. Once all the cards are hung on the clothesline, ask students to share observations about the final placement of all the cards. Are there cards that need to be moved? What patterns do students see? What challenges did they encounter?

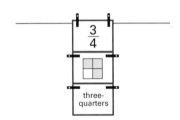

©P

Sample Clothesline Topics

Below is a list of clothesline activities you could do with your students. You can use any of these activities at any level by modifying the concepts on the cards.

For reproducible cards that could be used in clothesline activities, see the *Math Expressions* website: www.pearsoncanada.ca/ mathexpressions

Primary

- Provide students with cards showing shapes. Invite them to create an AB pattern using the cards.

- Provide shape cards that students can order from smallest to largest.

- Provide a variety of number cards. Invite students to choose cards to create a sequence of counting by 2s, 5s, or 10s.

- Create two heading cards for the clothesline: Symmetrical and Non-symmetrical. Hang one on the left and one on the right, with a strip of brightly coloured paper hanging in the middle of the string to separate them. Invite students to place an assortment of shape cards with the appropriate heading. The cards could hang down in a chain below the headings or be placed on the appropriate side of the dividing line. For this activity, you could use the shape cards from Line Masters 2.3 and 2.4 (Concept Attainment: Shapes with Line Symmetry).

Junior

- Hang a variety of shape cards on the clothesline. Provide groups with cards showing descriptive vocabulary words. Invite students to hang the word cards under the shapes that they feel the words best describe.

- Hang a group of numbers on a clothesline and invite students to identify the mean, median, and mode of the range of numbers.

- Invite students to order a set of cards from greatest to least. In addition to numbers, include cards with multiplication and division questions. Students will need to calculate the answers to determine the number that each card represents.

Intermediate

- Provide students with cards on which different numbers and images of decimals up to 3.0 are written. Invite students to place the cards in order from least to greatest. Hang reference cards of 0, 1.0, and 2.0 to assist students in sequencing their cards.

- Hang several algebraic expressions that create growing patterns on the clothesline. Provide each group with images that represent different terms in the patterns. Invite students to place their cards under or beside the appropriate expression to show the progression of the pattern. For example, for the expression $3n$, you could provide cards that show a 1 by 3 rectangle, a 2 by 3 rectangle, a 3 by 3 square, a 4 by 3 rectangle, and so on. For the expression n^2, you could provide cards showing a square, a 2 by 2 square, a 3 by 3 square, and so on.

Modifications and Extensions for Mathematical Clothesline

- Invite students to create clotheslines in small groups. Provide each group with a piece of string, clothes pegs, and cards to place in order. Once each group has organized their mathematical clothesline, they can present it to the whole class with one student holding it up at each end.

- Scaffold the activity by using the same colour for cards that should be grouped together. You can also do this if you have similar concepts, such as 0.50 and $\frac{1}{2}$, that need to be placed together.

- Record the appropriate vocabulary to accompany the numerical and/ or visual concepts on each card. Doing so can assist students in learning mathematical vocabulary.

STRATEGIES IN ACTION

Mathematical Clothesline

Grade 1

As part of a lesson on repeating patterns, a teacher provided her Grade 1 students with cards showing yellow circles and cards showing red circles. She invited groups of students to create patterns with the cards in their groups and then display the patterns on the clothesline for the rest of the class. The visual nature of this activity, in addition to the mathematical discourse that took place, enabled students to demonstrate their understanding of patterns and engage in rich mathematical discussions.

Mathematical Clothesline

This photo shows a section of the completed clothesline.

In a Grade 8 classroom, a teacher created cards with numbers, images, and words representing simple and mixed fractions, decimals, and whole numbers. She invited her students to work in small groups to place a set of cards in order from least to greatest on the clothesline. She hung 0, 1, and 2 on the clothesline as sequential references for her students.

Wanted Number

In this problem-solving activity, students process information to identify a number that satisfies a set of criteria. As the activity progresses, more criteria are provided. Students must check their number and make any changes needed so that the number satisfies all the criteria. If you do not have number tiles, ask students to write the digits 0 to 9 on small sticky notes. Using number tiles or sticky notes will allow students to move numbers easily as they try to figure out the Wanted number. This activity enables students to consolidate mathematical vocabulary, practise active listening, and develop an understanding of the different attributes numbers can have. It supports many facets of mathematical expression, including reading, writing, and talk. You can modify the criteria and vocabulary to suit the learning needs and mathematical knowledge of your students.

materials

- a set of clues you have written about a mystery number (see page 44 for samples)

- sets of number tiles for the digits 0 to 9 for each student or small sticky notes on which students can write digits

- chart paper and markers

- blank copies of Wanted poster (Line Master 2.8) (optional for extension)

Sample Implementation of Wanted Number

1. Create a set of clues that progress from very general to more specific, for example: *It is an even number… It is between 25 and 30.* Beginning with the most general clues will enable students to explore different attributes of the number before arriving at the answer.

2. Provide each student with a set of number tiles or small sticky notes on which to write the numerals 0 to 9. If your mystery number has repeating digits, provide extra sets of tiles to each student. Explain that students will be creating a number with the number tiles. They do not know what the number is. You will be giving them clues about it.

3. Read aloud the first clue and allow time for your students to create a number that satisfies the criterion. Write each clue on chart paper after you read it aloud so that, as new criteria are added, students can check to make sure that their number still complies with the previous criteria. Or, you may decide to prepare a list of clues ahead of time so that you can reveal them as needed, using an LCD projector or chart paper.

4. As you read each additional clue, allow more time for students to make changes to their number.

5. Once you have read all of the clues, allow time for students to check their number against all of the criteria listed. Then invite students to share what they think is the Wanted number.

6. Afterwards, you may ask students to look over the criteria and decide whether any clues are unnecessary. What is the least amount of clues they needed to arrive at the Wanted number?

Sample Clues for 29	Sample Clues for 325
• It is a 2-digit number.	• It is a 3-digit number.
• It is an odd number.	• It is an odd number.
• It is less than 40.	• The number is not a multiple of 10.
• The number contains one prime digit.	• Two of its digits are prime.
• It is a number with no repeating digits.	• No digits repeat.
• An even number is in the 10s place.	• The digit in the 10s place is less than the digit in the 1s place.
• It is a prime number.	• An even number is in the 10s place.
• Its digits add up to 11.	• Two of its digits are odd.
• It is a number between 25 and 30.	• There is an odd number in the 100s place.
	• The number is divisible by 5.

Modifications and Extensions for Wanted Number

- You may begin with a simple list of just three criteria, for example, a number that has 2 digits, is even, and is between 10 and 25. Many Wanted numbers satisfy these criteria, which makes it easier for students to understand the process. You can invite students to share all of the possible numbers that satisfy the criteria.

- Partway through providing a criteria list, you can stop and invite the class to create a list of all the numbers that satisfy the criteria thus far.

- You can create lists of clues for Wanted numbers that are decimals, fractions, or exponents.

- You may wish to invite students to draw a Wanted polygon that satisfies a set of criteria you have prepared. See the margin for sample clues that describe an equilateral triangle. This activity works best if students make sketches with non-permanent markers on plastic sheets or small whiteboards so they can easily make changes to their shapes as criteria are added. They can also use straws or toothpicks to create their shapes.

- Invite students to create wanted posters for different mathematical concepts that show a list of clues. Students can use Line Master 2.8 (Wanted!) as a rough draft, recording their wanted number in the square and the clues they create on the lines below. They can then create a larger poster showing the clues and drawing their own art to make it resemble a wanted poster.

Math Congress

Math congress is an instructional strategy created by Fosnot and Dolk (2002). Students work on a rich mathematical problem in pairs or groups of three, and then share their problem-solving solutions with the whole class during a *math congress*.

For this activity to be successful, it is critical to provide students with a rich problem to solve—rich problems invite multiple solution strategies and representations. They may also have multiple solutions. Such problems challenge students to think beyond the obvious and provide new learning opportunities. They can accommodate a variety of levels and learning styles. They should focus on a topic relevant to students' lives.

The math congress is a process by which students share and discuss each other's ideas. It is based on the three-part lesson plan, in which a problem is introduced, and students explore the problem and then share their solutions. The process provides meaningful opportunities for students to justify their ideas to others and consolidate their own mathematical understandings. It helps students realize that mathematical communication is not just descriptive narratives about how they solved

materials

- markers and chart paper for each group

- depending on the problem posed, possibly grid paper, manipulatives, or construction materials

See pages xiii–xiv of the introduction to this book for more information on the three-part lesson plan.

a problem; it also involves exploration and inquiry. Students must create precise arguments in which they present a clear rationale for their decisions (Ontario Ministry of Education, 2010). Furthermore, the process makes explicit students' strategies and mathematical thinking.

As the students work on their problems, circulate to facilitate student thinking. Make notes on student progress and the kinds of strategies they are using. Once students have completed their work, you can select two or three groups to share their mathematical solutions. Select the groups based on the learning needs of your students and the mathematical ideas derived from the students' solutions. In some cases, it may be an effective strategy that you would like the students to learn, a mathematical idea that should be highlighted, or a misconception in a group's work that is important to discuss and clarify. As students provide feedback and pose questions, the authors of the solution can make changes to their work to clarify ideas or improve their solution.

Sample Implementation of a Math Congress

1. Organize students in groups of 2 or 3.

2. Minds On/Getting Started: Present the class with a rich problem to solve. Depending on the problem and your students' needs, you may need to take some time to activate students' previous mathematical knowledge related to the problem they are about to solve. Ensure that students have access to a variety of tools that they can use to solve the problem. They also need to know that they may be presenting their ideas to the whole class.

3. Working on It/Action: Allow students ample time to address the problem. As students work on the problem, circulate and pose questions to challenge their thinking and prompt them to clarify their ideas and reasoning. As you engage in mathematical discussions with your students, you may make observational notes on the strategies they choose, their mathematical reasoning, and misconceptions or mathematical concepts the class needs to review. These notes will be useful when choosing groups to share during the math congress.

4. Preparation for Math Congress: Once students have completed their solutions and have rough notes and diagrams that demonstrate their thinking, invite them to create a math poster on which they include key points, examples, and strategies to share with the whole class. Unlike their working notes, which may include several different ideas, the large poster needs to be quite precise and present the key details of the solution they believe is the most effective. When students submit their math poster, ask them to include their working notes as well. These notes can provide you with additional information about the thinking processes that led to the solutions.

5. Once the posters are completed, choose 2 or 3 groups to share their solutions with the class the following day. Take time to look over the solutions and choose those that best suit your students' learning needs. Choosing 2 or 3 groups enables you to select key ideas that you want your students to discuss as part of the math congress. This process also saves time and allows you and your students to discuss key concepts and ideas in depth.

6. Consolidation/Math Congress: Clear a space where students can post their work as they share their solutions with the class. As each group presents, you can prompt students to pose questions, consider different mathematical ideas, and share comments about the mathematical strategies presented. See pages 26–28 in this chapter for more examples of effective questioning strategies.

- *Who used an approach similar to Mary and Alex's? Can you explain how the approaches are similar?*

- *I am not clear on how you counted the boxes. Can you explain this please?*

- *Mohammed and Julia, I noticed that you used a different strategy to add up the boxes. Please share your idea with our presenters Manmeet and Sonia.*

- *Can someone explain what Sheenu and Danielle just said? Please do so.*

It is important to note that the educator's role is to facilitate the discussion and allow students to pose questions and share mathematical ideas with each other. In addition to students sharing their work on paper, you may decide to take pictures of their work using a tablet, and share the images using an interactive white board or a screen. This will allow you or your students to make annotations directly on the image as you facilitate mathematical discussions. The images and documentation can be saved for future reference.

7. Once the math congress is completed, you may wish to invite students to write about what they learned in their journals or math notebooks. You may decide to record any final observations about the discussions or individual students. These notes can be used to inform your teaching and support student assessment.

Modifications and Extensions for Math Congress

- Before beginning the activity, you could conduct a math congress think-aloud where you demonstrate how to share a math poster using a poster you have created. Discuss what you chose to include in your poster and which elements you want to share and why. Invite students to explain what they think would be helpful to share and how they would present arguments in support of the strategy demonstrated in the sample poster. During your think-aloud, it may be helpful to create a list of different kinds of questions students could pose.

- You can differentiate your instruction by providing less or more guidance to each group in order to support and scaffold their learning. Some groups may require modifications or extensions to the problem to suit their learning needs.

To view more sample problems, see the *Math Expressions* website: www.pearsoncanada.ca/ mathexpressions

Sample Math Congress Problems

Here are some sample problems that would be suitable for a math congress. You may wish to modify the wording or content to suit the needs of your students and the concepts they are learning, or create your own rich problem.

- I was out with my family and we ordered pizza. After we finished our meal, $\frac{1}{3}$ of the pizza was left. Two family members wanted to eat it. How much of the whole pizza would each person get if they shared what was left equally?

- Danny, Melissa, and Jane have 8 cookies to share among themselves. They do not need to receive the same amount, but each person should receive at least 1 cookie. Assume that the children do not break any of the cookies. In how many different ways can they share the cookies?

- How many different ways can you divide a square in half?

- I want to buy fish for my large aquarium. At the store where I buy my fish, they have several kinds. The green fish cost $10 each. The blue fish cost $20 each. The small red fish cost $5 each. I want to buy at least 1 fish of each colour. How many different combinations of different-coloured fish can I buy if I spend exactly $20? $50? $100?

- How many different ways can you show the fraction $\frac{1}{2}$ on a geoboard?

- How many different ways can you make 55 cents using pennies, nickels, dimes, and quarters?

- There are 34 students in a class. There are 4 more boys than girls. What is the number of boys and the number of girls in the class?

- How would you share 2 of these chocolate bars with 3 people so that each person gets the same amount? How much does each person get? (Provide students with paper bars that they can cut up any way they wish. Intermediate students can name the fractional portion of the chocolate bar each person receives.)

©P

Bansho

Bansho, which means "board writing" in Japanese, is a Japanese teaching strategy that engages students in rich problem solving and mathematical discourse (Shimizu, 2007). Used as part of the three-part lesson, a Bansho provides a format in which students can share and discuss their mathematical ideas and solutions. Students work on a mathematical problem in pairs and then share their problem-solving solutions with the whole class. Like a math congress, a Bansho focuses on rendering explicit students' mathematical thinking. As with a math congress, it is critical to provide students with a rich problem to solve. Any of the sample problems outlined under "Math Congress" could also be used for a Bansho.

Student pairs record their solution process on a piece of legal-sized paper or chart paper placed in landscape format. As the students work, circulate and pose questions to support student problem solving. You will also decide which pairs will share their work.

As each pair explains its solution during the sharing process, the class analyzes the merits and limitations of each approach. Your role is to organize their solutions, as well as solutions from the rest of the class, in columns of similar mathematical ideas and strategies, as shown below. This visual allows students to become metacognitive of the different kinds of strategies. It is often recommended to order the groupings from left to right, beginning with solutions that contain simplistic ideas and less efficient strategies to those that demonstrate more complex and efficient ideas and strategies.

During the discussions, use sticky notes to annotate on and around the student work to make mathematical ideas explicit. These annotations may take a variety of forms, such as clear explanations, diagrams, symbols, and specific mathematical vocabulary. You may want to organize and classify the students' work ahead of time in columns and then invite students to identify and discuss the similarities and differences that they observe in each grouping. As you facilitate the Bansho, keep in mind key mathematical learning goals for the lesson. This helps you to focus attention on critical ideas in student work. A Bansho lesson can look different from classroom to classroom depending on the classroom culture and student needs.

materials

- sticky notes

- markers and legal-sized paper or chart paper

- depending on the problem posed, possibly grid paper, manipulatives, or construction materials

For resources about Bansho, see the *Math Expressions* website: www.pearsoncanada.ca/mathexpressions

Sample Implementation of a Bansho

1. Clear a space on the board where you can post student solutions.

2. Organize students in pairs.

3. Minds On/Getting Started: Present students with a rich problem that has many possible solutions or solution strategies. As with the math congress activity, you may need to activate students' prior knowledge of specific strategies or concepts related to the problem they will be solving. It may be a good idea to post the problem in the classroom.

4. Working on It/Action: Allow students ample time to address the problem. As students work on the problem, circulate and pose questions to challenge their thinking and prompt them to clarify their ideas and reasoning. As you engage in mathematical discussions with your students, you may decide to make observational notes on the strategies they choose, their mathematical reasoning, and misconceptions or mathematical concepts you feel the class needs to review.

5. Consolidation/Bansho: Once students have completed their solutions, select two or three for the class to analyze and discuss. Invite the authors to explain their solutions to the class. Students, including the authors, are usually seated while the teacher stands at the front organizing the student work.

6. As students explain their solutions, make any notations on or around the work that you feel may help clarify their thinking to the class. Encourage the class to pose questions and share comments about the solutions.

7. As the authors explain their work, invite the class to examine the different strategies pairs have used and determine how they are similar and different. Which strategies are most effective? Why?

8. Arrange the solutions that have been presented as well as solutions from the rest of the class into groups that show similar strategies. The samples are often arranged from those showing the least effective to those showing the most effective strategies. It often helps to label the groupings based on the strategies demonstrated. Invite students to identify the column in which each solution should be placed and to explain why the solution should be there.

9. Review the strategies and concepts that were highlighted during the Bansho.

Chapter 3

Reading in Mathematics

Indicators of Success

Goals for students include the following:

- Students can analyze, interpret, and summarize a variety of texts from different mathematical contexts such as the media, picture books, math textbooks, and word problems.

- Students can apply the information they have read to different learning situations.

- Students can make connections between math texts and their personal lives.

- Students can make connections between different math texts and identify similarities and differences between them.

- Students are able to interpret and decode the meaning of mathematical symbols, models, and pictures.

- Students are able to apply a variety of strategies to assist them in comprehending the mathematics they read.

For a reproducible version of these indicators of success, see the *Math Expressions* website: www.pearsoncanada.ca/ mathexpressions

What the Research Says About...
Reading in Mathematics

For resources about reading in mathematics, see the *Math Expressions* website: www.pearsoncanada.ca/ mathexpressions

Current research on reading tells us that reading is an interactive process influenced by a reader's prior knowledge and the personal life experiences the reader brings to the text. Readers also rely on their knowledge of specific vocabulary and how different texts are constructed (Hyde, 2006; Miller, 2002). Through this complex process, they make meaning. When I began teaching, I believed that because students were taught how to read in language arts, teaching reading skills in mathematics was unnecessary. However, text that students process in mathematics is different from what they read in other subject areas (Fisher & Frey, 2007). Mathematical text includes elements that students may not have encountered in their everyday reading experiences.

The organization and content of mathematical text is unique. Mathematical text contains more concepts per paragraph than other text and is often organized differently, forcing the eye to travel in different directions than the traditional left to right (Kenney, 2005). Mathematical text does not repeat information—repetition or redundancy can often assist readers to consolidate meaning and learn new vocabulary. Unlike images in stories, which provide information to support the storyline of the text, images that accompany mathematical text often provide only mathematical information. Furthermore, processing text effectively in mathematics requires readers to derive meaning from the words while creating mental mathematical models based on the words they read (Barton & Heidema, 2002). Because of these challenges, it is important to provide opportunities for our students to develop the skills necessary to read mathematics effectively.

Costa (2008) notes that true comprehension of what we read begins when we are able to merge our thinking with the content we are reading and react to the information. He points out that we make meaning by listening to the inner conversation that takes place as part of our interaction with the text—the voice in the head that speaks to us when we read. In mathematics this *inner voice* may sound like the following: *I do not understand this part of the problem. This number is important. I need to check this again as it does not make sense. That does not look like an obtuse angle.* By modelling this process with our students through think-alouds, we can help them develop strong thinking skills and become better aware of their own reading processes. Listening to a teacher clarify confusions during a think-aloud or explain that she does not have enough facts to solve a problem provides learners with key insights into the problem-solving and reading processes (Hutchins, 2011).

Assessing Reading in Mathematics

The ability to read and interpret mathematical text and pictures allows students to build on the concepts and activities they are exploring. The main goal in assessing this skill is formative: to collect information that enables you to improve instruction and identify student needs. You can use many of the strategies that you use in language arts to assess your students' abilities in this area. Through effective questioning about the mathematical text students are reading, you can gain insight into their understanding. You can do this as part of a class discussion, as you circulate supporting students during group or individual work, or in one-on-one interviews with students. You can also examine the work students produce in response to different mathematical texts they have read, such as solutions to word problems or verbal reflections on a newspaper article. What do their responses tell you? Do they have misconceptions about the information they read? Did they overlook key information? Did they incorporate information not relevant to the problem, text, or picture? Student responses can provide authentic observations that enable you to modify your teaching to assist students in becoming proficient readers of mathematics and, in turn, proficient learners of mathematics.

Providing indicators of success like those shown on the next page can assist students in becoming more metacognitive about their reading skills in mathematics. In this example, the indicators target word problems. You may wish to modify the wording or content of this list to suit your learners' needs. You may also find it appropriate to create different indicators of success for other forms of mathematical text. In many cases, the indicators we would use for reading in language arts would work with mathematics.

For a reproducible version of these sample indicators of success, see the *Math Expressions* website: www.pearsoncanada.ca/mathexpressions

Sample Indicators of Success for Understanding Word Problems
❑ Do I read the whole problem at least two times before working on the math question?
❑ Do I summarize or retell the problem in my own words before solving it?
❑ Do I create pictures in my mind to help me understand the problem?
❑ Do I think about where I may have had a problem like this in my daily life?
❑ When I complete my answer, do I reread the problem to see whether my work makes sense?

Facilitating Reading in Mathematics

Infusing Reading into Your Math Program

It is important that students understand that mathematical language can be expressed in many ways using a mixture of words, numbers, symbols, and pictures. By providing a variety of reading experiences, you can expand students' knowledge of mathematical concepts as well as their perception of the role of mathematics. Students begin to understand that mathematics exists outside the classroom and influences our world in many ways. Reading a variety of mathematical texts can also provide students with examples of different kinds of voices in mathematical writing. Picture books, chapter books, and advertisements are just a few examples of the kinds of materials you can infuse throughout your program. (A more comprehensive list is provided on the next page.)

Through different media, students can investigate significant issues in which mathematics plays a critical role. They can explore global issues such as poverty, environmental concerns, and the pros and cons of possible solutions to such concerns. They can also explore local issues that have a direct impact on the school community. In one Grade 3 classroom, a teacher read an article to the class on reducing garbage. The students decided to investigate how many students brought their lunch to school in reusable containers. They collected data, displayed the information using a variety of graphs, and compared their results to the information in the article. They then communicated their findings to the rest of the school to encourage students to decrease how much garbage they were producing each day.

- Graphs
- Pictures
- Floor plans
- Instruction booklets and diagrams for instructions
- Maps
- Picture books
- Novels
- Word problems
- Passages from a textbook
- Magazine and newspaper ads
- Advertisements on billboards or buses
- Weather graphs
- Magazine and newspaper articles

Supporting English Language Learners

As English Language Learners (ELLs) engage in learning mathematics, they are not only acquiring new language, but also processing how mathematical text and symbols are organized, which may be different from how similar text is presented in their native language and culture. Mathematical symbols are not universal and are not standard across all cultures. For example, in North America and many Asian countries, we write *21.16* to denote twenty-one and sixteen one-hundredths. In many countries in Europe, South America, and the former Soviet Union, as well as in French Canada, this number is written *21,16*. In Persian-speaking countries, a symbol that resembles a forward slash is used rather than a decimal point or comma. Similarly, currency symbols are usually placed before the number in English-speaking countries and many others, but after the number in some countries.

Bresser, Melanese, and Sphar (2009) point out that syntax and grammar can be confusing for ELLs. They note that a word problem like the first one shown in the margin can present challenges for non-native speakers. The possessive, indicated in Problem 1 by the phrase *Aunt Martha's*, may not be expressed using this structure in their native language. The use of the term *case* in the context of packaging juice or *brunch* as a meal may also be confusing. Cultural biases in word problems can also create confusion for ELLs. For example, students may be unfamiliar with the concepts of "birthday parties" and "loot bags" used in

Problem 1: *Jamal is bringing the juice for his Aunt Martha's family brunch. He decides to buy 12 bottles. There are 6 bottles of juice in a case. How many cases does he need to buy?*

Problem 2: *Selina is having a birthday party. She has invited 10 friends and will give each a loot bag. She wants to put 3 toys in each bag. How many toys does she need to buy?*

Problem 2. Furthermore, the word *loot* has multiple meanings in English, which can create misunderstandings. These challenges can be distracting and frustrating for students and may prevent them from focusing on the mathematical concepts (Brown, Cady, & Taylor, 2009).

We need to examine word problems for cultural biases not only to support ELLs, but all learners in our classrooms. We can assist students by inviting them to discuss the word problem and to seek clarification about its content. When completing word problems, we can also help ELLs by focusing on reading strategies in small groups comprised of both native speakers and ELLs (van Garderen, 2004). As they process and discuss mathematical ideas, allow students to use their native language if they wish. In some classrooms, we created word problems in the ELLs' native language. Doing so provided them with an opportunity to gain understanding of the problem and explore different strategies with native speakers in the class.

Reading math-themed picture books that relate to concepts you are teaching can help all students, particularly ELLs, consolidate their learning. The storyline nature of picture books provides a meaningful framework in which mathematical ideas are presented. The detailed images often found in picture books can assist students in learning new mathematical vocabulary. Unlike word problems, picture books often have repetitive text, which allows ELLs to check meaning and consolidate their understanding of vocabulary. As well, students often reread picture books to revisit ideas and storylines and thereby gain multiple exposures to the mathematical content.

The strategies that support ELLs with reading mathematical text provide rich opportunities for all learners to consolidate their understanding of mathematics and strengthen their comprehension skills. Some of these strategies are listed here.

Supporting English Language Learners with Reading in Mathematics

- Identify words with multiple meanings and clarify what they mean.

- Identify any cultural differences in the way symbols are used and clarify their use.

- Provide visual cues to help ELLs understand the context of the passage.

- Provide opportunities for ELLs to work in small groups with native speakers.

- Discuss the text beforehand, using simpler vocabulary to help students understand specific words.

- If possible, provide texts in their native language.

- Create a culture in which students feel comfortable to speak in their native language.

- Use drama to act out the text and explore different ideas and solutions.

- Use picture books as a tool to support the learning of mathematical concepts and vocabulary.

- Model the text using concrete materials.

Supporting Readers Who Struggle

Some students may find mathematical writing easier to read than stories because it contains less description and more factual information. Mathematical writing that includes pictures can also be easier for students to understand than words alone. Students who struggle with reading in language arts, however, will most likely experience difficulty reading mathematical texts. Some of these students who struggle with reading may work with numbers and mathematical symbols very efficiently. They may also excel at problem solving. It is their struggle with reading that can limit their ability to work to their full potential in mathematics.

How can we provide support to students who struggle with reading mathematics? One Grade 5 teacher always ensures that those who struggle with reading are paired with another student who can explain the problem verbally. She feels that this pairing provides support for the student who finds it difficult to read while giving the other student an opportunity to practise explaining mathematical texts. A Grade 8 teacher always begins her lessons with students explaining the problem verbally before beginning to solve it. She also invites students to represent the problem using diagrams and sketches. She finds that this approach enables all of her learners to understand the mathematical text through discourse, words, and visual representation. In some cases, it can be helpful to modify the text so that only the information needed to complete the mathematical activity is included. Many of the suggestions for supporting English Language Learners can also be adapted to help readers who struggle.

Building a Mathematical Word Wall

One challenge with reading mathematics is that most mathematical vocabulary is used only in mathematics and often cannot be acquired through conversational interactions (Ron, 1999). A word wall can be especially useful in teaching mathematical vocabulary and helping students in clarifying what different mathematical concepts mean.

For an online mathematics dictionary, see the *Math Expressions* website: www.pearsoncanada.ca/mathexpressions

A *word wall* is an organized collection of words displayed on a wall or other large display space in the classroom. The words are selected for instructional purposes. They serve as visuals that temporarily assist students with independent reading and writing. They consist of a growing core of words that become part of students' reading and writing vocabulary (Cunningham, 1999).

A *mathematical word wall* comprises words, symbols, and pictures that relate to concepts students are learning in mathematics. Each word is written in large, clear letters on a card. A picture that illustrates the concept represented by the word is usually included as well. Similarly, each symbol is written on a card along with a word that represents its meaning and, where appropriate, a picture. Cards are added to the wall as the teaching of different concepts progresses. We can even invite students to add their own cards to the wall (Harvey & Goudvis, 2007). Students frequently refer to the mathematical word wall when they engage in mathematical writing, reading, and discussions or when they complete various mathematics activities (Marks Krpan, 2008b).

Using Mathematical Picture Books

To view a list of picture books that explore mathematical concepts, see the *Math Expressions* website: www.pearsoncanada.ca/mathexpressions

Many picture books address and explore mathematical concepts in meaningful ways. By reading a picture book, we provide a common mathematical experience to discuss and examine with our students. Picture books also provide educators with opportunities for modelling reading and thinking skills (Harvey & Goudvis, 2007). The graphic nature of picture books and their often repetitive text help students of all ages to learn mathematical vocabulary and see how mathematical concepts connect to their daily lives. Use of picture books can be particularly beneficial for English Language Learners and learners who struggle. Picture books also create a sense of engagement that can motivate students and pique their interest.

As we read a mathematics picture book, it is important to engage the students in exploring not only the storyline but also the writing style of the author, specific expressions the author uses, and the kinds of illustrations in the book. At any grade level, these kinds of discussions can support students as they become effective communicators in mathematics. This approach can also assist students in understanding that, even though the book has a mathematics focus, literary elements are used to communicate the mathematical concepts.

Debbie Miller (2002) uses sticky notes in her classroom as a way to engage students to share their insights and questions about what they are reading. When you share a picture book with the class, you have a great opportunity to model the use of sticky notes. If you or your students notice a specific mathematics word or interesting part in the book, you can jot the information on a sticky note and place it in the book where you made the discovery. You can thereby help students understand how readers interact with print and how they use the information to make

©P

inferences. When reading mathematics picture books independently, students can use sticky notes to identify different math strategies or questions related to the mathematical content. They can also note additional mathematical knowledge or strategies related to the text. This approach seems to work well as it allows students to document their thinking and provides you with insight into how each student processes the text he or she is reading. Students can also share their insights with one another.

Traditionally thought of as an effective teaching resource for primary students, picture books can also address complex concepts for older students. I have often used picture books with my intermediate students to explore mathematical concepts that are not explicitly addressed in the text. Billings and Beckman (2005) note that books that may seem to address only simple mathematical concepts can be used to teach more complex ideas. For example, a book that addresses the concept of simple division through sharing, such as *The Doorbell Rang* by Pat Hutchins, can also be used to demonstrate the concept of algebraic equations. In this story, two children share 12 cookies. Each time a new guest arrives at the house, the children redistribute the cookies so each person gets the same quantity. The story can be used to teach the algebraic equation $y = \frac{12}{x}$, where x represents the number of people and y represents the number of cookies each person will get when the cookies are shared equally. There are also many picture books that explicitly address mathematical concepts for junior and intermediate grades.

See the Teaching Strategies section starting on page 63 of this chapter for further ideas about using picture books.

Reading in Mathematics: Skills and Structures

Key Reading Strategies

Researchers have identified several key reading strategies used by proficient readers (Daniels, 2011; Harvey & Goudvis, 2007; Hyde, 2007; McGregor, 2007). These strategies are critical for students to become efficient readers of mathematics. I have provided some examples of how these strategies can support the learning of mathematics.

Inferring and Predicting: Readers are able to connect their own knowledge to the text and draw conclusions about an idea, outcome, or theme in the text.

You can invite students to predict an answer to a problem or computation. Whatever predictions you ask students to make, be sure to explore the different strategies they use to arrive at their responses. What information did they use to make their predications? What knowledge guided them?

See "Visualizing Mathematical Text" on pages 65–66 in the Teaching Strategies section of this chapter.

Making Connections: Readers are able to draw upon their previous knowledge and experiences to make meaningful connections with the text.

When possible, invite students to reflect on past experiences related to the mathematical text being read. For example, you might ask when they have used a specific mathematical strategy, whether they have experienced an event similar to one described in a math text, or when they have seen information communicated in a graph similar to one in the text. In this way, you can help students to connect mathematical concepts to their everyday lives.

Visualizing: Readers construct meaning by creating mental images of the text.

You can invite students to visualize what specific mathematical concepts may look like and ask them to create models to represent their thinking. It is important that you consider different ways of modelling the same concept, including the use of concrete materials and pictures. You can also invite students to visualize mathematical text from a picture book or a textbook.

Self-Monitoring: Readers use metacognitive strategies to know when their reading makes sense and when it does not. When something is unclear to them, they are able to select an appropriate strategy to assist their comprehension.

Metacognitive strategies can be cultivated through discussions that engage students in exploring the mathematical strategies they use to solve problems or create non-standard algorithms, just to name a few examples. As students read mathematical texts, you can also invite them to discuss strategies they use to understand an unfamiliar word, theme, or idea.

Posing Questions: To clarify details, readers pose questions before, during, and after reading. They question the ideas, content, and problems presented in the text.

Clarifying details is a critical step toward developing a deep understanding of mathematical concepts. It is paramount that you encourage students to pose questions as they explore new ideas, whether they are completing a hands-on activity, reading problems, examining graphs and pictures, applying mathematical strategies, or exploring non-standard algorithms. Students' questions can also provide insight into possible misconceptions they may hold.

Identifying What Is Important: Readers focus on important information and connect it to what they already know.

As students study graphs and pictures, read problems, or explore mathematical equations, you can invite them to highlight which pieces they feel are most relevant and explain why. You may also assist students in observing mathematical patterns and reflecting on how what they have learned previously connects to their new learning.

Reading Word Problems

Many people assume that because word problems usually consist of only a few sentences, they are easy for students to read; however, word problems present some challenges. Kenney (2005) notes that in traditional paragraphs, the topic sentence is located at the beginning and the remaining sentences elaborate on details that support the topic. In word problems, the main idea often comes at the end and in the form of a question. This organizational change can create difficulties for students who are used to the traditional paragraph structure. They need to read through the problem to get to the main idea. Once they know the main idea, they need to read the problem at least one more time to determine which pieces of information are relevant. There is also very limited redundancy in word problems, which results in limited opportunities for readers to check their ideas and verify word meanings. Furthermore, words sometimes have different meanings when used in a mathematical context rather than in everyday usage. As students read word problems, they need to differentiate between these multiple usages and meanings.

Students are often taught to identify key words to determine which mathematical operation(s) they will need to solve a problem, but this approach is limited. When students use the key-word approach, they rarely read for meaning. Rather than making sense of the mathematical concepts and ideas in the problem, their thinking is reduced to finding a word to which they associate a specific operation. This approach can eliminate any opportunity for mathematical reasoning and can lead to incorrect solutions (Sowder, 1988).

We would not think it appropriate to teach our students to look for only one or two words in a story in order to understand the plot. Why then would we use this approach in mathematics? Another limitation of focusing on key words is that you may miss more subtle details in the question. For example, students may be told that if they see the word *times* in the question, they should multiply to determine the answer. However, for Problem 1 shown in the margin, this approach would not produce the correct answer. Students do need to multiply, but they must then calculate the difference between the product and another quantity to determine the final answer. In some cases, such as Problem 2, there are no words to suggest a specific operation (Clement & Bernhard, 2005). The key-word approach can create further confusion when the word problems are complex, involve several relationships, and include information that may not be relevant to the solution.

One way to help students interpret word problems is by reading problems aloud together before students work on their own or in groups to solve them. Invite students to explain what they think the problem is describing. Effective questions can draw students' attention to the words, pictures, and symbols used in the problems and clarify their meanings. Inviting students to share their interpretations can provide you with insight into what students understand, how they process the content,

Problem 1: *Mary made 5 times as many cookies as Parvinder. Parvinder made 6 cookies. How many more cookies did Mary make?*

Problem 2: *How many wheels do 5 cars have?*

and what they find confusing. By posing key questions before, during, and after reading a math problem, you can help students in understanding mathematical text features and developing important reading skills.

While the idea may sound a little odd, another way to help students struggling to interpret word problems is to provide them with the correct answer before they begin to solve a problem. In word problems, understanding the thought process behind the solution is as important as the answer. Knowing the answer lessens the anxiety many students feel about being wrong or having to reach the answer at the same time as their peers. In my research, I have found that this knowledge enables learners to focus on the strategies needed to arrive at the correct answer: they are more likely to explore a variety of strategies. This approach helps to improve group work and support learners who struggle.

See the Teaching Strategies section of this chapter beginning on page 63 for more activities involving reading, sorting, and creating word problems.

Reading Mathematical Symbols

In mathematics, students need to process and understand symbols and numerals as well as words. Decoding mathematical symbols can be challenging as symbols such as arrows, brackets, and subtraction signs can have different meanings in other subject areas and contexts (Marks Krpan, 2008b). David Sousa (2008) points out that the processing of numerals takes place in a different part of the brain than the processing of words. An implication of this is that the human brain comprehends numbers as quantities, not as words. Sousa explains that the brain converts a numeral instantly into a quantity.

It should be noted that English and other western languages are more challenging for learning number names than languages such as Cantonese, Japanese, Korean, Turkish, and Hungarian. For example, in English the names for the numbers 11, 12, 13 (*eleven, twelve,* and *thirteen*) have no correlation to the actual 10s and 1s. In the languages listed previously, the same numbers translate to *ten one, ten two,* and *ten three,* demonstrating a direct correspondence to the base ten system. Furthermore, in English we need 28 words to count from 1 to 100, whereas in Cantonese, only 11 are needed. This information is important to consider when working with English Language Learners.

When reading in language arts, students are expected to gain meaning from text, not just to understand individual words. Similarly, to visualize and model numerical expressions and equations, they need to do more than understand what each individual symbol or number represents. Students need to understand the meanings of the numbers and symbols and how they interact with each other. Students' ability to read numerical expressions and equations can be improved by modelling different equations using manipulatives and pictures, and by exploring non-standard algorithms. Students also benefit from opportunities to discuss or write about how they interpret and understand different numerical expressions: doing so allows them to clarify any misconceptions they may have. For example, a study conducted by McNeil and Alibali (2005) revealed that many students believed that the equal sign meant *the total* or *the answer*, instead of understanding it to mean *equal to* or *two amounts that are the same.*

Teaching Strategies

Picture Book Read-Aloud

Mathematical picture books are often structured with a storyline and a mathematical theme that is addressed throughout the text. The mathematical theme can be quite explicit, inviting the reader to answer questions and engage in mathematical problem-solving. When we share these books with students, it is important for us to model the key reading strategies described in the Skills and Structures section of this chapter beginning on page 59, but also to take the time to build on and discuss the mathematical concepts presented. You may decide to use a document camera as you read the story. This will allow you to make notes on the images using a whiteboard, as students share their thoughts.

The research on reading stresses the importance of enabling students to make text connections (Booth & Swartz, 2004; Miller, 2002). Text connections occur when readers make a personal connection between the text and something in their own life, another text, or the world. When reading mathematical picture books and other math texts, we also need to provide opportunities for students to make *text-to-mathematics* connections, in which they identify the mathematical concepts in the story and the role they play; *mathematics-to-mathematics* connections, in which they relate the mathematics in the story to mathematical concepts or strategies they have studied previously; *mathematics-to-self* connections, in which they relate the mathematics in the story to their own lives; and *mathematics-to-world* connections, in which they explore how math concepts in the story relate to events in the world. By posing questions that invite students to think about the mathematical vocabulary, images, and concepts presented in the book, we can assist them in developing mathematical thinking and stronger comprehension skills. These questions may also prove useful for other teaching applications in mathematics.

Sample Implementation for Picture Book Read-Aloud
These are examples of the types of questions you can pose during a read-aloud. You will need to adapt them based on the topic or storyline of the picture book you are using.

materials
- picture book that explores a mathematical concept your class is studying

To view a list of picture books that explore mathematical concepts, see the *Math Expressions* website: www.pearsoncanada.ca/ mathexpressions

Text-to-Mathematics

- What kinds of mathematical patterns do you see in this picture?

- Why do you think the illustrator drew this picture to represent $\frac{1}{2}$? Can you think of another picture that could show the same fraction?

- Why do you think it is challenging for the bugs to share 13 cookies? What number of cookies would be easier to share? Why?

- What algebraic equation can you use to represent this problem? Why?

- The author provides three examples of ways to get to 11. What other ways do you know to get to 11?

- What other examples of triangles could the author have mentioned?

Mathematics-to-Mathematics

- Where have we seen this idea before?

- How does this relate to what we have in the past done with fractions?

- Can you describe another strategy we have used that is similar to the one in the book? Please do so.

Mathematics-to-Self

- What does this remind you of?

- Describe a time when using addition has helped you.

- How have you used multiplication in your daily life?

- Have you experienced the same measurement problem as Frank in the book? What would you do differently to solve the problem?

- When do you think you will need to use ratios?

- How could the estimation skills that the author is sharing help you? When could you use these skills?

- Have you ever had to share some cookies or candies with a friend? How did you share them?

Mathematics-to-World

- How do you think data or graphs can help us to make good decisions in our world?

- Which mathematical ideas mentioned in the book do you feel are the most important for people to understand? Why?

- How do you think the geometric shapes in this story have influenced the way people design buildings?

- How can you use this strategy in other subject areas?

- How have Fibonacci numbers influenced our lives?

- This story is an ancient folktale from Egypt. Why do you think cultures have mathematical stories? Do you know of others?

Modifications and Extensions for Picture Book Read-Aloud

- Invite the class to create a mathematical picture book based on one you have read. Each student can create one page of the book.

- If the story focuses on a mathematical problem, stop partway through the story and invite students to think of solutions. You may invite students to work on their solutions in groups and then share with the class. When you finish reading the story, ask students to compare their solutions to the one the character in the book used. Was the character's more effective? Why? Why not?

- Invite students to write mathematical stories in their language arts program.

- Invite students to do Readers Theatre, in which they take part of the text and "perform" it. They can add actions, vary the sound level (louder and softer), create patterns (through repeating different parts of the text), vary the reading speed (slowly or quickly), and so on.

- Ask each student to examine a mathematical picture book, select their favourite sentence, and read the sentence to the class. Students need to explain their choice and how the sentence represents the mathematics in the book.

- Organize your students into groups of four and provide them with a mathematical picture book to read. Prompt each group to determine, through discussion, their favourite page of the text and why they like it. Invite a member of each group to read aloud the selected page and to explain why it is the group's favourite. Ask each group to determine their favourite mathematical picture in the book as well and then share and explain why they chose it.

Visualizing Mathematical Text

Visualizing text is an important reading skill that can help students in focusing more effectively on what they are reading and developing a deeper understanding of it. In mathematics, this approach also enables

materials

- mathematical text to inspire visualization

- sketching materials for students

students to develop visual models of mathematical concepts, which leads to stronger comprehension skills.

Sample Implementation of Visualizing Mathematical Text

1. Begin with a practice visualization of a noun such as the word *car*. Ask students to picture a car in their minds. Then invite students to share the different kinds of images they pictured.

2. Let students know that what they have just done is called "visualization." It is an effective strategy to use when reading any kind of text. Students can create images in their mind that reflect what they understand the text to mean or describe.

3. Explain to the students that you are going to read aloud a mathematical text and that they are to try to see in their minds what the text is saying. You may want to ask students to close their eyes.

4. Read a mathematical passage such as a paragraph from a textbook, a word problem, or a description of a mathematical concept.

5. Once you finish, ask students to sketch one or two images that they envisioned. Then invite them to share their sketches in pairs.

6. Engage students in a whole-class discussion about what inspired their sketches: the words and phrases in the text, as well as their own prior knowledge and experiences. This discussion will enable students to learn different ways to make connections to the text through images.

Modifications and Extensions for Visualizing Mathematical Text

- For younger students, you may want to do a whole-class activity where you read a simple mathematics passage and build up to one that is more complex. Students can describe their images.

- Conduct a think-aloud, where you read a passage and share the images that come into your mind as well as the specific parts of the text that triggered the images.

- Invite students to read short texts to a partner and then ask the listener to share what he or she visualized.

- Share a mathematical text with the whole class, with the text displayed so everyone can see it. As you read with the class, pause in different sections and invite students to share and explain the images that are elicited by the text.

Mathematical Text Paraphrasing

When reading word problems, students often begin to solve the problem before they read the whole text. They tend to focus on the numbers and key words. This activity helps students focus on the story in the problem and visualize what they are reading. You may need to review that *paraphrasing* means retelling in your own words and provide opportunities for students to relate this skill to what they have done in other subject areas. Using this approach as an integral part of exploring word problems in your classroom is helpful.

It is important that students focus only on the story of the problem and what it is asking. As an example, consider this problem: *Maya wants to buy 3 novels that cost $5 each. She has $15. How many can she buy? Prove your answer.* Here is one way to paraphrase the problem: *Someone wants to buy some novels. The problem is asking how many she can buy with the money she has. We need to explain why our answer is correct.*

Sample Implementation of Mathematical Text Paraphrasing

1. Organize your students in pairs. Explain that each pair will receive a word problem. One partner will paraphrase the problem verbally following instructions you will provide.

2. Distribute one word problem covered with a sticky note to each pair. Ask your students not to lift the sticky note until you tell them.

3. Once the problems are distributed, invite one student from each pair to read the problem silently and write on the sticky note three key words that will help in paraphrasing the problem. Explain that they are focusing only on the story of the problem and should not yet be recording any numbers.

4. Prompt these students to re-cover the problem with the sticky note.

5. Invite the students who have read the problem to paraphrase it to their partners, using the words written on the sticky note for guidance. Once the first student in each pair has provided a paraphrase of the problem, the partner shares what he or she heard.

6. Provide an opportunity for students to make improvements to their paraphrases. Then have the pairs read the original problem together to see whether their rewordings conveyed the story successfully.

7. Ask several students to share their paraphrases of the problem with the whole class. Invite students to share any personal experiences that relate to the story told in the problem. Doing this enables them to make personal connections to the text.

materials

For each pair:

- copies of word problems

- sticky notes large enough to cover the word problems

To view more sample word problems, see the *Math Expressions* website: www.pearsoncanada.ca/mathexpressions

8. You can repeat the activity, but reverse roles so that the students who paraphrased the problem are now the listeners. You will need to provide new problems for the pairs to use. Try to incorporate a variety of types of word problems.

Modifications and Extensions for Mathematical Text Paraphrasing

- Invite students to share and discuss their paraphrases with the whole class.

- Model this activity with the whole class before inviting them to do it on their own.

- You can vary the difficulty of this activity by using simpler or more elaborate word problems depending on the grade level and abilities of your students. You can also give each pair a different word problem to differentiate the instruction for the varying learning needs among your students.

- Consider using this technique with newspaper articles or excerpts from textbooks to assist students in summarizing mathematical texts from different genres.

- For English Language Learners or students who may be struggling with reading, you may want to provide visuals with the word problem.

Mathematical Text Sorting

materials

For each group:

- a copy of a set of math texts of the same genre (word problems, picture books, articles from newspapers) *or*

- a copy of a set of mathematical constructs of the same type (equations, word problems, numbers, geometric shapes, or graphs) printed on small cards or pieces of paper

- index cards

This activity requires students to sort math texts or constructs into groups based on common attributes. It helps them to recognize and understand the different features and characteristics of math texts or constructs. You can provide your students with the attributes they should be looking for or invite them to use their own. I often find when students choose their own attributes as categories, they identify more characteristics in the samples and provide me with more insight into their own learning.

In the sample implementation, students are sorting word problems, but you can replace word problems with a different text genre or a construct.

Sample Implementation of Mathematical Text Sorting

1. Organize your students into groups of 4 or 5.

2. Provide each group with 6 to 10 word problems. All groups should have the same set of problems.

3. Explain that they need to read the word problems and sort them into different groups based on common elements. You may want to establish a list of possible sorting criteria with your students and post the list in the classroom. Examples of criteria for word problems could be related to the storyline, question asked, operations used, mathematical strand, and so on. For younger children, it may be helpful to provide index cards on which the categories are written.

4. Allow enough time for students to sort the problems into categories and label each group, using index cards.

5. Once students have sorted their problems, invite each group to explain how they sorted them and the reasons for their categories.

6. You may want to choose one or two word problems and examine them in detail based on what your students observed.

Modifications and Extensions for Mathematical Text Sorting

- You may sort a group of math texts or constructs as a whole-class activity. Doing this helps to model the process and enables you to facilitate student thinking.

- Each group can work with a different set of texts or constructs, thereby allowing you to differentiate the activity for each group.

- Instead of sorting several texts or constructs, invite students to compare and contrast two items. They can list the similarities and differences on a T-chart and then share their ideas with the class. A sample is shown below for two word problems.

Problem 1	Problem 2
• is about buying something	• is about hanging pictures
• involves money	• involves measurements
• asks how much change	• asks about differences in area

What's the Problem?

For this activity, you provide students with a phrase (*5 pencils*) or a sentence (*Sunny has 3 more than Joel*), and invite them to create a word problem for which the phrase or sentence is the answer. Barlow and Cates (2007) note that for this activity to be effective, the directions need to be explicit and the answer needs to be more than a number. Rather than saying something like "The answer is 10. Write a mathematical problem or

materials
- none

story," provide more detail by saying "Write a word problem that has an answer of 10 cookies."

This activity enables students to explore different ways to construct word problems, which, in turn, strengthens their reading comprehension skills. It also provides students with opportunities to develop key problem-solving skills as they explore different ways to arrive at one answer. You may decide to have students exchange problems and solve the problem they receive to confirm that it has the desired answer. You can keep this activity open-ended or, depending on the grade level, provide guidelines or samples related to the complexity of the problem you want your students to write.

STRATEGIES IN ACTION

What's the Problem?

Grade 3

This sample problem was written for the answer "5 pencils."

Narges had 2 pencils and Usha gave her 3 pencils.

How many pencils does Narges have altogether?

Grade 7

This sample problem was written for the answer "5 pencils."

Joel had 27 pencils and decided to give one-third of them to his sister.

Then he gave 50% of the remaining pencils to his friend Jamal and 4 to his brother.

How many pencils does Joel have left?

Show Me the Math!

materials

- photographs showing math in our environment (see sample on page 72)

- chart paper and markers

This activity engages students in exploring how mathematics is everywhere in their environment if they take the time to *see* it or *read* it around them. By showing students a photograph that can be connected to several mathematical concepts, we can enable students to make meaningful mathematical connections in a variety of contexts. The open-endedness of this activity allows students to work to their own abilities and enables them to develop visual literacy skills.

Sample Implementation of Show Me the Math!

1. Show students an image.

2. Invite students to describe any mathematics they see in the image. You may get many different responses depending on the grade and knowledge of your students.

3. When students share, it is important to ask them not only to describe what they see, but also to explain their thinking. For example, if a student says that he or she sees parallel lines, invite the student to explain where the lines are and how he or she knows they are parallel.

4. You may want to record on chart paper all of the mathematical connections students identify in the image.

To view more sample photos of math in the environment, see the *Math Expressions* website: www.pearsoncanada.ca/mathexpressions

Modifications and Extensions for Show Me the Math!

- You may decide to direct students' attention to a specific mathematical concept or topic you are teaching. For example, say: *"We are studying parallel lines. Can you see any parallel lines in this photo? Where are the lines and how do you know they are parallel?"*

- Using an interactive whiteboard will allow students to draw or write on the image to show their mathematical thinking. If you do not have a whiteboard, you can place an image in a plastic sheet protector and students can use whiteboard markers to draw on it.

- Invite students to find mathematical pictures in magazines. You can also invite students to find images that show specific mathematical concepts such as different shapes and use of numbers.

- Students can make math collages of pictures that show examples of one concept.

- Invite students to create a math problem or story that is based on the picture you shared. You can also guide your students by stipulating the theme on which the problem should be based, perhaps fractions or probability.

- Show your students a graph and invite them to describe a story or an event that they feel the graph could represent. Encourage your students to explain why they think their story supports the graph.

- Invite students to share their own photos (perhaps from different countries) that they feel show mathematical concepts.

Show Me the Math!

The following are excerpts from discussions about the photo shown here.

In the first line, I see five plus two, which equals seven. (Kindergarten)

There are 35 yellow beads. (Grade 2)

I see a square. (Grade 3)

I see parallel lines. (Grade 5)

On the first row, the red beads represent negative numbers and the yellow are positive so the total value of beads in the first row is positive 3. (Grade 8)

The number of yellow beads could be represented by $5^2 + 10$. (Grade 8)

Mathematical Glyphs

This activity engages students in using symbols to communicate data and in reading data from symbols. Students will need a glyph key, which contains the different symbols and their meanings. In the implementation described here, students create a portrait of a classmate based on criteria related to the glyph key. This activity is a great way to build classroom community as students learn more about each other, explore commonalities, and celebrate differences. A sample glyph key that can be used for this implementation is provided in Line Masters 3.1A and 3.1B (Biography Glyphs). Depending on the needs and interests of your students, you may decide to use just the first master, both masters, or a glyph key of your own.

materials
- a glyph key (sample provided on Line Masters 3.1A and 3.1B: Biography Glyphs)

- art supplies such as brightly coloured paper, scissors, and glue sticks

Sample Mathematical Glyphs Implementation: Biography Glyphs

1. Begin the activity by inviting your students to share different preferences: *"Who likes to read as a pastime? Who likes spicy foods? Who has more than 3 people in their family?"* Discuss how our differences and similarities make us unique as individuals and as a group.

2. Explain that students will be creating a portrait of a partner. While the portrait will not necessarily look like the other person, it will communicate a lot of information about the partner.

3. Explain that students will use a key in order to know what kinds of eyes, ears, and other features to use in the portrait. Post the glyph key in the classroom or give a copy to each group. Invite students to read the key by asking questions, for example: *"If my birthday is in January, what would my eyes look like? If I prefer reading as a pastime, what would my nose look like?"* Or you may choose to display a completed portrait and invite the class to figure out how it relates to the glyph key.

4. Divide the class into pairs. Explain that students should collect information about their partners and cut out the appropriate features to create their partner's face based on the key. They can use different coloured paper for each feature. They will glue the features on the face they are creating.

5. Once students complete the portraits, invite them to post the portraits in the classroom.

6. You can use the portraits to pose questions. You might ask: *"Who in the class comes from a large family? Who in the class has a pet that is not listed?"* Ask students how they know this information. You will thereby be able to highlight specific features of glyphs and how they are used to read data.

7. Invite students to pose different questions to the class based on what they see in the portraits.

Modifications and Extensions for Mathematical Glyphs

- Students can create their own glyph key and create a self-portrait that conveys additional biographical information.

- Students can pair up and pose questions to each other based on what they see in their portraits.

- You can change the features in the glyph key and invite students to create snow people or monsters instead of portraits.

- You can invite students to create graphs to represent the data shown in the class portraits.

- Students can do research in other subject areas and create a visual that communicates information about their topic. For example, if students are researching countries around the world, they could develop a glyph key to present information for each country. The shape could represent the continent the country is in, the colour could represent a population range, and the pattern(s) (dotted, striped, and so on) could represent the official language(s) spoken in the country.

- Instead of creating portraits of each other, students can create portraits that represent historical figures or characters in a book. They can create a glyph key that represents information about the characters or people they are researching.

- If a glyph activity is too challenging, decrease the quantity of information in the glyph key. For example, have younger students create a portrait where the only attribute they need to add is the eyes.

- For older students, you can make the activity more challenging by using descriptions of the shapes instead of pictures. For example, rather than having an image of a triangle for the eyes to represent specific information, you can write *equilateral triangle, isosceles triangle,* and *scalene triangle* for the different choices. Students must then use their knowledge of different shapes to convey the desired information.

Mathematical Glyphs

Mathematical Recipes

Mathematical recipes are word problems that engage students in creating concrete representations of different quantities based on the relationships between the quantities. The recipes focus on linking different coloured cubes together to create *trains*. The number of cubes of each colour is based on the information the recipe provides. These recipes support the development of mathematical vocabulary as each recipe focuses on different quantitative language. The recipes on Line Master 3.4 involve whole number relationships, the recipes on Line Master 3.5 involve fractions and percents, and the recipes on Line Master 3.6 involve algebra.

   In some cases, the information in the recipe builds on previous information. For example, in the first recipe shown on the next page, the information that there are 6 yellow cubes is needed to determine the number of green cubes. In the second recipe, the problem solver is required to read the whole recipe to gather all the information necessary to create the train. With this recipe, you can invite your students to represent the different combinations of red and orange cubes that make the first statement true before reading the quantity of orange cubes in the third statement. Similarly, students can represent the different combinations of green and pink cubes that make the second statement true before reading the quantity of pink cubes in the final statement. They can then read the last two statements and modify the quantities of each colour of cube so that all the statements are true.

materials

- recipes printed on index cards (see samples on next page and on Line Masters 3.4 to 3.6)

- linking cubes in different colours

- blank index cards for students to create their own recipes

- copies of Line Masters 3.2 and 3.3 (Train Recipe Card and My Train)

Recipe 1

6 yellow cubes

3 fewer green cubes than yellow cubes

2 fewer black cubes than green cubes

3 more red cubes than black cubes

Recipe 4

3 more red cubes than orange cubes

3 more green cubes than pink cubes

5 orange cubes

3 pink cubes

Sample Mathematical Recipes Implementation

To view more recipes, see the *Math Expressions* website: www.pearsoncanada.ca/mathexpressions

1. Distribute linking cubes to students. Students may work individually or in small groups.

2. Write a simple recipe on the board or chart paper. Invite students to use their cubes to create a train based on the recipe.

3. After allowing time for students to complete their trains, invite volunteers to show their creations and explain the strategies they used to solve the recipes, and what they noticed about the text.

4. Repeat with a more challenging recipe.

5. Once students have completed a few trains, invite them to discuss which parts of the recipes were challenging or helpful.

6. Distribute more recipes to the students and allow time for further exploration. You can give different recipes to students to differentiate the instruction for varying learning needs.

7. Consider asking students to create their own trains and recipes. They can give their recipes to other students to complete. Students can provide feedback on how helpful the recipes were. Invite students to use Line Masters 3.2 and 3.3 (Train Recipe Card and My Train) to post their recipes in the classroom.

Modifications and Extensions for Mathematical Recipes

- For younger students, you may wish to create recipes that always indicate both the quantity and colour of the cubes, for example, 2 red, 3 green, and 5 yellow. The words in the recipe can be the colour of the cubes they are describing.

- For younger students, you may choose to complete different recipes as a whole class. For example, you could create three recipes that make different cube trains of 10 using only two colours. Doing this will enable students to see different combinations that make 10 and learn specific mathematical vocabulary.

- Let older students write more complex and detailed recipes by using 20 cubes in a train.

- Show your students a cube train and invite them to write a recipe. You may want to specify that all of the recipes relate to a specific mathematical concept you are teaching, such as fractions or percent. Invite students to share their recipes with the class. Doing this helps students see how one set of cubes can be described mathematically in many different ways.

STRATEGIES IN ACTION

Mathematical Recipes

Kindergarten

5 red

2 blue

3 orange

After creating different trains and writing recipes with her students as a whole-group activity, Jeanne decided to provide cubes, coloured square stickers, blank sheets of paper, line masters, and assorted markers as one of the activities at the math centre. Some students created their own trains using cubes or stickers, some drew their own trains, while others, like Sema, used the line masters to create theirs. Jeanne used the student work created at the centre as part of her mathematical discussions with her students about comparing different number quantities.

Mathematical Recipes

See sample for content.

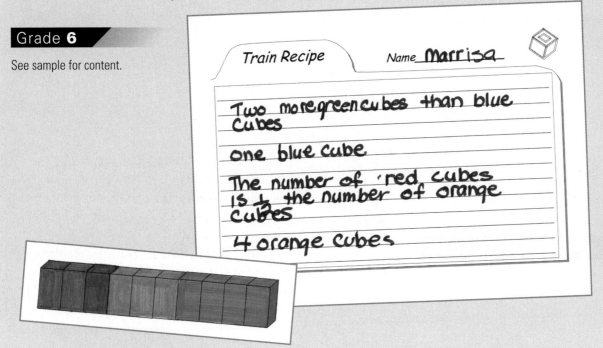

Train Recipe   Name Marrisa

Two more green cubes than blue cubes

one blue cube

The number of red cubes is ½ the number of orange cubes

4 orange cubes

In this sample, Marrisa organizes her clues in such a way that the reader cannot use the information from the first clue without reading more of the recipe to gain additional information. She employs the concept of fractions as well as more/less. Marrisa's teacher knows that she is capable of using more complex mathematical concepts in her recipe.

Sample Descriptive Feedback
Marrisa, your recipe accurately represents the train that you have created. I like the way the clues are mixed up so that the reader must read more than one clue to complete the train. You have included a fraction clue. I know that you have a solid understanding of fractions and decimals. How could you create a recipe that includes both decimals and fractions for the same train?

©P

Chapter 4

Writing in Mathematics

Indicators of Success

Goals for students include the following:

- Students can communicate their ideas clearly using a variety of writing formats such as conjectures, proofs, mathematical arguments, graphic organizers, and affective writing.

- Students use appropriate mathematical vocabulary.

- Students integrate pictures, words, and numbers meaningfully to support and demonstrate their understandings and ideas.

- Students provide effective rationales for their ideas.

- Students provide examples to support their mathematical ideas.

- Students are able to revise and rework their writing based on feedback from peers and/or teachers.

- Students can make connections to real-world applications.

For a reproducible version of these indicators of success, see the *Math Expressions* website: www.pearsoncanada.ca/mathexpressions

What the Research Says About...
Writing in Mathematics

For resources about writing in mathematics, see the *Math Expressions* website:
www.pearsoncanada.ca/mathexpressions

The benefits of engaging students in exploring their thinking through writing are recognized in many subject areas. The National Council of Teachers of Mathematics (2000) notes that writing needs to be an essential part of a mathematics program as it enables students to explore their own mathematical ideas and build on those of others.

Students' views of mathematics are often limited to numbers and procedural steps to remember (Aspinwall & Aspinwall, 2003). Writing about mathematics encourages students to investigate concepts from a variety of perspectives, broadening their understanding of what mathematics entails. Writing also affords students time to reflect, reshape, and rework what they know. As they organize and revise their writing, students can learn more about their own mathematical thinking and identify possible gaps in their mathematical knowledge (McIntosh & Draper, 2001; Sousa, 2008). As one Grade 7 student shared, "When I write about math, I really have to think about how I understand mathematics. I get to know myself in a different way."

As students communicate their mathematical thoughts through writing, they make implicit learning explicit, allowing educators to see how they understand and make connections between mathematical concepts. Unlike mathematical discourse, student writing also provides documentation of thinking. Students can revisit a piece of writing to see how their understanding of a specific concept has changed and modify their original response. Teachers can also use student writing to document student progress and assess the impact of specific teaching approaches. Encouraging student writing in mathematics enables all students to have an opportunity to share their thinking with the teacher and become engaged in their own learning (Zinsser, 1989).

Assessing Mathematical Writing

As described in the introduction to this book, student work can be used as assessment for learning, as learning, or of learning. How a piece of writing will be used depends on the goal of the activity that motivated the writing and the learning needs of your students. In all cases, students need to know beforehand the purpose of the writing activity and how it will be used for assessment. If their writing is going to be formally evaluated, it is essential that your students understand the assessment criteria. In addition, students need ample time to develop and practise their writing skills in the specific mathematical area that will be evaluated.

As you implement writing in your mathematics program, strive to establish a balance of assessments. Students are often more cautious and take fewer risks in their writing when they know it will be formally graded. If writing serves only as a summative assessment piece in your mathematics program, students may refrain from expressing themselves freely and write somewhat superficial entries. Students need opportunities to investigate their thinking without worrying about being evaluated.

As with all teaching and learning processes, it is critical that we empower our students to assess their own work. When students assess their own writing, they become metacognitive of their learning and are better able to make improvements and set personal learning goals. A list of indicators of success, written in student language and collaboratively created with your students, can be used to help students understand what is expected when they write in mathematics. A sample list appears below. This tool makes the self-assessment process transparent and accessible for all students. Developing the indicators with your students can help them to monitor their own learning and assess their work.

For a reproducible version of these sample indicators of success, see the *Math Expressions* website: www.pearsoncanada.ca/ mathexpressions

---

Sample Indicators of Success for Writing

❏ Is my writing well organized and easy to follow?

❏ Have I included mathematical vocabulary?

❏ Have I used mathematical vocabulary correctly?

❏ Have I used pictures effectively to explain my thinking?

❏ Have I used numbers effectively to show my thinking?

❏ Have I explained the reasons for my mathematical ideas?

❏ Have I included examples to help the reader understand what I am saying?

Facilitating Mathematical Writing

When students first arrive at school, they often lack personal experiences discussing, reading, and writing about mathematics. We need to teach students these skills by providing them with many different learning experiences in which they can communicate and reflect on their mathematical learning. As noted in Chapter 2: Mathematical Discourse, students require opportunities to discuss their ideas before expressing them in writing. Mathematical discourse plays an important role in developing writing skills in mathematics as it allows students to consolidate their thinking before they begin to write (Ediger, 2006).

Some teachers assume that if students know how to write in language arts, they will know how to write in mathematics. Mathematical writing, however, involves learning processes that may be unfamiliar to students. Students are required to analyze, make conjectures, use specific mathematical vocabulary, and explore their mathematical reasoning. In addition, students should be able to include pictures and numbers in their writing to represent abstract concepts and represent their thinking. As with writing in language arts, we need to provide explicit instruction to help students refine their writing. Students need lots of examples and support as they develop effective writing skills in mathematics. We must be sure to provide them with time to practise and become comfortable communicating mathematically.

Classroom Organization

Writing activities can be used as the main part of a mathematics lesson, as an introduction, or as a way of closing a lesson. Each writing activity in this chapter can be used to support any part of your mathematics program. Writing can be done individually, in small groups, or as a whole-class activity. What matters is that the writing you infuse is meaningful—it must not be an *add-on* to what the students are already doing.

There are several ways to organize writing in your mathematics program. For individual reflections, some teachers prefer to have students complete their writing in a journal. Adopting this approach would let you gain access to all of a student's reflections at once. You can observe and document how the student has progressed over time. Using a math journal also sends the message that students' reflections are valued enough to merit a special notebook. Alternatively, you may want to invite students to write their reflections in their math notebooks. Students can thereby record their ideas together with the work they are completing. You can see their reflections for that day alongside the mathematical activities that may have inspired them. Some educators prefer to have students write on separate sheets of paper or index cards. They like the flexibility of being able to group the writings and quickly see patterns in student thinking in the class. You need to determine the organization methods that will work best for you and your students.

Supporting English Language Learners

Writing is considered the most challenging of the literacy skills as it requires the simultaneous use of systems involving phonemes, syntax, and graphics, as well as orthographic, semantic, and discourse rules (Dyson & Freedman, 1991). Through careful planning, however, we can create opportunities for English Language Learners to experience success. ELLs often have stronger verbal than writing skills in English, so inviting them to explain their thinking verbally to another student who can then assist them in recording their ideas can be helpful. ELLs will often use drawings and diagrams to support the messages in their writing. These drawings can serve as a basis for discussion to elicit further elaboration and detail in their written work (Yedlin, 2004). In addition, consistent teacher feedback related to the content and form of the written work can be extremely beneficial in helping ELLs to develop strong writing skills. Listening to read-alouds, including math picture books, can also have a positive impact (Krashen, 2004). The use of a mathematical word wall with lots of visuals (see Chapter 3), as well as personal word cards (see Chapter 2), can enable ELLs to access specific mathematical vocabulary as they write (Marks Krpan, 2008b).

English Language Learners may not have experienced writing in mathematics in their homelands. By taking the time to model mathematical writing and verbalize your thinking as you do so, you can assist ELLs in understanding the elements and purpose of the writing process in mathematics. For students who feel comfortable writing in English, talk prompts like those shown in Chapter 2 can provide a structure around which they can organize their ideas.

Sentence frames (Bresser, Melanese, & Sphar, 2009), often used to help ELLs express their thinking verbally, can also assist with writing. Sentence frames are statements in which key math vocabulary is omitted, providing the learner with a meaningful context for mathematics vocabulary. Students are responsible for adding the key vocabulary to communicate complete thoughts related to their mathematical understandings. Frames can range from very simple to the more complex. Here is a simple frame: A _____ has _____ sides. (A *square* has *4* sides; a *triangle* has *3* sides.) Here is a more complex structure: A_____ might have equal _____, but always has _____sides. (A *hexagon* might have equal *sides*, but always has *6* sides.) It is important that students have opportunities to learn and explore key vocabulary so that they can apply it readily in the sentence frames.

As they begin to develop writing skills in English, many ELLs may feel most comfortable writing in their native language. Working in their native language can help students to express their ideas freely and empower them to participate fully in classroom activities (Gutiérrez, 2002). It can also help them to deepen their mathematical understanding and bridge the mathematical knowledge already acquired in their native language with what they are learning in English. In one school, teachers invited ELLs who were proficient in both the language of their homeland and in English to help translate what other ELLs had written.

Encouraging the Use of Pictures

When students communicate their thinking in mathematics, we want them to use pictures, numbers, and words, but in my research, I have noticed that students tend to rely mostly on numbers to represent mathematical ideas. To challenge students' communication skills and views of mathematics, I will sometimes ask them to use only pictures in a piece of written work. Other times, I invite students to draw on numbers, pictures, and words in order to choose the most effective methods for communicating their ideas. I then ask them to explain the reasons for their choices. It is important to use a balance of approaches as we want our students to be competent in using all three communication tools successfully in their mathematical writing.

Inviting students to visualize mathematics enables them to bridge concrete and abstract modes of thinking (Ben-Chaim, Lappan, & Houang, 1989). However, students are not always clear on the role of pictures and how they can communicate mathematical meaning. We expect students to include pictures in their work, but rarely take the time to teach them *how* to incorporate pictures in their written expressions or identify the characteristics that make a picture effective. Pictures can be used to represent problems and concepts as well as to model strategies and mathematical thinking. Lacking this understanding, students may include pictures as an afterthought to fulfill teacher expectations rather than using them as tool to explore mathematical concepts. In one study, we noticed that students included pictures as decorative pieces as opposed to representations of the mathematical ideas they were discussing in their work (Marks Krpan, 2008b). Developing a rationale for including pictures in mathematical writing can enable students to better understand the role pictures have in mathematics. Consider the rationale below.

Why is it helpful to include pictures in mathematics?

- Pictures can be used to represent problems, thoughts, and strategies visually.

- Pictures can make a complex idea easier to understand.

- Some people understand pictures more easily than words or numbers.

- Pictures can help the reader understand an idea that might be difficult to describe using words or numbers.

- Pictures can help the reader compare ideas to see things that are similar or different.

- Pictures can highlight something important.

- Pictures can support what is said in the writing in a different way.

Visual Models

Visual models are pictures that can be used to represent mathematical thinking. It is important that students become aware of efficient visual models. A few models you may decide to show your students and have them explore are described below.

Arrays

A rectangular array is a set of objects, symbols, or squares arranged in an orderly way in rows and columns. Arrays can be used to model a variety of mathematical concepts and strategies including repeated addition, multiplication, division, area, perimeter, and fractions. They can assist students in understanding and representing many mathematical relationships.

An array in a grid format in which the rows and columns are not shown is called an open array. Open arrays are drawn as rectangles with side lengths roughly proportional to the values they represent. See the next page for examples.

Modelling Multiplication and Division with Arrays

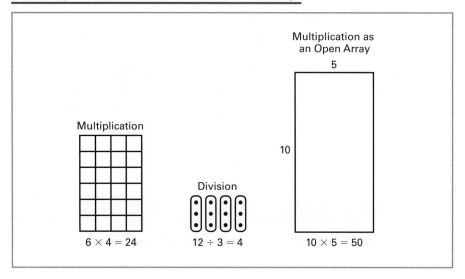

Multiplication

$6 \times 4 = 24$

Division

$12 \div 3 = 4$

Multiplication as
an Open Array

5

10

$10 \times 5 = 50$

Open Number Lines

Unlike traditional number lines, open number lines use approximations to represent spatial relationships between numbers. Addition and subtraction strategies can be modelled on the line using arrows. Only the significant numbers related to the mathematical operation being considered are recorded. Open number lines support the knowledge that numbers are spatially related to each other.

Modelling Addition and Subtraction on Open Number Lines

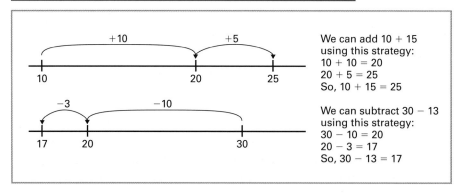

+10   +5

10   20   25

We can add 10 + 15
using this strategy:
10 + 10 = 20
20 + 5 = 25
So, 10 + 15 = 25

−3   −10

17   20   30

We can subtract 30 − 13
using this strategy:
30 − 10 = 20
20 − 3 = 17
So, 30 − 13 = 17

Five- and Ten-Frames

For a reproducible five-frame and ten-frame, see the *Math Expressions* website: www.pearsoncanada.ca/mathexpressions

Five-frames and ten-frames are one-by-five and two-by-five grids that can be used to model mathematical concepts and strategies, such as whole numbers, fractions, and algorithms. Because of their structure, five-frames and ten-frames are often useful in assisting students to visually represent numbers and model the composition and decomposition of numbers.

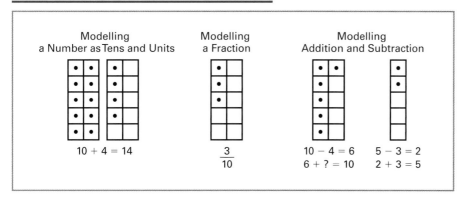

Modelling
a Number as Tens and Units

$10 + 4 = 14$

Modelling
a Fraction

$\dfrac{3}{10}$

Modelling
Addition and Subtraction

$10 - 4 = 6$ $5 - 3 = 2$
$6 + ? = 10$ $2 + 3 = 5$

Exploring Mathematical Pictures

Just as we need to provide opportunities for students to develop writing skills in mathematics, we need to provide them with support and guidance on how to create and use pictures when solving problems or communicating mathematical ideas. Students need opportunities to interpret and draw mathematical pictures and visual models in order to understand what makes a picture effective. The explorations described here provide opportunities to highlight specific attributes in a mathematical picture that communicate ideas and concepts.

- Prompt students to look through magazines and newspapers, or on the internet to find pictures that are used to communicate mathematical ideas. Invite students to share the pictures they find with the class. When students share their pictures, pose questions such as these: *What mathematical idea(s) does the picture show? In which kinds of media was it found? Do you think the picture is effective? Why? Why not?* Discuss the use of words and symbols such as labels, arrows, and colour. Invite students to explain how these elements help the viewer understand the picture.

- Ask students to sketch a picture to represent a mathematical concept. For example, you could invite each student to draw a picture that represents *area, multiplication,* or *patterns*. Once students have created their pictures, invite them to share the pictures with a partner and discuss the differences and similarities. Which pictorial elements were helpful? How could each picture be improved? You may want to have one or two pairs share their ideas with the whole class.

- Show a mathematical picture without a title and invite your students to discuss what they think it could represent. Ask them to explain what they saw in the picture that influenced their answer. You can choose a picture to suit the needs of your students and the topics under study. Possible examples include a graph with no title, a drawing of an object or place with dimensions labelled, a pattern, or a photograph of something students see in their daily lives.

- Organize your class in pairs. Ask one student in each pair to draw a picture to represent a specific math concept and the partner to guess the concept. After the activity, the guesser can provide feedback about which elements of the picture were helpful and which may have been confusing.

- Invite students to use specific models, such as an open number line or array, to model their thinking or the thinking of another student. Students can provide feedback to each other as to how effectively they represented their thinking using the model.

Once students have had a chance to explore mathematical pictures, you may wish to develop indicators of success for effective mathematical pictures that students can use to assess the pictures in their own work. A sample is shown here. You may wish to modify the wording or content of this list to suit your learners' needs.

For a reproducible version of these sample indicators of success, see the *Math Expressions* website: www.pearsoncanada.ca/mathexpressions

Sample Indicators of Success for an Effective Picture in Mathematical Writing
❏ Are my pictures clear and easy to read?
❏ Do I use titles and numbers effectively to communicate the message of the picture?
❏ Do I use arrows and labels appropriately to highlight different features of the picture?
❏ Does the picture effectively support the message of the text?

Modelling the Writing Process

A teacher-led think-aloud can assist students in understanding the thinking process required to create mathematical texts. To conduct a writing think-aloud, model the writing of a mathematical text on chart paper or on a whiteboard in front of the class. Throughout the modelling, share your decision-making and thinking processes. Once the text is complete, invite students to add ideas or provide feedback. Students gain insight into how you organize your thoughts as you rework and edit a piece of mathematical writing. This appreciation can be very beneficial, particularly for reluctant or inexperienced mathematical writers. The following are some excerpts from different writing think-alouds that teachers have conducted with students.

©P

Writing Think-Alouds

I have decided to draw a rectangle, a square, and a four-sided shape that has no equal sides to show what I think a quadrilateral is. Each picture provides a different example, some with equal sides and some without. I want the reader to know that I understand that quadrilaterals can have sides that are of different lengths, but all quadrilaterals have four sides. I will also write this in my explanation.

After I read my sentence I have decided that I am going to change it because I think it is confusing. I am going to replace it with one that is easier to follow. I am also going to include an equation to support what I am talking about.

I am drawing an array of 6 by 7 so I can use it to show how 6×7 and 7×6 both have the same answer.

For this part, I am going to include a chart that shows the differences between area and perimeter so that the reader can make the comparisons more easily.

I need to explain why I think $\frac{1}{2}$ is smaller than $\frac{3}{4}$. I think I should draw a picture and then explain what my picture is showing.

OK, I am going to look at the indicators of success to see if I have included everything that I need in my writing...

Mathematical Writing: Skills and Structures

Cooperative Writing

Sometimes students lack ideas or are unsure about how to organize their thinking. Sharing ideas through group writing can help students who are reluctant to write in mathematics. Before beginning a cooperative writing activity, you may want to engage students in discussing the writing topic with students who are not from their writing group. Doing this provides an opportunity for students to construct and organize their ideas. Sharing with students who are not members of their group may also enable them to bring different mathematical ideas to the group activity.

When first introducing this approach, provide a topic that is simple and open-ended so that all students, regardless of their level in mathematics, can write about it. This approach also avoids students becoming too focused on the content and allows them to develop a comfort level with the writing and cooperative processes.

As discussed in Chapter 1, cooperative placemats allow students to write individually and then share their ideas with the group to arrive at a final group response. Students each write their name and thoughts in one section, thereby allowing you to verify what they wrote as part of the group. What I like about this approach is that, in addition to hearing a variety of responses, each student can *see* how other students organized their writing—what pictures they included and the sentences and vocabulary they used. Once all the groups have completed their group response in the middle square, invite the groups to share with the whole class. The whole-class sharing provides students with more examples of mathematical communication.

Deciding what to include in the middle square can be challenging for students. In one junior class, one group decided to let each person contribute one idea to the centre square. Another group liked one student's answer so much that they asked that student to write it in the middle square and then the others each added something extra from their own answers.

Grade 6 Placemat Sample

Graphic Organizers

For resources about graphic organizers, see the *Math Expressions* website: www.pearsoncanada.ca/mathexpressions

Graphic organizers are a visual representation of a learner's knowledge and understanding of a specific topic. You can use these tools as an integral part of your teaching and assessment strategies in mathematics. The use of graphic organizers can improve learning and how the brain stores and retrieves information (Buzan & Buzan, 1993; Buzan, Buzan, & Harrison, 2006; Novak 1998). The visual nature of graphic organizers,

©P

combined with key word concepts, can assist students in reflecting on what they know and can deepen their understanding of the material they are learning (Ellis, 2004).

Graphic organizers not only communicate what a learner understands, but also help to identify misconceptions the student may have. You can use the information that students communicate in a graphic organizer to inform your own teaching and provide meaningful feedback to your students. For students to use graphic organizers effectively, we need to explicitly teach how to create them through teacher modelling (Gardill & Jitendra, 1999).

Verbal and Visual Word Association (VVWA)

Verbal and Visual Word Association (Eeds & Cockrum, 1985) is a graphic organizer that is used to help students develop a deeper understanding of vocabulary and concepts they are learning. VVWAs can assist students in making meaning through visual and personal connection. They can also be used to help English Language Learners consolidate new mathematical vocabulary. Examples of completed VVWAs are shown on the next pages. Line Master 4.1A is a blank VVWA you may wish to use with primary students. Line Master 4.1B is more suited to junior/intermediate students.

The VVWA chart is divided into four quadrants. The upper left quadrant is labelled *Math Word(s)*, where students write the word or concept they are exploring. The upper right quadrant is labelled *Pictures*, where students draw pictures that they feel best represent the word or concept. The lower left quadrant is labelled *Definition* (Line Master 4.1B) or *Description in My Own Words* (Line Master 4.1A), where students write their own definition or explanation of the word or concept. The lower right quadrant is labelled *Real-Life Example*, where students draw or write an example of how this concept or word is used in their daily lives. Once an organizer is completed, students can use it as a reference to review math concepts and vocabulary. You can also display a variety of completed VVWA charts in the classroom as part of a mathematical word wall (as described in Chapter 3).

Be sure that students know how to fill in the chart. Before you ask students to complete a VVWA, it is helpful to use a teacher-led think-aloud to demonstrate how to fill out each quadrant. Begin with a math word or concept that is familiar to your students. Once you have modelled the VVWA process, you may choose to complete another example working together as a class. Invite your students to provide suggestions for each quadrant. You could also divide the class into groups, have each group collaboratively complete a VVWA, and then invite groups to share their work using the gallery walk approach described in Chapter 1.

When students complete VVWAs, you may want to suggest that they fill in the definition quadrant (*In My Own Words*) last. Doing so allows students to reflect on the examples they have provided in the other quadrants to create a personal definition.

Verbal and Visual Word Association

Grade 3

Math Word(s): Bar Graph

Pictures: [Drawing of a bar graph that shows favourite ice cream]

In My Own Words: A graph that has bars that go up. It gives us information.

Real-Life Example: I can use it to know who likes what. You can compare.

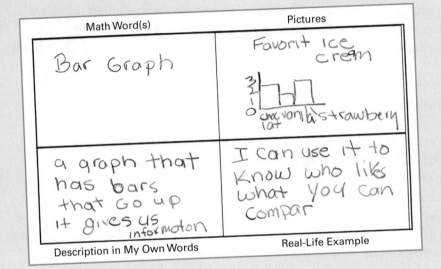

Math Word(s)

Pictures

Description in My Own Words

Real-Life Example

Danielle explains that a bar graph can provide us with information. She provides a good example of how she can use it in her daily life—learning what people like. She is also able to provide a rough sketch of a bar graph. Although her sketch is missing some elements, such as labels for the axes, it does include other elements such as a title, scale for the vertical axis, and labels for the bars.

Sample Descriptive Feedback

Danielle, you provide a good example of how we can use bar graphs— to know what people like. You tell us that bar graphs can provide us with information, which is important for your readers to know. You also mention that we can use them to compare. What can we compare with a bar graph? If you include this information in your example, it can help readers understand what you mean. I see you have numbers on the vertical axis. What are you counting? A label would help your readers know this.

Verbal and Visual Word Association

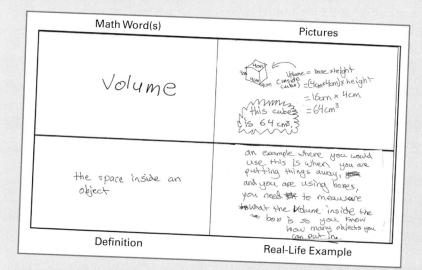

Grade **6**

Math Word(s): Volume

Pictures: [Drawing of a cube with sides labelled 4 cm and calculation of the cube's volume]

In My Own Words: the space inside an object

Real-Life Example: An example where you would use this is when you are putting things away and you are using boxes; you need to measure what the volume inside the box is so you know how many objects you can put in.

Frayer Models

The Frayer model, like the VVWA chart, can help students develop vocabulary and conceptual understanding in a variety of subject areas (Frayer, Quilling, Harris, & Harris, 1972; Wormeli, 2004). As students complete a Frayer model, they are challenged to think critically to identify non-examples that may cause confusion and lead to misconceptions. Examples of blank and completed Frayer models are shown on the next pages. Line Masters 4.2 and 4.3 provide blank Frayer models.

There are two different examples of the Frayer model. One model consists of a central oval surrounded by four quadrants. The word or concept to be explored is written in the central oval. The upper left quadrant is labelled *Definition*, where students write a definition of the word or concept in their own words. The upper right quadrant is labelled *Facts/ Characteristics*, where students describe what they know about the word or concept. The lower left quadrant is labelled *Examples*, where students record examples of the word or concept from their daily lives. The lower right quadrant is labelled *Non-examples*, where students record examples that do not represent the word or concept. The other model has *Essential Characteristics* and *Non-essential Characteristics* instead of *Definition* and *Facts/Characteristics*. In this case, students reflect on the key attributes of the concept or word and decide which are the most important and which are less critical to understanding the concept.

You may choose to introduce Frayer models using a similar process to that described for VVWAs, beginning with a teacher-led think-aloud and progressing to group or individual work.

Once you have introduced Frayer models, you may want to invite students to solve Frayer model mysteries, which help to develop critical thinking skills. Display a Frayer model that you have completed except for the central oval, which should be blank. Ask students to suggest a word that could belong in the oval and to explain their thinking. You may choose to discuss whether more than one word is appropriate. You can also invite students to create their own Frayer model mysteries. These could be shared in pairs, in small groups, or with students presenting the models to the rest of the class to solve.

In one of the schools I visit, teachers used Frayer models to review mathematical concepts in geometry. They posted the completed models, like the one shown here, in the classroom. Like the VVWA charts, you can post completed Frayer models as references for students as they work on mathematics activities.

Grade 3 Frayer Model

When students complete Frayer models, you may want to suggest that they fill in the *Definition* quadrant last. If they do, they will be able to reflect on the examples they have provided in the other quadrants to create a personal definition.

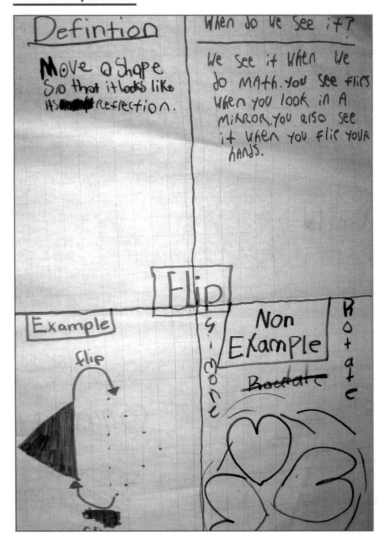

©P

Frayer Model

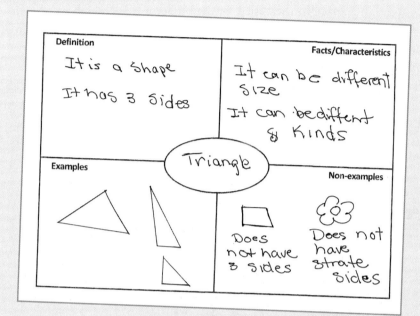

Triangle

Definition: It is a shape. It has 3 sides.

Facts/Characteristics: It can be different sizes. It can be different kinds.

Examples: [pictures of several different triangles]

Non-examples: [rough sketch of a square] Does not have 3 sides. [drawing of a flower] Does not have straight sides.

Jennifer included the key characteristic of a triangle—that it has 3 sides. She knows that triangles can be different sizes. It would be interesting to explore what she means by the word *kinds*. In her examples, Jennifer includes several drawings of different types of triangles. She also provides two non-examples and includes a reason why each is not a triangle.

Sample Descriptive Feedback

Jennifer, you have included some key information about triangles in your Frayer model—that they have 3 sides and can be different sizes. What do you mean when you say that they can be different kinds? I like how you included an explanation of why the non-examples are not triangles. This helps the reader understand why you included the pictures you did. What other facts do you know about triangles that you could include in your Frayer model?

See "Exploring Concept Circles" on pages 118–119 in the Teaching Strategies section of this chapter for suggestions on how to introduce concept circles to students.

Concept Circles

A concept circle (Allen, 1999, 2007) consists of a circle divided into sections, as shown here. In each section, the learner records pictures, numbers, symbols, or words that are examples of a concept. This main concept is recorded in a space in the centre of the circle or as a title above the circle. Like all graphic organizers, concept circles enable the brain to make key connections in the learning process. They also focus student discussions and engage learners in conceptual thinking (Allen, 2008; Vacca, Vacca, Gove, Burkey, Lenhart, & McKeon, 2011). Working with concept circles helps students to learn that mathematical concepts are interrelated; it also reinforces that there are different ways to represent mathematical ideas (pictures, symbols, numbers, and words) and encourages a deeper understanding of mathematical vocabulary. See Line Masters 4.4 to 4.9 for six concept circle variations.

Grade 4 Concept Circle

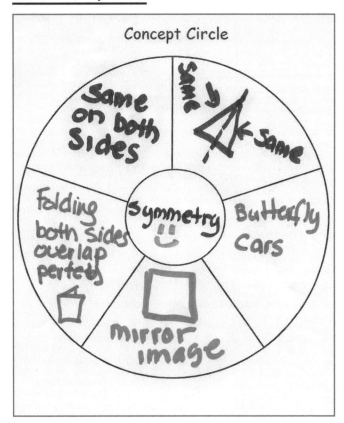

Mind Maps

Mind maps were developed by Tony Buzan after he discovered that traditional note-taking did not reflect how the brain naturally thinks and organizes ideas. A mind map is a graphic organizer that combines words, colour, and pictures to identify key ideas and how they relate to each other. The use of colour, pictures, and words engages the whole brain in the learning process, enabling the learner to make new connections. Buzan (1993, 2004) stresses that the mind map is a brain-friendly visual that helps students think, imagine, remember things, and plan and sort information.

Every mind map is a personal representation of how an individual connects ideas so no two mind maps are identical. As one student explained, "They are like a road map of my thinking!" To draw a mind map, record the map title and a picture representing the main idea in the middle of the map. Add branches that radiate from the main idea, connecting it to related ideas that are represented by words and pictures. These branches are drawn as lines or arrows. There is a hierarchical organization to mind maps—the ideas become more specific the further they are placed from the central picture.

See "Exploring Mind Maps" on pages 120–124 in the Teaching Strategies section of this chapter for suggestions on how to introduce mind maps to students.

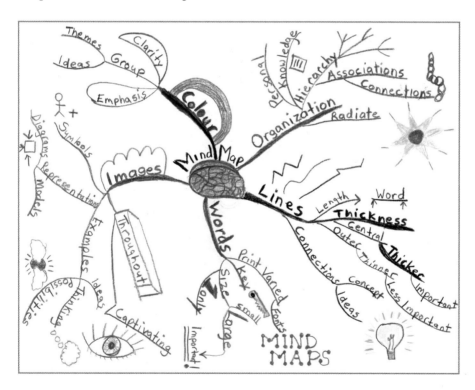

For a reproducible version of this mind map, see the *Math Expressions* website: www.pearsoncanada.ca/ mathexpressions

©P

Key Elements of a Mind Map

The following elements are essential to creating an effective mind map.

- **Main idea:** This idea is represented by a central picture and title to which all the branches connect.

- **Branches:** Branches or lines connect ideas. They can be any style or thickness and are often curved. As with a tree, thinner branches grow from the central branches. In a mind map, the thinner branches represent ideas that are triggered by or related to an idea on a central branch. The thicker the branch, the more significant the idea is to the topic. The learner can also use branches to connect different areas or sections in a mind map.

- **Pictures:** Pictures are vital in mind maps because they can convey more information to the brain than a word or a sentence. Pictures can be photographs, sketches, or computer-generated drawings. They can represent words in the map or introduce a new idea.

- **Key words:** Buzan stresses that limiting the written component to one word on a branch enables the brain to be more creative and make deeper connections. For example, a reader can make more connections to the word *money* than to a more specific concept such as *the money Parvinder has on his desk*. When adding words to a mind map, you can vary the printing style and size.

- **Colour:** Lines of the same colour can be used to denote a group of ideas that are related to one theme. Strategic use of colour renders the map easier to read and allows the learner to see connections and relationships more readily. Including colourful pictures and text makes the mind map more appealing and interesting to the brain.

Mind Map

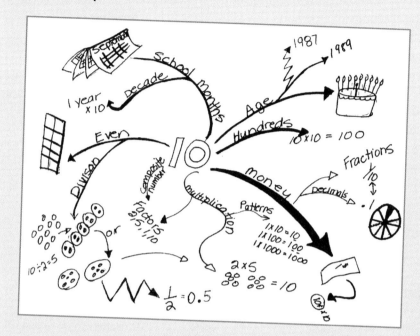

This is a mind map I created with a Grade 6 class to teach them about mind mapping, using a mind map think-aloud like the one described on page 121. I engaged the students in sharing what they knew about the number 10. Before they added each idea to the map, they discussed the different ways they could represent it and how they could connect it to the map in a meaningful way. During the lesson, many students became more comfortable with mind mapping and adding their own connections on the class map.

Concept Maps

A concept map is a graphic organizer in which concepts related to a specific topic are organized in a hierarchical fashion, with the key concept at the top. Lines link each concept in the map to one or more other concepts. Each line is labelled with a linking word that explains how the concepts are related. The farther concepts are from the key concept, the more specific they become. Concept maps can be used in note taking and studying as they allow students to organize material visually and logically on a page.

Concept maps can be used to communicate mathematical thinking, but do it somewhat differently than mind maps. A major difference is that concept maps require students to create a vertical hierarchy, while mind maps radiate from a central picture. Pictures are a key element in mind maps, while linking words are essential to concept maps. However,

See "Exploring Concept Maps" on pages 125–129 in the Teaching Strategies section of this chapter for suggestions on how to introduce concept maps to students.

For a reproducible version of this concept map, see the *Math Expressions* website: www.pearsoncanada.ca/ mathexpressions

you may choose to let students represent concepts in a concept map with pictures rather than with words.

Concept maps were developed by Joseph Novak in the 1970s to help students improve their thinking skills. Because concept maps are explicit representations of a person's thoughts, they help educators to identify what a student knows and what misconceptions he or she may have.

Like mind mapping, concept mapping engages many parts of the brain in organizing and communicating ideas. Novak asserts that the development of each relationship between concepts activates tens of thousands of neurons (brain cells). Neural connections are built, leading to better retention and retrieval of information.

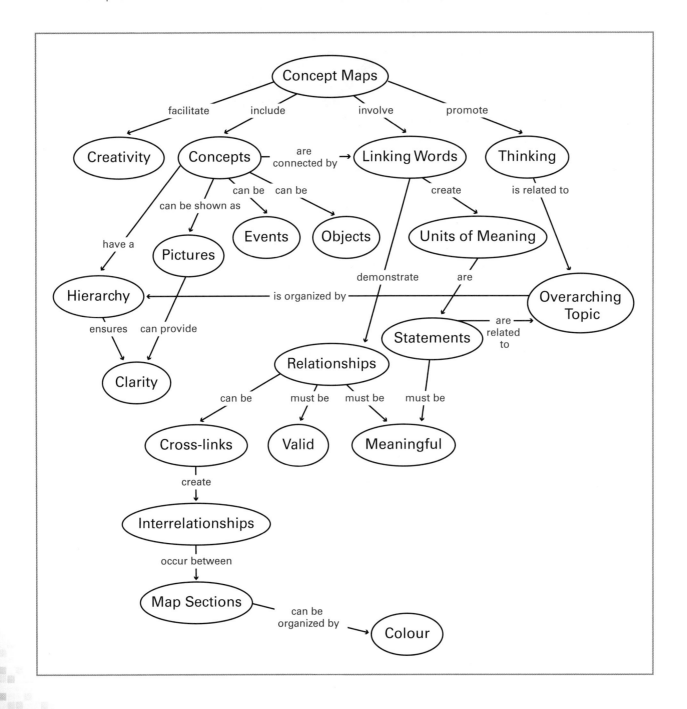

Key Elements of a Concept Map

The following elements are essential for creating an effective concept map.

- **Key concept:** The theme or topic of the map is recorded at the top of the map. The key concept is usually enclosed in a box or circle, as is each sub-concept.

- **Concepts:** To create a concept map, students need to understand what concepts are. Joseph Novak defines *concepts* as regularities in objects or events. For my students, I simplify the definition by explaining that concepts can be events (*adding* or *graphing*), objects or people (*triangles* or *mathematicians*), or attributes (*whole* or *symmetrical*). Proper names are not concepts, but can be used as examples of concepts. The concepts are placed in a vertical hierarchy, so that each level has more specific information than the level above it.

- **Connector lines:** These lines or arrows link related concepts. Unlike the curvy lines in mind maps that vary in thickness to indicate importance, the lines in concept maps are usually straight and similar in thickness. They often end in an arrow.

- **Linking words:** The words written on connector lines convey relationships between the concepts. They are commonly verbs or short verb phrases. When the linking words connect two or more concepts, they create meaningful statements. See Line Master 4.10 (Sample Linking Words for Concept Maps). Providing a list of linking words can assist students in creating concept maps and help them to understand the kinds of words that can be used.

- **Cross-links:** Connector lines can also link different sections of a concept map. When this happens, they are called "cross-links." Cross-links usually demonstrate high-level thinking in which the learner relates two topics in the concept map together.

Concept Map

See sample for content.

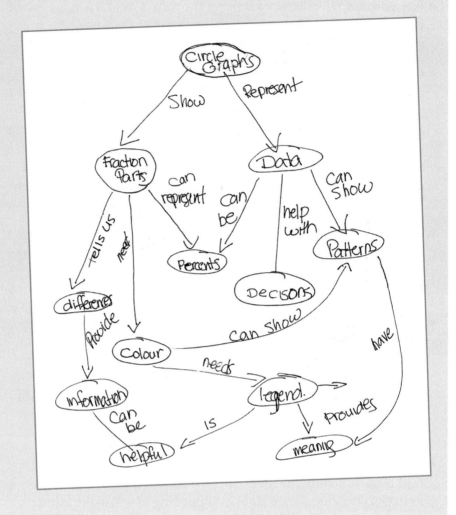

Comparing Mind Maps and Concept Maps

Many people confuse mind maps and concept maps, as both are used to represent a person's thinking; however, each organizer has specific elements that render it unique and effective in assisting students in developing critical thinking skills. The chart on the next page summarizes some of the different ways elements are integrated into each type of map.

©P

Comparing Mind Maps and Concept Maps

Element	Mind Maps	Concept Maps
Main topic	The main topic, identified as an image, word, or both, is placed in the middle.	The main topic is placed at the top.
Linking words	There are no linking words, but key words that represent ideas and themes are written on connecting branches.	Words are used to explain *how* the connecting concepts relate to each other.
Pictures	As a key element of mind maps, pictures are used to communicate ideas and reinforce concepts.	Pictures can be used instead of concepts, but are not a key element of this graphic organizer.
Concepts	Concepts are written on the branches that radiate from the central image.	Concepts are written horizontally on the map and connected by lines and linking words.
Lines	Lines are usually curved but can be straight. They vary in thickness, colour, and shape and radiate from the central image. They are often referred to as *branches*.	Lines can be curved (especially as cross-links) but are usually straight and pointing down from the main topic.
Hierarchy	Concepts are very general at the centre of the map and become more specific as they radiate from the central image.	Concepts are very general at the top of the map and become more specific as they near the bottom of the map.
Colour	Colour is a critical part of a mind map. It is used to embellish images and group similar ideas together.	Colour is not a critical element, but can be used to distinguish concepts from linking words or to group similar themes.

Teaching Strategies

Affective Writing Explorations

In affective writing, students describe their feelings about a math topic or activity. Emotions affect the learning process. If students feel anxiety and fear toward mathematics, their attention will be divided and

materials
• none

mental efforts are expended worrying about what will happen next. If an emotional threat is perceived, thinking remains at a concrete level and becomes disorganized (Pekrun, Goetz, Titz, & Perry, 2002). Baxter, Woodward, Olson, and Robyns (2002) believe that affective writing allows students to develop a comfort level with writing in mathematics before they move on to more complex stages, such as explaining or justifying mathematical ideas. Affective writing also provides the teacher with insight into how students feel about mathematics and what misconceptions they may have about their abilities or the subject.

Sample Ideas for Affective Writing

- How do you feel about mathematics?

- Are you good at mathematics? Why? Why not?

- What do you like or dislike about fractions?

- If you could improve one of your skills in mathematics, what would it be?

- How do you feel you did today in mathematics?

- What would you tell a new student about how to be successful in mathematics in our class?

- Do you like working in groups? Why? Why not?

- Do you like writing in mathematics? Why? Why not?

STRATEGIES IN ACTION

Affective Writing

Grade 4

James was responding to the question, "Are you good at mathematics?"

I think I am not good at math because I am a person that does not like challenges.

i think i am not good at maths because i am a person that does not like challedges

James may have a negative perception of mathematics. It is also possible that this student has misconceptions about his abilities in mathematics. It is important to follow up with James and explore what he is good at in mathematics. What does he find challenging? How can you assist James in having positive experiences in mathematics? What support can you provide to enable him to develop a positive self-image about his mathematical abilities?

Affective Writing

> 3) Yes I do like math because it's fun to be experimental with different numbers and find out different answers. I like expressing myself in this way. I enjoy having the knowledge to solve different equations. It helps me out daily and I couldn't live without it. Being able to get answers is very amazing. Math is a great experience. I also like math because it's simple, it all makes sense, there's always an answer. For example, it's fun to work with words, numbers and shapes, it makes everything easier to acknowledge. I'm more of a visual person so working with shapes really helps me to understand the concept at hand.

Hiba provides insight about the very positive way she views mathematics. She is able to explain why she finds mathematics enjoyable and is able to make connections to her daily life. Hiba also provides some insight into how she learns best—visually, using shapes. This information could be used to provide her with opportunities to use shapes in other areas of mathematics such as fractions and patterning with algebraic equations.

Grade 8

Hiba was responding to the question, "Do you like mathematics? Why or why not?"

Yes, I do like math because it's fun to be experimental with different numbers and find out different answers. I like expressing myself in this way. I enjoy having the knowledge to solve different equations. It helps me out daily and I couldn't live without it. Being able to get answers is very amazing. Math is a great experience. I also like math because it's simple, it all makes sense, there's always an answer. For example, it's fun to work with words, numbers, and shapes. It makes everything easier to acknowledge. I'm more of a visual person, so working with shapes really helps me to understand the concept at hand.

My Best Math Moment

In a Grade 8 classroom, I once saw a bulletin board of student reflections on their best math moment. Inviting students to think about their best math moment is a great way to engage them in celebrating their personal successes in mathematics. It also encourages them to make positive connections to mathematics. I have since explored this strategy with many students.

materials
- none

Ideas for My Best Math Moment

- Students can draw an image of their best math moment and invite others to guess what it is.

- Invite students to reflect on their best math moment outside of the classroom. They thereby gain an opportunity to relate mathematics to their daily lives.

• Ask students to reflect on a specific area of mathematics through writing or drawing. They might choose their best geometry moment or their best graphing moment.

My Best Math Moment

Grade 5

See sample for content.

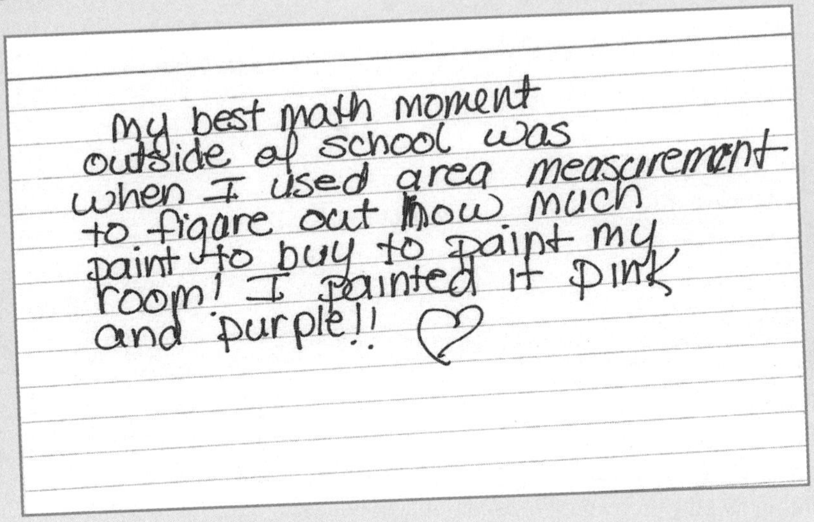

> My best math moment outside of school was when I used area measurement to figure out how much paint to buy to paint my room! I painted it pink and purple!! ♡

Defining a Mathematical Term or Concept

materials
• none

If you have introduced any of the graphic organizers described in the Skills and Structures section on pages 90–103 of this chapter, consider inviting students to record their ideas using a graphic organizer.

Teachers regularly use mathematical vocabulary and symbols in teaching mathematical concepts. If students do not take the time to reflect on the meanings of mathematical terms, they may use the terms in a rote fashion. By writing about what a term means, students make their personal understanding explicit. They are able to develop a personal awareness of how they believe specific terms and symbols communicate mathematical thoughts and ideas. They can then share their thoughts with others to verify their thinking.

Students' written definitions of mathematical terms can reveal misconceptions. When Ling, a Grade 6 teacher, asked her students to explain what 0.65 meant, one student wrote, "It's like 65 except there is a period in front. It is just another way of writing 65." Although this student could provide correct answers for math questions involving decimals, her writing revealed that she held significant misconceptions. Ling realized that she needed to integrate more opportunities for students to work with decimals in a variety of contexts. She began to have students represent decimals using concrete materials and sketches in order to consolidate their knowledge.

©P

Sample Ideas for Defining a Mathematical Term or Concept

- What is a triangle?

- What is a pattern?

- What does the symbol > mean?

- What do you think the term *data* means?

Defining a Mathematical Term or Concept

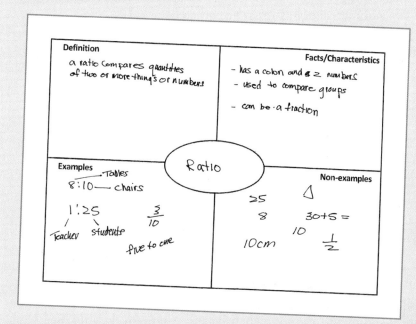

Grade 8

Centre oval: Ratio

Definition: A ratio compares quantities of two or more things or numbers.

Facts/Characteristics: Has a colon and 2 numbers. Used to compare groups. Can be a fraction.

Examples: 8:10 (tables to chairs); 1:25 (teacher to students); $\frac{3}{10}$; five to one

Non-examples: [sketch of a triangle]; $30 + 5 = $; 25; 8; 10; 10 cm; $\frac{1}{2}$

Jamal chose to use a Frayer model to record his definition of ratio. He has provided a clear explanation of what a ratio is, including some important facts and examples. He included a fraction in the non-example section, which is incorrect.

Sample Descriptive Feedback

Jamal, your definition effectively explains how a ratio is used. You also provide many good examples of ratios in different forms, including fractions. Based on the examples you included, do you think that $\frac{1}{2}$ belongs in the non-example category? Why or why not?

Lesson Feedback

materials

• none

Lesson feedback involves students writing personal responses to specific aspects of a mathematics lesson, theme, or teaching strategy they have experienced. Students can describe areas of the lesson that confused them as well as parts of the lesson that helped them. Obtaining this type of reflection provides you with feedback about your teaching approaches and the impact they have on your students.

By inviting students to provide feedback, teachers convey the message that they care about student learning and, like students, need to reflect on their personal strategies in order to improve. One teacher found that the information she gathered from student reflections enabled her to modify her lessons to address specific misconceptions that she identified in her students' writing. She also used their writing as further evidence to support any summative evaluations she gathered.

Sample Ideas for Lesson Feedback

- What did you find helpful in today's lesson?

- Describe one thing you learned about addition today.

- What part of my teaching helps you to learn better in mathematics?

- What questions do you still have about algebra?

Exploring Mathematical Proofs

materials

• depending on the statement to be explored, students may decide to use grid paper, manipulatives, or other materials

This activity is a form of persuasive writing, a technique students may use in language arts classes. Students explore a mathematical statement and decide whether it is true or false. Then they develop and present a mathematical argument to support their beliefs. Alternatively, a teacher may deem a statement true or false and then invite the students to provide an argument to support or refute the statement. This activity helps students to develop strong critical thinking skills and learn how to present mathematical arguments.

Sample Ideas for Mathematical Proofs

- Is the statement $2.3 + 0.07 = 3.0$ true or false? Support your answer with mathematics.

- Prove or disprove whether this 2-dimensional net will create a 3-dimensional cube when folded.

- Is $7 + 3 = 10$ correct or incorrect? Give reasons for your answer.

- Is ○○○■■■○○♦♦♦ a pattern? Justify your answer.

- Is $\frac{1}{5}$ greater than $\frac{3}{18}$? Prove your answer.

©P

Mathematical Proofs

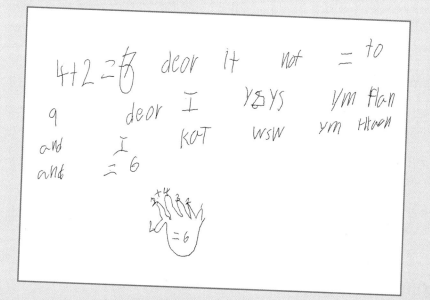

Jamena was responding to the question, "Is 4 + 2 = 7 correct or incorrect? Why?"

Because it is not equal to 7 because I used my hands and I counted with my fingers and it equals 6.

Jamena was able to explain how she arrived at her proof. She showed visually (using only one hand) how she counted on her fingers to determine that 4 + 2 = 6.

Sample Descriptive Feedback

Jamena, you did a great job in explaining that 4 + 2 = 6 and then you proved it by showing how you counted on your fingers. The picture with the numbers on your fingers really helped me to understand how you used your fingers to count and demonstrated that 4 + 2 cannot equal 7. Can you show how many fingers you used on each hand? What other pictures could you use to show that 4 + 2 = 6?

Lateral-Thinking Explorations

In 1967 Edward de Bono developed the *lateral thinking* concept as part of his research into creativity and the brain. Lateral thinking involves training the brain to make new connections and see things in different ways. Being able to think this way can help problem solvers generate solutions that would not be reached through traditional ways of thinking. De Bono (2010) believes that we do not teach our students how to think effectively and thus they use only a limited amount of their thinking potential. He argues that we need to provide students with specific activities that *train* the brain how to think. He points out that thinking skills can be taught regardless of someone's IQ. A person can have a high IQ

materials
• none

and poor thinking skills. De Bono likens this to someone who has a fast car, but does not know how to drive it.

Students often experience mathematics as a step-by-step process in which they follow certain procedures to get an answer with little opportunity to develop rich thinking skills. Lateral-thinking questions require students to think creatively about mathematical concepts and encourage the creation of new ideas and connections.

Sample Ideas for Lateral-Thinking Explorations

- If you could be any number, which number would you be and why? Support your answer with mathematics.

- If mathematics were an animal, which animal would it be and why? Support your answer with mathematics.

- If you could pick one geometric shape to represent happiness, which one would you pick? Support your choice with at least two mathematical reasons.

STRATEGIES IN ACTION

Lateral Thinking

Grade 4

Dai Cen was responding to the question, "If mathematics were an animal, what type of animal would it be and why?"

I think it would be birds. It would be birds because birds fly in a pattern. I think it could also be a butterfly because of the cool pattern on its wings.

If mathimatics was an animal, what type of animal would it be? Why?

I think it would be birds. It would be birds because birds fly in a pattern. I think could also be a butterfly because of its cool patterns on its wings.

Dai Cen is able to make a connection between mathematics and nature. Her sketches support her text. The birds are flying in a formation that is a growing pattern, and the pattern on each butterfly wing appears to be symmetrical with the other wing. Dai Cen's teacher invited her to share this piece of writing as she felt it was an effective way to review different kinds of patterns in mathematics.

Sample Descriptive Feedback
Dai Cen, you are able to effectively provide examples using words and pictures to explain why you would choose birds and butterflies to represent mathematics. Your pictures correctly show the different patterns for each animal. How many birds would be in the next step of your sketch? How do you know? What are some other animals that have patterns on their bodies?

Lateral Thinking

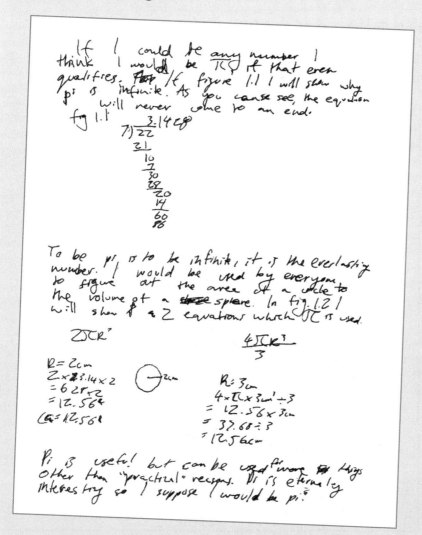

Mark wrote this response to the question, "If you could be any number, which number would you be and why? Support your choice with mathematics."

If I could be any number, I think I would be pi, if that even qualifies. In Figure 1.1 I will show why pi is infinite. As you can see, the equation will never come to an end…

To be pi is to be infinite, it is the everlasting number. I would be used by everyone to figure out the area of a circle (and) the volume of a sphere. In Fig 1.2 I will show 2 equations in which pi is used…

Pi is useful but can be used for more things other than "practical" reasons. Pi is eternally interesting so I suppose I would be pi.

Posing an open-ended lateral-thinking question allows students to think of mathematics from very different perspectives. The open-endedness of this type of writing exploration also enables advanced students like Mark to work at their own level.

Mark uses the qualities of pi to explain why it would be a good number to be. In his reasoning of why he would choose pi, he demonstrates a very solid understanding of the applications of pi. He includes some practical applications of pi and provides an example to support the fact that pi "will never come to an end."

Lateral Thinking with Pictures

materials

- a group of pictures that are not overtly mathematical (see samples)

For a reproducible version of this art, see the *Math Expressions* website: www.pearsoncanada.ca/mathexpressions

Another way to teach lateral thinking is to provide opportunities for the brain to make connections between seemingly unrelated things.

Sample Implementation of Lateral Thinking with Pictures

1. Display the pictures to your students. Some examples of the types of images you might use are shown below.

Mathematics is like…because…

2. Provide a prompt such as "Mathematics is like…because…" and invite students to choose a picture that they feel works best to support their ideas. Using an open-ended prompt to introduce lateral-thinking activities allows students who may feel unsure of mathematical content to share and make connections more readily.

3. Remind students that in addition to choosing a picture, they must support their answer with what they know about mathematics or the specific topic.

4. Once students have had enough time to think about their answer, invite them to share their ideas with the class or in small groups.

As they share, you can point out how some students may have chosen the same picture, but for different reasons.

5. You may decide to ask students to then write about their answers.

Modifications and Extensions for Lateral Thinking with Pictures
Once students are familiar with the approach, you can use more content-focused prompts to review what they have learned in a specific area or gain insight into prior knowledge before you begin a unit of study. For example, at the end of a data management unit, you could ask: *Which picture best represents data management? Support your answer with what you know about data management.* During a geometry unit, you might use this prompt: *An isosceles triangle is most like…because…*

STRATEGIES IN ACTION

Lateral Thinking with Pictures

I Thick a char because Math is relasing and a char is relasing.

Grade 2

Walter was selecting an image in response to the prompt, "Mathematics is like…because…"

I think [its] a chair because a chair is relaxing and math is relaxing.

Walter chose a chair as a metaphor for how he feels about mathematics and was able to explain his choice. Walter enjoys mathematics and he shares his sentiment in his reflection.

Lateral Thinking with Pictures

Grade 7

A skateboard links to algebra because everything needs to stay in balance or the equations will be thrown off. Also, for different people skateboarding can be easy or hard, just like algebra.

> A skateboard links to algebra because everthing needs to stay in balance or the equations will be thrown off. Also, for different people skateboarding can be easy or hard, just like in Algebra

The teacher used this activity to introduce a lesson. The class had completed some work on algebra in an earlier lesson and he wanted to see what the students understood thus far. Students were shown several images and asked to choose the one that best represents algebra and explain their choice. Students shared their ideas in pairs, then with the whole class. The students in this class did a lot of skateboarding, so the teacher included an image of a skateboard that he felt would be meaningful to the students.

Sujit makes an effective analogy between balancing equations and the importance of balancing on a skateboard. She is able to relate algebra to her everyday activities.

Recording Mathematical Discoveries

materials

- materials required for mathematical investigation students are completing

- discovery sheets (Line Master 4.13)

As discussed in the introduction to this book, students should be engaged in making discoveries about mathematical concepts on an ongoing basis. As students work on investigations, you may have them record their observations and personal discoveries in any writing format. In whatever format students are working, I refer to the place in which they are recording their personal discoveries in mathematics and science as *discovery sheets* or *research sheets*. I use these terms because they emulate the notes a scientist or mathematician might keep. You may have students use Line Master 4.13 (Discovery Sheet), sheets of paper, chart paper, or math journals.

Students can use individual discovery sheets whether working on their own or in groups. During an investigation, students should record each discovery as it occurs, rather than waiting until they have finished. For class or group inquiries, hanging large chart-paper discovery sheets in the classroom works well. Students and teachers have full view of all the discoveries taking place during the exploration process. By varying the types of discovery sheets and formats you use, you can provide your students with a range of writing experiences.

Remind students to keep their recordings brief during the discovery process. Encourage them to use a variety of recording techniques, such as jotted notes, simple charts or tables, a few words, or a sketch. Recordings should enhance the investigation process, not consume it. After the investigation, you may ask students to elaborate on their discoveries by writing about them in a more formal way.

A few ideas for mathematical investigations are provided here. You may choose to think of other ideas that meet the needs of your students. Some students may also write about the design or results of inquiries they have created in order to test personal mathematical predictions and theories.

Sample Ideas for Recording Mathematical Discoveries

- Explore with these Pattern Blocks and record what you discover.

- Record any discoveries you make about patterns as you create your own patterns using the buttons, string, and other objects at your table.

- Examine the numbers on the hundreds board. Record what you discover.

- Explore the radius, diameter, and circumference of each of the circles provided. Record what you discover.

Recording Mathematical Discoveries

Grade 2

When I explored with a triangle(s) this is what I discovered:
A trapezoid makes a triangle with a triangle.

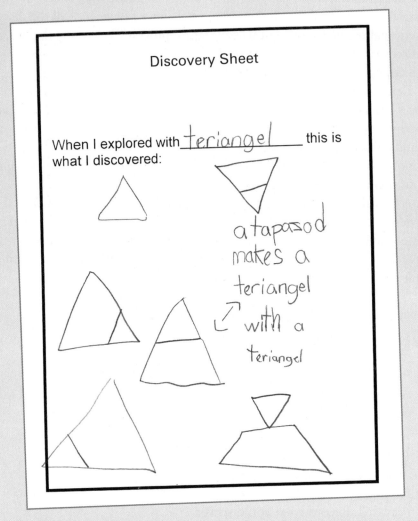

Discovery Sheet

When I explored with _teriangel_ this is what I discovered:

a tapasod makes a teriangel with a teriangel

After providing time for the class to explore with Pattern Blocks, Miguel's teacher invited students to record one or two discoveries they made. The teacher found that the discovery sheet was a nice way for students to reflect on their learning and record the discovery they liked the best.

Miguel made a key discovery: that we can combine different shapes to make new shapes. In this case, he used a trapezoid and a triangle to make another triangle. He also rotated the shape in his drawings.

Sample Descriptive Feedback

I like how you explained your discovery and made drawings to help us understand what you have done. The arrows are a great way to help the reader connect your words to your pictures. I also noticed that you have drawn the triangle in different positions. Please show me where you did this. What is different about the position of each triangle? What other shapes can you create using two different shapes? Using three different shapes?

Recording Mathematical Discoveries

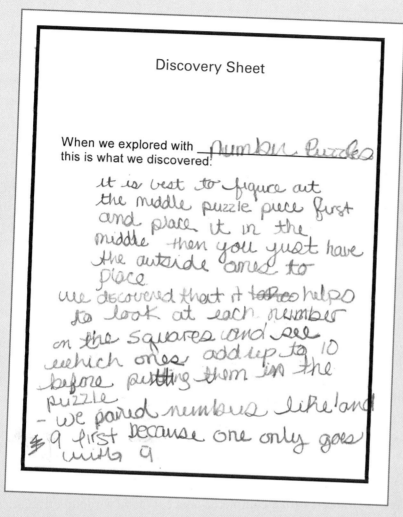

Discovery Sheet

When we explored with ___Number Puzzles___
this is what we discovered:

it is best to figure out
the middle puzzle piece first
and place it in the
middle then you just have
the outside ones to
place
we discovered that it ~~takes~~ helps
to look at each number
on the squares and see
which ones add up to 10
before putting them in the
puzzle
- we paired numbers like 1 and
9 first because one only goes
with 9

When we explored with number puzzles this is what we discovered: It is best to figure out the middle puzzle piece first and place it in the middle. Then you just have the outside ones to place. We discovered that it helps to look at each number on the squares and see which ones add up to 10 before putting them in the puzzle. We paired numbers like 1 and 9 first because only 1 goes with 9.

Students completed this recording after exploring a mathematical puzzle that involved 9 squares with a number between 1 and 9 written on each side of each square. The challenge was to create a 3 by 3 arrangement of the squares in which each pair of numbers on adjacent sides of the squares had a sum of 10. The teacher found that the discovery sheet was an effective way of building in accountability for learning with her students as they completed the puzzle. It also provided her with insight into their problem-solving approaches. She was able to read the students' reflections and invite them to share specific strategies with the class.

Pari and Nijel are applying specific problem-solving strategies and can identify them: for example, beginning with the combinations for which there is only one answer. They are also planning ahead by looking for different number combinations that add up to 10 before placing the squares together.

Exploring Concept Circles

materials

- chart paper and marker
- blank concept circles (see Line Masters 4.4 to 4.9)

See a description of concept circles on page 96.

You may wish to introduce concept circles by completing one together as a class.

Sample Introduction to Concept Circles

1. Choose a concept that is familiar to students. Prepare a large, empty concept circle on a sheet of chart paper. Divide the circle into as many sections as you feel are appropriate for the concept and your students.

2. Record the main concept either as a title or in the centre space, depending on which style of concept circle you have drawn.

3. Invite students to suggest related concepts that could be recorded in the sections of the circle. You may find it helpful to record an idea in one of the sections as an example for students before asking them to offer suggestions.

4. You can record students' suggestions in the concept circle yourself or invite them to add their own recordings.

5. The finished concept circle can be displayed both as a visual reference for the concept and as an example of how to complete a concept circle.

Modifications and Extensions of Concept Circles

Once students are familiar with concept circles, consider introducing some of the following activities. These activities require students to think critically as they problem solve to complete each concept circle. It is important that they share how they arrived at their answers.

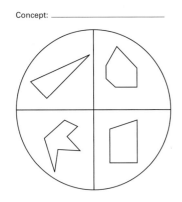

Concept: _____

- Present students with a completed concept circle without a title, such as the one shown here. Invite them to determine the concept. Provide opportunities for students to explain their thinking.

- Present students with a completed and titled concept circle that includes one non-example. Invite students to identify which concept does not belong in the circle. Provide opportunities for students to explain their reasoning.

- Present students with a concept circle that is complete except for one or two sections. Invite them to think of possible examples to put in the empty section(s). They cannot repeat any of the existing examples.

- Provide students with a concept and a blank concept circle and ask them to complete the circle. Students can share their circles with the class or in small groups. Doing this allows them to see the different examples each student uses to represent the same main concept and the different ways of recording these examples. You may choose to create a bulletin board with the completed circles.

- Use concept circles as part of your mathematical word wall (see Chapter 3). The sections of the circle are used to record examples that convey the word's meaning.

Exploring Concept Circles

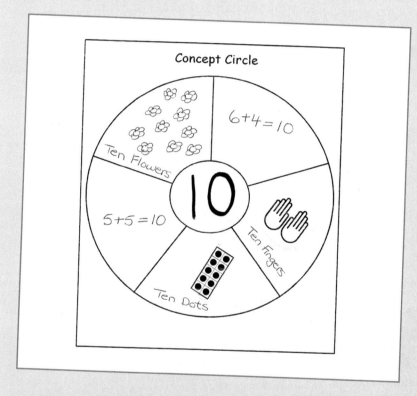

Kindergarten

See sample for content.

The teacher decided to create a large concept circle and complete it as a class activity. She posted different images on the wall—some that represented the concept 10, and some that didn't. She wrote the number 10 in the middle of the concept circle, and then invited her class to choose different items that represented 10 to place in the blank sections. Students chose the images of the fingers and dots and provided reasons for their choices. For the rest of the sections, she invited the class to provide suggestions of what they could include—they suggested 6 + 4 and ten flowers—and then she recorded their ideas in the concept circle. Each day, the class worked on a concept circle for a different number. She posted each completed concept circle in the class and used them to teach different number concepts.

Exploring Mind Maps

materials

- observation sheet (For a more guided discovery, you may decide to have students use Line Master 4.11: Mind Map Elements.)

- index cards, chart paper, and markers

For students to use mind maps effectively, they need explicit instruction in what mind maps are and how to construct them. Some teachers of younger students may decide to introduce the concept of mind maps less formally. One way to do this is by completing only the Sample Mind Map Think-Aloud portion of this activity.

Sample Introduction to Mind Maps

Invite students to examine several examples of mind maps and to identify the characteristics or elements of the maps. You can use the samples included in this book as examples, or create a map of your own to share with students. Students can create an observation sheet by recording the title "Characteristics of a Mind Map" and listing their observations, or you can distribute copies of Line Master 4.11 (Mind Map Elements). Alternatively, you may choose to show students just one example of a mind map. In any case, facilitate a discussion about the elements students discover and what they think the purpose of each might be. You can use questions such as these:

- What do you notice about how this mind map is organized?

- What do you think the topic of this mind map is? How do you know?

- What are some ideas or topics that are connected to the main topic? How do you know?

- Why do you think the author of this mind map included pictures? How do they help us to understand the mind map?

- What do you notice about how the branches are organized? Are they all the same length and thickness? Why or why not?

- What are two ideas that are connected in this mind map? How do you know?

Once students are familiar with the structure of a mind map, a teacher-led think-aloud to construct one will highlight key aspects of the mapping process. Here is one approach you could take.

See a description of minds maps on pages 97–98.

Sample Mind Map Think-Aloud

1. Choose a topic. Use a familiar mathematics topic to allow students to focus on the mind-mapping skills. Invite students to suggest a picture to represent the topic. Sketch the picture in the middle of a piece of chart paper and record the map topic below the picture.

2. Invite students to suggest an idea that connects to the central topic. Using a new colour, add a branch radiating out from the central picture. Write a word to represent the idea on the branch.

3. Invite students to suggest a picture to represent the branch you have just drawn. Add the picture near the end of the branch or have a student add it. Encourage the use of colour.

4. Ask students to share sub-topics that are related to the theme of the branch you have just drawn. To allow the free flow of thought, do not correct students as they offer ideas. Add sub-topics to the mind map as branches labelled with words and pictures, radiating from the first branch. Explain that you are using the same colour for these sub-branches to show that the ideas are related to the same theme.

5. Invite students to suggest ideas to add to the map, both as new branches and as sub-branches. Each time you change themes on the mind map, use a new colour for the branches.

6. When you have a few themes on the map, you may want to ask students if they can make any cross-connections between them.

7. Once students feel more confident, invite them to add their own branches and images to the map. Continue until students have provided all of the information they want to add.

8. When the mind map is complete, invite students to assess the information the map displays. You may also choose to discuss how the map demonstrates the key elements of a mind map.

Extension: Cooperative Mind Maps

When students begin to create their own mind maps, you may want to have them work collaboratively. Provide each student in a group with 4 or 5 index cards on which to record pictures or words to be included on the group's map. Once students have shared and organized their ideas from the cards, they can use chart paper and markers to create the final mind map, including at least several ideas from each group member. Groups can share their completed maps using the gallery walk approach described in Chapter 1.

Once students have some experience creating mind maps, you may decide to work collaboratively with them to develop indicators of success for mind maps. A sample is shown here. You may wish to modify the wording or content of this list to suit your learners' needs.

For a reproducible version of these sample indicators of success, see the *Math Expressions* website: www.pearsoncanada.ca/mathexpressions

Sample Indicators of Success for an Effective Mind Map

❑ Connections and information that I include in my mind map make sense.

❑ I use a variety of branch styles.

❑ I use images and key words correctly to communicate my ideas.

❑ I use colour effectively to organize my map.

❑ All key concepts/ideas I include are related to the main topic and radiate from a clear central image.

❑ I include cross-links to correctly connect different ideas.

❑ My mind map is well organized and easy to read.

©P

Exploring Mind Maps

When asked to share his mind map about mathematics, Luka explained (going clockwise):

"The top line shows how I use my fingers for math. The one beside it shows how I used times. The next part of my mind map shows how I use my notebook. I drew pictures of my mom and dad because they help me with my math at home. I also put some Grade 4 math because it has a lot of numbers like 600. I also drew all the pages of work they have to do."

It is evident that Luka understands the concept of mind mapping, as he has included all the necessary elements. The map even has some branches connected together (*times* and *XXXX*). He also correctly used the "not equal to" sign between the two different sets of fingers he drew. His work demonstrates that a graphics-based writing format, such as mind mapping, often allows young learners to communicate their mathematical understandings, even if they have not developed significant writing skills.

Exploring Mind Maps

See sample for content.

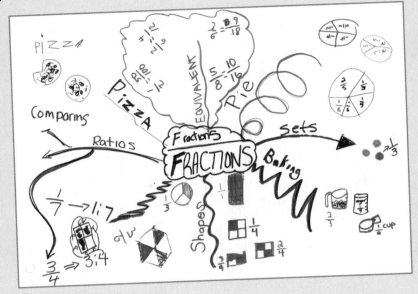

This group of students created a mind map after they had explored fractions as part of a mathematics unit. Their teacher wanted them to create a mind map to see what they had learned and to identify any misconceptions they had. She did not provide them with any specific concepts to include, as she wanted to see what they felt was important and relevant based on the unit they had just completed.

These students were able to relate fractions to a variety of concepts including sets, shapes, and ratios. Their teacher would like to see some representation in the mind map of operations with fractions, such as addition or multiplication.

Sample Descriptive Feedback

Your mind map is well organized and demonstrates a good use of pictures, words, and colour. I think the strength of the mathematics you included is that you have incorporated many examples of what fractions are beyond shapes and pizzas. Please explain to me how fractions can be ratios and how your image of the four squares with the arrows supports your ideas. We completed a lot of work on the addition, subtraction, multiplication, and division of fractions. How could you represent some of these concepts visually in your map using shapes?

Exploring Concept Maps

For students to use concept maps effectively, explicit instruction in what concept maps are and how to construct them is needed. Some teachers of younger students may choose to introduce concept maps less formally. One way of doing this is by completing only the Sample Concept Map Think-Aloud portion of this activity.

Sample Introduction to Concept Maps

Invite students to examine several examples of concept maps and identify the elements or characteristics of the map. You can use the samples included in this book as examples, or create a map of your own to share with students. Students can create an observation sheet by recording the title "Characteristics of a Concept Map" and listing their observations, or you can distribute copies of Line Master 4.12 (Concept Map Elements). Alternatively, you may show students just one example of a concept map. In any case, facilitate a discussion about the parts students identify and what they think the purpose of each might be. You can use questions such as these:

- What do you notice about how this concept map is organized?

- What do you think the topic of this concept map is? How do you know?

- What are some ideas or topics that are connected to the key topic? How do you know?

- What do you notice about how the connector lines are organized? Are they all the same length and thickness? Why or why not?

- What is written on the connector lines? What do you notice about these words?

- What are two ideas that are connected in this concept map? How do they relate to each other?

- What information does this map communicate? Provide some examples.

Once students are familiar with the structure of a concept map, a teacher-led think-aloud to construct one will highlight key aspects of the mapping process. Here is one approach you could take. I will model the think-aloud process using the topic *Shapes*, but you can choose any topic you feel is relevant and familiar to your students.

materials

- observation sheet (For a more guided discovery, you may decide to use Line Master 4.12: Concept Map Elements.)

- Line Master 4.10: Sample Linking Words for Concept Maps

- sticky notes on which you have recorded concepts for mapping

- blank sticky notes, chart paper, and markers

See a description of concept maps on pages 99–101.

Sample Concept Map Think-Aloud

1. Choose a topic or key concept. On sticky notes, record about 10 related concepts, one on each note.

2. Arrange the concept sticky notes randomly on a whiteboard or chalkboard. Ask your students to name the topic for the group of concepts. Note the topic, in this case *Shapes*, on a sticky note and place it on the board away from the group of concepts.

3. Take two concepts from the group and place them side by side with a space in the middle. For example: *Triangles* _____ *Angles*. Invite students to explain how these two concepts relate to each other. Ask them to suggest words to go in the space between them, stressing that they should not use sentences as linking words. Record the words students suggest. For example: *Triangles* contain *Angles*. *Triangles* have three *Angles*.

4. Repeat the connecting process with a variety of concepts until you feel your students are comfortable with it.

5. Now begin the concept map. Take a concept from the group, perhaps *Polygons*, and place it below the main topic *Shapes*. Ask students how these concepts connect or relate to each other. Student may suggest phrases such as *Shapes* include *Polygons*, or *Shapes* can be *Polygons*. Draw a line from the key concept *Shapes* to *Polygons* and write one of the suggested connector words or phrases on the line.

6. Invite students to choose a concept they can connect to *Polygons* and provide the linking words they would use. Record their ideas on the concept map.

7. Continue this process for each of the concepts until you have created a class map with connections to the key concept and sub-concepts that uses a variety of linking words. You may invite students to add the concepts, lines, and linking words. Encourage students to make cross-links, connecting different sections of the map.

8. When the concept map is complete, invite students to share information that the map conveys and correct any errors they notice.

Extension: Cooperative Concept Maps

As a follow-up, you may wish to invite students to create a concept map with a partner. Provide each pair with a piece of chart paper, markers, sticky notes, a copy of Line Master 4.10 (Sample Linking Words for Concept Maps), a key topic with which they are familiar, and a list of 7 to 10 mathematical concepts related to the key topic. Invite students to add their own concepts to the map. Once they are finished, invite students to share their maps. You may choose to explore how the same concepts can be arranged differently in each map.

Once students have some experience creating concept maps, you may want to work collaboratively to develop indicators of success for concept maps. A sample list is shown here. You may wish to modify the wording or content of this list to suit your learners' needs.

Sample Indicators of Success for an Effective Concept Map

- ❏ I place my main topic at the top, leading to more specific concepts at the bottom.
- ❏ I use a variety of linking words and concepts.
- ❏ My linking words correctly describe how the concepts connect to each other.
- ❏ I use cross-links that correctly connect concepts from different sections in my map.
- ❏ I include additional concepts that support the main topic.

For a reproducible version of these sample indicators of success, see the *Math Expressions* website: www.pearsoncanada.ca/mathexpressions

Exploring Concept Maps

The students created this concept map to answer the question, "What do you know about shapes?"

(Left to right) Triangles have sides. Triangles have angles. Shapes can be circles. Circles are symmetrical. Circles don't have sides. Circles are round. Squares have sides. Squares have lines. Squares are symmetrical. Shapes are symmetrical.

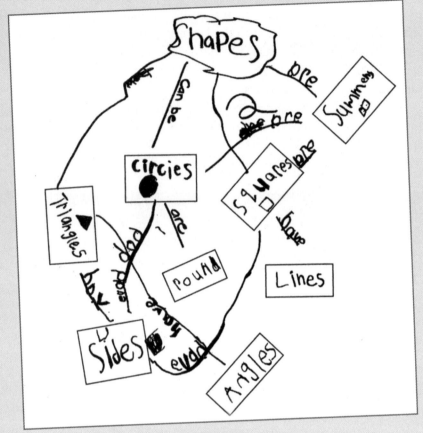

This was a first attempt for a group of Grade 1 students creating a concept map. They had completed a unit on shapes. Before they began this activity, their teacher created a concept map with the whole class on a topic they had studied in science. For the concept map on shapes, the teacher posted a list of concepts and linking words in the classroom. She also invited her students to add their own concepts and linking words.

This group has included the key elements of a concept map. At the start of this activity, their teacher assisted them with the wording for the links in "Shapes can be circles" and "Circles are round." The students then created the rest of the map on their own. They included two cross-links.

The first one links *symmetrical* and *circles* and the second one links *squares* and *sides*. This map also demonstrates what the students know about shapes and their attributes.

Sample Descriptive Feedback

You have used pictures and words effectively to show how the different concepts can go together. For example, in your map you tell me that shapes are symmetrical and that triangles have angles. Are all shapes symmetrical? How do you know? Your map is easy to read because you organized it well and wrote the connector words clearly. You also included a new connector word, "have." I see cross-links in your concept map. Cross-links can help the reader see connections between different ideas. Please show me where they are. Which ideas did you connect with your cross-links?

Exploring Concept Maps

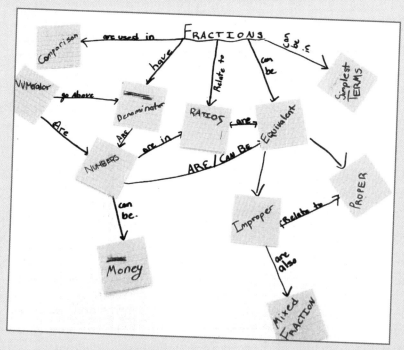

Grade **7**

Fractions are used in comparison.

Fractions can be in simplest terms.

Fractions have denominators. Numerators and denominators are numbers that can be money and equivalent and are in ratios.

Fractions are related to ratios which can be equivalent.

Fractions can be equivalent/ improper. Equivalent fractions can be proper fractions. Improper fractions are also mixed fractions. Improper fractions are related to proper fractions.

This was Manpreet's first concept map. His teacher modelled a concept map on shapes with the class, then provided students with a list of concepts related to fractions as well as a list of connector words. Students were encouraged to add their own concepts and connector words.

Manpreet's work demonstrates the elements of a concept map, including several cross-links and a variety of connector words. He communicates that ratios are related to fractions and that fractions can represent money values. Including some examples would provide further evidence of his understanding. Manpreet indicates that improper fractions are also mixed fractions. He may mean that they can be converted to mixed fractions. It is through questioning that this point can be clarified.

Sample Descriptive Feedback
Manpreet, you have effectively incorporated key elements of a concept map, including cross-links and a variety of connector words. I like the way you made specific connections to ratios and money as this shows that you can relate the concepts to your life outside of the classroom. How could you add some examples to your concept map to support your ideas? What examples could you use to show simplest terms, equivalency, proper fractions, and improper fractions? You indicate that improper fractions are also mixed numbers and are related to proper fractions. Please explain what you mean.

Mapping Your Learning

If your students have explored mind maps and concept maps, you may decide to use these graphic organizers throughout your mathematics program. Here are a few examples of opportunities to include mapping activities.

- Invite students to create a mind map or concept map at the beginning of a unit of study. You can thereby gain insight into students' prior knowledge. At different times during the unit, ask students to revisit their maps to add to them or revise them to reflect new learning. This documentation of ongoing learning can be done individually, in small groups, or with a class map.

- Use a mind map or a concept map to introduce a mathematics lesson. You can create the map collaboratively, or use one you have already created. Consider using the map to prompt discussion about the topic you are introducing.

- Invite students to create a mind map or concept map at the end of a unit or lesson to summarize what they have learned.

- Invite students to create a mind map or concept map as part of a summative assessment activity. You can provide a list of concepts for students to include in the map along with their own ideas.

- Invite students to participate in a map carousel. Divide the class into groups of 4 or 5 students. Ask each group to begin a mind map or concept map, with all groups working on the same or a different topic. After 10 minutes, invite the groups to pass their maps to another group. Groups read the map they receive and add ideas to it. After several exchanges, the groups return the maps to the original authors who can read the different ideas each group has added.

- Present the class with a mind map or a concept map that includes some conceptual errors, perhaps incorrect concepts, linking words, pictures, or connections. Invite students to identify and correct the errors.

Math on the Back

This activity is an effective way of using mathematical discourse to support writing. It also helps develop strong questioning skills and mathematical vocabulary.

materials
- chart paper and marker
- stickers on which you have written numbers or words related to one mathematical concept
- clipboards or notebooks to write on

Sample Implementation of Math on the Back

1. You may wish to demonstrate the activity with the whole class. Ask one student to stand with her or his back to the board. Write or draw a whole number, fraction, geometric shape, or math word on the board and announce the general concept, such as whole numbers.

2. Invite the student who has not seen what you have written to pose yes-or-no questions to the class. A question such as "Is the number an even number?" is appropriate, but one such as "What kind of number is it?" is not. Record the questions and responses on chart paper.

3. Once the student guesses the correct word or number, invite the class to look over the questions posed. Which questions were the most effective? Which ones were less effective? Why? Keep the list of questions posted so students can use them as a guide during the rest of the activity.

4. Place a sticker on each student's back with a word or number related to a familiar mathematical concept. Announce the concept. Each student's goal is to determine what is written on the sticker by asking yes-or-no questions of other students. Encourage students to carry a clipboard or notebook they can use to record the questions and responses. If students are not sure if their answer to a question is correct, they can say "Pass." This avoids providing incorrect information that might influence the questioning process.

5. Allow time for students to circulate and gather information. If students think they know what is written on their back, they can tell the person they are talking to and explain the reasoning behind their idea. If they are not correct, they can continue to pose questions. If they are correct, the partner can remove the sticker for them to verify their answer.

6. At the end of the activity, students will have collected key information they can use to write about a specific math word or number.

Modifications and Extensions for Math on the Back

- You may decide to impose a limit on how many guesses students can have. By doing so, you can lessen the likelihood of students guessing without posing questions or taking the time to carefully think about what the mathematical concept could be.

- You can organize the concepts so that those who struggle have a simple concept and those who are more comfortable with a topic have a more complex concept.

- Students can also do this activity seated. Provide each student with a concept noted or drawn on an index card in an envelope. Their partner can look inside the envelope to find out what the concept is. Students can take turns posing questions in order to guess what is on their card.

Sample Ideas for Math on the Back

- Vocabulary related to a specific topic

- Different kinds of graphs

- Whole numbers

- Fractions

- Pictures of geometric shapes

- Decimal numbers

Line Masters

Cooperative Math Chart

Skill	Looks Like	Sounds Like	Feels Like
	👁	👂	❤
Listening to others			
Sharing my thinking			
Disagreeing in a positive way			
Including everyone in the process			
Posing good questions during presentations			

**Cooperative Group Roles
for Mathematics**

Role	Your Job
Timekeeper	You keep the group on task. You keep track of the time.
Materials monitor	Only you can get materials for your group and return them. You show your group how to use the materials. You organize the cleanup.
Advice seeker	Only you can ask the teacher questions. You make sure that your group understands the answers.
Recorder	You write down or draw your group's ideas.
Checker	You make sure that the group's answers make sense. You make sure that everyone understands the answers.
Presenter	You present the group's answers to the class or other groups.

Cooperative Group Roles for Mathematics

Role	Responsibilities
Timekeeper	You keep the group on task and keep track of the time. You let your group know when they are halfway through the activity and when the time is almost up.
Materials monitor	You collect, organize, and return the materials for your group. You explain to your group how to use the materials. You organize the cleanup for your group.
Advice seeker	If a question needs to be asked of the teacher, you are the only member of your group allowed to ask it. Before you ask the question, you check that no one in your group already knows the answer. You make sure that everyone in your group understands the teacher's answer.
Recorder	You record information for your group. You check the information you record with group members.
Checker	You check to make sure that the group's ideas or answers make mathematical sense. You make sure that everyone in the group understands the answers.
Presenter	You present the group's answers to the class or other groups. You verify what you will say to make sure that it accurately represents your group's ideas.

Math Expressions: Developing Student Thinking and Problem Solving Through Communication

**Observation Checklist
for Cooperative Work**

Teacher Comments							
Accepts others' ideas/suggestions							
Asks group members to clarify ideas							
Listens to others' ideas							
Helps to resolve group conflicts							
Disagrees in a positive way							
Completes agreed-upon work							
Stays on task							
Contributes relevant ideas							
Student Name							

R = Rarely   S = Sometimes   F = Frequently   C = Consistently

Math Expressions: Developing Student Thinking and Problem Solving Through Communication

Student Discourse Observation Sheet

Teacher Comments							
Can provide sound reasons for mathematical decisions							
Builds on the contributions of others							
Poses insightful questions that promote thinking							
Can explain why something is correct/incorrect							
Self-corrects ideas based on feedback							
Uses appropriate mathematical vocabulary							
Provides sound and easy-to-follow descriptions							
Makes meaningful contributions to discussions							
Student Name							

R = Rarely   S = Sometimes   F = Frequently   C = Consistently

Interview Sheet

Student Name _____   Date_____

Success Criteria

The student can

- explain his or her mathematical thinking clearly

- apply problem-solving strategies to different learning contexts

- use appropriate mathematical vocabulary

- identify the strategies being used and explain why they work or do not work

- describe models/diagrams and how they represent mathematical ideas

Explain how you solved this problem/completed this activity.	Why do you think your strategy works?	What do you think was the most challenging part of this problem/activity? Why?
Observation notes:	Observation notes:	Observation notes:
Can you do this another way? Please show me.	Can you model this idea using the _____? Please show me.	Q:
Observation notes:	Observation notes:	Observation notes:

Concept Attainment: Shapes with Line Symmetry

Yes Examples

**Concept Attainment: Shapes with
Line Symmetry**

No Examples

Concept Attainment: Shapes with Area Less Than or Equal to 6 Square Units

Yes Examples

Concept Attainment: Shapes with Area Less Than or Equal to 6 Square Units

No Examples

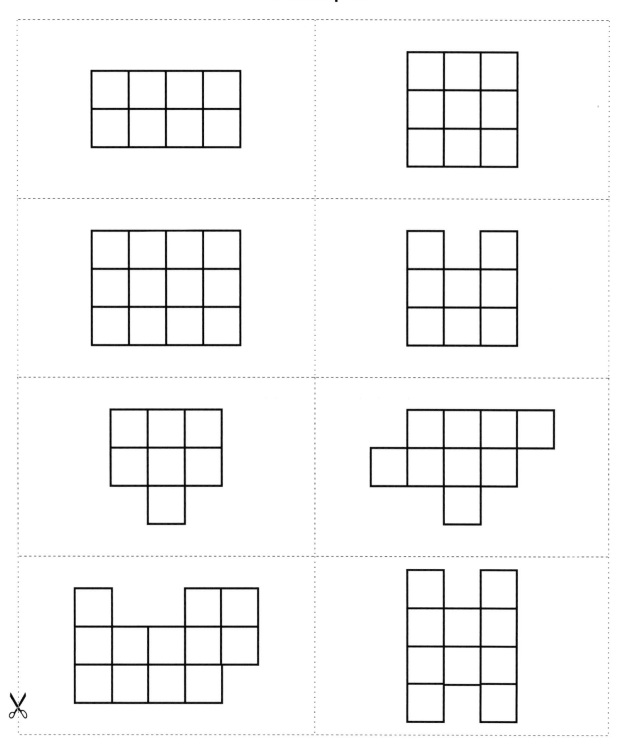

Concept Attainment: Prime Numbers

Yes Examples		No Examples	
11	17	12	16
23	43	24	45
59	61	60	87
97	101	93	100

Name _____   Date _____

a. _____

b. _____

c. _____

d. _____

e. _____

f. _____

g. _____

h. _____

i. _____

j. _____

Line Master 3.1A

Biography Glyphs

Eyes: Birthday

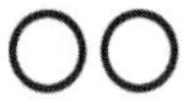	January or February
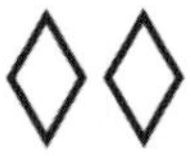	March or April
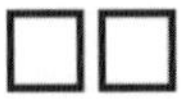	May or June
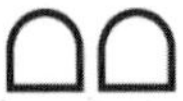	July or August
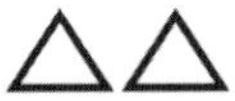	September or October
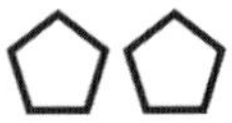	November or December

Hair: Family Size

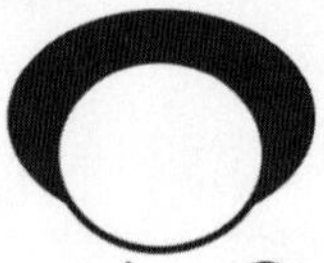	2 people
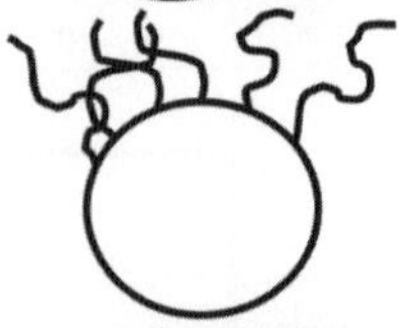	3 people
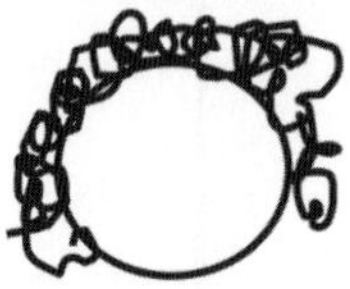	4 people
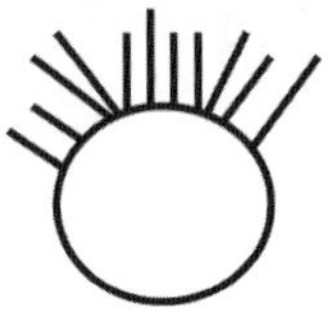	More than 4 people

Nose: Favourite Pastime

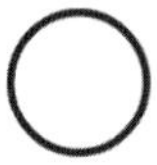	Playing sports
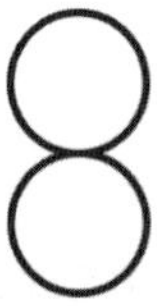	Reading
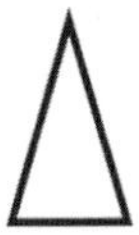	Playing games
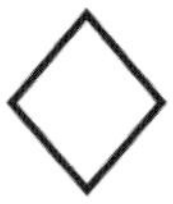	Watching TV or movies
	Doing something not listed

Mouth: How I Get to School

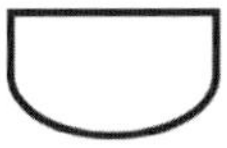	I walk.
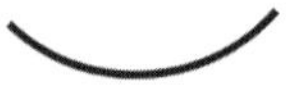	I take the bus.
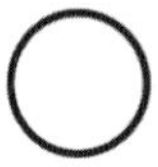	I get driven in a car.
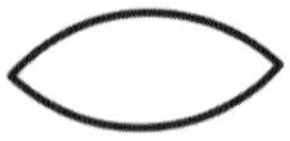	I ride my bicycle.
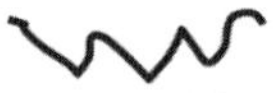	I use a different way.

Biography Glyphs

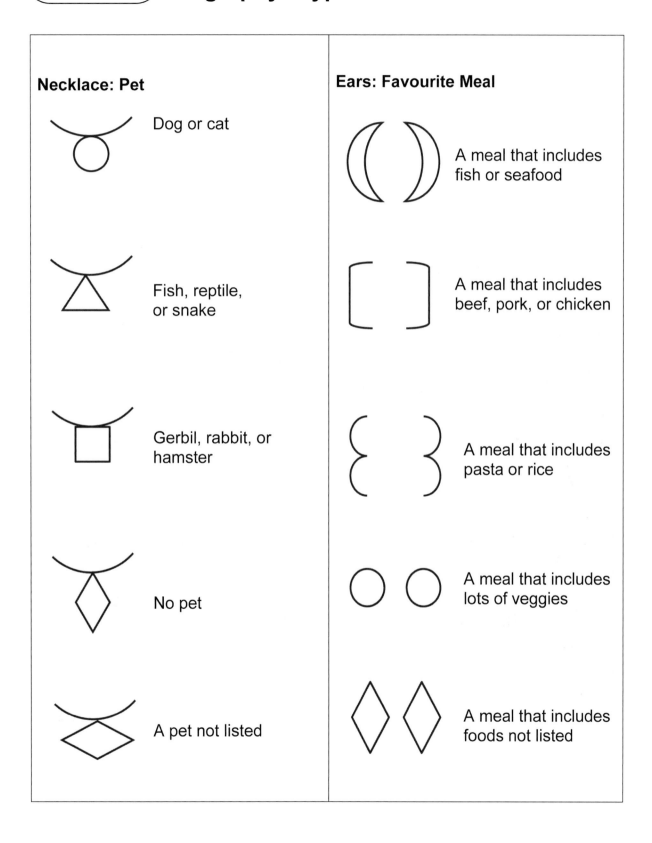

Necklace: Pet

Dog or cat

Fish, reptile, or snake

Gerbil, rabbit, or hamster

No pet

A pet not listed

Ears: Favourite Meal

A meal that includes fish or seafood

A meal that includes beef, pork, or chicken

A meal that includes pasta or rice

A meal that includes lots of veggies

A meal that includes foods not listed

Train Recipe Card

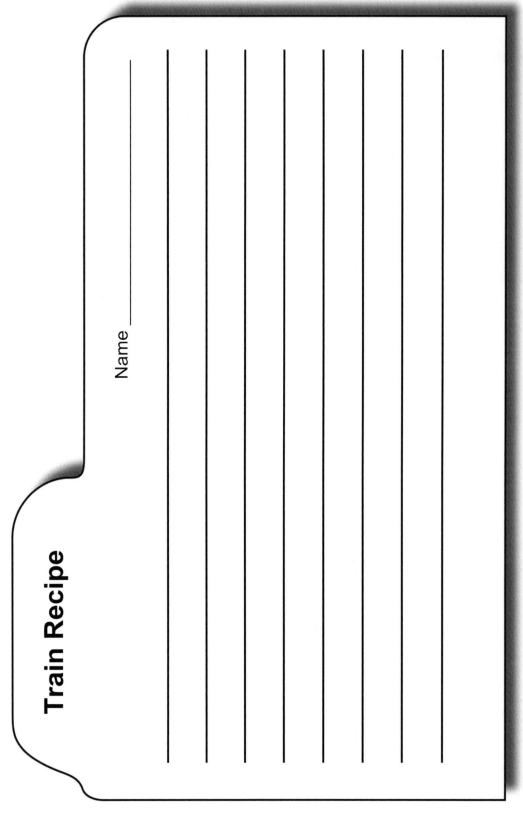

Name

Train Recipe

Name_____

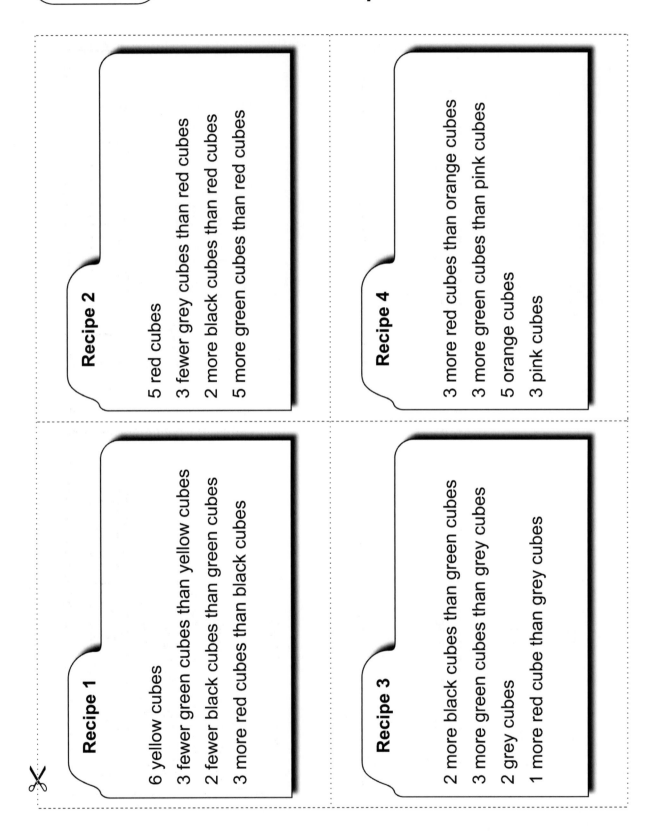

Recipe 2

5 red cubes

3 fewer grey cubes than red cubes

2 more black cubes than red cubes

5 more green cubes than red cubes

Recipe 4

3 more red cubes than orange cubes

3 more green cubes than pink cubes

5 orange cubes

3 pink cubes

Recipe 1

6 yellow cubes

3 fewer green cubes than yellow cubes

2 fewer black cubes than green cubes

3 more red cubes than black cubes

Recipe 3

2 more black cubes than green cubes

3 more green cubes than grey cubes

2 grey cubes

1 more red cube than grey cubes

Mathematical Recipes

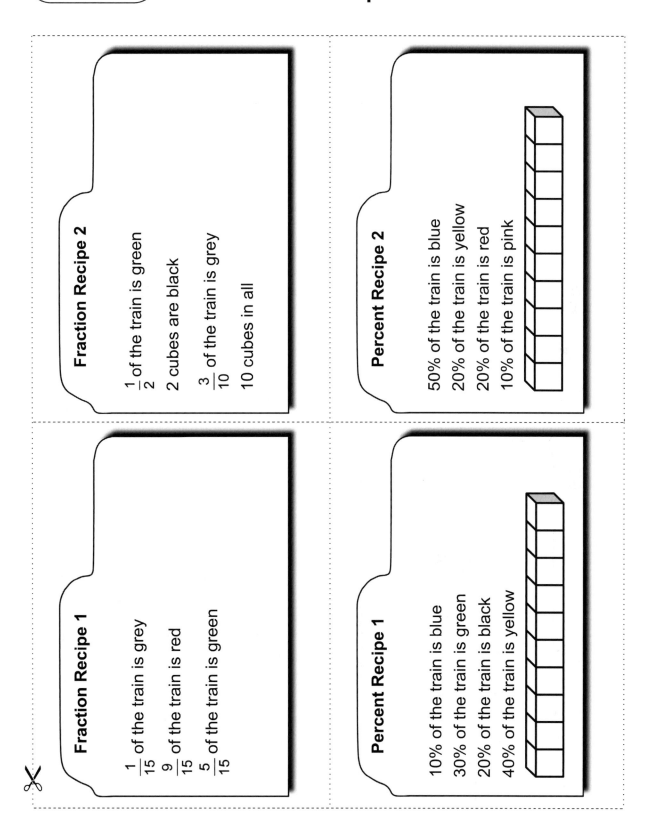

Fraction Recipe 2

$\frac{1}{2}$ of the train is green

2 cubes are black

$\frac{3}{10}$ of the train is grey

10 cubes in all

Percent Recipe 2

50% of the train is blue

20% of the train is yellow

20% of the train is red

10% of the train is pink

Fraction Recipe 1

$\frac{1}{15}$ of the train is grey

$\frac{9}{15}$ of the train is red

$\frac{5}{15}$ of the train is green

Percent Recipe 1

10% of the train is blue

30% of the train is green

20% of the train is black

40% of the train is yellow

Line Master 3.6 Mathematical Recipes

Algebra Recipe 1

$r = 2p + 1$
$p = 2(b - 1)$
$b = 3$

r = number of red cubes
p = number of pink cubes
b = number of blue cubes

Algebra Recipe 2

$r = y^2 - 4$
$y = b + 2$
$b = 1$
$p = 3b - 2$

r = number of red cubes
y = number of yellow cubes
b = number of blue cubes
p = number of pink cubes

Algebra Recipe 3

$g = b^2 - 6y$
$b = 2y$
$y = 2(6 - 5)$

g = number of green cubes
b = number of blue cubes
y = number of yellow cubes

Algebra Recipe 4

$b = 2(y^2 + 5) - 12$
$y = 2g - 2$
$g = 2$
$p = b - 4$

b = number of blue cubes
y = number of yellow cubes
g = number of green cubes
p = number of pink cubes

Verbal and Visual Word Association (VVWA)

Name _____   Date _____

Pictures	Real-Life Example
Math Word(s)	**Description in My Own Words**

Verbal and Visual Word Association (VVWA)

Name _____ Date _____

Pictures	**Real-Life Example**
Math Word(s)	**Definition**

Name _____   Date _____

Facts/Characteristics

Non-examples

Definition

Examples

Frayer Model

Name _____   Date _____

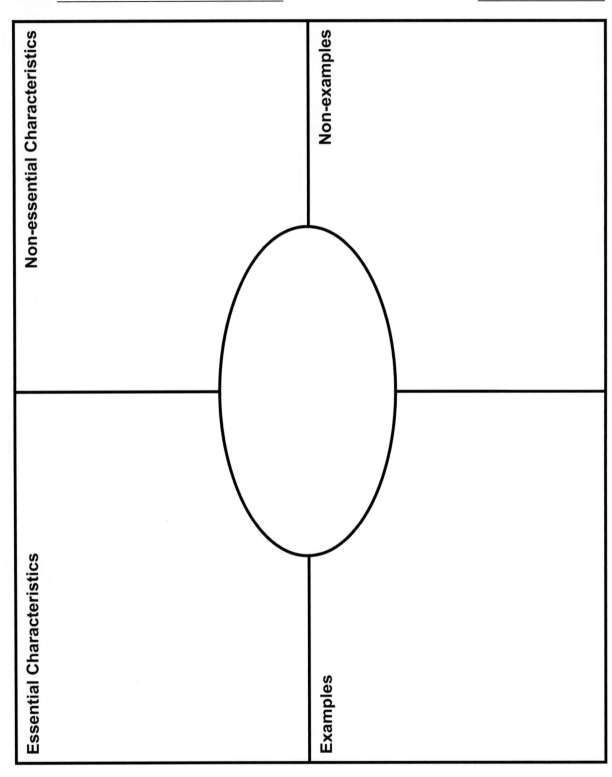

Non-essential Characteristics

Non-examples

Essential Characteristics

Examples

Three-Part Concept Circle

Name _____   Date _____

Concept: _____

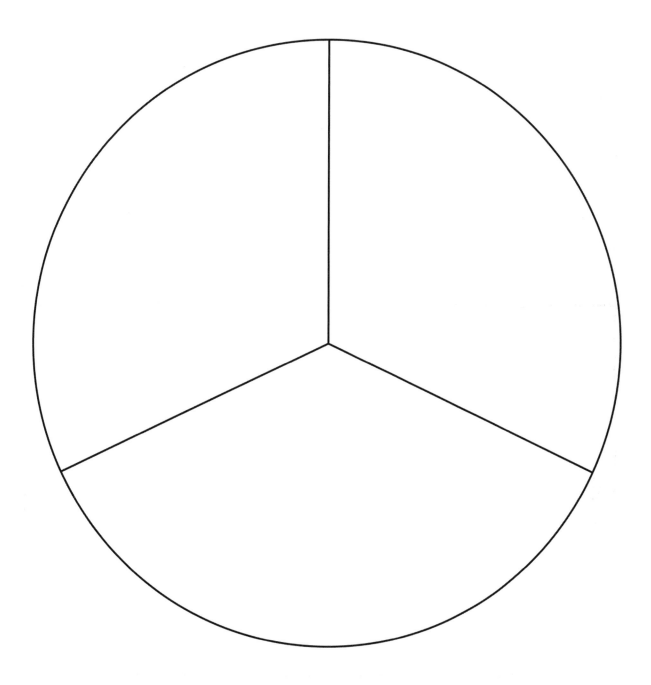

Four-Part Concept Circle

Name _____   Date _____

Concept: _____

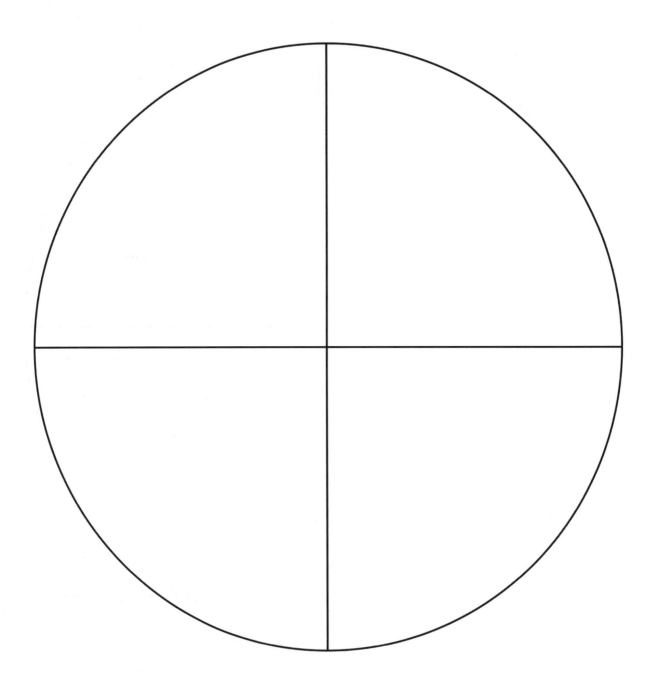

Four-Part Concept Circle

Name _____   Date _____

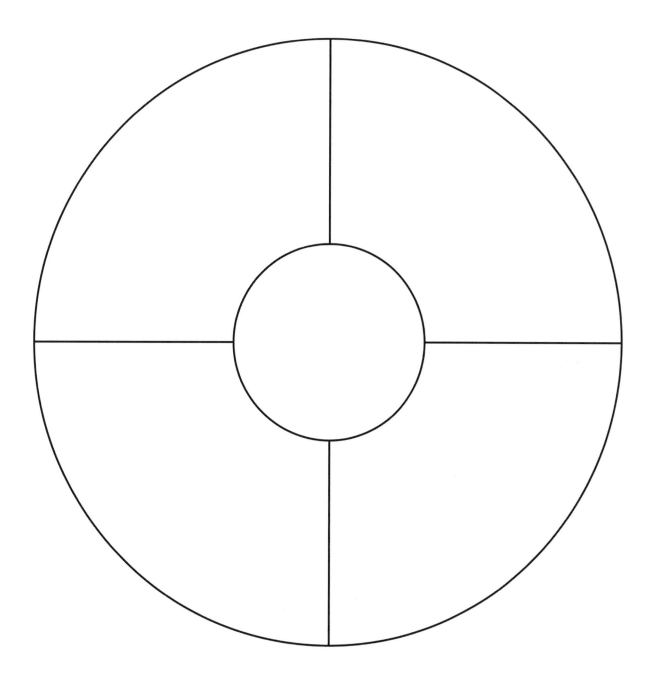

Five-Part Concept Circle

Name _____   Date _____

Concept: _____

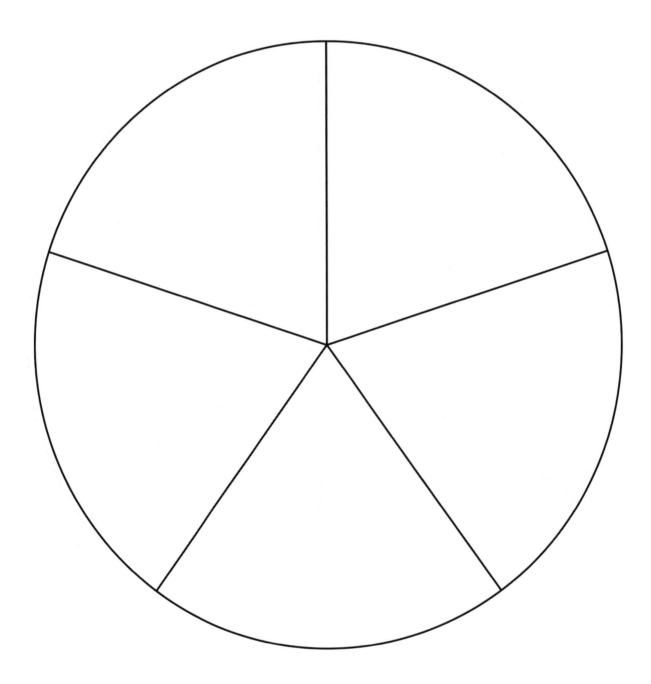

Six-Part Concept Circle

Name _____   Date _____

Concept: _____

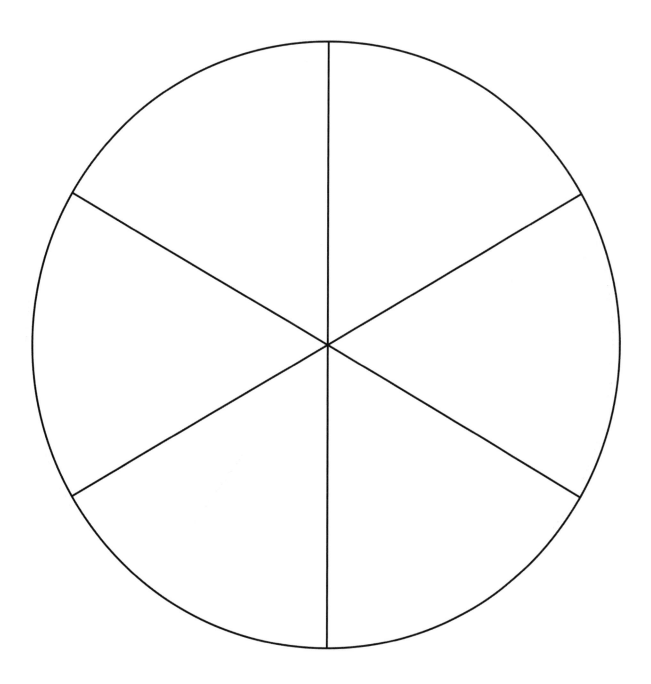

Eight-Part Concept Circle

Name _____   Date _____

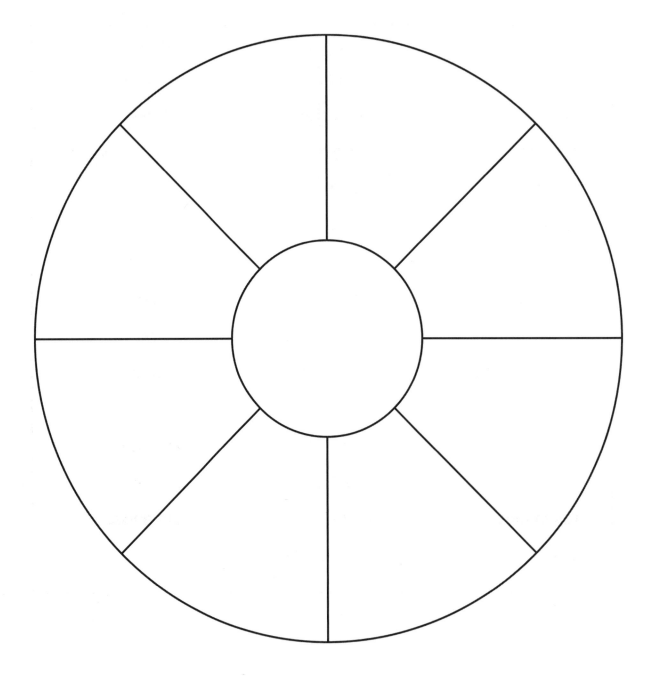

Math Expressions: Developing Student Thinking and Problem Solving Through Communication

Sample Linking Words for Concept Maps

Name _____   Date _____

Add your own words to this list. Use the back of the page if necessary.

is	has	tells us
is not	is equal to	provides
are	can have	shows
are not	can be	is important for
contains	cannot be	to
is part of	cannot have	adds
is made of	must have	divides
consists of	needs	equals
is less than	measures	means
is greater than	is measured in	represents
belongs to	uses	helps
does not belong to	related to	improves
like	such as	involves
resembles	due to	enhances
similar to	is crucial to	

Math Expressions: Developing Student Thinking and Problem Solving Through Communication
Copyright © 2013 Pearson Canada Inc.
This page may have been modified from its original.

Line Master 4.11

Mind Map Elements

Name ______________________________ Date ________________

How and where is the main topic identified?

How are the concepts organized?

How are the following elements used in the mind map?

Words

Pictures

Lines

Colour

Other things noticed about the mind map:

Line Master 4.12

Concept Map Elements

Name ______________________________ Date ________________

How and where is the main topic identified?

How are the concepts organized?

How are the following elements used in the concept map?

Words

Pictures

Lines

Colour

Other things noticed about the concept map:

Line Master 4.13

Discovery Sheet

Researcher(s)

____

____

Date ____________________

When we explored ____________________________

we discovered this:

Allen, J. (1999). *Words, words: Teaching vocabulary in grades 4–12.* Portland, ME: Stenhouse.

Allen, J. (2007). *Inside words: Tools for teaching academic vocabulary.* Portland, ME: Stenhouse.

Allen, J. (2008). *More tools for teaching content literacy.* Portland, ME: Stenhouse.

Allsopp, D., Kyger, M., & Lovin, L. (2007). *Teaching mathematics meaningfully.* Baltimore, MD: Paul H. Brooks.

Aspinwall, L., & Aspinwall, J. (2003). Investigating mathematical thinking using open writing prompts. *Mathematics Teaching in the Middle School, 8*(7), 350–353.

Barlow, A., & Cates, J. (2007). The answer is 20 cookies, what is the question? *Teaching Children Mathematics, 13*(5), 252–255.

Barton, M. L., & Heidema, C. (2002). *Teaching reading in mathematics* (2nd ed.). Aurora, CO: Mid-continent Research for Education and Learning.

Baxter, J., Woodward, J., Olson, D., & Robyns, J. (2002). Blueprint for writing in middle school mathematics. *Mathematics Teaching in the Middle School, 8*(1), 52–56.

Ben-Chaim, D., Lappan, G., & Houang, R. T. (1989). The role of visualization in the middle school mathematics curriculum. *Focus on Learning Problems in Mathematics, 11*, 49–60.

Bennett, B., Rolheiser, C., & Stevahn, L. (2001). *Cooperative learning: Where heart meets mind.* Toronto, ON: Educational Connections.

Billings, E., & Beckman, C. (2005). Children's literature: A motivating context to explore functions. *Mathematics Teaching in the Middle School, 10*(9), 470–478.

Booth, D., & Swartz, L. (2004). *Literacy techniques for building successful readers and writers.* Markham, ON: Pembroke.

Borgioli, G. (2008). Equity for English language learners in mathematics classrooms. *Teaching Children Mathematics, 15*(3), 185–191.

Bransford, J. D., Brown A. L., & Cocking, R. R. (1999). *How people learn: Brain, mind, experience and school* (Expanded ed.). Washington, DC: National Academy Press.

Brenner, M. E. (1998). Development of mathematical communication in problem solving groups by language minority students. *Bilingual Research Journal, 22,* 214–244.

Bresser, R., Melanese, K., & Sphar, C. (2009). *Supporting English language learners in math class: A multimedia professional learning resource, Grades K–5.* Sausalito, CA: Math Solutions.

Brown, C. (2005). Equity of literacy-based math performance assessments of English Language Learners. *Bilingual Research Journal, 29*(2), 337–363.

Brown, C., Cady, J., & Taylor, M. (2009). Problem solving and the English Language Learner. *Mathematics Teaching in the Middle School, 14*(9), 532–539.

Bruner, J., Goodnow, J., & Austin, G. A. (1956). *A study of thinking.* New York, NY: Wiley.

Buckley, P. A., & Ribordy, S. C. (1982, May). Mathematics anxiety and the effects of evaluative instructions on math performance. Paper presented at the meeting of the Midwestern Psychological Association, Minneapolis, MN.

Buzan, T. (2004). *Mind maps for kids: Rev up for revision.* London, UK: HarperCollins.

Buzan, T., & Buzan, B. (1993). *The mind map book.* New York, NY: Penguin Group.

Buzan, T., Buzan, B., & Harrison, J. (2006). *The mind map book: Unlocking your creativity, boost your memory, change your life.* London, UK: BBC Books.

Casteel, J. D., & Stahl, R. J. (1973). *The Social Science Observation Record (SSOR): Theoretical construct and pilot studies.* Gainesville, FL: P. K. Yonge Laboratory School.

Chapin, S., O'Connor, C., & Anderson, N. (2009). *Classroom discussions: Using math talk to help students learn.* Saulsalito, CA: Math Solutions.

Clement, L., & Bernhard, J. (2005). A problem solving alternative to using key words. *Mathematics Teaching in the Middle School, 10*(7), 360–365.

Cohen, D., & Ball, D. L. (2001, September). Making change: Instruction and its improvement. *Phi Delta Kappan,* 73–77.

Cohen, E. G. (1994). Restructuring the classroom: Conditions for productive small groups. *Review of Educational Leadership, 64*, 1–35.

Costa, A. (2008). The thought-filled curriculum. *Educational Leadership, 5*(65), 20–24.

Cummins, J. (2009). Multilingualism in the English-medium classroom: Pedagogical considerations. *TESOLQuarterly, 43(2),* 317–321.

Cummins, J. (2001). *Negotiating identities: Education for empowerment in a diverse society* (2nd ed.). Los Angeles, CA: California Association for Bilingual Education.

Cunningham, P. M. (1999). *The teacher's guide to the four blocks.* Greensboro, NC: Carson-Dellosa.

Daniels, H. (2011). Welcome and introduction. In H. Daniels (ed.), *Comprehension going forward: Where are we? What's next?*(pp. 1–7). Portsmouth, NH: Heinemann.

de Bono, E. (1967). *The use of lateral thinking.* London, UK: Jonathan Cape.

de Bono, E. (2010). *Think! Before it's too late.* London, UK: Random House.

Downey, C. J. (2000). Top 10 instructional strategies for achievement. *Leadership, 30*(2), 11.

Dyson, A. H., & Freedman, S. W. (1991). Writing. In J. Flood, J. Jensen, D. Lapp, & J. R. Squire, (eds.), *Handbook of research on teaching the English language arts* (pp. 754–774). New York, NY: Macmillan.

Ediger, M. (2006). Writing in the mathematics curriculum. *Journal of Instructional Psychology, 33,* 120–123.

Eeds, M., & Cockrum, W. A. (1985). Teaching word meanings by expanding schemata vs. dictionary work vs. reading in context. *Journal of Reading, 28*(March), 492–497.

Ellis, E. (2004). *What's the big deal about graphic organizers?* www.graphicorganizers.com

Ellis, E., & Howard, P. (2005). Graphic organizers: Power tools for teaching students with learning disabilities. *Graphic Organizers and Learning Disabilities 1,* 1–5.

Fisher, D., & Frey, N. (2007). *Improving adolescent literacy: Strategies at work* (2nd ed.). Upper Saddle River, NJ: Pearson Merrill Prentice Hall.

Fosnot, C. (2005). *Turkey investigations: A context for multiplication.* Portsmouth, NH: Heinemann.

Fosnot, C., & Dolk, M. (2001). *Young mathematicians at work: Constructing number sense, addition, and subtraction.* Portsmouth, NH: Heinemann.

Fosnot, C., & Dolk, M. (2002). *Young mathematicians at work: Constructing fractions, decimals, and percents.* Portsmouth, NH: Heinemann.

Fosnot, C., & Dolk, M. (2006). *Sharing submarine sandwiches: A context for fractions.* Portsmouth, NH: Heinemann.

Frayer, D. A., Quilling, M. R., Harris, M. L., & Harris, C. W. (1972). Experimental approaches to establishing the construct validity of tests of concept attainment (Theoretical Paper No. 34). Madison, WI: Wisconsin Research and Development Center for Cognitive Learning.

Furner, J., & Duffy, M. (2002). Equity for all students in the new millennium: Disabling math anxiety. *Intervention in School and Clinic, 38*(2), 67–74.

Gardill, M. C., & Jitendra, A. K. (1999). Advanced story map instruction: Effects on the reading comprehension of students with learning disabilities. *Journal of Special Education, 33*(1), 2–17, 28.

Gibbs, J. (2001). *Tribes: A new way of learning and being together.* Windsor, CA: Center Source Systems.

Gibbs, J. (2006). *Reaching all by creating Tribes learning communities.* Windsor, CA: Center Source Publications.

Greenan, M. (2011). *The secret of success criteria.* Retrieved from http://www.cpco.on.ca/News/PrincipalConnections/PastIssues/Vol14/Issue3/SuccessCriteria.pdf

Gutiérrez, R. (2002). Beyond essentialism: The complexity of language in teaching mathematics to Latina/o students. *American Educational Research Journal, 39*(4), 1047–1088.

Harlen, W. (2006). On the relationship between assessment for formative and summative purposes. In J. Gardner (ed.), *Assessment and learning* (pp. 103–117). Los Angeles, CA: Sage Publications.

Harvey, S., & Goudvis, A. (2007). *Strategies that work: Teaching comprehension for understanding and engagement.* Portland, ME: Stenhouse.

Hiebert, J. (1999). Relationships between research and the NCTM standards. *Journal for Research in Mathematics Education, 30,* 3–19.

Hiebert, J., Carpenter, P., Fennema, K., Fuson, D., Wearne, D., Murray, H., …Human, P. (1997). *Making sense: Teaching and learning mathematics with understanding.* Portsmouth, NH: Heinemann.

Hufferd-Ackles, K., Fuson, K., & Sherin, M. (2004). Describing levels and components of a math-talk learning community. *Journal for Research in Mathematics, 35*(2), 81–116.

Hutchins, C. (2011). Thinking, talking our way through the words. In H. Daniels (ed.), *Comprehension going forward: Where are we? What's next?* Portsmouth, NH: Heinemann.

Hyde, A. (2006). *Comprehending math*. Portsmouth, NH: Heinemann.

Hyde, A. (2007). Mathematics and cognition. *Educational Leadership, 65*(3), 43–47.

Jensen, E. (2005). *Teaching with the brain in mind*. Alexandria, VA: Association for Supervision and Curriculum Development.

Johnson, D., & Johnson, R. (1989). *Cooperation and competition: Theory and research*. Edina, MN: Interaction Book Company.

Johnson, D., & Johnson, R. (2005). *Teaching students to be peacemakers* (4th ed.). Edina, MN: Interaction Book Company.

Johnson, D., Johnson R., & Holubec, E. (2008). *Cooperation in the classroom* (7th ed.). Edina, MN: Interaction Book Company.

Kagan, S., & Kagan, M. (2009). *Kagan cooperative learning*. San Clemente, CA: Kagan Cooperative Learning.

Kazemi, E., & Stipek, D. (2001). Promoting conceptual thinking in four upper elementary mathematics classrooms. *Elementary School Journal, 102*(1), 59–81.

Kenney, J. (2005). *Literacy strategies for improving mathematics instruction*. Alexandria, VA: Association for Supervision and Curriculum Development.

Knuth, E., & Peressini, D. (2001). Unpacking the nature of discourse in mathematics classrooms. *Mathematics Teaching in the Middle School, 6*(5), 320–325.

Krashen, S. (2004). *The power of reading: Insights from the research*. (2nd ed.). Westport, CT: Libraries Unlimited.

Lambert, M. (1990). When the problem is not the question and the solution is not the answer. Mathematical knowing and teaching. *American Educational Research Journal, 27*, 29–63.

Marks Krpan, C. (2001). *The write math*. Parsnippany, NY: Pearson Education.

Marks Krpan, C. (2008a). Critical talk that matters in mathematics. In D. Booth (ed.), *It's critical: Classroom strategies for promoting critical and creative comprehension* (pp. 109–110). Markham, ON: Pembroke.

Marks Krpan, C. (2008b). Exploring effective teaching strategies for ELLs in mathematics classrooms. In C. Rolheiser (ed.), *School university partnerships: Creative connections* (pp. 24–28). Toronto, ON: Ontario Institute for Studies in Education.

Marks Krpan, C. (2009). Exploring mathematics talk in elementary classrooms. In C. Rolheiser (ed.), *Partnerships for professional learning: Literacy & numeracy initiatives* (pp. 5–14). Toronto, ON: Ontario Institute for Studies in Education.

Marks Krpan, C. (2011). Supporting struggling learners: Collaborative problem solving in mathematics. In C. Rolheiser, M. Evans, & M. Gambhir (eds.), *Inquiry into practice: Reaching every student through inclusive curriculum* (pp. 101–117). Toronto, ON: Ontario Institute for Studies in Education.

McGregor, T. (2007). *Comprehension connections: Bridges to strategic reading*. Portsmouth, NH: Heinemann.

McIntosh, M., & Draper, R. (2001). Using learning logs in mathematics: Writing to learn. *Mathematics Teacher, 94*, 554–557.

McNeil, N., & Alibali, M. (2005). Knowledge change as a function of mathematics experience: All contexts are not created equal. *Journal of Cognition and Development, 6*, 285–306.

Miller, D. (2002). *Reading with meaning*. Portland, ME: Stenhouse.

Montgomery County Public Schools, Division of ESOL/Bilingual Programs. (2004). *Questioning strategies for English language learners*. Rockville, MD: MCPS, Department of Curriculum and Instruction.

National Council of Teachers of Mathematics (NCTM). (2000). *Principles and standards for school mathematics*. Reston, VA: Author.

Novak, J. (1998). *Learning, creating and using knowledge*. Mahwah, NJ: Lawrence Erlbaum Associates.

Novak, J.D. & Gowan, B. D. (1984). *Learning how to learn*. New York: Cambridge University Press.

Ontario Ministry of Education, Literacy and Numeracy Secretariat. (2010). *Growing success: Assessment, evaluation, and reporting in Ontario schools*. Toronto, ON: Queen's Printer for Ontario.

Pekrun, R., Goetz, T., Titz, W., & Perry, R. P. (2002). Academic emotions in students' self-regulated learning and achievement: A program of qualitative and quantitative research. *Educational Psychologist, 37*(2), 91–105.

Rigleman, N. (2007). Fostering mathematical thinking and problem solving: The teacher's role. *Teaching Children Mathematics, 13*(6), 308–314.

Ron, P. (1999). Spanish–English language issues in the mathematics classroom. In L. Ortiz-Franco, N. G. Hernandez, & Y. De las Cruz (eds.), *Changing the faces of mathematics: Perspectives on Latinos* (pp. 23–34). Reston, VA: National Council of Teachers of Mathematics.

Rowe, M. B. (1987). Wait time: Slowing down may be a way of speeding up. *American Educator, 11*, 38–43, 47.

Rubenstein, R., & Thompson, D. (2002). Understanding and supporting children's mathematical vocabulary development. *Teaching Children Mathematics, 9*(12), 107–112.

Shimizu, Y. (2007). How do Japanese teachers explain and structuralize their lessons? In M. Isoda, M. Stephens, Y. Ohara, & T. Miyakawa (eds.), *Japanese lesson study in mathematics: Its impact, diversity and potential for educational improvement* (pp. 64–67). Hackensack, NJ: World Scientific Publishing.

Sousa, D. (2001). *How the brain learns*. Thousand Oaks, CA: Sage.

Sousa, D. (2008). *How the brain learns mathematics*. Thousand Oaks, CA: Sage.

Sowder, L. (1988). Children's solutions of story problems. *Journal of Mathematical Behavior, 7*, 227–238.

Stahl, R. J. (1990). *Using "think-time" behaviors to promote students' information processing, learning, and on-task participation. An instructional module.* Tempe, AZ: Arizona State University.

Stahl, R. J. (2009). Retrieved from http://pcboe.net/les/elderweb/READINGCOACHFILES/StudentEngagement/thinktime.pdf

Stein, C. (2007). Let's talk: Promoting mathematical discourse in the classroom. *Mathematics Teacher, 101*(4), 285–289.

Tobin, K. (1987). The role of wait time in higher cognitive level learning. *Review of Educational Research, 57*(1), 69–95.

Turner, J., & Meyer, D. (2004). A classroom perspective on the principle of moderate challenge in mathematics. *Journal of Educational Research, 97*(6), 311–318.

Vacca, J., Vacca, R., Gove, M., Burkey, L., Lenhart, L., & McKeon, C. (2011). *Reading and learning to read* (8th ed.). Columbus, OH: Allyn & Bacon.

van Garderen, D. (2004). Reciprocal teaching as a comprehension strategy for understanding mathematical word problems. *Reading and Writing Quarterly, 20*(2), 225–229.

Wolfe, P. (2001). *Brain matters: Translating research into classroom practice.* Alexandria, VA: Association for Supervision and Curriculum Development.

Wormeli, R. (2004). *Summarization in any subject: 50 techniques to improve student learning.* Alexandria, VA: Association for Supervision and Curriculum Development.

Yedlin, J. (2004). Teacher talk: Enabling ELLs to "grab on" and climb high. *Perspectives* (January/February). Retrieved from http://www.mec.edu/mascd/docs/yedlin.htm

Zaslavsky, C. (1999). *Fear of math: How to get over it and get on with your life.* New Brunswick, NJ: Rutgers University Press.

Zinsser, W. (1989). *Writing to learn.* New York, NY: Harper & Row.

Zolkower, B., & Shreyar, S. (2007). A teacher's mediation of a thinking-aloud discussion in a 6th grade mathematics classroom. *Educational Studies in Mathematics, 65*(2), 177–202.

©P